I0819633

Modern Southeast Asia Series
Stephen F. Maxner, General Editor

Also in the series

After the Killing Fields: Lessons from the Cambodian Genocide, by Craig Etcheson

An Loc: The Unfinished War, by General Tran Van Nhut with Christian L. Arevian

The Battle of Ngok Tavak: Allied Valor and Defeat in Vietnam, by Bruce Davies

David and Lee Roy: A Vietnam Story, by David L. Nelson and Randolph B. Schiffer

Fragging: Why U.S. Soldiers Assaulted Their Officers in Vietnam, by George Lepre

Hog's Exit: Jerry Daniels, the Hmong, and the CIA, by Gayle L. Morrison

The Mayaguez *Incident: Testing America's Resolve in the Post-Vietnam Era*, by Robert J. Mahoney

Military Medicine to Win Hearts and Minds: Aid to Civilians in the Vietnam War, by Robert J. Wilensky

Operation Passage to Freedom: The United States Navy in Vietnam, 1954–1955, by Ronald B. Frankum, Jr.

Vietnam and Beyond: A Diplomat's Cold War Education, by Robert Hopkins Miller

Vietnam Chronicles: The Abrams Tapes, 1968–1972, transcribed and edited by Lewis Sorley

Vietnam Labyrinth: Allies, Enemies, and Why the U.S. Lost the War, by Tran Ngoc Chau with Ken Fermoyle

The Vietnam War: An Assessment by South Vietnam's Generals, edited by Lewis Sorley

Window on a War: An Anthropologist in the Vietnam Conflict, by Gerald C. Hickey

CHARLIE ONE FIVE

A Marine Company's Vietnam War

Nicholas Warr

Foreword by Scott Nelson

Texas Tech University Press

Unless otherwise indicated, all maps by Lt. Col. Richard L. Cody, USMC (Ret).

This book is typeset in Minion Pro. The paper used in this book meets the minimum requirements of ANSI/NISO Z39.48-1992 (R1997). ∞

Designed by Kasey McBeath
Cover photographs appear courtesy John Rusth (top) and Rich Lowder (bottom).

Library of Congress Cataloging-in-Publication Data

Warr, Nicholas, 1945–
Charlie one five : a Marine company's Vietnam War / Nicholas Warr ; foreword by Scott Nelson.
pages cm.—(Modern Southeast Asia series)
Includes bibliographical references and index.
ISBN 978-0-89672-797-7 (hardcover : alk. paper)—ISBN 978-0-89672-798-4 (e-book)
1. Vietnam War, 1961–1975—Campaigns. 2. United States. Marine Corps. Marine Regiment, 5th. Battalion, 1st . Company C—History. 3. Vietnam War, 1961–1975—Regimental histories. I. Title.
DS558.4.W37 2013
959.704'345—dc23

2013011226

Printed in the United States of America
13 14 15 16 17 18 19 20 21 / 9 8 7 6 5 4 3 2 1

Texas Tech University Press
Box 41037 | Lubbock, Texas 79409-1037 USA
800.832.4042 | ttup@ttu.edu | www.ttupress.org

This book is dedicated to all Vietnam veterans, especially those who served "in country"—in the rice paddies and jungles, up the rivers and off the shores of Vietnam—during one of the most difficult, divisive, and costly foreign wars in American history.

You, the Vietnam veteran, chose service over self-interest; you faced fear nearly every day you spent there and didn't waver in its face. Your courage and determination resulted in victory after victory against a very capable foe who would just not give up, despite near annihilation which came at great American cost on too many battlefields.

The tragic outcome of this war, from the American point of view, had nothing to do with you. Clearly, our national leaders failed our country, failed to honor our commitments to the South Vietnamese people, and failed you miserably when you came home. Your reputation was tarnished by a few who chose politics and antiestablishment vitriol over a desire actually to understand anything about Vietnam and those who fought there. Many young people ran away from their responsibilities and hid from the challenge of service in the military, mocking your commitment. Yet despite all of that, you persisted and succeeded on every battlefield. You came home to, at worst, outright hostility from your fellow Americans and, at best, a universal apathy from the silent majority, yet you continue to serve to this day, in many ways, in your communities and for your country.

You did not ask what your country could do for you; you stepped up and did your job despite extreme risk and sometimes terribly dangerous and incredibly challenging circumstances.

I honor you all for your service and sacrifices. You are my brothers and sisters.

Welcome home.

Contents

Illustrations ix

Maps x

About the Maps
  Lt. Col. Richard L. Cody xi

Foreword
  Scott A. Nelson xvii

Preface xxiii

Acknowledgments xxvii

Prologue 3

1: The Early Days and Operation Jackstay, December 1965–Early 1966 7

2: Sparrow Hawk and Operation Colorado, June–December 1966 19

3: Changes of Command, November 1966–March 1967 33

4: Changes of Weaponry, April 1967 51

5: Operation Union I, 21 April–9 May 1967 65

6: The Battle for Hill 110, 10 May 1967 91

7: Dying Delta and the Move to Hill 51, 11–17 May 1967 147

8: Operation Union II, 26 May–5 June 1967 156

9: Operation Swift, 4–15 September 1967 186

10: Hoi An Days, 1 October–25 December 1967 217

11: Incoming! Phu Loc 6 Combat Base, December 1967–March 1968 247

12: Lang Co Village and the Phantom Mortar Crew, 16 January–10 February 1968 274

Afterword 292

Appendices *297*

Notes *303*

Index *305*

Illustrations

The swamps of the Rung Sat Special Zone 9
Gunnery Sgt. Marcelino Rivera-Cruz and two Marines 40
Lance Cpl. Leonard Roberson and Pvt. Kevin Rohring 56
Hill 54 Combat Base 57
Charlie Company tent, Hill 54 58
Bill Edge, Jim Reed, and Lance Cpl. John Rusth 95
Viet Cong sign, summer 1967, Que Son Valley 96
Cpl. Nick Tague and Harvey Cunningham 97
Mortar crew at Hill 51 Combat Base 151
Living quarters, Hill 51 Combat Base 152
Poncho Hooch on Hill 51 153
Hill 51 158
Nui Lac Son 159
Marines in a bunker atop Nui Lac Son 160
Sgt. Rodney M. Davis, USMC 211
1/5 Vietnam Veterans gather at Sgt. Davis's gravesite 212
Sgt. Rodney M. Davis, USMC (MOH) Memorial Monument 213
1/5 Marines prepare to go on patrol, Hoi An Combat Base 221
Sand berm and concertina wire perimeter, Hoi An 222
Hard point bunkers on the perimeter, Hoi An 223
Village near Charlie Company compound, east of Hoi An 224
M109A2 155 mm self-propelled medium howitzer,
Delta Company combat base 248
2nd Lt. Rich Lowder beside a truck convoy 249
Severe switchback, Hai Van Pass, Highway 1 250
Marines of Charlie 1/5 prepare for patrol, Phu Loc 6 251

M50 Ontos in a defensive posture, Phu Loc 6 252
2nd Lt. Rich Lowder in front of the Lang Co Bridge 276
2nd Lt. Nick Warr and 1st Lt. Scott Nelson 277
Nicholas Warr, Maj. Gen. Admire, and Staff Sgt. John Mullan 278

Maps, following p. 164

Map 1. I Corps Tactical Zone with Inset Depicting the Republic of South Vietnam and All Corps Tactical Zones
Map 2. Chu Lai TAOR, the Chu Lai Airfield and Combat Base, and Tam Ky
Map 3. Rescue of Staff Sgt. Jimmie Howard's Recon Team on Hill 488
Map 4. Que Son Valley, Battle for Hill 110
Map 5. Operation Union II
Map 6. Operation Swift
Map 7. Da Nang and Hoi An TAOR and Vicinity
Map 8. Phu Loc 6 Combat Base TAOR and Phu Bai Combat Base

About the Maps

Maps are a vital part of any book that describes military operations. They make verbal descriptions meaningful by visually depicting the relationships of place locations, unit positions, and terrain features. Maps also provide the reader with a feeling for the time and distance involved in maneuvering and delivering fire support. All of these factors are key elements in military strategy and tactics. The maps in *Charlie One Five*, which are gathered together in this book's color section, are designed to do just that—to graphically support the descriptions of the operations in which Charlie 1/5 participated. As the old saying goes, "A picture is worth a thousand words."

But maps only show the lay of the ground. Heat, humidity, rain, cold, snow, and all the other things that impact operations and the troops involved combine with terrain to form the complete war-fighting environment. The following brief is offered to provide general highlights of the environment that American warriors experienced in the Vietnam War. It also explains the features and names shown on the maps. The rest of this book expands on this and describes in vivid detail what the Marines of Charlie 1/5 encountered and how they dealt with living and fighting in "The 'Nam."

Of Provinces and Hamlets

Working from top to bottom politically, Vietnam is organized into provinces (equivalent to US states), which are broken down into districts (roughly the same as counties). Urbanites and suburbanites live in cities and towns. In the country the people live in villages. The larger villages are subdivided into hamlets. Each hamlet is identified by the village name and a number. Thus, the village of Phu Lac consists of the hamlets of Phu Lac (1), Phu Lac (2), Phu Lac (3), Phu Lac (4), and Phu Lac (6). In the field Americans tended to get down to the basics and refer to any cluster of buildings or huts as a village or "ville," regardless of size.

Although the residents of Vietnamese cities and towns live in Western-style houses and apartments, this is not necessarily so for the country folk. During the Vietnam War a rural hamlet may have had a proper building or two, but the average Vietnamese farmer lived in what can best be described as a thatch-roofed wood or bamboo hut with a dirt floor—a humble abode called a "hooch" by American troops. Visions of these hooches, clustered together in villes that dotted the rice paddies and mountain valleys, are deeply etched in the memories of American veterans of this war.

The Maps

The maps in this book are designed to provide snapshots of the terrain in which the Marines of Charlie 1/5 lived and fought. Their purpose is to provide visual references that complement the text. To achieve this, the maps are of two basic types: strategic (or area) and operational (or tactical).

Strategic maps are high-level views that show the locations of major places and areas. Operational maps drill down to the tactical level. These maps depict the ground in enough detail to show the terrain features that influenced troop movements and fire support. Symbols representing clusters of huts are used to show the countless hamlets that dotted the terrain as they dramatically influenced operations, but only the names of selected villes are displayed to make the maps easy to read in the space available. Similarly, minor streams, trails, and secondary roads that are not important to the story are not shown. Military-style contour lines outline the shapes of mountains and hills. Bench marks (which are identified with a +) are placed to indicate elevation in meters.

Place Names

The place names used are those that veterans of the 5th Marines would most likely recognize. For example, when asked, "Did you operate near the Thu Bon River?" a Charlie 1/5 rifleman might appear a bit puzzled at first, but ask about the Song Thu Bon and his eyes will light up with instant recognition.

In Vietnamese *song* means "river." *Nui* is "mountain"; thus, Nui Lac Son translates as Lac Son Mountain. American troops sometimes used the Vietnamese name and sometimes the English version. Occasionally the troops would assign an American-style nickname that reflected their impression of a feature or area, such as Charlie Ridge, Arizona Territory, Hill 55, Alligator Lake, and so on. So the maps use a mixture of several languages: Vietnamese, English, and troop jargon. The following table lists a few Vietnamese words that are used for common terrain features:

Common Vietnamese Geographical Terms

Vietnamese	English
vung	lagoon, pool (Vung Da Nang translates to Da Nang Lagoon)
vinh	bay, gulf
bai	beach, shore (Bai Chuoi is Chuoi Beach)
ho	lake
song	river (Song Ly Ly is the Ly Ly River)
mui	point of land (Mui Chon May Dong is Chon May Dong Point)
nui	mountain, mountain range, ridge (Nui Tron is Tron Mountain)
thung lung	valley
duong	ocean
be, bien	sea
ga	railway station (Ga Lang Co is the Lang Co railway station)
hon	island (Hon Son Tra is Son Tra Island)

Vietnamese is a lovely, soft, singsong, tonal language. The written form uses a complex variety of accent marks to indicate how a word is pronounced. The Vietnamese names on the maps in this book do not include the accent marks. It is a technical limitation associated with the English language word processing and drawing tools employed. It is by no means intended as an insult to this ancient and beautiful language. For the scope and context of this book, the omission of the accent marks does not affect the meaning of the words that are used to Americans—nor, we hope, any Vietnamese readers, either.

Map Symbols and Unit Identification

Standard US military symbols are used to depict the type and size of units. US Marine rifle companies and artillery batteries organic to regiments within the Corps are traditionally identified by their letter and regimental designation without reference to battalion assignment. This is because the letters are consecutively assigned within the entire regiment. In the table of organization in effect during the Vietnam War, Companies A, B, C, and D were organic to the 1st Battalion; E, F, G, and H to the 2nd

Battalion, and I, K, L and M to the 3rd Battalion. Therefore, it is only necessary to state Company F, 5th Marines (abbreviated as F/5 Mar, or simply F/5), and all hands know without saying that Company F is part of the 2nd Battalion, 5th Marines. By the way, all Marine regiments—infantry and artillery—are assigned numbers that are unique within the Corps. The 11th Marines is an artillery regiment, and no other Marine regiment bears that number. Therefore, the words *infantry* (Inf) or *artillery* (Arty) are not used as part of a Marine regiment's name. Other arms in the Corps are not organized into regiments but are formed as independent battalions or companies. They incorporate their arm of service in their designation, such as 1st Tank Battalion, 3rd Tank Battalion, 1st Reconnaissance Battalion, and so on.[1]

The maps in this book use the company/battalion/regiment designation, such as F/2/5 Mar or F/2/5.

Informally, Marines often refer to their companies using the phonetic alphabet. In the phonetic alphabet, *C* is Charlie. Hence, we have Charlie Company, or, as with the subject of this book: Charlie 1/5.

Units are organized for combat to accomplish specific missions. This task organization process involves attaching units from one organization to another to provide the capabilities required for the job at hand. Therefore, units can get mixed up at times, such as Charlie 1/5 finding itself fighting under the operational control of 2/5 for a particular operation. When a unit detaches one or more subordinate units, it is noted as being minus (–); on the other hand, a unit with attachments is reinforced (+). A unit can be both minus (–) and reinforced (+) at the same time. Task organization is temporary, and parent unit designation and the administrative chain of command never change: Charlie 1/5 remains Charlie 1/5 even if it is under the operational control of another battalion.

Final Thoughts from the Map Maker

Determining how to design supporting maps for *Charlie One Five*, and what to include in them, was a labor of love. It brought back a lot of memories. I served two tours in Vietnam. The first, 1965–66, found me as an infantry advisor to the Army of the Republic of South Vietnam (ARVN)—specifically, to the 2nd Battalion, 2nd Infantry, 1st ARVN Division. The regiment was based in Dong Ha, and we operated in northern I Corps along the DMZ from Gio Linh on the coast all the way west to Khe Sanh and Lang Ve near the Laotian border. My second tour was in 1968, when I had the honor of commanding Company A, 1st Battalion, 5th Marines (Alpha 1/5), a brother company of the subject of this book. In that tour I operated in the An Hoa Basin, which includes the infamous Arizona Territory.

In compiling the map data, I consulted standard 1:250,000 maps of Vietnam, the excellent multivolume *US Marines in Vietnam*, published by the Historical Division, US Marine Corps, and many books written about the war by historians and veterans. Often the information in these sources conflicted. When that occurred, I used my best professional judgment and personal experiences to resolve the issue. In the latter case, I was fortunate to have fought with both South Vietnamese and US Marine units. The former gave me a feel for the Vietnamese language and what the ARVN soldier called the places of his homeland. The latter gave me insight into the mixture of Vietnamese, English, and Leatherneck jargon that my fellow Marines used to name the mountains, hills, paddies, jungles, and villes of a land that was foreign to us. I made a particular effort to indicate the location of those places fought over and given famous nicknames by American grunts, such as Antenna Valley, Dodge City, and Charlie Ridge. This should bring back old memories to many veterans of this faraway and long-ago war. Any errors or omissions in drawing the maps are my responsibility, but please be gentle, as they were not intentional.

Semper Fi!

Lt. Col. Richard L. "Bill" Cody, USMC (Ret)

Foreword

When I first arrived in South Vietnam in late January of 1968, my first assignment was to command the legendary Marine rifle company Charlie Company, 1st Battalion, 5th Marines—Charlie One Five—a truly awesome responsibility. I wasn't new to the command of Marines, as I had served in the Marine Corps for well over a year at that point and was an experienced platoon commander, but it would be my first command in a combat situation, and it would be my first command of a Marine rifle company. When I graduated from Platoon Leaders Class and completed my training at the Basic School in Quantico, Virginia, I transferred to the 2nd Marine Division based at Marine Corps Base, Camp Lejeune, North Carolina. I spent many months as a platoon commander in Echo Company, 2nd Battalion, 2nd Marines. During that time our battalion went afloat on a Caribbean cruise, and we sailed the warm waters of the Caribbean Sea participating in training activities, including amphibious assaults on the island of Vieques, near Puerto Rico. As always, this Marine infantry training proved arduous and effective. We worked hard and we fine-tuned our infantry skills.

After that I went to the Civil Affairs Advisory School in Fort Gordon, Georgia; we sarcastically referred to that school as the Live Longer School. I had recently married and had been promoted to first lieutenant. I knew that I would ultimately go to Vietnam, so I didn't mind taking those extra few weeks in school to learn about how the Marine Corps reconstituted things and interacted with civilian populations after the battles ended. My arrival in a combat zone, and subsequent assignment to the 1st Battalion, 5th Marines, was a very rude awakening for this young first lieutenant.

When I found out, at 1st Marine Division headquarters, that I was headed to the famous 5th Marines, I felt quite honored but a bit awestruck. My fellow lieutenants and I learned a lot about Marine Corps history during our training, and the Fighting Fifth is very strongly represented in that legendary history. I also learned that the 1st Battalion of the 5th Marines (1/5) had a reputation as a fine fighting force, so I felt very fortunate to join their ranks. However, I wasn't quite sure what to make of my welcome "briefing," conducted by the commanding officer of the 5th Marines, Col. Robert D. Bohn.

After I was ushered into his office in the Da Nang area, Colonel Bohn personally greeted me. A big and impressive guy with real military bearing—just the sort of officer one might expect to lead the battle-hardened 5th Marines—he stood up as I entered, shook my hand firmly, and asked but one simple question: "Lieutenant Nelson, do you know why you are in Vietnam?" I answered him by repeating what we learned stateside and said that I was there to liberate the country, to set the people of South Vietnam free for democracy, or something along those lines, and he quickly countered with, "No! You're here, Lieutenant, to kill the enemy." After a somewhat stunned silence, I kind of looked at him funny, but then I thought to myself, "There it is," and said to him, "Aye, aye, sir." He then asked me if I had any questions, and I said, "No, sir," and he dismissed me with a warm "Good luck!" That was it. Welcome to Vietnam. My job was to kill the enemy, plain and simple.

The 5th Marines assigned me to their 1st Battalion, put me on a helicopter, and sent me to 1/5's combat base on 29 or 30 January 1968. I stayed there for three days, and during that entire time Phu Loc 6 Combat Base came under heavy attack. Enemy mortars and rockets exploded everywhere, the Marine artillery battery and mortar units returned fire, people rushed to and fro, and it seemed like all hell had broken loose—my baptism by fire. I can remember sitting in a damp, dark bunker during those three days, having no command, having no control, just stuck there waiting to leave. I somehow remained very detached about it all, but I could smell real trouble all around me, and I found it difficult to just sit there with all the incoming and outgoing fire. That last morning was especially harrowing, because 1/5's battalion commander got hit and was severely wounded, and several reaction forces went out to try to get him, resulting in the deaths of many 1/5 Marines. I can remember, like it was yesterday, the bodies brought back into the combat base on mechanical mules, stacked up like cordwood.

I found the situation at Phu Loc 6 Combat Base unbelievably chaotic. The sights and the sounds were surreal. All I could really think about was getting out of that basin flanked by mountains and taking command of my rifle company, Charlie Company, located way down south in an area called Lang Co. Many of the bridges of Highway 1 had been destroyed, so road travel was out of the question. I tried to catch a chopper, but the combat base's landing zone (LZ) was too hot for anything other than emergency medevacs, so I stayed at that combat base for those three long and harrowing days.

I left Phu Loc 6 by helicopter late on the afternoon of 1 February 1968. It was by now crystal clear in my mind that this was no training session. This was real. This was combat. Death and destruction were the order of the day. As I rode that helicopter toward my new command, my thoughts turned inward, and I found myself asking myself, "How do you 'do' company commander?" My training experience had always been commanding an infantry platoon, a force of about fifty Marines. Now I would lead an infantry company, a force of about two hundred Marines. I really never wondered why I, as a first lieutenant, got this command, because I had learned that only two captains, both busy with their own infantry companies, currently served in the battalion, and another first lieutenant commanded the other infantry company; so I wasn't really surprised, although the table of organization indicated that company commanders should carry the rank of captain. Interestingly, I also wasn't really concerned about my ability to lead a company of Marines. Confident in my abilities to lead, I felt that I had received great training, and I knew that I had been assigned to a good outfit. Maj. Len Wunderlich, the battalion operations officer (S-3), took some time out of his busy schedule to brief me about Charlie Company and our mission in the Lang Co area, so I knew I was fortunate to get command of Charlie Company.

Eventually, I answered my own question by thinking that it wouldn't really be much different than leading a platoon; rather than three squads, I would have three platoons. In my mind I looked at my new command as just a big platoon. I would have maneuver elements, point elements, flanks, rear guard, communications, and logistics; it was just that each element was bigger. I also knew that I would have good NCOs, whose experience would be invaluable. After all, they had been there and done that.

I felt prepared for command and determined to take command the right way—the Marine way. I knew that, just to survive, I would have to rely heavily upon the officers and NCOs who led the Marines of Charlie Company, and I felt I was the kind of leader who would listen and who didn't know it all. I came there with the view that I wouldn't dominate but would put a team together and take care of business. I knew I couldn't do that by myself, but on the other hand I didn't want to appear unsure of myself or unable to do the job, so I probably threw up a mask there for a while.

One of my earliest memories of my command of Charlie Company was hearing fragments of stories about the combat operations that 1/5 had conducted during the very eventful year of 1967. Combat veterans like to compare war stories; it seems as though the combat operations *you* experienced were always much worse than those that others experienced. There seemed to be a somewhat perverse sense of humor about all of that comparing, a sort of warped pride about how bad things got.

When I arrived at Lang Co village late that afternoon, there was an awful lot going on all around us. The bulk of the Marines of 1/5 were still fighting the NVA at Phu Loc 6 Combat Base, and the Marines of Delta 1/5 were struggling with them at their company firebase as well.[1] The fast-moving events of the NVA's Tet Offensive continued to unfold all over South Vietnam. But things remained fairly peaceful at Lang Co village, and that inevitable comparing was going full force. The Marines of Charlie Company were vigorously comparing the past few days' events with combat operations I had never heard of, operations called Colorado and Union and Swift and battles for obscure terrain features such as Hill 110 and the Que Son Valley. Although I knew next to nothing about those operations and battles, I would learn about them from my Marines during the days and weeks to come. The Marines of Charlie 1/5, those lucky enough, or tough enough, to have survived those past encounters with enemy forces just loved to tell us new guys how tough and terrible those battles had been. I knew that some of what I heard might be a little exaggerated, because Marines love to tell these stories, and it seemed as though the stories got better each time they were told. But I also knew that most of it was fact, and the harsh realities and tough lessons of combat were there, in the stories. So I listened, and I learned.

Although Marines come from every walk of life and every part of our country and appear different in many ways, the one thing they have in common is this love of telling war stories. I attribute part of it to a perverse sense of humor, a warped competitiveness, and a love of bragging about how very, very tough *their* experiences had been in comparison. Another, perhaps more important part of it was a sense of history, of a deep and abiding respect for Marine Corps history, drilled into every Marine's skull from the earliest days of boot camp or OCS. And that history taught us that we were tough warriors, capable warriors, and warriors who would be victorious. It could never be otherwise.

This book is written by one of those warrior Marines. When I took command of Charlie 1/5 at Lang Co village, one of my platoon commanders was 2nd Lt. Nick Warr, the author of this book. Nick had arrived in Vietnam in mid-November of 1967 and had commanded 1st Platoon since then. Nick was seasoned and in control, and I immediately viewed him as a platoon commander I could definitely count on. He displayed a sort of professorial view of the war, and he commanded the respect of each of his troops. I shared that respect and frequently counted on Nick's wise guidance, absolute sense of direction in the most difficult of terrains, and even temperament to get us through some very difficult dilemmas. Moreover, I counted on Nick's tactical prowess and ability to look ahead. After all, he and I were both really only kids with flak jackets, weapons, and access to thunderous firepower from the air, sea, and ground and a huge amount of life-and-death responsibility. But in my book he was a real salt and someone to listen to. So, I did. I admired Nick as a combat officer then, and I admire him now as he leads the 1/5 Vietnam Veterans in the formation of a new association, as he promotes esprit de corps and assistance for all Marines, and as he authors enormously popular Marine Corps books and articles depicting the brave history of our Corps. Over these many years, he has never laid his Marine officer's sword aside, and for that I am most grateful.

When I look back on my experiences during the Vietnam War, during which time I led two different infantry companies in combat, served on the battalion's staff, and also served as 1/5's Battalion S-3 Alpha—and even as their operations officer for a few weeks—as a first lieutenant, I feel honored to have led those Marines in combat. I do feel very deep regret about the inevitable loss of life; death is always a part of warfare and was a terrible consequence of the Vietnam War. I regret the fact that many of those sacrifices came under my command, and I also deeply regret the terrible effect those deaths and injuries had on the parents and wives and children of those outstanding young Americans. I'm very proud of those Marines, and I believe that we did a good job under very difficult circumstances.

This book tells the story of some of the Marines who served in the 1st Battalion, 5th Marines during the early years of the Vietnam War. It records, for history, the events of the combat operations that 1/5 conducted from the time they landed near Chu Lai in late 1965 until we left the Phu Loc 6 Tactical Area of Responsibility (TAOR) and headed north toward the NVA who waited for us, in force, inside the citadel fortress of Hue.

Semper Fidelis!

Scott A. Nelson

Preface

My friends and family have often asked why I must tell these stories. First and foremost, I'm determined to write the truth about the Vietnam War as I experienced it—how it tasted and smelled, looked and felt, and how it is remembered by those who rose to the challenge of serving their country, risking everything in that worthy endeavor. Much of what has been written and most of what was made into movies about the Vietnam War focuses on caricatures of aberrations: a renegade general being pursued by a drunken army captain; drugged-out sergeants turning on each other, Americans killing their own. These lurid stories are mostly made up; if incidents similar to them did occur, at least in my experience, they were the rare exceptions, not the rule. For the most part, those who experienced combat in Vietnam served their country and the South Vietnamese with honor and then returned home and went on with their lives. That's the Vietnam War I choose to write about.

When asked to describe the fighting during the battle for Iwo Jima in the South Pacific in World War II, Adm. Chester W. Nimitz summed up the Marine fighting spirit with these few powerful words: "Uncommon valor was a common virtue." These words aptly describe the vast majority of the Marines who fought in Vietnam.

I write about the Vietnam combat veterans of the 1st Battalion, 5th Marines because they are true Americans who have done some rather amazing things as they served their country and Corps with honor and distinction and because they are my friends. I will never forget the Marines of Charlie One Five. All of them seemed so very young, yet many of them displayed an awesome courage, a gut-wrenching toughness and determination that allowed them to stand up in the face of certain death and somehow overcome their fears and push forward toward the sounds of gunfire. Over and over I witnessed these young Americans as they overcame those all-too-real fears to defy the enemy trying to kill them, somehow overcame adversity, and, in virtually every single battle during the Vietnam War, emerged victorious.

I also can not forget the exotic sights, smells, tastes, and sounds of the beautiful country called Vietnam. If ever a place fit the description of an exotic foreign land, Vietnam does. A picture taken from almost any spot in Vietnam could instantly become a best-selling scenic picture postcard. Vietnam's coastlines boast hundreds of miles of palm-lined, white sandy beaches splashed by the clear, blue green water of the South China Sea. Her western highlands are dominated by towering, jungle-covered mountains overlooking huge expanses of emerald green rice paddies, and beautifully framed, nearly magical villages and hamlets are interspersed throughout the lowlands. Yes, Vietnam was and is a beautiful, exquisitely scenic place, although many disturbing blemishes scarred its countryside during the war.

I can not forget the smell of death and the constant and shattering scenes of destruction that the war machines of both sides wreaked upon this beautiful but unfortunate land. Nearly every day of my thirteen-month combat tour in South Vietnam I witnessed, up close and personal, just how ugly a picture postcard scene could become when blasted by a 250-pound bomb, or some daisy-chained 105 mm artillery shells set up as a command-detonated bomb, or napalm, or mortar fire, or the sustained concentration of small arms fire from machine guns and other automatic weapons—or worse, when littered by shattered animal and human bodies. Many such scenes remain etched in my memories, and in my soul, indelibly, forever.

But most important, I can not, and I will never, forget the US Marines, the young American heroes who served with Charlie One Five during the Vietnam War. I can't forget what they said and what they did. I have forgotten some of their names, but I can't and won't forget what they looked like. Their faces appear as canvases in my memories—canvases upon which the complete scale of human emotions played out.

I saw laughter and happiness on those faces, because even in the most difficult and trying circumstances, those guys could somehow find humor. I saw the joy and elation of survival on those faces, but almost always those particular emotions became shaded with guilt, because they experienced joy from a victory in battle, which meant that they had killed other human beings. Their faces often showed another form of guilt, generated by an involuntary but very human elation that overwhelmed them when they had somehow survived another battle but their buddy had not. I saw their faces filled with anger, with hatred, with frustration, with fear, and with abject terror. I saw the facial etchings of hunger and fatigue, the dark shadows of sleep deprivation surrounding their wary eyes. I saw the quick acquisition of deep lines of physical exhaustion on their young but rapidly aging faces, oftentimes caused by physical deeds that they seemed uncertain they could do—but that, somehow, they did.

These emotions came not only at the hands of our enemy, the Viet Cong and NVA soldiers, but also from our other enemy, the very land we fought to protect. The extreme terrain and weather conditions as well as the exotic and dangerous wildlife and supposedly domesticated animals of South Vietnam sometimes took a greater toll on us than our Viet Cong and NVA enemy.

Another emotion I invariably witnessed on the face of the Marines I met was love: love of America; love of the Marine Corps; love of freedom; love of a buddy. The reason didn't matter one bit. Love simply resided there, in their hearts, every day. Love and deep friendship became determination, which became courage, which became the bravery to act in the face of certain death. And act they did, on many, many occasions. Some came home; too many didn't.

These are their stories.

Semper Fidelis. Always Faithful.

Acknowledgments

My heartfelt thanks go out to all of those combat veterans who went above and beyond the call of duty to assist me in this project. Returning to those distant days, if only in memory, was difficult for many of them, and I want them to know exactly how much I appreciate their courage then and today and their dedicated service to our Corps and country. Their combined efforts added significantly to this work, contributing to US Marine Corps history by providing a wide range of perspectives to the events that are recorded herein. Any errors of fact and grammar are mine alone.

Col. Marshall Buckingham "Buck" Darling, USMC (Ret), platoon commander, company commander (19 March 1941–20 June 2004)

Keith Vollendorf, squad leader

Hillous York, platoon sergeant, acting platoon commander

Lt. Gen. Arthur C. Blades, USMC (Ret), platoon commander

James K. "Blooper Man" Coxen

Col. Peter Hilgartner, USMC (Ret), battalion commander

Lt. Col. Dave McInturff, USMC (Ret), company commander

John "Rusty" Rusth (Navy Cross), fire team leader

Maj. Russell J. "Jim" Caswell, USMC (Ret), company commander

Harold L. Thrasher, rifleman

Delbert L. Best, fire team leader

Richard L. Schlagel, rifleman

David Babb, rifleman (deceased)

Brig. Gen. Jerry McKay, USMC (Ret), battalion communications officer, company commander

Rick Zell, platoon commander

Craig Jackson, platoon sergeant

Sgt. Maj. Dale Hatten, USMC (Ret), 81 mm mortar platoon commander (9 July 1936–29 May 2005)

Bruce C. "Cole" Morton, Ontos platoon commander

Gary Petrous, assistant machine gunner

Randy Leedom

Scott Nelson, company commander

I also wish to acknowledge the excellent assistance I received from several combat veterans and other writers while writing, editing, and revising this book. I have great appreciation for their help and friendship. When writing books, I believe it is critical to have a "true surface" off of which ideas and manuscripts can be bounced. I owe my eternal gratitude to Lt. Col. Joe Cody, USMC (Ret) (deceased); Lt. Col. Alex Lee, USMC (Ret); Maj. Jim Caswell, USMC (Ret); Col. Pete Hilgartner, USMC (Ret); Rick Zell; Craig Jackson; and Lt. Col. Dave McInturff, USMC (Ret), as well as to 1/5 Vietnam Veterans members Steve Colwell and Scott Nelson, for reading the original rough manuscript and providing me with invaluable critiques and feedback and to Scott, my skipper, for writing the Foreword to this book.

In particular, I wish to thank John D. Hollis for providing me with information he obtained from his investigations into the circumstances surrounding the death of Medal of Honor recipient Sgt. Rodney M. Davis. John is married to Sergeant Davis's niece, Regina, and he is in the process of writing a book about the life and courage of this great American hero.

Thanks to manuscript readers Lt. Col. Richard Bianchino, USMC (Ret), and author Spencer C. Tucker, Texas Tech University Press made the decision to publish this book, and to them I will always owe a debt of gratitude. The editorial and production staff at TTUP, including Robert Mandel, Jada Rankin, Joanna Conrad, and their entire team, also deserve kudos for their excellent work. As any writer knows, the writing and publishing of books is truly a collaborative effort, and the task cannot be completed without a significant team effort.

Many thanks also go out to Lt. Col. Richard L. "Wild Bill" Cody, USMC (Ret), for his outstanding contribution by creating all of the maps contained in this book.

I also wish to thank Staff Sgt. John "Mother" Mullan, USMC (Ret) for his leadership and help in completing my on-the-job training in South Vietnam during those early months and for his steadfast support of the 1/5 Vietnam Veterans. I owe you a huge debt of gratitude and friendship, Mother. Thanks for taking such good care of our Marines.

And last, but assuredly not least, thanks to my beloved wife, Pamela, for being a sharp-eyed editor, that perfectly true surface, and for representing all those readers who do not have direct experience in the military.

You have all made a huge difference in this work.

CHARLIE
ONE
FIVE

Prologue

The giant spider remained perfectly still. The tarantulalike arachnid's brown coloring and yellow and green markings matched its surroundings, allowing it to remain virtually invisible against the bark of the huge jungle tree trunk it clung to. Through instinct and experience, the frighteningly ugly creature knew that food would come; it just had to stay perfectly still until the humans came and went. Then the inevitable and frantic scattering of the small birds and mammals that lived in the area, as they fled the humans' approach, would inexorably draw one of them into the giant spider's web, ingeniously constructed atop the low growth on the jungle floor. Once entangled in its web, the prey invariably proved easy to kill. The eight-inch-diameter spider carried a large amount of very toxic venom, and it excelled at clinging to hapless small animals and pumping them full of that poison. Patience; that's all the giant spider needed to obtain food.

Several hours later, the jungle noise slowly died away as three heavily camouflaged Marines moved with tense anticipation toward the waterhole, their bodies hunched slightly under the weight of heavy packs, weapons at the ready. The point man knelt beside the placid pool, noticed the receding sounds of the jungle, opened his two canteens, and filled them with cold, crystal clear water. He reholstered both canteens, warily stepped away from the waterhole, and continued down the mountain trail. His companions took their turns replenishing canteens, then one went quietly to the left, the other right, and both disappeared into the low jungle foliage. No one spoke.

One minute later, seven more Marines—a four-man fire team, the squad leader, a corpsman, and a radio operator—cautiously approached the waterhole and spread out to provide security. Each took turns to fill his two canteens or watch the surrounding area.

While they worked, the squad leader spoke into a radio handset in a low but clear voice. "Cottage Charlie Six this is Charlie One Alpha. Have reached and secured the water source. We are replenishing. Will maintain security and finish water resupply. Plan to depart in five mikes, over." There followed a moment of low static from the radio, and then a brisk, acknowledging reply, "Roger. Out." Security had been established around the waterhole for the Marine infantry company approaching it from the mountain above. None of them had noticed the perfectly camouflaged spider clinging to the side of the tree trunk twenty feet above their heads.

The giant spider stayed calm; it was in no hurry. From its vantage point above the Marines it could see everything clearly. More Marines approached—a lot of them.

The spider had also seen the other two humans, the ones who arrived very early that morning, the ones who had spent a few minutes at the edge of the waterhole and then had slid back into the jungle. The giant spider had watched the two men creep well back into the low brush covering the jungle floor, and it knew that they remained there, hidden.

A final group of Marines in the squad, a four-man fire team and a three-man machine gun team, arrived at the waterhole. As they started their water resupply, the squad leader and his group proceeded down the trail, leaving the point fire team to provide security and then bring up the rear of the squad.

As each Marine holstered his full canteens, he quietly continued down the trail, staying within view of the man in front of and in back of him, displaying the natural choreography of a well-trained and very experienced Marine infantry squad.

The giant spider remained perfectly still. The constant jungle noise, having diminished somewhat during the time the humans had spent at the water hole, started to rise in volume and then died off again.

The point squad's security fire team silently withdrew from their hidden positions around the waterhole and trailed the rest of the squad down the hill toward open rice paddies.

Once again, the jungle noise around the deserted waterhole rose in volume as birds and insects briefly reclaimed their domain. The cacophony died when a group of twenty Marines descended the steep mountain trail and made a beeline toward the clear water. Most, parched, had finished both of their canteens an hour or more before, and the heat overwhelmed everything. With the area declared secure by the point fire team, no one in this group, the main element of the 1st Platoon of Charlie Company, 1st Battalion, 5th Marines, thought about setting up security. Thirst dominated their minds after humping for hours up and down this damnable mountain trail, in merciless heat and humidity.

The spider sensed the heat and sweat of the humans below him and sensed the increasing agitation and stress of the other two, still trying to remain hidden.

As their leaders, 1st Sgt. Louis U. Pellizzari and 1st Lt. Lawrence D. "The Crocodile"

Knuth followed the Marines into the open, chills ran down their spines despite the heat when they saw thirsty Marines, *their* Marines, in violation of the first rule of combat: "Spread out!" NCOs and officers constantly harped on their Marines to stay spread out whenever they found themselves outside the relative safety of a combat base. The two ran forward, hollering and screaming at the Marines.

"Get the fuck away from the waterhole!" yelled Pellizarri's gravelly voice. "Spread out, spread out, goddammit!"

"Who put security out? Get away from the water!" shouted Knuth.

Instinct saved the spider; it had sensed something calamitous was about to happen, and it moved quickly from the front of the tree into a deep crack in the bark on one side.

Suddenly a hideously blinding white light flashed, caused by a huge explosion. In an instant, concussion and fire from a command-detonated bomb turned the idyllic pond into a mud-filled abattoir filled with shredded bodies. Bloody, screaming men stumbled drunkenly or lay among the broken trees and shattered jungle vegetation surrounding what was left of the pond.

At the fringe of the chaotic scene, the two Viet Cong soldiers crawled away and vanished within the foliage, their mission accomplished.

The giant spider remained in its safe haven for several hours and then resolutely moved away from its destroyed habitat to find another home.

1: The Early Days and Operation Jackstay, December 1965–Early 1966

1st Lt. Marshall Buckingham "Buck" Darling arrived in South Vietnam in early 1965 as one of the three platoon commanders serving in C Company, 1st Battalion, 5th Marines (Charlie 1/5). The battalion was afloat at the time, serving as a Marine expeditionary unit (MEU) off the coast of South Vietnam.

Buck Darling had graduated from the University of California at Santa Barbara in June 1963. Buck had then lived and worked on a ranch until he learned that the Marine Corps, in his words, "gave away weapons and paid guys to hunt full time." He liked the whole military idea. Inspired by a local recruiter in Barstow, California, he joined the US Marines.

Darling graduated from the Basic School with a regular commission because he had done well in the Platoon Leaders Course (PLC), which he had taken during the summers before his junior and senior years in college, and in the Basic School. Buck requested an infantry MOS (military occupational specialty) and received orders to the 1st Battalion, 5th Marines.

Although 1/5 was based at Camp Pendleton, California, when Buck joined the battalion, it soon received orders to join the other units of the 1st Marine Division already in Vietnam. Once they arrived in WestPac (the Western Pacific) in 1965 and took responsibility as the infantry component of the MEU, 1/5 became responsible for special landing force (SLF) missions and remained afloat for about seven months. The Marines of 1/5 acted as the reserve force for virtually every combat operation in I Corps during that period because they had embarked with a full load of equipment, ammunition, and supplies and they even had raid gear. They had everything necessary for rapid reaction to virtually any combat situation. For example, 1/5 acted as one of the reserve forces for Operation Starlite, the first major American combat operation in South Vietnam, conducted by the 7th Marines shortly after the landings in Da Nang in early 1965.

For several long months, 1/5 sailed up and down the coast of South Vietnam. If something happened in Da Nang, they would go there as fast as possible. They might move rapidly north to Cap Ferrer, south to Cap Saint Jacques, and then back to Cap Ferrer. To Buck Darling, it seemed like every morning when they woke up they had a new "deal," as he called it.

In late spring of 1965 the battalion boarded a troop ship bound for Hawaii. They stayed in Hawaii, spent several weeks training, and then boarded the USS *Princeton*, sailing from Hawaii with a squadron of Frogs (CH-46 helicopters). In Da Nang they traded the Frogs in for a squadron of CH-34s. Shortly thereafter, in Subic Bay, a huge US Navy base in the Philippines, a large group of new people joined 1/5 as advisors. Once 1/5 put out to sea, the advisors revealed to the battalion's officers their destination: the infamous Rung Sat Special Zone (RSSZ) down around Saigon. The operation was to be called Jackstay.

Lt. Col. H. L. "Al" Coffman, the battalion commander, launched Operation Jackstay with the mission to conduct search-and-destroy operations to find and eliminate Viet Cong (VC) installations and to capture or destroy VC personnel in the RSSZ, a densely covered mangrove swamp area of approximately four hundred square miles. The native population of approximately fifteen thousand people lived in nine villages located on the relatively few dry islands in the area. The only road in the zone crossed the Long Thanh Peninsula. An extensive waterway system provided the only real transportation for the locals, by boat. Dense vegetation severely limited access to interior areas, and extensive flooding at high tide impeded the movement of foot troops, who had to cut paths through the soggy vegetation. The shallow water of the relatively few navigable channels forming the main shipping route upriver to Saigon, about twenty-five miles to the north, provided the only approaches to the RSSZ from the sea.

Although several VC installations had been identified in the RSSZ, their organization and strength varied considerably from day to day. Bunkers, ammunition and gun factories, caches, and VC units of company size populated the area. In addition, VC engineer units operated in the area on a regular basis in an attempt to block the shipping channel to Saigon. During late February and early March, the VC attacked shipping in the channel on several occasions.

Operation Jackstay, an amphibious operation, launched surface-borne and helicopter-borne assault forces on 26 March 1966. The initial phase of the operation focused on securing three objectives within approximately two days. Phase One dictated that a provisional rifle company, accompanied by an artillery battery, land over Red Beach and establish blocking positions. At the same time, the Marines of Charlie Company helilifted into LZ Sparrow and established blocking positions. Alpha Company landed at LZ Robin to secure the LZ and provide a defensive perimeter for subsequent landings. Bravo, Delta, and Headquarters and Service (H&S) Companies

The swamps of the Rung Sat Special Zone; photo taken in 2004. Courtesy of Mike Mavar.

and other combat support and service support elements followed Alpha Company into LZ Robin. Phase Two operations largely depended on the situation as it developed, the availability of helicopters and surface craft, and the time and space factors dictated by the terrain and weather.

Cpl. Keith Vollendorf from Wisconsin had served in Charlie 1/5 for over two years when the battalion arrived aboard ship off the coast of Vietnam. Keith had made squad leader (a billet that normally carries the rank of sergeant, E-5) a few months before, while afloat. Although Keith served in a different platoon from the one Buck Darling commanded, they knew each other well, because they had both been in Charlie Company for over a year.

Buck Darling loved his job as a leader of Marines in combat, and he took every aspect of it very seriously. Known as a ferocious fighter, Buck believed in thorough planning and determined execution. Keith Vollendorf proved also to be a natural-born leader who men would listen to and follow without argument or discussion under extreme conditions.

Keith wrote home regularly, sending several detailed letters to his family about his adventures, his fears, his plans, and his dreams. These letters home provide an excellent snapshot of the life of a US Marine in combat during this period of the

Vietnam War. One of his earliest letters home contained a brief but thorough diary of events during Operation Jackstay:

March 24, 1966,

Dear Family, It's about time I get busy and write a letter. This will be the last letter for approximately 3 weeks. Our operation starts on Saturday, March 26th. The name of the operation is JACKSTAY. Don't know if it will be in the papers or not, but imagine it will. We've got about 3 reporters aboard the ship right now.

My Platoon will be the first one to land in Vietnam. So, I'll be in the 1st wave of choppers to land. We don't expect too much resistance when we land, but then we're not sure. We're going to set up ambushes and then Bravo Company is going to push the Viet Cong towards us. It's going to be like a deer hunt; we'll watch them being pushed right into our positions. I just wish it was as easy as that.

This operation is taking place about 40 miles south of Saigon, on a peninsula just east of the Saigon River. The only extra gear we're taking along for ourselves, besides what we have on, is 3 pairs of socks and a toothbrush. So we're going to be some dirty and cruddy people in 3 weeks.

Just came back from chow. Tastes just as bad as it always does. Just got myself a haircut. Heard that tomorrow night they are having some sort of a celebration for us. Don't know what it will be though, probably a bunch of food and stuff. Right now we're sitting about 200 yards off the coast, but I don't know exactly where it's at.

If anything should happen to me, they will send you a telegram. I'll write as soon as I get back and let you know I'm okay. Just don't worry yourself about me, I'll be okay. We've got the best hospital ship in the world with us and our medical facilities are real good, so no sweat there.

6 April 1966

Dear Family, Well, here I am and still all in one piece! The operation just got over today. It lasted for about 12 days and they were the most miserable days I've ever spent in my life. I suppose you've been reading about it and watching it on TV. They told us it was really making the headlines back in the states.

Today when we got back aboard the ship, General Westmoreland came and talked to us all and congratulated us. We really screwed up the VC. My company is the one that found the hospital. It was really neat the way they had it set up in the jungle. We just wrecked the shit out of the whole place. It was a real big [enemy] hospital.

Right now I don't feel much like going into details about the operation 'cause I'm dead tired and just want to sleep. I'll explain it to you when I feel a little better. One man in my squad was killed the first night we went out. He was only about 20 yards from me and he got shot through the neck. We kept him alive for about 45 minutes but he died before the chopper could get there. I didn't lose any more people after that. Anyway, it's all over for a while and I'm damned happy to be here. Sure hope I don't have to go through that for quite a long time. Right now we're heading for Subic Bay and 2 weeks of R & R. So when I get there I'm going to do plenty of party timing!!

8 April 1966

Dear Family, Today we went to Chu Lai and dropped off a helicopter squadron and are now en route to Subic Bay. Here's a little breakdown about Operation JACKSTAY.

1st day—We got up at 0300 and drew our ammo. My squad had about 3,000 rounds and we each had 2 grenades, plus rifle grenades, smoke grenades, and I had a radio. We also had armored vests, helmets and packs. They really had us loaded down. 0600 rolled around and they called my team up on the flight deck and we got into a chopper. Everybody was scared. We were ready to go and it started to rain so they held it off for a while. By then everyone was getting a little jumpy. It cleared up in about 10 minutes and we were on our way. It took us about 15 minutes to get to the LZ (Landing Zone). We came in and I was the first one out. I ran across the opening and into some bushes. Nobody was firing at us so we set up around the LZ and waited. About 2 hours later I got the word to take my squad out and set up an ambush on the river. The rest of the company stayed at the LZ. We waded through mud that was waist deep and everybody was dead tired. We made it to the river and I set my men in. Everything went good for the rest of the afternoon, but then something bad happened—night came! It was just about everybody's first time in combat and we were all jumpy. Then the firing started—all I could hear was bullets whizzing over my head. It would stop for a while, then start all over again. Most of the fire we were receiving was from our own men back at the LZ. We weren't too far away. At 8:30, Hill was shot, so I called in on the radio to have a chopper get out there real fast. The choppers were out on the ship and they couldn't make it in time. Pfc. Richard K. Hill of Seaford, Delaware, was dead. I didn't tell the rest of the men that he had been shot. A few of them knew it. Then at 0300 all hell broke loose again 'cause they thought they saw something on the river. All I did was pray that daylight would come. It finally came at 0700. I swear to God it's the longest night I've ever spent in my life and ever will be. We made a litter and carried Hill's body back to the LZ. Sweeney said I looked like a ghost when I came in.

2nd day—Then they told me that two more men had been killed, Lance Corporal Anthony G. Velardo, from Wakefield, Massachusetts, and Lance Corporal David Colvin, from Indianapolis, Indiana, had been killed at the LZ. There were 4 men on a machine gun and one rolled over in his sleep and hit a land mine. It blew him in half and tore the hell out of the guy beside him. He got it in the back and in the head. He died aboard the ship that night. Another one got hit in the knee. The 4th one was lucky; all he got was a hole in the eardrum. He's in the Saigon hospital. He is a real good friend of mine. We crapped out for the rest of the day. Then they flew in choppers and we were lifted out to Red Beach. It had already been secured. We then caught boats to an LST (a type of ship). We stayed there that night. They finally got wise and we left our packs, helmets, armored vests and anything else we didn't need aboard the LST. We were going to travel real light.

3rd day—We boarded boats and headed for Blue Beach—we had to take this one. An NBC reporter was on my boat, a reporter with a camera, taking pictures. We hit the beach but received no fire. We ran into about 40 booby traps and we had to disarm them. Progress was real slow and the mud was waist deep. We moved inland for about a mile and stayed for the night. Still no contact with the VC.

4th day—We moved out again and headed for a big river where we were supposed to pick up boats. We walked all day long and finally came to a VC hut. All we did was blow it up. We finally came to the river. We were then informed that we would not be picked up until the next day. So we went out on an ambush patrol and 30 minutes later all hell broke loose. We got 4 VC in a sampan. The VC didn't even know what hit them. One was a doctor 'cause we got all his surgical equipment. We hung the body on a pole like a deer and brought him to our camp to show everybody our first VC. A chopper came in and dropped us 11 cans of beer for about 300 men (one of the good moments). All I got was a little sip though. It got dark again, and we went out on another ambush. 6 more came from the other way in a sampan; we got them too.

5th day—Morning came and we caught boats and they took us to a village, which was our battalion headquarters. We rested that day. I went to church and communion between two rice paddies in the mud.

6th day—We moved out at 1st light through the swamps again. The muddy water was up to our waist and higher all day. It got late and we stopped for the night. I volunteered to go out on an all night ambush. It was another miserable night, but no contact was made with the VC.

7th day—Moved out along the river and the swamps really became bad. The water was up to our necks. This did save us from a lot of heat casualties. We finally had to call in an airplane to find us some high ground. We got to the high ground and stayed for the night. We didn't send out any more ambushes that night.

8th day—Moved out again through the swamps for awhile and then we finally hit high ground. It was so nice to be walking on solid ground. We then came to a VC training center that had been bombed by B-52 bombers two days before. It was a relief to see that place destroyed. They had fortified bunkers all over the place. If the VC had been there we would have lost some people. We then moved on and by pure luck we came upon this field hospital. At first we didn't know what it was. Then we found all kinds of equipment. They must have heard us coming 'cause no one was there. We collected up anything that might be valuable information and saved it. Then we started wrecking the buildings. It was fun doing that and we didn't leave anything standing. We spent the rest of the night there.

9th day—We moved back to the VC training center that had been bombed and cleared an LZ for our choppers. We sat in there all day. At night we sent out an ambush patrol and killed more VC coming down a stream in their sampan. Captured rifles and some more gear.

10th day—That morning I had to take out a patrol and see if any VC were trying to get close to us. I didn't see any so I came back. Then they flew in choppers and were taking us back to the village for some more rest (we needed it). I had to keep my squad at the LZ until the whole company was flown out. We had to stop any VC trying to shoot at our choppers; those big birds make nice targets. We made it back to the village that day. The next day we were supposed to go to our last objective, but they decided to keep us in reserve, 'cause we had done more than any other company. So far, that made us real happy (not the officers, though).

11th day—We stayed at the village.

12th day—Flew back to the USS Princeton and took my first shower after 12 days and changed my clothes for the first time. We really smelled raunchy!

> All the time we were out there, one day was like all the rest. Walking through the waist deep water and mud, mosquitoes, bugs and big red ants. Maybe it doesn't sound too bad on paper, but I left out all the little things that really made it miserable. If you had ever had someone trying to kill you, you would probably know what I mean. Anyway, it's all over now, I'm here and still alive, and as far as I'm concerned that's all that counts. The Marine Corps can shove this war right up their ass! I don't want any more of it. I don't need that extra $65 per month for combat pay. I would just as soon be broke as to earn it that way. If the VC knew what they were fighting for and knew what they were up against, they wouldn't even be there. Well, enough of my gung-ho war stories for now.

Buck Darling also remembers those long, soggy days in the swamps of the RSSZ. The battalion stayed ashore for almost two weeks in the swamps during Jackstay. Buck's 3rd Platoon of Charlie 1/5 was assigned as a main maneuver element responsible for establishing the blocking positions.

A tough and determined young second lieutenant, Buck got better at his job with each day that passed. He took pride in the fact that his platoon, and later the companies he led, got their job done with very few casualties. "Third Platoon didn't lose any people during Jackstay," he said. "We ran ambushes and patrols day and night, and we killed a whole bunch of Cong. We patrolled the Rung Sat Special Zone during that operation for about ten days, and there was nothing good about it. It was a nasty, horrible place. But our company took no casualties that I was aware of. We had three or four good days, striking and ambushing, striking and ambushing, day and night. It seemed like every five minutes we made contact and killed Viet Cong."

Buck Darling strongly believed that every day was a good day, every day of his life, before, during, and after Vietnam. Every day was a good day, but on some occasions, when bad things happened to his men, it became much harder to maintain that attitude.

As planned, on 6 April 1966 the Marines of 1/5 withdrew from the RSSZ and went back aboard the USS *Princeton*. According to the combat after-action report compiled by Lieutenant Colonel Coffman, Operation Jackstay accounted for at least sixty-three Viet Cong killed by 1/5 Marines and probably sixty more either killed or wounded. In addition, Battalion Landing Team 1/5 captured and/or destroyed a substantial amount of enemy equipment and material. The RSSZ proved to be a very difficult area in which to conduct combat operations. But overall, the Marines of 1/5 accomplished their mission with great success and took very few casualties, which proved the Marines were up to the task.

On 27 April 1966, 1/5 departed the USS *Princeton* for the mountainous jungles of I Corps, assigned to another search-and-destroy mission, Operation Osage. On D-Day, 1/5 helilifted to LZ Crow, located on the top of Bach Ma, one of the dominant mountains located north of the Hai Van Pass and south of Phu Bai in the Phu Loc district. An old French compound sat atop Bach Ma, complete with a swimming pool and a cluster of very substantial buildings.

Located only about eight kilometers from the Dam Cau Hai coastal bay, the steep, jungle-covered mountain peaks in the Bach Ma area soared 1,250 to 1,300 meters high, over four thousand feet in elevation. The Marines searched the compound and quickly determined it was deserted, so they did not stick around long. They worked their way northward, down toward the coast. Temperatures rose, so each man carried as much extra water as possible.

"One Five really took a long, slow hike, but we didn't see anything up there," Buck Darling recounted:

> We finally got down into the plains, and someone called in and said, "See that hill over there? Well, get on top of it." Our battalion commander, Lt. Col. Al Coffman, served during the Korean War and used 1:5,000 maps in Korea; we used 1:50,000 maps in Vietnam, so, to him, a foot on a map measured out a short distance. He never really understood the distance a foot represented on our maps. But he was the boss, so when he told us to get on top of this hill, we had to go. We started toward our objective and immediately ran into thick, vine-covered jungle and very steep terrain. We reached a point ten feet from the top when somebody threw a grenade at us. Sergeant Sweeny had the point squad, and Sweeny went over the top like a tiger with about ten Marines right behind him. We never did catch the guy. About that time, battalion called again and said, "Get down off there." Everybody said okay, and we turned around and someone flying around in an airplane called down and told us to go down this trail. So we started down that damned trail.

Meanwhile, Vollendorf's squad of Marines humped for hours up and over a steep jungle-covered mountain trail. When they started their forced march, they had the trail position in the rear of Charlie Company, but they took point later that morning.

By the time the squad reached the top of the "hill," in reality a small mountain by anyone's standards, Keith had drunk his own canteens down to a swallow or two. He knew that, despite his constant lectures on water conservation, his men had probably finished every drop of their water from all of their canteens because of the nearly unbearable and monstrous heat. They had to find a source of drinkable water soon, or they would start taking heat casualties. Battalion had put pressure on Charlie

Company to move fast, and since they had put his squad on point, both the battalion and company commanders kept demanding that the point squad's pace stay at a brisk speed.

As they neared the bottom of the hill, much to Corporal Vollendorf's amazement and delight, a beautiful pool full of clear spring water came into view. It looked just like a picture postcard. Vollendorf and his squad had seen other beautiful locations during their previous operations down south in the RSSZ, as well as in the countryside northwest of Chu Lai, an area known as VC Valley, but this setting raised the bar on pure scenic beauty. Lush vegetation, exotic flowers, and thick clumps of shimmering green ferns surrounded the clear pool. A huge, ancient tree towered above their heads from its base behind the pool, draped with nature's threads of jungle foliage.

Vollendorf's Marines went into a practiced routine, an automatic mode, and quickly secured the area around the pool; the point fire team filled up first and fanned out around the pond a short distance. Then they proceeded down the trail toward the bottom of the mountain. The rest then filled their canteens with practiced and efficient movements. The mountainside remained perfectly quiet except for the occasional shriek from a bird or small animal in the heavy growth nearby. Vollendorf beckoned to his radio operator, took the handset of his squad PRC-25 radio, and called his platoon commander, First Lieutenant Knuth, to give him a brief situation report.

About a hundred meters behind Vollendorf's squad, the main body of the 1st Platoon (point element for Charlie 1/5) stopped to take a brief break. Buck Darling's 3rd Platoon Marines acted as the rear element of Charlie Company, still well behind them up the steep mountain trail, but Buck had come forward to coordinate with Knuth. Buck Darling sat on a rock beside the trail, his pack still on, talking quietly with his friend, Larry "The Crocodile" Knuth. The nickname had evolved as a result of Knuth's appearance and demeanor. Larry Knuth and Buck Darling had spent many long nights and arduous days together as officers in Charlie Company and had become very close friends.

After some good-natured bitching about the heat and terrain, Crocodile surprised Buck by getting serious for a few moments. Buck shook his head as he remembered this conversation with a damning clarity, but when it occurred it seemed like just one of those infrequent moments, a snippet of conversation, when a guy had gotten deadly serious but you didn't register the change, you didn't really pay close attention to what was being said. For Buck Darling, it became one of those moments that haunted him for the rest of his life.

"He and I were just about the best friends that ever lived," Buck continued. "We had taken a short break before starting down the hill. Knuth and I sat down on a rock beside the trail. As we sat there, the Crocodile handed me his loot, you know, a stick, some stuff he had collected, and he handed me this stuff and said, 'Here, take this stuff, and if you don't see me again, keep it.' "

Buck didn't think much of it, just agreed to carry the stuff, so a few moments later, when Corporal Vollendorf's situation report to Knuth came over the company net, Buck forgot about what Larry Knuth had said and about the extra baggage he now carried for his friend.

Despite the constant scratchy static background noise that always accompanied radio communications via "Prick-25s," Corporal Vollendorf's voice came in clearly with a very welcome report. "Cottage Charlie Six this is Charlie One Alpha. Have reached and secured a water source. We are replenishing. Will maintain security and finish water resupply. Plan to depart in five mikes, over." Knuth tersely acknowledged the message: "Roger. Out."

First Lieutenant Knuth passed the word to the company CP. Everyone in Charlie Company was thirsty, so they didn't have to say it twice. Buck watched as his friend, Larry Knuth, 1st Sgt. Louis U. Pellizzari, and several other enlisted Marines, some surrounding the company commander with radios on their backs, started down the path. Buck and his 3rd Platoon Marines waited until the following 2nd Platoon Marines passed through his position, and then his Marines followed the others down the trail. As they started forward, Buck heard Vollendorf's second situation report come in over the company net, indicating that his squad had completed their water resupply and had moved further down the trail to visually make contact with the next objective and to secure the open rice paddy area to their northeast.

Buck Darling had awful memories of that terrible day. When that bomb went off, Buck instantly thought back to that brief, subdued conversation with his friend Larry Knuth only a few minutes before. The Crocodile apparently had a premonition.

> We were all green as hell, only in country for a short while. Knuth and his radio operator arrived at the bottom of the hill, and he saw about thirty Marines bunched up around this spring. We were all thirsty as hell, and people were taking advantage of the fresh water supply. The Crocodile started bellowing at his people, telling them to get away from the spring and to spread out. I guess the guy at the other end of the wire figured out that this was about as many guys as he was going to get, so he triggered that bitch.
>
> About fifteen minutes before this happened, Knuth and I were having that conversation. Now, here he was, jelly. I don't know the makeup of that bomb. It didn't seem to have much shrapnel in it, but it was a very large bomb, probably a bunch of C-4. It had a huge amount of explosive power, and our people had bunched up really close, crowded around that water, and the bomb took

> out the spring, killed seven of our people and wounded about fifteen more. Our company commander wasn't in very good shape. He had been pretty close. Knuth was pretty much jelly from the waist down. The Crocodile and 1st Sergeant Pellizzari had tried to get people spread out, but it was too late.
>
> A big cloud of smoke came up. The people within a hundred meters were pretty shell shocked, you know, standing around in a daze. So, the corpsmen from 2nd and 3rd Platoons started working on the wounded. I got down there within a minute or so. We laid out the casualties and started calling in the medevacs. The explosion transformed this beautiful spring into a black, muddy hole filled with people's bodies. Sergeant Westmoreland and I fished the Crocodile's body out of the muddy hole.

Keith Vollendorf's terrible memories of that day won't ever go away. He said, "While we carried the bodies, the company fought with the VC on the hill. The VC killed one more Marine and wounded one. Altogether, Charlie Company lost seven killed and seven wounded. I then moved my squad further down the line. I saw two VC run into a cave, and I fired two grenades right in behind them. Don't know if I got them or not. We finally got the VC, so we pulled out. That evening they brought in three more companies to help us. We'd been hit bad, so they kept us in reserve for the next two days, which I didn't mind at all."

The seven Marines killed by that command-detonated bomb on 29 April 1966 during Operation Osage include 1st Lt. Lawrence D. Knuth, from Boynton Beach, Florida; 1st Sgt. Louis U. Pellizzari, from Solvay, New York; HM2 Bob E. "Doc" Pogre, from San Francisco, California; Pfc. Harry D. Haskins from Dayton, Ohio; Pfc. James C. Wiskur from Winthrop, Illinois; Pfc. Loren E. Bradley from Granite City, Illinois; and Sgt. David D. Gummere, from La Habra, California.

That day, 29 April 1966, went down as one of the deadliest single days for Charlie Company, 1st Battalion, 5th Marines during the Vietnam War. Many such bloody days lay ahead for the Marines who served with Charlie 1/5, but those who were there would long remember the day the VC set off that devastating command-detonated bomb, instantly transforming a peaceful, idyllic place into a Dantesque scene from hell.

2: Sparrow Hawk and Operation Colorado, June-December 1966

Buck Darling's career continued to advance steadily. Promoted to first lieutenant in early June 1966, Buck became the Charlie Company executive officer, and a week later Lieutenant Colonel Coffman made him the company commander of Charlie Company. The Marines of 1/5 went back aboard ship and a few days later got orders to organize another combat operation. The TAOR for Operation Desoto/Deckhouse V was out in a very bad area in the Quang Ngai province.

The enemy shot down two helicopters during Desoto/Deckhouse V, but 1/5 didn't take many casualties, and they killed many Viet Cong soldiers. The operation started when the Marines took over a hill that a South Vietnamese Regional Forces (RF) company held. The Marines started patrolling right away, and that didn't sit well with the regiment or so of Viet Cong that had occupied the area around the hill. The VC had stayed fairly safe because they operated so close to this hill, which was inside a save-a-plane area.[1] Very rapidly, an entire regiment of Marines landed in that area to fight the VC.

The Marines, expanding the perimeter at Chu Lai, moved west toward the mountains. When Operation Desoto/Deckhouse V concluded, 1/5 stayed at Da Nang for a day or two and then went back to Chu Lai. Almost immediately they moved to Hill 54, located a few kilometers northwest of Chu Lai, and started building a new combat base there. Fairly flat, and not a very dominant terrain feature, Hill 54 was completely surrounded by rice paddies, so the Marines of 1/5 stayed secure there. Later on, when it started raining, it got muddy, but other than that, life at Hill 54 Combat Base seemed good.

"Except for that damned bomb that got the Crocodile and the others," Buck Darling said, "we hadn't taken any casualties until we got to the Chu Lai area. After we set up the combat base at Hill 54, we started having problems with enemy snipers and started to take casualties. We had a sniper named Terry Redic, a Marine who I had trained in Hawaii. I told Terry to go out there before dawn one morning, and when that Viet Cong sniper started shooting at us, Terry took him out from a range of about twelve feet. The Cong had fired a couple of rounds at us, and tried to run away right over Terry, but it didn't work out very well for him."

Combat activities continued at a steadily increasing pace for 1/5 in the area surrounding Chu Lai Combat Base complex. May and early June staggered forward, one long, hot, dangerous, sweaty day after the other. Then, in early June, 5th Marines assigned Charlie Company to a "Sparrow Hawk" mission. Those assigned to Sparrow Hawk formed a rapid reaction unit that would stand by, loaded up and ready to go at a moment's notice, in the event something bad happened and friendly forces needed help. In addition to the commanding officer, 1st Lt. Buck Darling, the leaders of Charlie Company included 2nd Lt. Rob Enaiko, 1st Platoon commander; 2nd Lt. Ronald W. "Stumpy" Meyer, 2nd Platoon commander, and Staff Sgt. John Gall, 3rd Platoon commander.

On 16 June 1966, something very bad happened. The reconnaissance team of Staff Sgt. Jimmie E. Howard stepped on a hornet's nest, a main force NVA battalion. The recon team, surrounded and overwhelmingly outnumbered, tried futilely to break contact with the enemy. The large enemy force of an estimated five hundred soldiers had trapped Staff Sergeant Howard and his twenty-man recon team, intending to systematically destroy them. Immediately, the call went out for the Sparrow Hawk team.

Buck Darling remembers this day with great clarity: "I got a call about 0300," he said, "informing me that a recon team had gotten hit and that they were surrounded and in grave danger of being overrun and wiped out. All kinds of rumors about where we were going flew around the combat base. It turned out to be a very large lift, with about forty CH-34 helicopters; seemed like damn near every one of the CH-34s located in the Da Nang/Chu Lai AO [area of operations]."

Even given the dire circumstances of Staff Sergeant Howard's recon team—surrounded, outnumbered, and suffering—the Sparrow Hawk rescue effort became hampered by issues of communications and coordination fairly common to the movement of troops and equipment in Vietnam. Buck Darling and his officers had maps of the Quang Ngai province area a few kilometers south of Chu Lai, but their helicopters lifted off and started flying in the opposite direction. Fortunately, he had encountered this so often that they had acquired their own 1:100,000 maps of the entire I Corps TAOR, and his wife, Linda Darling, had recently supplied plastic laminate from the States to protect them.

Buck knew that Staff Sergeant Howard and his Marines were in deep trouble and running out of ammunition. He wanted to save as many of that recon team as he could, but the rapid reaction nature of their mission, and the typical chaos of war, combined to create more confusion. When Buck got to the helipad, he saw the air officer controlling the liftoff and asked him which helicopter was the lead helicopter. The air officer yelled, "Yellow Back Number 19," or something like that. Buck saw a CH-34 with the number 19 painted on it, ran over to it, threw two people off, grabbed his radio operator, and climbed on.

This massive armada of CH-34 helicopters flew north and circled Tam Ky for about half an hour, and Buck got antsy. So he moved forward in the very noisy helicopter, took out his notepad, and wrote out a message for the pilot: "Where are we going?" He reached up and tapped the pilot on his knee. The pilot's hand came down, and Buck put his note in his hand. A few seconds later his note came back down, and on the back side of the note was written, "Damned if I know!" Buck turned it over, and wrote, "You're the lift commander, right?" Buck lifted it up, tapped his knee, and a few moments later the reply came back down that said, "No, I'm barely a hack." Buck ripped off another page, and wrote, "I'm the troop commander!"

About that time, the crew chief, who had watched this written dialogue with great interest, took off his headphones and handed them to Buck, providing him with voice communications directly with the pilot. Once again, Buck asked him their destination, and the pilot confirmed that he really didn't know but that they were circling because the save-a-plane area hadn't been established yet, as everyone in the area was pounding the target with artillery. They had been hitting the area with artillery for most of the night. Buck looked off to the west of Tam Ky and saw Willy Pete (white phosphorous) explosions and asked the pilot if that was their target area, and, once again the pilot said, "Damned if I know."

Trying not to show his disgust, Buck then asked the pilot to get in touch with the lift command pilot, so he did. He got permission to move toward the front of the lift formation, and a few moments later Yellow Back Number 19 moved forward and took up the command position on point.

Buck and his Sparrow Hawk rescuers loitered airborne so long before they reached their planned landing zone that all forty choppers had to land in nearby Tam Ky to refuel and take off again, a major exercise. "When we got back airborne," Buck said, "we finally got the word that we now knew the location of Staff Sergeant Howard's team, that supporting arms were about to fire their last artillery mission at the target, and then we would make our landing. The target area, called Nui Vu, was quite a ways west of Tam Ky. We found a landing zone. Helicopters on the north side of the hill reported taking quite a bit of flak, so we decided to land three or four birds at a time on the south side in a big area of elephant grass on a gently sloping ridge that went to the southwest."

Buck knew from radio reports that the stranded recon team could not hold out much longer. Most of their men had been killed or wounded. "I sent the 1st Platoon around the side of the hill to see if they could get below the enemy and cut them off and kill them. I then sent Stumpy Meyer up to the top of the hill with the 2nd Platoon, where the recon team was still fighting the enemy, and told him to help them get control, treat their wounded, start the process of getting medevacs in, and then stay put. I then sent the 3rd Platoon around the other side of the hill to see if they could cut the enemy off on that side."

The Marines of Charlie 1/5 managed to fight their way up to Sergeant Howard's position on the hill, finally stopping the destruction of the small recon team. It was not until later that the true ferocity of this battle became evident. Buck remembers, "It was a tough fight. Something like a dozen Cong got inside Sergeant Howard's perimeter; they were later found dead, killed with KA-BAR knives and entrenching tools. The VC had a lot of weapons and ammo, and the Marines expended most of their own ammunition during the melee, but they somehow managed to collect some AK-47s from dead Viet Cong and used them against their enemy. The Viet Cong, so certain that they would kill everyone in Howard's patrol, continued attacking them even as we landed in the helicopters a click [kilometer] away."

Despite their overwhelming advantage in numbers, the enemy had been pinned down on the hill all night long by artillery fire. Howard's Marines fought like Devil Dogs with M14s and hand grenades. They continued to attack when Charlie Company arrived on the battlefield; the NVA, certain they would win, just kept coming. When Buck and his Marines got to Howard's position, he saw live enemy soldiers within five feet of Howard's position, some of them feigning death. Buck calmly shot one of them, an NVA lieutenant playing dead who was getting ready to shoot Howard.

In the aftermath of the battle, the Marines discovered they had been fighting an enemy entrenched in a nest of foxholes dug overnight at the base of the hill. It took about two or three hours for Charlie Company to get them out of those holes and to kill them. "When we 'policed up' Howard's hill that day," Buck said,

> we found a whole shitload of guns there; we ended up putting 150 enemy weapons on the helicopter. We left behind a couple of hundred enemy bodies. Staff Sgt. Jimmie Howard and his corpsman were the only two Marines able to walk out of that position; we carried the rest of them down that hill.
>
> Our casualties included my sniper, Lance Cpl. Terry Redic, from Anderson, Indiana; Terry stood up to get a better shot and someone took him out with a machine gun. 2nd Lt. Ronald W. "Stumpy" Meyer, from Dubuque, Iowa, really wanted a Silver Star. Stumpy collected up a bunch of hand grenades and went hunting. He went down the hill, ran right into the teeth of the enemy positions, but unfortunately he ran out of hand grenades before he ran

out of enemy. He went down in the open at the bottom of the hill, dead. One of his Marines said to me, "Sir, the Lieutenant's out there, and we've gotta go get him." So I told him to keep his head down, and we crawled down to the bottom of the hill and got his body. Stumpy Meyer got his Silver Star for throwing all those hand grenades, but he earned it the hard way.

Cpl. Keith Vollendorf's Charlie One Alpha squad found themselves right in the middle of this action, as he wrote home a few days later:

June 17, 1966

Yesterday morning we were called out to help get a Recon team out of trouble (20 men). I'm sure it's hit the news back home. It was unbelievable what those 20 Marines did. A battalion of VC attacked them at two in the morning and they fought them off until we got there (about 7:30 am). We still had to fight the VC off. There were bodies all over the hill, Marines and VC. There were only three Marines left that could walk out of there on their own power. Two of those were wounded. They were just about all out of ammo when we reached them. One man had 8 rounds left and another guy had 7. One guy came up to us and started crying, and he said, "Oh, God, I never thought you'd get here." He said he didn't think he'd ever see civilization again.

Those Marines put up such a terrific fight you can't even imagine what it was like. There are a lot more little details, but they are hard to explain. I just wish we could have gotten there sooner to help them out. Something like that really makes you "proud" to be a Marine.

A whole battalion of NVA had completely surrounded Jimmie Howard's recon team, but the recon team did an excellent job of calling in artillery support and defending their hill ferociously. Combat after-action reports of this battle indicate that the recon team and the Marines of Charlie 1/5 killed over two hundred NVA soldiers. Staff Sgt. Jimmie Howard, awarded the Medal of Honor, and his heroic recon team are considered the most highly decorated military unit in American history.

Memories of the events of 16 June 1966 stayed firmly in the back of the Charlie 1/5 Marines' minds, but they were quickly forced from conscious thought. The Marines knew by now that they had to pay attention, to remain alert, to fight the fatigue and distractions surrounding them. They all knew that just about the time the deceptive peacefulness of the countryside and the humid heat of Vietnam lulled them, the enemy would surely strike again, often when least expected.

The ensuing months in the Chu Lai area passed in routine skirmishes and oppressive heat. After the Sparrow Hawk operation, Charlie Company continued combat operations in and around the Chu Lai TAOR. A few days after their fight on Hill 488, the Marines of Charlie Company found themselves on a remote outpost dubbed Snaggletooth Island.

The area was actually a cluster of small islands just north of Chu Lai. The outpost included a Hawk (antiaircraft missile) battery, colocated with a Combined Action Platoon (CAP) unit. The Marines of Charlie 1/5 patrolled that area for a month or so. They captured more weapons than they killed Viet Cong, because the enemy mainly traveled the area aboard boats, so even when the Marines hit them hard, a lot of the bodies floated away in the river.

Keith Vollendorf, soon to be promoted to sergeant, remembers some parts of his Vietnam experience as fun:

20 June 1966

Dear Family, We're having a big exciting day today. John Wayne is coming here. I guess he's not bringing any women with him, so I don't imagine it will be too much. I think they are afraid to bring women out to this hill (Ha!).

I received your package and Grandma's yesterday. The sausage tastes real good. I got two things full of cookies from Grandma and they were real good. It only takes 4 or 5 days for a package to get here, so it doesn't take long at all.

Last night the VC had a mortar attack on our Regimental Headquarters. It's about 5 miles down the road from us. We lost 3 KIAs and about 22 WIAs. This morning they found about 10 VC tangled up in the barbed wire. Now they're getting all shook up here, 'cause they think they will hit us pretty soon. I guess I'll have to agree with them. Sure hope they hit with mortars after I leave, 'cause those mortars can really be rough.

Still haven't heard for sure when I'm coming home. Lots of rumors, but half of those aren't true. So, I'll just have to wait until my orders come in.

I told you I was going on Operation 'KANSAS' a few days ago. Well, about an hour before we were to leave they cancelled it. The VC were tipped off and had moved out of the area. So it didn't make much sense going in.

Keith's letters home continued to roller coaster along, matching the savage up-and-down emotions felt by the Charlie 1/5 Marines as they marched into the hellish heat of the summer of 1966:

26 June 1966

Dear Family, I finally scraped up enough energy to write a letter. It gets so damn hot around here you just don't feel like doing much of anything.

27 June 1966

Dear Family, As you can see, I didn't get this letter finished yesterday. A few things came up so I didn't have much time.

Things have finally turned for the good around here. I'm no longer on Hill 54 anymore. Our Company was moved into Chu Lai to guard the airstrip. I don't even think there are too many VC in the area. We're supposed to be here for 5 weeks, so it should be some pretty slack duty.

By the time we're due to leave here, I should be ready to come home. So my chances of getting shot around here are pretty nil.

p.s. My letter was sent in for me to make Sergeant, but it hasn't returned yet. Maybe I'll get it in a few days.

As Corporal Vollendorf prepared for his promotion to sergeant and his return ride home, many hundreds of replacements began rotating through the ranks of 1st Battalion, 5th Marines. When America first committed its ground forces to the war, US Marine Corps battalions arrived in South Vietnam intact. When the 1st Battalion, 5th Marines arrived off the coast of South Vietnam and began their amphibious operations, the infantry companies were at nearly full strength. The Marines had trained together for months and, in some cases, for years as a Marine infantry battalion. The Marines knew each other; commanders at all levels knew the names of their subordinates, along with their strengths, weaknesses, tendencies, and idiosyncrasies. They possessed the mental spirit of a family as well as that of a combat fighting unit.

As the war took its inexorable toll on the Marines of 1/5, new men joined this family. As the individual rotation system took full affect through the mid- and late 1960s, the original feeling of family diminished somewhat as new men arrived and old hands departed almost daily. To 1/5's great fortune, many of the replacements proved to be outstanding Marines, including officers, enlisted men, and NCOs. One of the earliest replacement Marines to join 1/5 was an NCO with a rather famous name, Sergeant York. This Sergeant York arrived in South Vietnam and joined the 1st Battalion, 5th Marines at the end of July 1966.

Sgt. Hillous York, a distant cousin of the famous Sgt. Alvin York of World War I fame, enlisted in the Marine Corps in January, 1965. Born and raised in Tennessee, right across the river from Alvin York's Kentucky clan, Hillous proved to be a natural combat leader in the great tradition of the York family and therefore received meritorious promotions on several occasions.

Hillous didn't actually enlist in the Marine Corps. He received a draft notice and dutifully reported to the local induction center for processing and a physical. After his group had been examined thoroughly and had passed the physical, Hillous remembers, strange events eventually led him into the Marine Corps: "There were two doors in the examining room," Hillous said,

> There must have been about fifty of us standing in that room. An army sergeant stood at one door, and a Marine sergeant, standing at the other door, made an announcement: Everyone who wanted to go in the army would go through the left door, and everyone who wanted to go in the Marines would go through the right door. So I thought, well, heck, if I'm going to have to go to Vietnam, I might as well go with the Marines. So I walked over toward the door guarded by the Marine sergeant, and I heard all this snickering and laughing going on behind me. So I turned around and looked to see what they were laughing about and saw that I was the only one who had chosen the Marine Corps. Every other guy in that room had chosen the army, and they all laughed at me. I thought, well, shoot, I'm going to stick with my decision. I got my own laugh a few moments later when the Marine sergeant went over to the big mob of guys who had chosen the army and said, "You, you, you, and you. You are now in the United States Marine Corps."

Hillous also recalls that he took a lot of ribbing because of his name and because he had gone in the Marine Corps instead of the army. Hillous's father and brother and all of his cousins, as well as most of the other York boys from Tennessee and Kentucky, had done their military service in the army, following in the footsteps of their famous relative, Sgt. Alvin York. His buddies in the Marine Corps got a lot of mileage out of the fact that "Sergeant York" had chosen the Marines over the army.

Another replacement Marine with much combat in his future was 2nd Lt. Arthur C. Blades. He arrived in South Vietnam on 10 July 1966, fresh from his training in the United States, and caught a ride with a driver and a staff NCO from S-1 (Administration) who were going to the 1st Battalion, 5th Marines headquarters about ten miles up the road. The driver and staff NCO carried only personal weapons. Blades asked if he should be armed but was assured that the road was safe.

Upon arriving at battalion, 2nd Lieutenant Blades reported to the S-1 officer. The S-1 told Blades that his relief had finally arrived and that he would be taking command of a platoon. Blades asked the S-1 who his relief was. The S-1, a captain, looked at Blades and said, "That would be you, Lieutenant." Blades asked if that was negotiable and stated that he had not come to Vietnam to be an S-1. The captain said, "The decision has been made, Lieutenant, and you should learn to accept that fact."

After waiting a few more minutes, Blades reported into the battalion command post (CP) to meet with Lieutenant Colonel Coffman. Lean, tanned, with steely blue gray eyes, the battalion commander welcomed the lieutenant to the 1st Battalion, 5th Marines. After exchanging minor pleasantries, Coffman officially informed Blades about his assignment as the battalion S-1 and how important it was to the battalion. After that announcement, Blades stood up and came to attention, saying, "I wish to request mast with the regimental commander in order to transfer to a fighting unit."

A dead silence followed, and one could see a storm building inside Lieutenant Colonel Coffman. In a very tightly controlled voice, Coffman leaned over his desk and asked Blades to repeat his request, which he did. The lieutenant colonel also rose to his feet, looked Blades straight in the eye, and said, "Well, Lieutenant, if you want to see combat so badly I will grant you your wish. You are hereby assigned to Charlie Company, the assault company for the battalion. Charlie Company sees the most combat, Lieutenant, so you are sure to see as much combat as you want. Charlie Company also has the highest officer attrition rate. I am making this assignment, Lieutenant, with only one condition. That condition is if you should ever be unfortunate enough to get killed, you will have to promise not to come back and haunt me." Lieutenant Blades, at a loss for words, stuttered, "Aye, aye, sir." That minute, Art Blades was assigned as the platoon commander of 1st Platoon, Charlie 1/5.

With that, Blades left Coffman's office and returned to the S-1. The S-1 told him he would like serving as the S-1. As Blades told the S-1 the plans had changed, the phone rang from the CP confirming his new assignment to 1st Platoon, C Company, 1/5, under the much-touted combat leader Capt. Marshall Buckingham Darling III.

As the long, hot summer of 1966 progressed, the ebb and flow of human lives, marked by the arrival and departure of rotating Marines, continued without interruption. Newly promoted Sgt. Keith Vollendorf's final letters home represented the thoughts and dreams that all these young Americans experienced during their final days in a war zone:

> 31 July 1966
>
> Dear Family, I'm making Sergeant tomorrow. It was a meritorious promotion. So I'm pretty happy now. It should make life back in the states a lot easier.
>
> Our Regiment is going out on Operation COLORADO on the 4th of August. You better have a lot of cold, cold beer on hand for when I reach home! Because I'm going to be in the mood for a little beer drinking.

8 August 1966

Dear Family, This is my last sheet of paper, so guess this will have to be my last letter. Instead, I'll present myself in person. Guess that's better than a letter anyway. Well, just two days left on the Hill. Sure feels good knowing I'll be leaving here soon. I've been waiting for this for an awful long time. Our whole battalion went on the operation and they only left a handful of people back here to man the hill. So now they are really worrying about an attack here. If they ever are going to do it, this would be the perfect time. Sure hope they don't while I'm still here.

Sergeant Keith Vollendorf left Hill 54 and his buddies from Charlie 1/5 on 9 August 1966 and started his long journey home; Keith was headed back to "the World," as they called it. On 10 August 1966, Hillous York, A. C. Blades, Buck Darling, and the rest of the Marines of Charlie 1/5 began Operation Colorado. Seven Marines of Charlie 1/5 lost their lives that day.

Operation Colorado required the Marines to search out the enemy by sweeping through areas north and west of Tam Ky in an attempt to rout any hidden Viet Cong. These sweeps involved the entire regiment, all three battalions, making their own positions quite clear to the enemy at the same time. Using the strategy of baiting the enemy, these maneuvers successfully resulted in engaging the Marines with their enemy, but not always as they expected.

Buck Darling recalls, "It was about three o'clock in the afternoon, and we were done for the day. Colonel Coffman passed the word to dig in, so we dug in. The Viet Cong, of course, saw this happening. It turns out that the Viet Cong and NVA dominated the Tam Ky area of operations. None of us had seen them, but they were all over the place out there around Tam Ky this whole time. They didn't even shoot at us. They watched us constantly and always knew our exact locations. We operated out there in the sun about four or five days, and they never shot at us once."

Even though the troops had already dug in for the night, Col. Charles F. Widdecke, commanding officer (CO) of the 5th Marines, ordered his men to return the five or six kilometers to Tam Ky and to do it quickly.

Following Colonel Widdecke's instructions, Charlie Company, on point, launched out of their dug-in night positions. Buck said, "I've got the company spread out about fifteen hundred meters wide, and we're going like a bat out of hell, and we walked into this ville as the Viet Cong ate dinner. They had watched us dig in; they figured that we weren't going anywhere that night, so they were eating chow; they had no clue that we were on the move. We walked right into their CP. The 1st Platoon had already moved through their CP before anyone realized what was happening. A few

VC were running away from them, but there had not yet been a shot fired. Third Platoon was on the right, and they didn't see anything." Although caught by surprise, the elusive VC scattered; some of them ran away to fight another day, but many of them stood and fought.

As Buck and his men walked deeper into the village, they began to realize it wasn't just a ville:

> I stayed right in the middle, right behind the lead platoon, and there's a well there and one of my Marines said, "Hey, sir, there's a well. Can I go fill a couple of my canteens?" I threw him my canteen and he walked over to the well, stopped cold and said, "Sir, there's an AK-47 leaning against this well." Somebody else said, "Hey! There's three more leaning against that tree," and somebody else said, "Hey, there's a machine gun over here," and about that time the residual Cong got the word and started shooting at us.
>
> Several months before, when we rescued Jimmie Howard's recon team off that mountain, the enemy had just come from North Vietnam off the Ho Chi Minh Trail. They had the gray uniforms, the full bit; they were NVA soldiers. On Colorado the enemy wore black pajamas; they were locals, probably main force VC but definitely not from North Vietnam. They fought hard despite being really outgunned. We fought that afternoon in a downpour like a cow pissing on a flat rock. We couldn't cover all the escape routes, so we hollered at regiment to get this other battalion off its ass and plug the hole. We had a chance to kill them all. They didn't do it. Colonel Widdecke sent the reserve out there the next morning, too late; most of them got away.
>
> We had been very lucky. We managed to quickly destroy their crew-served weapons, scatter their CP group, and capture their rice. It took us the rest of the afternoon to root the rest of them out. They had pretty good positions, but we really caught them off guard. They had watched us closely, saw us dig in for the night, so they were supremely confident that their attack, planned for the next morning, would hit us hard. They had a couple of reckless [recoilless] rifles and a whole bunch of machine guns, mortars, all that kind of stuff. First Platoon took most of the casualties that day. The enemy documents indicated that an enemy battalion occupied that village, and 1st Platoon walked right into them. Charlie Company had seven KIAs and many WIAs that day, but we tore the heart out of a Viet Cong battalion. Anyway, the next morning we had about eighty enemy weapons or so—a big pile of rifles, and a whole bunch of crew-served weapons. We counted about a hundred enemy bodies when the shooting finally died down.
>
> Charlie Company's 1st Platoon commander, A. C. Blades, earned a Silver

Star that day on Operation Colorado. He and his platoon sergeant, a guy named Spawn, Staff Sgt. Warren Spawn, those two guys together became a killing machine. Initially, almost immediately, in the first full phase of the shooting, they killed a bunch of Cong. A few weeks later, our battalion commander, Lt. Col. Al Coffman, called me and asked me if I had a lieutenant who would make a good company commander, and I said, without blinking, "A. C. Blades." That was it; A. C. Blades immediately took command of Alpha Company.

1st Lt. A. C. Blades took command of Alpha 1/5 on 20 October 1966 and served in that position until 13 February 1967. On 18 March 1967, Capt. A. C. Blades became the battalion S-4 officer, and he later took command of H&S Company before completing his first thirteen-month tour in South Vietnam. Blades returned to Vietnam in 1971, serving a second tour as a helicopter pilot, having made the transition to aviation. "In 1970–71," Blades said, "Buck Darling served as the S-3 of the 7th Marines at LZ Baldy. I had transitioned to helicopters and would fly resupply missions to the various combat bases or support operations in the Que Son Mountains, and I had the opportunity to land in the combat base I had left three years prior." After a thirty-year career in the US Marine Corps, Arthur C. Blades honorably retired as a lieutenant general of Marines.

The seven Charlie 1/5 Marines who lost their lives during Operation Colorado include Cpl. Douglas B. Haddix, from Springfield, Ohio; US Navy corpsman HN Lawrence T. "Doc" Steiner, from Houston, Texas; Lance Cpl. Gregory M. Howard, from Greenway, Virginia; Lance Cpl. Robert D. Higbee, from Drexel Hill, Pennsylvania; Pfc. David L. Faught, from Grand Rapids, Michigan; Pfc. Melvin Rolle, from Miami, Florida; and Pfc. Paul E. Sudsbury, from Corinna, Maine.

In the succinct shorthand of the combat after-action report on Operation Colorado, the 1/5 battalion commander reported that Charlie Company stayed in constant contact with the Viet Cong from 1515 to 1845 that afternoon, when they were ordered to return to the battalion perimeter. Lieutenant Colonel Coffman reported thirty VC KIA confirmed and estimated that they probably killed another eleven VC and likely wounded thirty-five more during this engagement. In addition to the seven Marines who lost their lives, an additional twenty-seven Marines were wounded in action that day.

New arrivals continued to join the Marines of 1/5 in late 1966. James Keith Coxen enlisted in the Marine Corps, made it through boot camp in San Diego, and received orders to WestPac. Born and raised in eastern Oregon in the small town of Hermiston, situated on the southern bank of the Columbia River, Jim spent a lot of time as a boy hunting and fishing in the nearby mountains and forests. His hunting experience served him well, and he rapidly grew into a very proficient Marine and quickly earned promotion to lance corporal.

Upon arriving in South Vietnam in October, 1966, Jim reported to Charlie Company, 1st Battalion, 5th Marines while they operated in and around the Chu Lai TAOR. Assigned as a grenadier in the 1st Squad of the 2nd Platoon, he carried the M79 40 mm grenade launcher during his entire thirteen-month combat tour. The other Marines of the 1st Squad of Charlie Two called him Blooper Man because of his outstanding proficiency with the breech-loaded weapon, which the Marines called the Blooper due to the sound it made when fired. Buck Darling still commanded Charlie 1/5 when Coxen arrived and joined them.

The individual rotation system continued changing the personnel of all the Marine units, and eventually this led to a change in command for the 1st Battalion, 5th Marines. An iron disciplinarian, the outgoing battalion commander, Lt. Col. Al Coffman, had led his Marines from the moment they arrived in Southeast Asia through many difficult and dangerous combat operations. He worked hard and stayed closely involved with his Marines, both inside and outside the combat base. His men knew he was an outstanding battalion commander.

The importance of strong leadership is most appreciated in the absence of it. Following in the path of such large shoes, his replacement prompted a difficult time for the Marines of 1/5 at Hill 54. Buck Darling recalls:

> We got a new battalion commander after Lieutenant Colonel Coffman left. Our new battalion commander, a white-haired gentleman, turned out to be a very *nice* gentleman. When I received my promotion to captain, he had a really nice party in his hooch with, like, Ritz crackers with a piece of cheese and a slice of horse cock sausage. After all the food disappeared, he said, "You company commanders stick around," so everyone else left, and he said to us company commanders, "Okay, what do you boys want to do?" And I said, "I'm going on patrol." He said, "Okay." Charlie Company went to the field and stayed in the field; everybody else did whatever they wanted. We stayed in the field, I think, a month. We went over to the mountains, way out west of the combat base. We went so far west we became the outer screen. We stayed out there for a really long time, just to get away from the combat base. This new guy was really relaxed. A couple of bad things happened to him that probably were not his fault. We had a couple of accidental discharges; we shot a mortar round into one of our own tents. That's one of the crazy things about war: if you shoot a mortar round at the enemy, it's a fifty-fifty chance it will go off at all; if it does go off, it's about a ten percent chance it will kill any people within

the casualty radius. But if you accidentally drop it in your own tent, it functions perfectly. This one killed everyone within the casualty radius.

So a bunch of bad things happened there for a while. A patrol south of the combat base was accused of rape. As a matter of fact, five guys ended up going to jail. And all that bad stuff happened on this new guy's watch. I mean, you know, in the real world, none of it was his fault; but in another way, all of it was his fault, because he didn't take command in some senses. Lieutenant Colonel Coffman had left, and I had no confidence in our new battalion commander. I just wanted to stay out in the field and out of the way.

Division sent Hilgartner up to, basically, take this leaking bag of shit and straighten it out. This happened sometime in November 1966. Charlie Company stayed out in the field for another week after he arrived at Hill 54. I learned from the grapevine that he had already relieved most of the other company commanders by the time I got ready to come in from the field. We had a fun time that day. When I arrived at the base camp that morning, I thought he was going to relieve me, as I knew he had already relieved most of the other company commanders and he thought everyone in the battalion was a piece of shit. I came in from the field, and there he was, waiting for me. He wanted to go on patrol, so I had the company fall out, and we moved him about twelve clicks in about two hours, complete with flank security and everything. Then he left us out in the boondocks and took another company out because he wanted to relieve *that* company commander. So he took them out and relieved the company commander, stayed out there with them the rest of that night, and then brought them home the next morning. But he was impressed with how Charlie Company got around. From there on, Charlie Company just became permanent point.

After surviving the Sparrow Hawk mission and Operation Colorado, Buck Darling survived Hilgartner's management purge and continued to serve as commanding officer of Charlie 1/5 until 4 December 1966, when a new Marine captain reported in to the battalion.

3: Changes of Command, November 1966–March 1967

Maj. Peter Hilgartner arrived in Vietnam in August of 1966. Hilgartner enlisted in the Marine Corps on 8 October 1945 and served as an enlisted Marine for nearly two years before he reported to the US Naval Academy, from which he graduated with the class of 1951. Hilgartner immediately reentered the Marine Corps and went to war. He served as an artillery forward observer as a second lieutenant during the Korean War and earned a Bronze Star for his actions in combat. Upon his arrival in Vietnam, the very senior Major Hilgartner became the operations officer of the 7th Marines.

Peter Hilgartner vividly remembers his first introduction to the 1st Battalion, 5th Marines:

> One Five was widely regarded at that time as the worst battalion in the 1st Marine Division. Our regiment, 7th Marines, had taken operational control over 1/5 in October 1966. We sent them out on a search-and-destroy operation one day. I remember that day very vividly because Roy Rogers and Dale Evans happened to be in Vietnam, visiting us at the time, and I had lunch with them. I got called to the regimental tactical operations center (TOC) and found out that, basically, 1/5's battalion commander had turned tail in the face of the enemy. Colonel Snowden, the CO of the 7th Marines, went into a rage and stormed out of the operations tent. A short time later, Snowden called the division commander and then summarily relieved 1/5's battalion commander of his command.

Then Colonel Snowden turned to Major Hilgartner and said, "Pete, I'm giving you command of 1/5." Hilgartner requested two officers from the 7th Marines staff, Maj. Dick Alger and Maj. Gerald Turley, officers Hilgartner knew and trusted, because he knew he needed help. He knew that taking command of 1/5 under these circumstances would be difficult.

Pete Hilgartner took command of 1/5 on 3 November 1966 at Hill 54 Combat Base and appointed Major Alger as the battalion operations officer (S-3) the following day. Major Turley stayed with the 7th Marines.[1] Colonel Snowden felt that if Pete took Turley, the regimental staff would suffer too much by losing all three majors at the same time.

Hilgartner knew that in order for him and his battalion to succeed, they would first have to shed the tarnished image earned, unfairly, by a battalion commander clearly out of his element. One Five's reputation as an outstanding infantry unit under fire while serving all those months in combat under Lieutenant Colonel Coffman had now changed for the worst, and Pete determined to get that behind him as rapidly as possible. That meant that he would have to make some changes. He met the executive officer (XO) and told him that he would keep him around for a couple of weeks, and then the XO could rotate to the rear, which turned out to be fine with the XO.

Pete Hilgartner was determined to clean house, and he did. He went through that battalion, in his words, "Like Grant through Vicksburg." He knew from long experience that no commander succeeds by himself. He knew they could only succeed if he had confident and competent officers around him. Hilgartner wanted the best officers, and he wanted the best NCOs that he could find. Absolutely determined to accomplish the battalion's missions, Hilgartner had also privately made the decision that his battalion would do things right, that they would do things well, and that they would send home as many Marines as possible, alive and well. That was Pete's philosophy when he took over the battalion.

Hilgartner first fired the battalion mess sergeant. When he assumed command and arrived at the battalion's location, he saw immediately that he had a problem. Hilgartner knew that Marines fought, largely, on their stomachs. Combat Marines during the Vietnam War bitched endlessly about their C-rations, but they ate them and got the energy they required. When in a rear area, a combat base, the boredom of C-rations became instantly intolerable. Marines expected three hot meals a day, or at least two, and the battalion mess sergeant's job was to provide exactly that.

At Hill 54 Combat Base, the battalion mess sergeant had set up an officer's mess tent, with a parachute lining the top inside of the canvas shelter, chairs and tables, tablecloths, and all the other amenities one could reasonably expect under such circumstances. Further, the officers did not eat the same food as the troops.

When Hilgartner inspected the area where the enlisted Marines ate, he found a much different situation. The troops ate in a mess tent at stand-up tables, and they stood in about six inches of mud. Worse, their mess area smelled like a pigsty. Hilgartner ordered all the mess tents torn down, the officers' as well as the enlisted men's. The mess sergeant came to him and started to complain bitterly about what Hilgartner had done. Hilgartner took one look at the sergeant and said, "I know you are probably not responsible for this mess. But while I am the battalion commander, the officers and enlisted men will eat the same food, and they will be taken care of equally." And then Hilgartner fired him. Then he fired the battalion operations officer and installed Maj. Dick Alger in that position.

Over the next few weeks, five changes of command took place in 1/5's infantry companies, the direct result of Pete Hilgartner's housecleaning program. Pete's evaluations of company commanders took place "up close and personal" in the field. He would simply show up at a company area, inform the company commander that they had orders to conduct combat operations, and accompany the Marines to the field. If Hilgartner liked what he saw, the company commander kept his job. If not, a change of command would take place immediately.

Buck Darling survived the purge of company commanders carried out by the new battalion commander, but his tenure as the Charlie Company CO was about to end. About three weeks into Hilgartner's command, Buck heard a bellowing voice holler, "Darling, get up here!" So Buck reported to the battalion commander, and Hilgartner gave him new marching orders. "You're going to take command of H&S Company," Hilgartner said, "because I'm sick of this hill. I'm sick of the damned Combined Action people doing anything they want. You're going to sit on this place and fix it!" Buck respectfully but forcefully tried to refuse this order. "Sir," he said, "I just extended to keep Charlie Company." To which Hilgartner replied, "Well, you didn't extend with me. Besides, you've still got a company, it's just bigger." H&S Company of any infantry battalion has more Marines on paper, but Buck knew that many of those Marines, those manning the crew-served weapons (81 mm mortars, flamethrowers, 3.5-inch rocket launchers, heavy machine guns, and so on), were often attached to the line companies. When he remembered this story, Buck let out one of his hearty laughs. Buck Darling knew a done deal when he heard it, so he knew there was no use getting all hot and bothered by it.

"I used to call Hilgartner 'The Dragon,'" Buck said. "He could roar really loud, and he nearly always got his way. He brought Tricky Dick Alger with him. A. C. Blades, J. J. Carty and M. T. Cooper served as the other company commanders in 1/5 during this period. Carty, Cooper, and Blades all stayed in the Marine Corps, made a career of it; Carty retired as a colonel; and Art Blades and Matthew T. Cooper retired as lieutenant generals."

Capt. Jim Caswell took command of Charlie Company, and Buck Darling took command of H&S Company around Christmastime of 1966. One Five had been about a year in country, and everybody who had served in the battalion since the

Okinawa phase a couple of years before had rotated home. When 1/5 started combat operations up and down the coast of Vietnam, the rotation clock started. By the middle of summer of 1966, the battalion was losing large numbers of Marines due to this rotation clock, and 1/5 got thirty-five replacements from another outfit. These replacements had served up around the DMZ and had gotten shot all to hell up there.

The Marines of 1/5 had served together for a long time with relatively low casualties, with the exception of those two bad days during Operations Osage and Colorado, and, in the words of Buck Darling, "We had kicked some serious VC butt during that time. All of a sudden we get these new guys, these jackasses, who went out on patrol and said, 'Well, that's not the way we did it up at the DMZ with our old outfit.' I and others said back to them, 'Hey, guys, the reason you're down here now is because you got your ass shot off up there, so pay attention. We don't do that down here. We send patrols out, we have flank security out when we move, and you will do it this way.' "

The rotation system meant the arrival of new Marines in country as 1/5's Marines rotated back to the States or were otherwise lost to the violent vagaries of war. In December 1966, 1/5 received another outstanding Marine, one who would later play a significant role in 1/5's combat operations.

Lance Cpl. John "Rusty" Rusth, from Klamath Falls, Oregon, joined the Marine Corps in July of 1966. John graduated from boot camp at Marine Corps Recruit Depot (MCRD) San Diego, a Hollywood Marine (a condescending nickname given to Marines who went through boot camp at MCRD San Diego by those who graduated from boot camp at MCRD Parris Island). Following his training, John immediately departed to Vietnam, arriving there in December 1966. Among about two thousand Marines, Rusty boarded the USS *Gaffney* on 9 December 1966 in San Diego and sailed across the Pacific Ocean directly to the war zone. Rusty said, "*Gaffney* was an old troop ship, so it took until Christmas to arrive in Vietnam, but it actually wasn't bad, since all the NCOs and officers got quarters up above the deck; all the enlisted men stayed in racks below decks."

When Rusty arrived in the war zone, he received orders to the 1st Marine Division and was assigned to 1/5. As a private first class with a 0311 (infantry) MOS, he was assigned to Charlie Company as a rifleman in 3rd Platoon. Rusty remembers a humorous but somewhat morbid occurrence before boarding ship, when a staging battalion colonel at Camp Pendleton had everyone line up in formation and told all the privates that they had just been promoted to private first class. "He told us he was promoting us," John explained, "because he hated to see someone get killed as a lowly private."

Buck Darling remembered the losses, those lost to hostile fire and those lost to the now constant influence of the individual rotation policy:

We lost all the captains in the battalion, almost all at the same time. I especially hated to see M. T. Cooper go, as we had been friends since Hawaii. Cooper's wife hated him drinking and smoking, but when the battalion was stationed in Hawaii, our battalion commander demanded happy hour. So when M. T. got screwed up during happy hour this one time, his wife wouldn't let him back in the house; we had to take him over to the BOQ to sleep it off. When we got on the ship to go to Vietnam, M. T. Cooper said, "No fucking way, I'm never going to have another cigarette, and I'm never going to have another shot; I'm not drinking anymore, and I'm not smoking anymore, period. Not ever. I'm done. I'm clean." And he did; he quit drinking and smoking, cold turkey.

During Operation Colorado, M. T.'s company was positioned on my right. He had the ville, rounds were flying, and I literally had a pigpen. I mean, we were fighting in pig shit. But M. T. Cooper had a cement house in the ville. So we're out there and about five reckless rifle rounds come over our heads and impact wherever, and a whole bunch of mortar rounds came down on the battalion CP group and really did a lot of damage. The mortar barrage killed a couple guys that I knew pretty well, Marines who had served in my platoon in Hawaii. A little while later, Coop comes walking over to my position and says, "Got a cigarette, Buck?" I had some C-ration stuff in my helmet, so I pulled out the Pall Mall four-pack and gave it to him. And he smoked them up. I mean, he's chain smoking, you know what I mean? So I say, "Hey Coop, what's the matter?" He says, "I just damn near died." I say, "What's the deal?" and he answers, "When the bullets started flying, I got on my radio because battalion was calling me. So, I go over to the radio, I'm bending over the radio and holding the handset when this reckless rifle round comes through the door, goes right between my feet, and hits the wall. Wham!" That recoilless rifle round missed Coop by about four inches from several spots on his body. So, I dug in my pack and pulled out a four-pack of Lucky Strikes and gave him those as well.

I was very happy I had been stuck in the pigsty. Coop had been really well off in the nice hooch until the shit hit the fan. Earlier, this Marine named Rios and I had dug a foxhole in this pigsty, a nasty place, filled with pig shit. Situated on low ground, the earth stayed muddy as hell. Before the shit hit the fan, I slept in a hammock close by, but when the shit started I woke up and found myself in this muddy, shitty hole. Rios was in there, too. Rios had heard my conversation with Cooper, and he looked over at me and said, "Our shithole ain't so bad now, is it, Skipper?"

Capt. Russell J. "Jim" Caswell arrived in Chu Lai, South Vietnam, in October of 1966. Caswell, another US Naval Academy graduate (class of 1958), volunteered for duty in Vietnam in his quest to command a Marine rifle company in combat. Jim felt that his whole life during the previous eight years in the Marine Corps had been spent focused on preparing him for this important role, and nothing in life compared in importance to his quest to command, except perhaps his wife and three children.

After graduation from the Naval Academy, Jim received orders to join the 4th Marines in Kaneohe, Hawaii. Jim served in the 1st Battalion, 4th Marines (1/4) for three years. He felt that he received excellent training in small unit tactics, as he occupied every company-level position during those three years. During Jim Caswell's tenure as a company commander in 1961, his battalion became the "aggressors" (the enemy force) for a landing exercise involving the entire 1st Marine Division at Camp Pendleton, and later the exercise continued in the deserts of Twentynine Palms, California.

Caswell served as a series officer for a short time at his next duty station, MCRD San Diego, and then he served as the director of Sea School, also located in San Diego. After that, Captain Caswell received orders to become the commanding officer of the Marine detachment aboard the USS *Midway* (CV-41). This *Midway*, the third US Navy ship to carry the name, had been commissioned on 10 September 1945, so she was an aging but still very capable ship.

One of the last World War II–era aircraft carriers in commission, *Midway* served during the Vietnam War, sailing the South China Sea conducting combat operations against enemy military and logistics installations in North and South Vietnam. *Midway* achieved a notable first through aviators of the ship's Attack Carrier Wing 2, who on 17 June 1965 downed the first three MiGs credited to US Forces in Southeast Asia, illustrative of the major contribution the carrier made to the campaigns of the free forces to repel Communist aggression. *Midway* also carried a squadron of A-1H Skyraiders, propeller-driven attack aircraft, a flight of which managed to team up and shoot down a MiG-17 three days later.

Jim Caswell served on the USS *Midway* for two years, the last nine months on an extended cruise. During the cruise, considered by all to be a combat tour, the *Midway* became the second aircraft carrier to fly air strikes over Vietnam from Yankee Station in 1965.

Since that cruise was considered to be an overseas combat tour, under normal circumstances Jim would not have been eligible to go overseas for additional tours for at least another year. After Amphibious Warfare School, however, Capt. Jim Caswell volunteered for duty in Vietnam. He knew by then that he probably would make major sometime soon, and if he didn't go now, he might never have the opportunity to command a Marine infantry company in combat. Jim considered himself a career professional, highly trained and very well prepared for this role, and he would hate to miss his chance to lead a company of Marines in battle. So he asked to go back to WestPac.

All of his experiences over those eight years had taken place while Jim was "in command." While aboard the *Midway* during shore visits in the Philippines, Jim took his detachment into the jungle for training from the Negrito tribesmen. While in California, Jim's outfit had the use of a ranch on the coast north of San Francisco for small unit combat training, and they used it every chance they could get. Whenever Jim had time on his hands while aboard ship, he read everything he could find of the accounts of the French in Indochina fighting the Viet Minh and of the British Royal Marines fighting the guerrillas in Malaysia (a very successful campaign). Jim had devoted his entire life toward the study and practice of infantry command and control, strategy, and tactics, and he considered himself ready to step into the most important job of his life.

When he arrived in Chu Lai in October of 1966, Capt. Jim Caswell immediately started his search for an infantry battalion that needed a company commander. It took a while, but after two months of serving as a staff officer at the 1st Marine Division headquarters, Jim ran into Maj. Dick Alger, by then the XO of the 1st Battalion, 5th Marines. Jim had attended Amphibious Warfare School with Alger, and he pleaded with him for a command position in 1/5. Staff work was important, and the work was okay, but Jim felt very strongly that his training and preparations were being wasted, and he sorely wanted to escape staff duty. Dick Alger let Lt. Col. Pete Hilgartner (who had earned promotion to lieutenant colonel shortly after taking command of 1/5) know that Jim was available, so they asked for him by name, and in December 1966 Jim received orders to 1/5. Within a couple of days of joining the battalion, Jim Caswell took command of Charlie Company from Buck Darling.

Captain Caswell quickly figured out that he had assumed command of an excellent infantry company. Within a few days of his arrival he would find out just how good they really were. Between the Christmas and New Year's "cease fires" of 1966, regiment and battalion operations planners decided to send out a heavily reinforced rifle company on a quick, one-day search-and-destroy mission to a known VC stronghold and training area in the mountains to the west of the Chu Lai TAOR.

This operation targeted the village of Trung Tin, located in the mountains about fifteen kilometers west of Chu Lai. The company would land by helicopter in the morning, search the village, and return to its base that same night. Charlie 1/5 received orders for the mission. A forward air control team, a scout/sniper, a unit from division recon battalion, and a combat photographer would reinforce it. Their normal forward observer (FO) teams, both artillery and mortar FOs, would also accompany them.

Captain Caswell realized that with all these attached units, the company command

Gunnery Sgt. Marcelino Rivera-Cruz (*left*) and two Marines from 1st Recon Battalion deal with a captured VC sniper. Courtesy of the National Archives.

group would be enormous, as big as a rifle platoon. Handling his platoons, his radios, his fire support, and this huge command group of about forty Marines simultaneously could prove a daunting task. He assembled the Marines who comprised the command group and told them that they would take their orders from the company gunnery sergeant. Gunnery Sgt. Marcelino Rivera-Cruz, known to the troops simply as Gunny Cruz, glared at the group of newcomers and said only, "Five meters interval. Watch me at all times. If I run, you run. Half of you will board the chopper with the skipper, and half with me."

At first light the designated point platoon and the company CP group boarded the first wave of CH-46 helicopters at the airstrip in Chu Lai. Captain Caswell noticed that all of the small details that make a good unit had been attended to. Helmet chinstraps stayed buckled; every man wore a flak jacket buttoned all the way up. All types of grenades were in evidence: fragmentation, smoke, and tear gas. The weapons looked clean, and the Marines carried plenty of ammunition on their persons.

Jim put his heliteam in the first wave, as training dictated. That meant they would land with just one rifle platoon. It would never have occurred to him to come in with the second wave.

As the helicopters sped over the jungle, Jim realized that he would have his first opportunity to say "the words" soon. The words were a ritual among infantrymen—both Marine and army—and no one else except perhaps the Navy SEALs said them. They were as ritualistic as the salute of an aircraft pilot sitting on the catapult of an aircraft carrier to the catapult officer when ready to launch. No one would have dreamt of leaving them out. A Marine or army infantry NCO or officer would say these powerful words many times during a combat tour. Hollywood had long since romanticized and bastardized the words for movies and television as "rock and roll," or other nonsensical phrases. But he would always remember each time he said them because of the faces that watched him earnestly. Many of those faces might not live out the day, and the Marines inside those faces knew it.

Capt. Jim Caswell realized that everyone on the helicopter that morning stared at him intently. Were they wondering how many of them he would get killed as he learned his trade? They had trusted Buck Darling because Buck had proven himself in combat on many occasions. Who is this new guy?

Jim looked at them. They looked confident, but afraid. Then he said the words: "Lock and load!" Faint smiles crossed twenty faces as they slipped magazines into their M14 rifles and let the bolts go home. They felt better, ready. As his helicopter touched down, Caswell spoke again, not shouting but loud enough to be heard over the racket: "Keep low. Follow me. Good luck." Then he jumped off the back ramp into the rice paddy with his heliteam close behind him. As he ran out of the LZ, he saw Marine A-4 Skyhawk jets circling the LZ, dropping bombs and firing rockets along the high ground that dominated the terrain around them. Wave after wave of CH-46s came in, touched down in a cloud of dust, and disgorged running Marines. No one fired a shot.

The platoons organized quickly and headed for downtown Trung Tin. Reaching the outskirts of the hamlet, they formed up into the prearranged assault formation and assaulted through the hooches. One man tripped a booby trap, which blew him high into the air, but no one fired. The man who tripped the booby trap had only minor shrapnel wounds on his arms because he wore his flak jacket properly buttoned up.

After searching Trung Tin thoroughly and finding little of any military significance, the Marines formed into a tactical column and headed onto a mountain trail that led back to the coast. Although almost 250 Marines mounted the long, spread-out column with point and flank security, they made hardly a sound.

Several hours into the march, the point and flank security teams signaled the column to halt. The point then signaled for silence. Not a single Zippo clicked; no rocket tube clanked against a helmet; not one radio gave off the telltale static hiss that could have given away their positions. No one made a sound.

The column watched in disbelief as two Viet Cong soldiers came into view, walking along the streambed next to the trail. The VC smoked and talked quietly, their carbines slung on their shoulders. They knew they were safe, since no Americans had come down the trail ahead of them. They wore the distinctive shallow conical hats and black pajamas of the peasants, completely unaware of the 250 pairs of eyes watching them like cats watching mice.

Suddenly, the Marines sprung the trap. They captured one VC unharmed, with his weapon and equipment. The other escaped despite the hail of gunfire shot in his direction.

It was a very big event to capture a prisoner in 1966, because it did not happen very often and because the interrogations of VC prisoners usually provided much-needed intelligence for future combat operations. As the Marines of Charlie Company filed into the combat base late that night, the battalion commander congratulated them personally on a job well done.

Lieutenant Colonel Hilgartner worked hard to try to increase the morale of his Marines. On one occasion he arranged for a visit from a very famous Marine general. One day in late December, Lt. Gen. Victor H. Krulak, USMC, the commanding general of III Marine Amphibious Force (III MAF), came to visit 1/5. During the visit, Hilgartner installed Krulak as an honorary member of 1/5. Pete had worked for Krulak in the past and believed this visit might give the battalion a boost. He received a nice letter from General Krulak a few days later thanking 1/5 for their hospitality and expressing appreciation for the honors.

Capt. Jim Caswell made good use of his training and preparations as well as the experience and outstanding professionalism of his Charlie 1/5 Marines. He had seen what worked and what didn't. Combining those observations with his years of excellent training, Jim arrived at a set of tactical and operational principles that he thought best suited the men of Charlie Company and his own training and experience and were not prohibited by any regulation. Another of Jim's friends, Capt. John Carty, commanded Delta 1/5. John Carty and Jim Caswell had become close friends at the US Naval Academy and later as carpool buddies at Amphibious Warfare School. They thought alike, and they trusted each other implicitly.

John Carty and Jim Caswell, and thus the Marines of Delta and Charlie Companies, alternated the privilege and responsibilities of the assault company in helicopter-borne operations. They communicated constantly on each other's company radio nets, avoiding excess traffic on the battalion tactical network (Tac Net). Charlie and Delta Companies often went to the field together as a task force.

The operating standards that Jim Caswell adopted for Charlie Company mostly came from the lessons learned by the Royal Marines fighting in Malaysia. First, Charlie Company's Marines never exposed themselves at daybreak in the same location they had been seen in the previous day at dusk. They set up in their defensive positions at dark, sent out listening posts (LPs), observation posts (OPs), and ambush positions after dark, and always started down the trail without fires or light of any kind well before sunup. No one cooked his breakfast; a hungry Charlie 1/5 Marine ate cold C-rations. No one smoked until Jim Caswell lit a cigarette, and when he did you could always hear dozens of Zippos clicking immediately.

Second, they never returned to the combat base by the same route, trail, or road on which they had left. If possible, they used some other exit point than the last patrol or company had used. They tried not to use the same route to any location twice in succession. They tried to heli-lift out and walk back, if at all possible. Thus, they usually found the enemy's booby trap markers in place.

Third, whenever they could, they worked at night. They left the combat base in the dark and tried to reach a tactical objective, a suspected enemy position, before first light. The Marines of Charlie Company became very good at nighttime operations. They could even ford rivers without incident in the pitch dark. They used artillery illumination rounds to mark the corners of grid squares (very far away from their own positions) so they could keep track of their location.

These operational procedures proved very effective. During one long night Charlie Company moved eleven kilometers and forded two rivers in good order and without incident. These tactics succeeded in helping to reduce casualties from mines and booby traps. They also proved effective in meeting groups of VC leaving their girlfriends' beds in the early morning hours. Charlie Company's Marines always shot faster and straighter than their enemy did.

Captain Caswell also called in artillery concentrations, or naval gunfire concentrations, every night without fail, using illumination rounds. Thus, if they needed artillery fire support in a hurry, they just called in a preestablished concentration number and adjusted fire from there. Whenever they made a helicopter assault, they used fixed wing aircraft on station with rockets, bombs, and guns. These preparations often became arduous and difficult, but from Jim Caswell's point of view they were very worthwhile in saving Marine lives. However, despite his constant vigilance and expertise, the Charlie 1/5 Marines still took casualties. They were, after all, in a war zone; people get hurt, people die during wartime, and this was no exception. The pain of taking casualties at the hands of the enemy is horrible, but the pain of taking casualties as the result of friendly fire is many times worse.

One night in early 1967, Charlie Company lost one of their best squad leaders at the hands of one of our allies, the marines of the Republic of Korea. Jim Caswell remembers that terrible night well: "Despite our swapping liaison officers with the

ROKs and laying wire from CP to CP, the Korean Marine companies decided they could fire H&I [harassment and interdiction] fires all night long, anywhere they wanted, with their 60 mm mortars. Suddenly we got incoming mortar fire in the middle of the night that killed the best squad leader in Charlie Company. It was a big blow, a huge loss—he was well-liked, and extremely capable."

Caswell asked the battalion commander, Lieutenant Colonel Hilgartner, over the wire to make sure that the Koreans weren't mortaring Charlie Company. Hilgartner called back in a couple of minutes and said they were not. It went on like that for a while, back and forth. Charlie Company kept getting incoming mortar rounds every so often. John Carty's Delta Company Marines were situated between the Koreans and Charlie Company. All of a sudden, Carty came on the wire and forcefully stated that the mortar fire *was* coming from the Koreans' hill. He asked Hilgartner to "put the goddamn liaison officer on the phone. I want that fire stopped." Hilgartner told him to calm down.

Then more rounds dropped on Charlie Company's positions, and battalion assured Caswell once again that the ROKs weren't firing at his Marines. Carty came back on the radio and said, "I have a man holding a 60 mm round in one of our mortar tubes, aimed at the Koreans' hill. The 'enemy' mortar rounds are coming from the Koreans' hill. We can see the sparks as their rounds leave their tubes, and they *are* hitting Charlie Company's positions. If one more round leaves their tube, we will drop ours. Out!" Hilgartner threatened John Carty with relief for insubordination, as he often did. But someone got through to the ROKs, because Charlie Company received no more mortar fire that night.

On another search-and-destroy operation conducted in early 1967, 1/5 worked with both the ARVN Rangers and South Korean Marines. As Charlie Company moved through their zone of action toward the next objective, a small hamlet across some rice paddies, they saw green-clad troops exiting the village. The lead elements informed Captain Caswell about this development, and all the Marines automatically dropped behind some paddy dikes, took up firing positions, and watched. These people appeared to be Asian soldiers, but they carried American weapons, packs, helmets, and equipment. Luckily, no one fired. They turned out to be Korean Marines. After much smiling and handshaking and waving, both units went on their way, in opposite directions.

The Koreans had actually passed through the American Marines, who moved forward to secure the hamlet the ROKs had just left. Captain Caswell felt this was truly the most screwed-up operation he had seen so far. With somewhat lackadaisical security, the Marines of Charlie 1/5 moved across the rice paddy on line toward the hamlet.

As the line of troops reached the outskirts of the hamlet, they entered a large area, filled with jumbles of cattle pens, water buffalo pens, chicken coops, and so on, where the hamlet's animals apparently lived. As Captain Caswell and the other Marines (fortunately, well spread out) crossed this open area, several automatic weapons opened fire on them. The Viet Cong had been trailing the ROK Marines, spotted Caswell and his Marines, and immediately started shooting. Men dove behind logs, a watering trough, pigpens, or whatever cover or concealment they could find. There wasn't much.

As the Marines returned fire, Caswell called his reserve platoon commander, who was following behind the main part of the company. He ordered the reserve platoon to move above the hamlet into a tree line, to form up on line, and assault through the village. Caswell hoped to surprise and kill or capture the people firing on them. The two platoons he stayed with would provide a base of fire while the reserve platoon assaulted. It was going to be a textbook solution, Caswell thought, just like at the Basic School.

Bullets whined, zipped, smacked, and thudded all around them. The main force of Charlie 1/5 Marines kept up a heavy return fire with M14s, M60 machine guns, and M79 grenade launchers. They waited, and they continued to fire on the suspected enemy positions. They waited and waited and continued to fire, but nothing happened. The assault platoon wasn't in position.

Finally, one of the Marines in the open, Sgt. Juan Sanchez, could stand it no more. Picking up an M60 machine gun and firing short bursts from the hip, he walked toward the hamlet. Between bursts, he yelled, "Are you bastards going to lie here all day?" The entire unit got to their feet as one unit and, firing from the hip, followed this crazy Marine into that hamlet. Somehow, Charlie 1/5 did not take a single casualty that day.

Captain Caswell recalls, "Sergeant Sanchez was an amazing person. One night a few days earlier, as we crossed a dangerous, deep river with a heavy current, I saw the top of a helmet coming across the water. Above it, lurching out of the water, two arms held an M60 machine gun to keep it dry. As this Marine methodically plodded across the river bottom and floundered out onto the bank, I asked who the hell that crazy Marine was. A voice in the dark said, 'That's Sergeant Sanchez, sir. He can't swim a lick, neither.' Again, just a few days later, Sergeant Sanchez stood up, the first to rise and assault the enemy in the face of heavy enemy fire."

Captain Caswell remembers Sergeant Sanchez as a fairly quiet Marine, but one he could always count on when the chips were down. Almost any day Charlie 1/5 spent in the field, which was almost always, you could always find Sgt. Juan Sanchez somewhere in the column carrying an M60 machine gun. As he was the Weapons Platoon sergeant, acting Weapons Platoon commander, and acting section leader for mortars, machine guns, and rocket launchers, his rightful place would have been somewhere near the company commander. Sergeant Sanchez didn't see it that way. He wanted to help his troops carry and employ the heavy crew-served weapons.

Jim Caswell's operational procedures and precautions included his carrying a rifle and not wearing any rank insignia. His radio operators carried their radios disguised inside their packs, and they wrapped their short antennae around their helmets. Thus, any enemy observing Charlie Company from a distance would find it difficult to pinpoint the position of the command group.

These precautions, and the fact that Captain Caswell never slept in a house or a hut while in the bush, should have ensured a company commander's anonymity. (Caswell had found himself inside a stucco house in a hamlet once, early during his command of Charlie Company, when they received a nighttime mortar barrage; he vowed never to sleep in a house again.) Surely no one would try to assassinate a commander they couldn't recognize. Actually, the Viet Cong had no difficulty in recognizing troop leaders by careful observation, if they could get close enough, contrary to what Americans may have thought. The VC simply had to watch carefully, and they could figure out who the unit revolved around. That was the commander.

While on a battalion operation during the early part of Caswell's tour, Charlie Company set up defensive positions around a small hamlet, where they found it necessary to spend several days. The company gunnery sergeant decided to reprovision his troops. His orders included getting new radio batteries, replacing worn-out boots, and obtaining new jungle utilities for those torn by the thorns and briars ever present in the thick bush; he also ordered any needed ammunition, grenades, or rations. Since the company had already been in the field for a week, he also knew he could order sundry packs for his troops. These highly prized packages consisted of cigarettes, cigars, candy, and chewing gum for those troops spending considerable time away from their home combat base, away from the delivery of mail.

After the helicopters delivered all the ordered supplies, the gunny handed them out to the platoon sergeants, who in turn handed them out to the squad leaders and their troops. The village children found the packs of gum and candy fascinating, while the village elders eyed the cigarettes with envy. The soft-hearted Charlie 1/5 Marines began handing out their own candy and cigarettes to the children and the village elders, generating many smiles of gratitude.

Meanwhile, Capt. Jim Caswell and his radio operators occupied a chicken coop next to the largest stucco house in the hamlet. As far as Caswell knew, no one knew who they were. They looked like everyone else. Charlie Company finally left the hamlet amidst much waving and laughter.

A few days later, Caswell realized that Charlie Company's new orders sent them back to the same hamlet. There was nothing unusual in that; it happened all the time. As he and his radio operators and the gunny reached the dirt courtyard in the center of the village, they noticed no children playing. Then they started to notice that all the visible villagers were huddled near the walls of the stucco houses. Still no alarms went off in Jim's mind. But as they looked at the big house where they had stayed in the chicken coop, he saw the old lady who owned the house standing next to a wall holding a rope in one hand and a heavy stick in the other. The rope she held looped around the neck of one of the village dogs. That was odd. The Vietnamese never tied up their dogs or used leashes. Caswell slowly began to realize that the Marines of Charlie 1/5 were standing in a killing zone.

The old lady suddenly hit the dog several times with the stick. The dog set up a fearful wailing. Simultaneously the gunny and Captain Caswell started running for cover, with the two radio operators in hot pursuit. After a few heartbeats, the courtyard exploded in shattering geysers of dirt, dust, and hot shrapnel. Bullets zipped and sang around their heads. Then they heard the staccato bursts of firing, saw the powder flying from the stucco walls that the villagers hid behind, and jumped over a hedgerow into a ditch. Bullets whined and thumped everywhere, and then they heard the first 3.5-inch rocket fired by the Charlie Company Marines explode, followed by a huge volume of outgoing fire.

As Caswell called for his artillery FO to pound the tree line across the rice paddy with artillery fire, he checked to see how the gunny and the radio operators had fared. They all looked at each other in astonishment; not one of them had a scratch. Jim Caswell said, "Thank God the enemy had carbines."

During World War II the United States shipped hundreds of thousands of M1 Garand rifles, Browning automatic rifles (BARs), and M1 carbines to their allies who fought the Japanese in Asia. These allies included Mao Tse Tsung and the Chinese Communists as well as the French during the war in Indochina. The Viet Minh had defeated the French, and now the Viet Cong used these very same weapons to kill Americans.

Because of their small stature, the Viet Cong preferred the M1 carbine, a lighter, smaller weapon. The Marines were happy about that, because the M1 carbine fired a low-powered cartridge that rarely penetrated a flak jacket. When the VC used M1s, BARs, and AK-47s, the Marines suffered much worse casualties.

"And thank God they couldn't hit their asses with a handful of rocks," replied the gunny. The VC's notorious poor aim also pleased the Marines.

Out of the corner of his eye, Jim saw his interpreter, a Vietnamese Army staff sergeant, with his pistol up to the old lady's head, about to pull the trigger. Jim Caswell waved him off and told him to leave the old lady alone. The 155 mm rounds blew the tree line into piles of sticks. The Marines of Charlie 1/5 moved out. So much for the anonymity of company commanders.

Except for machine gunners, mortarmen, and radio operators, every Marine in

Charlie 1/5 carried a 60 mm mortar round or a 3.5-inch rocket round strapped to the outside of his pack over his already heavy load of ammo and provisions. At a given command, the Marines would all drop their extra rounds at a designated location, and the crew-served weapons would have some additional firepower.

Every Charlie 1/5 Marine also carried a one-half-pound block of C-4 (plastic explosive) or TNT. NCOs and officers carried primer cord, fuses, and detonators. Division standard operating procedure (SOP) required all officers and NCOs to attend the division demolition school taught by the engineers. Explosives were dangerous, but they were necessary for such things as blowing up the seemingly endless enemy bunkers, ammo caches, and booby traps the Marines found.

Before an operation the troops could draw as many C-ration meals as they wanted, with the understanding that they would only expect resupply every third day. Charlie Company did not resupply every other day, as did some of the other units. On many occasions, resupply operations in the field by helicopters (the normal method) proved hazardous, since the enemy watched the helicopters as they flew around the countryside, sometimes able to pinpoint the Marines' positions by where the helicopters landed. Captain Caswell wanted to mitigate this necessary evil by allowing resupply only every three days. Whenever they left a combat base, the Marines of Charlie 1/5 carried six C-rations for three days, and they learned to live on that.

Standard operating procedure in Charlie Company dictated that every officer, staff NCO, and NCO check the lines every night whether they occupied the static bunkers of a combat base or hastily dug positions in the field. That way it got the leaders off their asses and made them confident where their sectors of responsibility stood, and it made the troops realize that their leaders actually cared about them. Jim Caswell also checked lines every night, whether in garrison or in the field.

When returning inside the wire of a combat base, Jim required each NCO to check every chamber of every weapon to ensure that they were empty. All grenades were turned in and stored in a bunker where they could quickly be issued again for patrols, ambushes, bunker duty, or combat operations. While under Jim Caswell's command, Charlie Company had no accidental discharges or accidental grenade explosions in their tents.

During his six months as the CO of Charlie 1/5, Jim Caswell came to realize that as a company commander he experienced another set of difficulties, and his memories of those days have never left him:

> In 1967, Marine company commanders operated under a reign of terror—not that imposed by the enemy, which was plenty terrifying, but by our own chain of command. From the president of the United States to the secretary of defense, to the division, regiment, and battalion commanders, edicts were

regularly announced as to what our troops would do or would not do, or else. These edicts were always accompanied by threats, usually that the company commander would be humiliated, degraded, and relieved of command. That would be the end of his career. Apparently, President Johnson and Mr. McNamara would rather have been company commanders than whatever it was they were supposed to be doing. On a weekly (or more frequent) basis the chain of command warned us of the list of heinous crimes that, if committed by our men, would result in our demise. Simultaneously, they educated us about the duties that our men *would* perform, the failure of which would also result in our ignominious relief. Company commanders had to walk a very stressful tightrope, balancing what had to be done with what better not happen, or else they could kiss their careers goodbye.

It seemed that on every holiday, from Lyndon Johnson's birthday to the Ascension of Buddha to Heaven, company commanders received the dreaded Rules of Engagement and were ordered personally to read them to their troops. That way, if any violations occurred, the higher-ups would have a company commander to flog. On 24 December 1966, a few days after he had taken command, Capt. Jim Caswell read the Rules of Engagement to all his night ambush patrols and the men manning the defensive bunkers at the combat base. For the first and last time in his Marine Corps career, two hundred Marines laughed at Jim Caswell. It quickly became obvious to him that you could follow orders and lose the trust of your men, or you could disobey orders and be relieved in disgrace. Since he received so many edicts and dictates, Caswell assumed that his seniors were very competent at their jobs and sure of what they were doing. Under the worst possible conditions, he discovered this to be a terribly faulty assumption.

Buck Darling remembered very well the day Captain Caswell joined 1/5:

After Jim Caswell took over Charlie Company, I took over H&S Company. I was, in effect, the headquarters commandant—pretty much in charge of everything in the rear area combat base. That spring we must have had half a dozen Mickey Mouse operations, walk-arounds through the boonies, that sort of thing. They named these combat operations mostly after the presidents, like Polk, Clay, names like that. One Five went through company commanders like they were going out of style. One older captain came in to the battalion, took over Bravo Company, spent about two days in the field, got shot in the leg, and we never saw him again. So they gave me Bravo Company for two or three days out around Tam Ky. We patrolled, most of the time, on the southeast side of Tam Ky, but occasionally we moved up around Nui Lac

> Son. They had brought us the M16s by that time, so we had to turn in our M14s; we issued M16s to about seventy-five percent of the guys, but they let us keep one M14 per fire team. We still had quite a few M14s around, at least for a while. We're back in the rear, and one of the other companies was out there thrashing through the bushes coming toward the compound. A guy named Franklin Pierce, my radio operator at the time, says, "Damn, Skipper, lookit, there's a gooner." Sure enough, I see there's someone hiding in those bushes with an AK aiming right down the paddy dike. So, I say, "Don't tell me about it, shoot the bitch!" So Pierce fires his M14 rifle, *blam*! Unfortunately his flash suppressor was located about three inches from my right ear. I was a sick puppy for two or three days, bleeding out of my ear. The doc got all over me, giving me pills, whatever, but it finally went away. The hearing out of that ear went away, too. I still can't hear any high frequency noise out of that ear to this day.

While Buck Darling temporarily lost his hearing to a carelessly fired M14, many more losses would be attributed to the defective and deadly M16 rifle.

4: Changes of Weaponry, April 1967

The changeover from the M14 to the new and untested M16 rifle caused a great deal of uproar and made a significant negative impact on the 1/5 Marines' daily lives. During April 1967 a total of 946 brand new M16 rifles were issued to the Marines of the battalion. Within the first few days of the month, all personnel within the battalion armed with the M14 rifles received M16 rifles, and all M14 rifles (except for a handful) were sent to Fleet Landing Support Group B at Tam Ky. This dramatic change in the basic weapon of the combat Marines fighting in Vietnam would cause some consternation and much discussion and uncertainty amongst the Marines.

The M14 had long since proven itself to be an utterly reliable and powerful weapon in a combat situation. All Marines knew that in any combat zone, under any circumstances, with any weapon, keeping your weapon clean was very important, but in some situations the Marines confronted in Vietnam, this became difficult if not downright impossible. The Marines had come to love the M14, not only for its sturdy feel and looks, but also because it would always fire when needed, even under very adverse conditions. Some Marines told stories of accidentally dropping their M14 in the mud while taking cover under fire, only to pick it up and fire it at the enemy. It worked every time. But it was heavy, weighing (with full magazine, cleaning equipment, selector, and bipod) 11.85 pounds.

This new M16 seemed a very different beast altogether. First of all, it looked like a toy. Made out of black plastic and metal parts, as opposed to the M14 with its traditional wooden stock, the M16, at just under eight pounds (with sling and loaded thirty-round magazine), weighed much less. Marines knew that when it came to long patrols, your combat load needed to be balanced with speed. It looked like you would be able to carry much more ammo, maybe giving you an edge. But the M16 just looked like it wouldn't stand up to the stresses and demands of combat in Vietnam. It had too many spare parts, jammed easily, and was damned hard to clean, and the stock was too short for many Americans, so the Marines tended to shoot high. Lieutenant Colonel Hilgartner recently put the M16's combat effectiveness in its early usage into stark perspective. He stated, very bluntly, "We lost many good men because of that piece of crap."

The Marines of 1/5 made the change as quickly and smoothly as possible, under the circumstances, to the new M16. Like Marines from all eras, they understood that "ours is not to reason why, ours is but to do or die." As a hedge against the unknown reliability of the M16, Lieutenant Colonel Hilgartner tried to feed as many M14s into each unit as he could get away with.

In the first few months of use, many problems with misfires, double-feeds, and other jams in the M16 rifle cropped up. Some veterans contend that some bad lots of the 5.56 mm ammunition arrived along with the new weapons, which only made a bad problem worse. At some point, an important spring in the firing assembly proved defective, requiring replacement.

The most important lesson learned about the M16 rifle was that it needed to be cleaned almost constantly, an impractical requirement in any combat zone. If clean, it worked well most of the time; if dirty, it could easily jam and ruin your whole day.

Because the M16's too-short stock caused the Marines to shoot high, after Operation Union I, Lieutenant Colonel Hilgartner mandated that a tracer round be loaded every fifth round in an M16 magazine. That way the NCOs and officers could see exactly where their men's shots were going and make adjustments accordingly. This order stuck, and it became standard operating procedure.

Hillous York, outspoken about the changeover from the M14 to the M16, said, "Shortly after I rejoined the company at Tam Ky, just before Union I kicked off, we gave up our M14s and received M16s. Some reporter came in and wanted to do a story on the new weapon because of some reports of jamming. I told him that it was a good jungle weapon but that it would get even better when they got the bugs out. I knew that my mouth had nearly gotten me in trouble, because they told us to say only favorable things about the M16. I didn't get court-martialed for saying what I said, so I knew that I had skirted the problem."

Although the M16's combat effectiveness improved during the Vietnam War and a much-improved version of the M16 is considered an excellent military weapon today, those who had to rely on it daily for survival in 1967 and 1968 constantly worried about its shortcomings. The problems were worked out; unfortunately, they were too often worked out on the battlefield, causing the tragic and unnecessary deaths of many Marines.

Many more Marine replacements arrived in South Vietnam in March 1967 and joined the Marines of 1/5. Pfc. Harold L. Thrasher enlisted in the Marine Corps in September of 1966 and reported to MCRD San Diego for boot camp. Harold, another Hollywood Marine, graduated from boot camp, underwent ITR (infantry training regiment), and spent some time in the staging battalion at Camp Pendleton, California, before his assignment to duty in WestPac. Upon his arrival in South Vietnam, Harold reported to the 1st Battalion, 5th Marines and joined Charlie Company on 25 March 1967. Private First Class Thrasher became a rifleman in the 1st Squad of the 2nd Platoon, under squad leader Sgt. John Lynch.

Harold would quickly learn one of the second natures of a Marine in a combat zone, that of constant movement from one temporary home to another. Before ending his thirteen-month tour in South Vietnam, Harold's rear area "home" moved no fewer than fourteen times.

> When I joined the company, we were at a place we called Snaggletooth Island. An inlet from the South China Sea lay close by, and we would go down there and swim in the salty but pleasant water. We were somewhere around Chu Lai, but I'm not exactly sure of the location. Private first class riflemen didn't have a lot of access to maps. They told our squad leader and platoon commander where to go, and we just followed them.
>
> Shortly after arriving at Snaggletooth Island, a gung-ho second lieutenant joined the platoon and became our platoon commander. He immediately had us training in the sand for warfare. We weren't into the war games very enthusiastically due to the heat, and most of the Marines in the 2nd Platoon had already lost their cherry status; we were all combat veterans by now. Despite being green and very gung ho, this man meant well. I remember one day he had us practicing assaulting bunkers, using our own ammo bunker, which had concertina wire around it and an entryway. We just assaulted the bunker without taking any cover, and we ran through the entryway. We took the easy street. This wasn't good enough for our new platoon commander, and he reprimanded us for taking the easy way. We asked him how he wanted us to do the assault. "Use available cover and work towards the objective, and then when you have an obstacle you go *over or through*, not around it." We asked him to demonstrate. He immediately and enthusiastically obliged, using the deep ruts the amtracs cut into the sand for cover. When he got to the ammo bunker, he jumped up and leaped over the wire headfirst as if in gymnastic mode, and hit, rolled up into a ball, and sprung back up on his feet in a flash. He was impressive. But then one of the squad leaders pointed out that with seventy-five pounds on our back and a helmet and flak jacket on, we would break our necks if we tried something like that. Really, we were just giving him a hard time. He took one look at our smirking faces and said, "Men, it takes guts to be a Marine. If you lose a leg you hop to the objective on the

other leg. If you lose both legs you crawl to the objective." We all looked at one another in amazement at this statement, and we all began to wonder about his leadership.

Pfc. Delbert L. Best, a tall and very lean string bean of a man from Missouri, joined the Marine Corps in September of 1966. Yet another Hollywood Marine, Del Best served in Charlie 1/5 for an entire thirteen-month combat tour.

Del boarded the USS *Upshur*, an old US Navy "dependent" ship, in San Diego in early March 1967 and slowly crossed the Pacific Ocean, finally arriving in the war zone in late March. Not a part of a coherent unit while aboard ship, Del was just one Marine among thousands of Marines and soldiers who made their journey from America to South Vietnam aboard US Navy ships.

Del's trip across the Pacific took twenty-eight days. The USS *Upshur* cruised directly to Okinawa from San Diego harbor, made a brief stop in Okinawa, and then made the fast run across the South China Sea and dropped anchor in Da Nang Bay. "We slept in bunks stacked up seven high," Del recalled. "It got really bad down there when we hit a typhoon. We were literally locked up down in the bottom of the ship with hundreds of other guys during that storm. Fortunately, I didn't get seasick, but a lot of the other guys did."

Assigned as a rifleman in the 1st Squad, 2nd Platoon of Charlie 1/5, Del served under Sergeant Lynch. As a rifleman, fire team leader, and eventually squad leader, he fought in some of the fiercest battles of the war. Del was severely wounded and eventually medevaced during Operation Hue City in February of 1968. Fortunately, Del recovered from his wounds and returned to duty with Charlie Company, and he left the war in one piece as a decorated sergeant of Marines.

Pfc. Richard Leroy Schlagel enlisted in the Marine Corps in September 1966. Another Hollywood Marine, Richard completed his boot camp training at MCRD San Diego and his infantry training at Camp Pendleton, California.

On 19 March 1967, Richard arrived in the Republic of South Vietnam and became an 0311 rifleman with Charlie 1/5 as a part of the 3rd Fire Team, 3rd Squad, 3rd Platoon. Richard says, "That made it easy to remember; I was in the third of the third of the third. I don't remember the name of my Squad Leader, but I remember that the platoon sergeant was Sergeant York, and my fire team leader was Lance Cpl. John Rusth. We called him Rusty."

Richard's memories, like those of many combat Marines from this era, stay somewhat jumbled. He remembers many things very clearly, but since he spent thirteen months with Charlie 1/5 and fought in many, many firefights and large combat operations, he has found it very difficult in later years to communicate specific details with his recollections. Some things, however, Richard remembers with clarity that he would just as soon have disappear. During the hot summer and fall of 1967, Richard fought in Operations Union I, Union II, Swift, Pike, and Cochise and was eventually wounded in action during Operation Hue City in February 1968, receiving the Purple Heart medal. Richard Schlagel fought in some of the most deadly combat operations of the entire war.

In the Chu Lai TAOR Marine rifle companies could be given one of two assignments: bunker duty as security for the massive Chu Lai airstrip or island duty, which included the occupation, patrol, and protection of several small islands in an estuary located beyond the north end of the runway. Both of these assignments could prove exceedingly boring, so the troops never took them seriously, no matter how much the officers and senior NCOs ranted and raved. The companies rotated the assignments every week or two, and commanders and troops looked forward to the end of each assignment, because most of their conduct problems occurred during those boring times. It became extremely hard to keep the troops motivated during bunker and island duty, and thus the assignments were considered by leadership to be very dangerous.

One of the very few booby trap/mine incidents during that period occurred during a Charlie Company patrol on Snaggletooth Island. Capt. Jim Caswell recalls:

> When we occupied these islands, since there were several of them, we had to split into platoon- and squad-sized units, sent via LVTP [landing vehicle tracked personnel carrier] to their assigned island home. We called the largest of these islands Snaggletooth because of its irregular shape. We called one of the adjacent islands Cigar Island because it looked like a cigar on the maps. The patrol routes on all of these islands were very limited, and they could not be varied easily. One of my patrols tripped a booby-trapped 250-pound GP [general purpose, high explosive] bomb that had fallen from an American aircraft and failed to explode. Our enemy knew how to make them explode. Most likely command-detonated, this one yielded devastating results. That single bomb killed three Charlie Company Marines. During the remainder of my command tenure, several more months, we had only two other booby trap incidents.

John "Rusty" Rusth remembers those early days as well:

> One Five operated around the Chu Lai area. We traded off between guarding the Chu Lai airstrip and going out on some small operations east and west of Hill 54. The countryside actually remained fairly peaceful in early 1967. I mean we always had the threat of land mines, but for the most part we ran a

Left to right: Lance Cpl. Leonard Roberson (KIA 8 August 1967), unknown rocket man, and Pvt. Kevin Rohring (KIA 27 March 1967). Courtesy of John Rusth.

lot of patrols and night ambushes around Hill 54 Combat Base. Snaggletooth Island, located about six or eight kilometers northwest of Chu Lai, had a permanent compound with tents and bunkers. It was almost like R&R out there. We didn't have much if any contact with the enemy for a long time. The only way to get over to Cigar Island, short of swimming, was by amtrac. The amtracs would carry us back and forth as we moved from Snaggletooth to Chu Lai or to Hill 54 and back. A small village sprawled close by the compound.

Hill 54 Combat Base. Charlie 1/5 company office in left background. Bill Edge (*foreground front*), Sergeant Tigue (*left*), Lt. Jack Jewell, and Dietz (in the white T-shirt). Courtesy of John Rusth.

When we patrolled around the Snaggletooth Island area, there wasn't ever anything going on, but when we went over to Cigar Island, we ran into a lot of mines. The vegetation on Cigar Island grew very dense. We didn't like going over to Cigar Island at all because something bad always happened over there.

Rusty vividly remembers one patrol in particular, which took place on 27 March 1967:

Charlie Company tent, Hill 54. *Left to right*: Lt. Jack Jewell, unknown Marine (bending down), Lance Cpl. Walter Munns (KIA 27 March 1967), Sergeant Tigue, Ricky March, Bob Johnson (with camera), and Joe McQueen. Courtesy of John Rusth.

They sent us out on a two-squad patrol. The village on Snaggletooth Island seemed very friendly, and the area around the village was a very beautiful setting. A lot of water, sunshine, ocean breezes, and white sand beaches; it seemed very pleasant there. We knew that some of these people, the friendly Vietnamese villagers next door, knew that we planned to go over to Cigar Island that day. We spent a lot of time with them, and, in retrospect, we just talked too much about things. After Worley's squad got hit by that command-detonated 250-pound bomb, we knew that someone in our "friendly" village had tipped the VC off, and our enemy got there ahead of us.

I walked second man back from point; Bill Edge walked point. We took a quick break and Worley rearranged the order of the patrol, putting Munns on point, Rohring second in line, and Worley followed them. Not more than two minutes after Worley had changed us around, that damned bomb went off, killing the first three men on the patrol. Munns and Rohring died instantly.

Worley lived for a little while, but he died before the helicopter could get him back to the hospital. The helicopter pilots called us and let us know that Worley had died on the helicopter. Someone back behind us on the patrol saw the VC run away and took a few shots at them, but I think they got away.

John Rusth remembers that awful incident as if it happened yesterday, although it happened more than forty-five years ago, shortly after he joined the Marines of 1/5: “Worley Hall was just blown up by the bomb, along with Pvt. Kevin Rohring, from Buffalo, New York, and Lance Cpl. Walter Munns, from Winston-Salem, North Carolina.”

The death of Cpl. Worley Wayne Hall devastated Sgt. Hillous York, a close personal friend of Hall. To make matters worse, Hall had taken out the patrol to which York had initially been assigned:

My friend Cpl. Worley Wayne Hall had gone to NCO school in Okinawa. The day he got back, I had run two patrols already and was getting ready to go out on a third. I told Worley to take an ammo run up to Hill 54, but he refused to go. He said that I looked very tired, that he would take the patrol, and that I should go on the ammo run, that I could get some sleep in the amtrac on the way there and back. I took the ammo run and managed to get some sleep. Worley died on that patrol. He was my friend; we were two guys from Tennessee.

After that, Captain Darling sent me on R&R. He came over and told me to get on the chopper, and we almost got into an argument. After he told me twice to get on the damned chopper, that I *would* go on R&R, I got on the chopper. I wanted to go back out to Snaggletooth Island and get back into the area where Worley had died, but Captain Darling knew that I needed to take a break; he was the CO, and I had to obey his orders. So I got on the damned chopper.

When I came back from R&R, Charlie Company had moved up around Tam Ky. I hitched a ride on a resupply chopper from Chu Lai to Tam Ky, and when the chopper landed and I jumped out, I found myself in the middle of a firefight. Captain Darling, now the H&S Company commander, came running across the LZ, and he only said one thing to me. I had shaved off my mustache while on R&R. The fire was flying like crazy. Here comes Captain Darling running through the battle, and he took one look at me and hollered, “Get that damned mustache back on!” So, of course, I grew my mustache back.

Buck Darling’s eighteen-month tour with 1/5 eventually came to an end:

About April, Hilgartner started to feel sorry for me because I'd spent so much time out in the field. So he sent me to Da Nang to find all our awards and to get them moving along. I spent two days working with these three sissy majors at division in the awards section, moving our awards along. I found out that more Bronze Stars had been given out there at division than to those out in the field. Hell, they had all the typewriters at division, and they used them, all the time, to write medal citations with.

The rear moved from Chu Lai at about that time. Hilgartner sent me back to do the command chronology for April, that kind of stuff. My rotation date was 10 May. The battalion was searching for the enemy north of Nui Lac Son and a little way west of Que Son, and my rotation date came around.

I remember that Pete Hilgartner had us put sand on a field so we would have a parade deck. Maj. Gen. Herman "The German" Nickerson came out to the field and conducted an awards ceremony. The word that we had received before he got there was that General Nickerson had a reputation as absolutely the meanest son-of-a-bitch that had ever lived. The day before he came out there, I had about four or five stars show up at our position, you know, to make sure I wasn't going to fail this visit. Colonel Widdecke stayed out there most of the day, worrying about it. Anytime we spent more than a couple of days in any one place, we had bunkers, we dug communication trenches, you know, we always stayed ready to go. So, after he got there General Nickerson walks around our position, and he says, "This is a damn fine company position, Captain. Now, when I leave here, is there any place that you don't want me to fly over, so I don't cause you any trouble?" I told him where our Marines patrolled and asked him to avoid flying over them, so he said okay, got in his helicopter and flew away. I thought, "There's nothing wrong with this guy. He's a tactical guy, he's a pretty good guy. Everyone was afraid of him, but I'm not sure why."

We awarded one of the 1/5 Marines the Navy Cross during this award ceremony. I still find it hard to believe we were out here in the middle of the war, marching on a parade deck, but Hilgartner told me, "Let me show you a little about protocol, Captain." So we had this full-scale award ceremony out in the middle of a war zone.

Finally we got a resupply chopper out there, and Capt. H. Gaylen Lyles got off the chopper and said, "I'm your relief." And so I hopped on that helicopter and went home.

Buck Darling returned to Vietnam in 1970 and put in another thirteen-month-long tour. Buck served the Marine Corps with distinction for nearly thirty years and retired honorably as a full colonel of Marines.

For all the action that Buck Darling saw in Vietnam, one of his clearest memories was of an incident that occurred in the rear. Buck felt that Lieutenant Colonel Hilgartner, who had been dubbed "Highpockets" by his Marines because of his tall stature, knew fire support and was good with a map; he was an excellent, maybe superb tactical commander. He was also greatly feared, because he could be very forceful in getting his way. One night, just before Buck left Vietnam, Hilgartner called the captain over to his hooch and said, "Have a beer."

He broke a beer out of his refrigerator and handed it to Buck. After a couple of chugs, he said, "I want you to get rid of that mustache, Captain."

Buck said, "I don't think so."

Hilgartner said, "That's an order."

So Buck said, "Okay, I'll take that order in writing."

Hilgartner, taken aback, said, "What?"

Buck repeated, "I'll take that order in writing."

Hilgartner asked why he wanted the order in writing, and Buck said, "Because I'm going to request mast to the division commander."

Hilgartner turned red, and said, "Well, goddammit, I'm trying to get the mustaches off these Marines, and I can't do it if I have one of my captains walking around with a mustache."

So Buck said, "You can't do that either."

Highpockets, now starting to get very angry said, "Goddammit, Buck, here you are drinking my beer and you're telling me what I can't do?"

And then Hilgartner sat down, leaned back, finished the last swallow of his beer, and said, "Okay. You want another beer?"

Buck Darling crossed paths with Peter Hilgartner many times during the remainder of their Marine Corps careers. Hilgartner rotated back to the United States around Christmas 1967, reported to Headquarters Marine Corps, where Buck was stationed, and took charge as the director of Plans Division, J-3. "Around Christmas," Buck said,

> we had our fiscal year budgeting going on, so things had been hellish since about November and we were scrambling to get our budget completed for the first of the year. Hilgartner always ended up putting me on a program objective memorandum (POM) team. I told Pete that we've got to have a better solution for this particular problem, and Hilgartner was capable of killing people to get his way. This guy came in with a bunch of paperwork and said we're doing this, this, this, and so forth, and Hilgartner listened for a minute and then said, "That's bullshit! Get outta here." So the guy fled the room. I asked him, "Why did you do that? I mean, we have to work with these guys,

> right?" He said, "Aw, hell, I don't know. I go out there and yell, and if they dive for cover, they're probably wrong. What would you have done if I had yelled at you about that?" And I said, "I'd tell you to jam it up your butt!" And Highpockets said, "I wonder why he didn't?" Hilgartner wanted what he wanted, all the time. If somebody wasn't doing his job, he'd relieve them, that was it. I think the battalion was better for it. Within a month of Hilgartner's arrival, 1/5 had become known again as a battalion that had its shit together.

Buck Darling's Marines would all agree that Buck had a unique quality, a knack for leadership that came as naturally as his sweat. He was a hybrid animal, the merging of a bulldog and a water buffalo—strong and belligerent like a waterboo and tenacious and stubborn like a bulldog. He was also a Marine commander who loved his Marines, and he did everything in his considerable powers to help them and protect them. His high days in Vietnam were those that included some of the fiercest fighting during the early days of the war, every one of them marked by victory over the Viet Cong and the NVA and by very few American casualties. His low days, which were few, were those marked by tragedy and loss, the loss of his beloved Marines. Buck Darling was a true warrior and a natural-born commander of US Marines.

Capt. Jim Caswell also proved to be a warrior and a natural-born leader of men, and he picked up the torch that Buck Darling handed off to him without missing a beat. The Marines of Charlie 1/5 considered themselves very fortunate during 1966 and 1967 in that they served with outstanding company commanders. This was especially critical because good officers were sometimes hard to come by during those years. Jim Caswell remembers:

> We received very few lieutenants while I commanded Charlie Company, and when we did get a lieutenant they didn't seem to last very long for a number of reasons. If they learned quickly and aggressively pursued the enemy, battalion snapped them up for staff positions. Many were wounded, but none died while I had the company. For a short time we had a couple of recently commissioned lieutenants, former staff NCOs, one of whom served as my executive officer. I found that many of these "mustangs" did not like to stand out or take initiative, and they seemed uncomfortable around other officers. They were probably good staff NCOs who would have proved more useful to the Corps had they stayed put. So mostly staff sergeants or gunnery sergeants served as platoon commanders in Charlie Company; to a man, they made excellent platoon commanders. They were quick, aggressive, positive thinkers, under control, and visibly fearless—overall, very good leaders. Occasion-

ally I had to use sergeants as platoon commanders, and once, later on during Operation Union I, I had to ask a corporal if he would try to handle a platoon. He tried and did a pretty good job until he died a few days later, killed by a sniper he was trying to eradicate.

During Jim Caswell's tenure as the CO of Charlie Company, they stayed in the field most of the time or occupied the small outpost called Nui Lac Son. They spent very little time in the larger combat bases. Most of that time Charlie Company operated as an independent combat force, which kept them at a distance from their parent battalion, or any other battalion, for that matter. Like Buck Darling, Captain Caswell felt this freedom of movement to be a good thing, giving him more independence than any company commander could ever ask for.

One of the first major combat operations that Charlie Company participated in during Jim Caswell's command was Operation DeSoto/Deckhouse VI. During his briefing he received a warning that he might encounter VC in reinforced concrete bunkers. Caswell found that hard to believe, but nonetheless he called for the battalion flamethrower section. In short order the flamethrower section found their weapons, filled them with napalm, and joined Charlie Company. Caswell ran each platoon through tactical training, refreshing their stateside training focused on attacking fortified bunkers, ending with the flamethrower operators firing their napalm at the bunkers. Caswell told Hilgartner that he might call for the flamethrowers if he needed them.

When Operation DeSoto/Deckhouse VI kicked off, Caswell's Marines received the mission to occupy a village located in the Quang Ngai province south of Chu Lai at first light. Viet Cong supposedly defended this village in concrete bunkers, so Captain Caswell arranged for an air strike at first light. Caswell moved his Marines up to a railway trestle, situated about one hundred meters from the village, in the early morning hours and waited for the fixed-wing aircraft.

Captain Caswell recalls that his air strike seemed very effective and provided good coverage of the target:

> At first light the aircraft showed up on station, right on time. The flight leader told me that they had five-hundred-pound GP bombs aboard, so I told him to start his runs. The flight leader asked me my location, and I gave him the coordinates at the railroad trestle about one hundred meters outside the village. At first the flight leader refused to drop his bombs, saying that we were too close to the target, so I assured him that since we were all behind a twelve-foot-high embankment, we were safe. Shortly thereafter, the aircraft started their bombing runs. I told everyone in the company not to look over the

> embankment under any circumstances. Of course, one of my Marines became just too curious for his own good and wanted to watch the bomb run, so he looked over the top and was immediately knocked cold from the concussion. Once we got him back on his feet, and the bombing run ended, we walked quietly into the village without firing a shot. Shortly thereafter we ran into a squad of VC, and the Charlie Company Marines, with all their packs and flak jackets and equipment, went into a dead run after them. We maintained a perfect attack formation for more than an hour as we chased down and killed almost every member of the VC squad, capturing their weapons. We never saw any concrete bunkers, and we never again called for the flamethrower section.

Lieutenant Colonel Hilgartner had assembled a good group of officers around him, and he felt confident. So by the time Hilgartner's Marines were committed to Operation Union I, they had become an outstanding battalion of fighting Marines.

Hilgartner felt that he had earned the confidence of the new CO of the 5th Marines, Col. Kenneth J. Houghton, Jr., but during early 1967 Houghton had not yet committed 1/5 to any major operations. Hilgartner suspected that this lack of battalion-sized combat operations experience might have given Colonel Houghton the impression that the Marines of 1/5 were still not ready for coordinated battalion operations at the regimental level.

Finally, Hilgartner could stand it no longer. He called for his driver, told him to bring up the jeep, and instructed him to get a case of beer and put it on the back seat. He then hopped in the jeep, and away they went to regimental headquarters. Colonel Houghton sat working behind his field desk when Hilgartner stormed into the operations tent with the case of beer under his arm.

"Colonel!" he blurted out, "The 1st Battalion is ready to fight, sir! In fact the men are on the landing pad now, packed and ready to go. I don't know what it's going to take to get us committed, but if it's a case of beer, here it is."

Hilgartner then slammed the case of beer on Houghton's desk. Houghton's eyes opened wide, and he looked at Hilgartner with a startled expression. Pete thought, well here it comes; I'm fired. Instead, Colonel Houghton started to chuckle and said, "Cool down, Hilgartner. I'm glad to hear you're ready. You'll be on your way shortly."

The Marine infantry battalion known as One Five had undergone drastic changes during the month of April 1967, receiving both new leaders and new weapons. Now they were headed into harm's way once again.

5: Operation Union I, 21 April–9 May 1967

Lieutenant Colonel Pete Hilgartner got his wish, but it didn't start off the way he had hoped it would. On 21 April 1967, 1/5's Alpha and Charlie Companies became chopped (attached) to 3rd Battalion, 5th Marines, augmenting Marine forces fighting in Operation Union I. Alpha Company's Marines proceeded to the 3/5 combat base and worked for 3/5 for the next couple of weeks. Charlie Company went to the field, assigned as battalion reserve to take up the drag position, responsible for 3/5's rear security. Nine long days later, Hilgartner got his Marines back and took command of the operation in the field.

The terrain west of the combat bases at Chu Lai and Hill 54 consisted largely of farmed rice paddies intersected by hedgerows and tree lines and dotted with small hamlets. Wildly spread green vegetation, including grass, brush, jungle growth, and bamboo, covered the hill masses in the area. Occasionally, sugar cane fields dotted the lowlands, interrupting the paddies. The jungle in the higher elevations of the Que Son Valley, the TAOR of Operation Union I, consisted mostly of single- or double-canopy growth—not the heavy, dense, triple-canopy jungle prevalent further inland.

The inhabitants of the hamlets in 1/5's TAOR seemed friendly near the coast and less and less friendly the farther inland 1/5 patrolled. In the friendlier villages along the coast, the women often gave the Marines pineapples as they passed through. On one operation, a village family burned their own house down and begged the Marines to protect them. The Viet Cong had threatened their lives. The Marines took them to safety. Now, the Marines of 1/5 marched inland into an area that had become known as VC Valley.

The objective of Operation Union I was to find, fix, and destroy enemy forces and supplies in the objective area, the Que Son Valley, a large, rugged area of mountains, valleys, and villages located about forty kilometers west of Tam Ky. During Marine Corps training stateside, Marine instructors often referred to this type of operation as a three F operation. The three Fs stood for, "Find 'em, fix 'em, and fuck 'em up real good."

Several critical terrain features dominated the Operation Union I TAOR, including Nui Lac Son (Hill 185), Nui Da Ham (Hill 218), and Nghi Ha Sa (Hill 110). The dominant rice paddy land in the Que Son Valley, surrounded by densely forested mountains with elevations of between 100 and 445 meters, was interspersed with hills thickly covered with brush. Many rivers and streams traversed the operational area, presenting potential obstacles. Trails in the area were considered good to excellent for foot troops, providing easy avenues of approach for both the Marines of 1/5 and their enemy. No unusual problems were expected during cross-country movements. Throughout the operation, the weather forecast predicted partly cloudy skies and hot and humid conditions with, for the most part, unrestricted visibility.

When Operation Union I kicked off, the Marines of Charlie 1/5 had been patrolling the area around the combat base at Hill 54, providing security for the rice harvest. Additional duties included acting as the Sparrow Hawk rapid reaction force, so the company's Marines always carried a full load of rations and ammunition, and they stood nearly at full strength except in officers.

The 1st Platoon was commanded by a first lieutenant named Kirkpatrick, and the 2nd Platoon by a new second lieutenant who had just joined the company. But the 3rd Platoon lacked an officer as its leader. For a short time 3rd Platoon had an E-5 sergeant, Hillous York, as its platoon commander, and then a replacement gunnery sergeant took command.

On 21 April 1967, Captain Caswell received a warning order that he was about to be chopped to 3rd Battalion, 5th Marines (3/5), and needed to get his men ready to climb aboard helicopters. So Caswell quickly and efficiently secured an LZ for CH-46s and broke his company down into heliteams. Shortly afterward, a wave of CH-46s landed and started ferrying the Marines of Charlie 1/5 into LZ Condor, located about twenty kilometers west of Hill 54. Charlie 1/5 became part of 3/5 until further notice.

After landing at LZ Condor, Charlie Company quickly secured a perimeter around the LZ, and Caswell reported to the 3/5 Battalion commander and the battalion S-3. After hasty introductions, the S-3 issued Caswell his map thrust points, phase lines, and objectives.

Charlie 1/5, along with all the other Marines of 1st Battalion, 5th Marines, had recently received the new M16 rifles, supposedly much more effective than the M14 for fighting in jungle. Although his Marines had begged him not to take their M14s away from them, Caswell was given no choice in the matter, so the Charlie 1/5 Marines found themselves out in an enemy-dominated combat zone, under operational control of a new battalion, and armed with a new and unfamiliar weapon. Although when they fired the M16 for familiarization they had not experienced any serious problems with it, the men did not trust it. The black plastic M16s looked like they would break if you looked at them crosswise. Caswell remembers that day, the day his men had the M16 forced upon them, as one of the worst days of his Marine Corps career. Other bad days would follow, some of them made terribly worse by the poor initial performance of the M16 and a bad lot of ammunition.

Pushing the continuing bitching of his men about their suspicious new weapons into the back of his mind, Caswell received his orders and kicked off toward his assigned objectives in Operation Union I. Charlie 1/5 would operate semiautonomously, screening 3/5's rear and acting as their battalion reserve force. Caswell doesn't remember seeing much of the 3/5 command group during those early days of Operation Union I; mostly the company stayed on the periphery of the battalion, covering its rear and flanks.

Charlie Company's Marines operated independently in their own assigned TAOR from 21 April until 1 May under the ostensible command of 3/5. The remaining Marines of 1/5 would join Charlie Company on 1 May, except Alpha Company, which would catch up with the rest of the battalion on 6 May.

At that time, Sergeant Hillous York served as the platoon sergeant of 3rd Platoon of Charlie Company. In various actions before May 1967, Hillous had proven himself in combat many times and had, at one point, served as the acting platoon commander of the 3rd Platoon. His two combat promotions demonstrated Sergeant York's outstanding abilities as a Marine NCO under very difficult conditions.

Shortly before the start of Union I, due to the scarcity of lieutenants in 1/5, Gunnery Sgt. Marcelino Rivera-Cruz became the platoon commander of the 3rd Platoon. Sergeant York became the permanent platoon sergeant, a position usually filled by an E-6 staff sergeant.

Sergeant York knew that the leaders he had served under in combat, during his on-the-job training in late 1966 and early 1967, especially Capt. Buck Darling and Sgt. Frank Parks, had taught him well. Hillous attributes his success as a combat leader to their outstanding example and leadership.

From Sergeant York's perspective, since Charlie Company mainly worked on its own for most of Operation Union I, working under the command of 3/5 made very little difference to him and his Marines. "As a platoon sergeant," York said, "I really didn't know the locations of any of the other companies, or what they were doing. We had fought in so many battles leading up to Union I that the end of one operation and the start of another operation had very little distinction."

A few days into the operation, Captain Caswell remembers that the battalion's direction of attack took them up a very large mountain. It would take all day to climb it. The map showed a round meadow near a hamlet at the top of the mountain. Although the hamlet had several pens of cattle, none grazed in the grassy meadow. 1st

Marine Division recon units had probably used it many times for insertions or extractions.

Charlie Company remained in ambush positions at the bottom of the mountain for a while to see if any VC trailed the battalion. The VC often used the tactic of trailing the Marines to keep informed of our troop movements and locations. After ensuring that no one trailed them, the Marines of Charlie 1/5 started the long climb to join 3/5 at the top of the mountain.

The troops climbed for several hours. Then, suddenly, a number of explosions shattered the labored silence. The huge blasts caused the troops automatically to scatter and seek cover, but none of the explosions hit their side of the mountain. The top of the mountain was exploding. More explosions shattered the afternoon as the Marines of Charlie 1/5 continued to trudge toward the unmistakable sounds of Marines dying.

At the top of the mountain they found 3/5 medevacing almost a whole platoon, about forty men. The VC had planted antipersonnel mines, those particularly nasty ones called Bouncing Betties, just under the surface of the ground throughout the big meadow, rigged with trip wires. When someone's foot snagged a trip wire, the Bouncing Betty fired a cartridge, which simultaneously armed the mine and propelled it straight up in the air. At a height of four to six feet, chest- to head-high on a Marine, the mine exploded, sending hundreds of lethal ball bearings in a 360-degree swath, killing or maiming anyone within a few yards of the mine. The point platoon of the lead company of 3/5 had gone into the inviting grassy meadow instead of moving around it. After the initial mines exploded, more would explode as the Marines tried to extricate the wounded and the unharmed from the field, resulting in a bloody disaster.

Jim Caswell witnessed this catastrophe, and he remembers these thoughts: "As a company or platoon commander watching this awful scene, you had to ask yourself, 'Would I have read the signs correctly? Would I have stopped my people from entering the meadow?' Many of us would agonize over those questions for many years to come."

On 1 May 1967 Charlie Company finally reverted back to the control of 1st Battalion, 5th Marines. The remainder of 1/5's companies landed by helicopter into LZ Condor while Charlie Company provided LZ security.

The mission assigned to Lieutenant Colonel Hilgartner when he assumed command of Operation Union I on 1 May 1967 was to commence search-and-destroy operations in a westerly direction to kill or capture the enemy, their weapons, and their supplies. Captain Caswell received his orders from Hilgartner, and his men continued their semiautonomous movement west toward the very remote town of Hiep Duc.

Under the Union I operational plan, 1/5 received solid support from artillery and air units. The 1st Marine Air Wing (1st MAW) provided air support, with both fixed-wing aircraft and helicopters flying out of the Chu Lai Air Base. Batteries D and F, 2nd Battalion, 11th Marines, who had established a firebase about twelve kilometers west of Highway 1, provided artillery support via their 105 mm artillery pieces.

First Marine Division Intelligence (G-2) provided 1/5 with detailed estimates of enemy strength, location, and disposition in the objective area. Elements of the 2nd NVA Division, the 3rd NVA Regiment, and the RQ-20, RQ-22, and RQ-24 NVA Battalions had been detected in this TAOR. Estimates of actual enemy strength totaled about 1,250 men, including VC and NVA units. According to G-2, all enemy cadre and soldiers displayed a high degree of self-sufficiency and appeared ready to put forth a determined defense.

For the next two and one-half weeks, the first half of May 1967, 1/5 Marines would fight under the control of the 5th Marines and stay fully committed to Operation Union I. These two and one-half weeks would be eye-openers for the Marines of 1/5 as they fought North Vietnamese Army (NVA) regulars in strength for the first time since arriving in Vietnam two years before.

Marine planners and commanders responsible for the security of Chu Lai Combat Base and its mile-long runway had long worried about the Que Son Valley. Many American and ARVN small unit patrols and recon units had traveled through the Que Son Valley and had experienced brief but intense firefights with what were assumed to be Viet Cong forces. The American and South Vietnamese forces long suspected the Que Son Valley harbored Viet Cong base camps and hid enemy resupply routes. Those VC forces in the Que Son Valley, the Hiep Duc Valley, the Thang Binh Valley, and the mountains that ringed and separated these valleys constantly threatened the viability of Highway 1, the primary logistical lifeline between Da Nang and Chu Lai.

Thirty kilometers west of Highway 1, the terrain of the Que Son area consisted of rice paddies and hedgerows dotting the lowlands, with dense undergrowth on the foothills of the surrounding mountains. Thick jungle foliage covered most of the higher mountains in this area. In short, the Que Son Valley provided excellent cover and concealment for a guerilla force located only fifty kilometers northwest of Chu Lai and only thirty kilometers west of Highway 1 at its nearest point. Viet Cong forces hiding in the Que Son Valley could easily strike a serious blow at any target along Highway 1 within a single day's march. Operation Union I would locate and destroy those enemy forces, thus reducing enemy threats to the Chu Lai airfield, Fleet Logistics Support Group at Tam Ky, Hill 54 Combat Base, and the critical supply convoys making their way north and south along Highway 1.

As the Marines of 1/5 moved steadily westward toward the VC and NVA lairs in the Que Son Valley, their battalion commander moved with one company for a couple of days and then moved with another company, shifting his physical presence from company to company. Lieutenant Colonel Hilgartner, "Highpockets," looked like a Marine commander, but he had one quirk: he no longer carried any weapon, not even a .45-caliber pistol. It seems that early in his command tenure as he tried to cross a swollen stream, he lost his footing while trying to hold his .45 out of the water and got swept downstream in the heavy current. Finally able to grab the limb of a tree, he pulled himself to safety, but his XO, his sergeant major, and Capt. John Carty all chewed his butt out. So he made the decision to turn in his .45, and from that day forward he carried only a walking stick. He figured that he had all those Marines defending him, so he didn't need to carry a weapon.

Sgt. Hillous York remembers those days very well:

> When Union I kicked off we helilifted west. My main focus each day was to keep my men in good fighting shape and to know our location but not necessarily to know where anyone else was. I never really knew the bigger picture of Operation Union I. It didn't really matter what battalion we were with at the time. My main focus stayed on the chain of command: those above me and those below me. I had come to realize that war is about the impact zone. It was about where an artillery shell lands, where a bomb blows up, where a bullet hits. Combat is about the impact zone. I had to know where we were, where 3rd Platoon was, where the company was. I had to know exactly where my men and I were. The bigger picture was not important to me at that time. What I focused on was what was happening to my men, my platoon, and my company.
>
> During Operation Union I we went into an area that had all types of terrain. We tromped across miles and miles of rice paddies interspersed with small villages. (We called them islands, because they sat on slightly higher ground completely surrounded by rice paddies.) We climbed over scrub-covered foothills, and we also searched for the enemy on the sides and tops of jungle-covered mountains. The sun, when we moved out into the open country, just broiled us with heat and humidity. We didn't have to deal with as much mud as we had during the monsoon season, but occasionally, at night when it rained, it got quite cold. It seemed like when it did get rainy and damp and miserable, the Viet Cong would pick those times to hit us.
>
> The countryside that became the battlefields of Operation Union I was populated by many civilians—as in most of the rural areas of South Vietnam, some of them friendly, some of them stand-offish, and some of them would try to do you in if you turned your back. From my perspective, the civilians needed to just get out of the damned way. It seemed like the VC would always

try to put the civilians between them and us. Some of the civilians acted friendly, but most of them were scared, and we couldn't trust any of them.

Some of the civilians turned out to be outright VC. They would work in their paddies by day, hiding their AK-47s and carbines, and then break out their weapons at night and try to kill us. Those guys were the "light" enemy. They didn't have much depth to them. The VC formed small units, squads or platoons of twenty or thirty soldiers. When we ran into the enemy at Hill 110, we found that they were hard-core NVA, extremely well equipped and armed to the teeth. They also traveled in very large groups.

Sergeant York's memories of those long, hot days include a rather bizarre confrontation with another hazard of the bush:

One of the other things we had to worry about was the water buffalo. You could tell when you were upwind from a water buffalo; his nose would turn up, and you knew that he had gotten a whiff of you. Once, one of these damned animals charged us. A bunch of us started shooting at him, and although we hit him several times, he kept charging us. So I dropped down into the prone position, took careful aim, and shot him in the nose. He came to a screeching halt about twenty meters from my nearest Marine, and then turned and withdrew. I heard other stories about the exotic animal life of Vietnam, like snakes and tigers, but fortunately I never saw any of those, just water buffalo and mosquitoes, lots and lots of mosquitoes.

We humped every day, mile after mile, searching the countryside for the enemy. We found him, nearly every day. We got shot at and engaged in many firefights almost every day. We questioned every villager, and took many of them into custody as detainees because they just looked suspicious or they didn't have the right paperwork. Sometimes they were innocent civilians, but many times these people proved to be the enemy. It was impossible for us to tell the difference simply from appearances.

John Rusth, still serving in the 3rd Platoon of Charlie Company, mainly remembers the heat and some very interesting human behavior when they left Hill 54 for Operation Union I:

When Operation Union I kicked off, we patrolled the Que Son Valley for three weeks or more. It seemed like we just moved a lot, we walked all the time. We had a few brief firefights here and there, a sniper or two, that kind of thing, but pretty much nothing happened for the first three weeks or so.

As we continued to move north, toward Hill 110, we came into more and more contact with the VC. I personally believe that they wanted to draw us toward Hill 110. As we walked down this long trail one afternoon, at the tail end of a very long column, we stopped for a few minutes' break. The VC sniped at us constantly. During that break, Pfc. Clarence Washington, a very large, very tall black Marine, a friend to everybody, captured a VC. All of a sudden, Clarence started hollering, and he reached down behind some brush, reached down into this hole, and pulled a VC out of the hole. Clarence was big enough to pull this guy up out of that hole with only one hand. Everybody had walked by this guy in the hole, but Clarence had *smelled* him; he pulled that VC up out of that hole with one hand and disarmed him with one big swipe of his other hand. At least a hundred Marines had walked by this very effectively camouflaged enemy soldier hidden just a few feet off the trail, and no one had a clue about his presence.

Clarence Washington could carry a really heavy load. We sloshed in and out of rice paddies during Union I, crossing rivers, humping constantly across the hot countryside. We had a lot of problems with heat casualties; we had to medevac a couple of guys due to heat exhaustion. But at one point word came down that they weren't going to medevac any more heat casualties; we knew we had to keep our canteens full, drink our water, and take our salt tablets. During conditions like this, Pfc. Clarence Washington often carried two extra packs. He would load himself up with belts of machine gun ammo, anything another Marine couldn't carry because of heat problems. He did this because it let us keep going. One of the nicest guys in the platoon, Clarence was by far and away the strongest.

On some occasions the Marines of Charlie 1/5 would engage in abrupt and violent clashes with hard-core Viet Cong soldiers. On every occasion, the Marines came out ahead. Sometimes, amidst the sheer terror of combat, amazingly funny things happened. Sergeant York reflects:

Early in Union I, Lieutenant Colonel Hilgartner accompanied Charlie Company. We reached the edge of a large rice paddy that the battalion would have to cross. Charlie Company, on point for the battalion, had to cross the paddy first. A small "island" village sat a few hundred meters across the paddy, and Lieutenant Colonel Hilgartner knew that we would have to secure the village before the battalion could move safely across the paddy. Highpockets called Captain Caswell and gave him the order; Captain Caswell called my platoon commander at the time, Lt. Jack Jewell, and gave him the order, and

Lieutenant Jewell looked at me and said, "Sergeant York. You're up. Cross the paddy and secure that village."

My men all looked at me, and I could tell from the looks on their faces that we had the same thought: "Oh, shit!" But, we also knew that we had to follow orders, and that truly the battalion could not safely cross the paddy until we secured the village, so we took off and headed for the island village.

When we got to about fifty meters from the hedgerow that bordered the village on this side, the VC opened up on us. I instantly knew that we couldn't hit the dirt there, because we would get pinned down and would take a lot of casualties. We took off running, as fast as we could, right at the enemy positions. Rounds hit the paddy water all around us. They fired at us with everything they had, and we fired back at them as best we could as we ran in file down the paddy dike toward their positions. As we reached the hedgerow, I could see the muzzles of their weapons sitting atop the trench line dug right behind the hedgerow, and I could clearly see the muzzle flashes. Since I couldn't run through the thick hedgerow, I jumped over it. It wasn't easy to jump over it, because of the weight of my combat load and pack, but I guess the adrenaline kicked in and I made it. I landed with my feet straddling their trench line, looked to my right, and almost cracked up at what I saw. A bunch of VC ran frantically away from us, trying to get away down the trench. As this mob tried to get around the corner of the trench to safety, they had bunched up. The VC in the back of the mob double-timed in place, desperately pushing at the VC in front of them, only about twenty feet from the point where I jumped over the hedgerow. Unfortunately for them, they were unable to move, because the corner was plugged with frantic VC.

Sergeant York remembers that scene as hilarious, but that didn't stop him from doing his duty. These enemy soldiers looked at that moment like a bunch of bumbling Keystone Cops, but they had tried to kill him and his men just a moment before. Without hesitation, Hillous took careful aim and killed as many of them as he could before the rest of them escaped. He said, "The VC that made it around the corner got away, but the VC in the back of the mob, well let's just say that they didn't do any more fighting after that."

Delbert Best, a lance corporal fire team leader, remembers the Que Son Valley very well:

VC Valley was considered a free fire zone, allowing us to shoot first and ask questions later. If anyone ran away or acted in a threatening way, we had orders to shoot to kill. We took a lot of sniper fire throughout the valley as well.

We found an NVA flag out there in the Que Son Valley, and I had it in my backpack for a long time, but when I got wounded and medevaced, it disappeared.

Del Best's recollections remain vivid to this day:

VC weapons included an old French rifle and a couple of carbines, and I think one guy had a shotgun. Their grenades were much different than ours. I can remember one grenade that had a string attached to it, like for a pin. I don't even know how they used the thing. The VC in the Que Son Valley wore black pajamas, nothing fancy.

Early in Operation Union I we walked through this really brushy area, using a path, and for some reason here comes a water buffalo charging down the path. Where he came from I have no idea, he just came running right down the trail, and we had to jump off the path to avoid getting run over. The guys behind me eventually had to shoot him, and they killed him, because the water buffalo tried to kill them. It was kill or be killed, that's for sure.

I remember those damned ants. You would sit down at the side of the trail, and the next thing you knew you had a swarm of little red fire ants all over you, stinging you. I sat down and didn't pay any attention to where I sat, and the next thing I knew I had ants stinging me all over my body.

Del Best also remembers his very colorful new platoon commander:

The first day of Union I, as we sat on the chopper, our platoon commander hollered at us about the LZ. He said it was going to be hot. After we took off, I set my helmet down on the floor of the CH-46 between my feet, feeling pretty safe with my helmet on the floor until we started to rotate into the LZ. But after the lieutenant started hollering, I reached down and grabbed my helmet by the chinstrap and put it on my head. The chopper rotated into the LZ, and we all ran off the back ramp toward our assigned part of the perimeter. I didn't notice until a few minutes later, after I had charged off the chopper and ran a few dozen yards and hit the dirt behind a little mound, that I only had my thin fiberglass helmet liner on. The steel pot, the part of the helmet that actually provides the protection, still sat on the floor of the chopper, on its way back to Tam Ky.

The lieutenant had scared the hell out of me. He said the LZ was hot, which meant we should expect a big firefight as soon as we hit the LZ, but nothing happened at all after we landed. After a few minutes of total calm and quiet, I got up off the ground and started walking around like everyone else. One of

> the other guys walked up to me and asked me where my helmet was. I told him that it was on my head. He said, "No, it's not." That's when I realized that I had left the steel part of my helmet in the chopper. The lieutenant chewed me out. He called me a boot.

Jim Coxen had served in the 1st Squad, 2nd Platoon for over six months when 1/5 joined Operation Union I. His squad leader, Sgt. Richard Lynch, a Marine NCO who had received his first combat experience during the uprising in the Dominican Republic in 1965, was a damned fine squad leader, from Coxen's perspective.

Jim wasn't actually with the company when Union I started, because he got sick. He remembers:

> Some intestinal parasites attacked me, and I damn near died. They medevaced me, and I spent some time in the hospital. So when I finally rejoined the company, I was still not in very good shape. I can remember doing a lot of humping [marching], a real drudgery. I had hitched a ride on a resupply chopper out of Tam Ky, but I'm not sure about the company's location when I finally rejoined them a few days before we got hit on Hill 110. It just seems like we walked for a really long time.
>
> As we moved through the valley, the surrounding countryside had pineapple plants growing, some watermelons, and some green banana trees, so we lived off the land to some degree. I'm sure that the villagers were not happy about it, but they tolerated us. Most of the villagers in the Que Son Valley seemed generally friendly to us, but since our hunger led us to eat from their trees and plants, they were probably not very happy about that.
>
> I wish I could remember the kid's name, but one time one of our guys got too close to a herd of water buffalo, when one of them decided to go for him. He put twenty rounds into him, and a bunch of the other guys unloaded their M16s into that damned waterboo, but it kept charging and managed to knock that poor kid off the paddy dike before it finally fell over and died. Scared the hell out of him, but he didn't get hurt.

John Rusth, promoted to lance corporal in early April 1967, had already been assigned as a private first class to fire team leader:

> Some of the squads only had six or seven guys, about half the normal strength of a Marine rifle squad. They made me a fire team leader because I had quite a bit of experience in the bush by now and I had managed to survive the first few months. We were always short of people.

At the beginning of Union I, we humped so far west that the Vietnamese people in the area were very friendly. Actually, they hadn't seen Caucasians like us in this area since the French left. As a matter of fact, in the beginning of Union I, some of the older Vietnamese we ran into thought we *were* the French. We had a guy there who could speak some French. We called him Frenchy, as you would probably expect. He talked with the villagers fairly easily in French. I thought it pretty unique that we ran into people out there in the Que Son Valley who thought we were the French from the fifties.

We continued to run into VC throughout late April and early May. We would see evidence of NVA having moved through an area, but most of the contact we had was with VC, mostly scruffy little guys carrying carbines, M1s, and BARs. Sometimes they had women with them who would carry weapons and act as nurses. We came across .50-caliber machine guns. The VC had packs on their backs, floppy hats, sandals, and they constantly harassed us, constantly sniped at us. They would shoot at us and run, hoping we would pursue; they tried to move us into a bad situation. They would stay ahead of us and try to get us to go into a specific area that they may have booby-trapped or mined, although we didn't see much of that. We moved constantly, all day, every day; we moved all over the Que Son Valley, with the VC sniping at us and worrying us incessantly.

Pfc. Richard Schlagel recalls those distant days of Operation Union I with the near total recall but somewhat fragmented memories that only a combat veteran can understand:

It was hot and humid in April and May of '67. I tried to adjust and acclimate from coming over from the States. I don't know if it was really hot for that time of the year, but it really felt hot and humid to me.

It seemed like we walked forever. We walked through rice paddy after rice paddy, over the hills and the mountains, seemingly forever. I couldn't believe all the greens: incredible, dark green, light green, and every shade of green imaginable. The countryside in the Que Son Valley was a beautiful setting. It hit me really hard that we were fighting a war in the middle of all this beautiful scenery. It seemed like we always found ourselves in areas that gave our enemy the cover and concealment they needed to ambush us.

Another new private first class in country, Harold Thrasher, recalls:

Around the middle of April we moved back to the combat base at Hill 54, and then on the 21st of April we started an operation out in the "VC Valley."

Assigned to a few patrols around Snaggletooth, I had never patrolled out in this new area. Our squad leader told us that we would always see a lot of action out in VC Valley.

During the first twenty days of Operation Union I, it seemed like we humped forever across the countryside. We only took one bath during that whole time, in a dried-up river. We stayed very hot and smelly. We only had two C-ration meals a day. At one point, our resupply let us down. The helicopters brought us plenty of ammo but no C-rations, so we instantly became scavengers and tried to live off the land.

Private First Class Thrasher learned some of the lingo of combat operations the hard way:

One night we marched all night long and approached this village early the next morning somewhere out in the middle of VC Valley. The company had taken a few casualties but hadn't experienced any major contact with the enemy at that point. The Vietnamese in this village had some geese, and the geese started cackling as we approached; they sounded like trained watchdogs. Then a bell started ringing in the village. But the village was vacant; there was no one there. It was a little spooky.

From the village, we went down this path, through some bushes, out into a clearing. A VC sniper opened up on the point squad, and this one Marine ahead of me, a corporal, started ditty-bopping across the clearing as if he felt invincible, showing how brave he was at not being scared, and the sniper shot him right in the throat. The sniper got lucky; the corporal ended up losing his life. The corpsmen came up immediately and started working on him as another squad started firing on the sniper and maneuvering in his direction. The company commander called in a medevac. Still pretty green, I didn't really understand the lingo. When they first called in the medevac, they called it an emergency medevac, as this Marine had been hit pretty badly. A couple of minutes later, I overheard another radio transmission, changing the status of the medevac from emergency to routine. I turned to one of the Marines next to me alongside that trail and said, "Good. It looks like he's going to be okay." Then the other Marine looked over at me and said, "No, he's dead. That's what a routine medevac means. It's not an emergency anymore." I felt just awful. That's when reality hit me, and I realized for the first time that I was in a war. Since they had downgraded the medevac to routine, our helicopter diverted to some other location, and we had to carry that dead Marine for nearly that entire day. We made up a stretcher using a couple of bamboo poles and a poncho and took turns carrying this poor guy's body for the rest of the day. Still considered a "greenie," I got the body carrying detail most of the day. The poncho didn't completely cover up his head. I remember thinking to myself, what the hell have I gotten myself into? I think that was Corporal Robert L. McCamble from Mobile, Alabama, twenty-two years old.

New replacement Marines continued to arrive in South Vietnam and report for duty at 1st Battalion, 5th Marines. Second Lt. Rick Zell was one of them. Rick Zell was born in the Bronx, New York. When he turned eight, Rick's family moved to Queens, so his entire upbringing centered in the New York City area. After graduating from high school, Rick briefly served some time in the US Army, taking his basic training at Fort Dix, New Jersey. He got out of the army early to go to college at Polytechnical Institute of Brooklyn and spent four years there earning a bachelor's degree. Polytechnical Institute of Brooklyn (later renamed Polytechnical Institute of New York) was an engineering school. While attending Polytechnical Institute, Rick joined and served four years with the Army ROTC.

Just before graduation, Rick decided that he wanted to serve in the infantry, but the US Army had other ideas. He was about to receive an engineering degree, the army needed engineers, and as far as the US Army was concerned, that was the end of that. Rick Zell was destined to become an engineer in the Army Corps of Engineers. Although Rick graduated with an engineering degree, he actually hated engineering, and he really wanted to serve his country as an infantry officer.

A friend of Rick's father, a Marine Corps major named Kuykendall, just happened to be the head of the officer's selection committee for the Marine Corps in the New York City area. During a casual conversation at a local bar, Major Kuykendall told Rick's father that according to an obscure Department of Defense regulation, because Rick had earned "distinguished military student" status in Army ROTC, he could apply for a regular commission in the Marine Corps. Although Rick could receive a reserve commission in the army infantry, that was not acceptable to him. He wanted to serve, he wanted infantry, and he wanted a regular commission. Rick planned to make a career out of the military, and he knew the importance of a regular commission to a military career. When his father first told him about the opportunity to apply for a regular commission in the Marine Corps, he thought the idea was nuts. Rick had spent the past six years of his life, including his brief stint as an enlisted man and then during his ROTC training, thinking about and preparing for a career in the US Army. He hadn't thought anything about joining the Marine Corps.

Rick met with Major Kuykendall several times, and they talked at length about this idea for Rick to join the Marines. Finally, Rick told the major, "If you can get me a regular commission in the Marine Corps, and they can guarantee me an infantry MOS, then, what the hell. I'll do it." Rick, still committed to joining the army, filled out a bunch of paperwork, but then he really didn't think much about it, because he didn't actually think it would happen. Then, just before the end of the school year, he got a letter from the Marine Corps congratulating him on receiving a regular commission and guaranteeing him an infantry MOS. He received orders to report to the Basic School by the end of June 1966. Rick was excited but shocked; he didn't have a single Marine Corps uniform. All of his military gear was US Army issue. Basically, he had to start all over again.

Rick Zell married his sweetheart, Bernadette, on 8 June 1966. After a very brief honeymoon, he reported to Quantico, Virginia, for officer training at the Basic School on 11 June. With the help of Major Kuykendall, he had hastily purchased a set of dress blues. He got married in his brand-new dress blue uniform (his only Marine Corps uniform at the time), packed up his new wife, and headed for Quantico.

When Rick reported in to the Basic School, he knew that he had a lot to learn and that he would have to power through his learning curve quickly. Armed with his dress blue uniform and his army fatigues (which he quickly converted into Marine Corps utilities by removing his US Army patches), he set his mind toward this fairly daunting task. All of the other second lieutenants who would comprise his Basic School class had the advantage of having already learned, during OCS, the basics regarding how to act and dress like a Marine Corps officer. Worse, the course studies included in the Basic School curriculum proved intense and daunting. A typical day at the Basic School started at dawn and ended well after dusk, and all of the young second lieutenants stayed extremely busy in classroom studies and field exercises. Rick Zell would have to handle all of that, as well as learn the basics of how to act like a Marine Corps officer, on the fly. It was one hell of a learning curve, but Rick proved up to the task, and he graduated from the Basic School well up in the rankings of his peers in late November 1966.

Upon graduation from the Basic School, Rick received orders to WestPac and proceeded directly to Camp Pendleton, California. Rick's pregnant wife, Bernadette, didn't want to be separated from her new husband, so she made the cross-country trip, and they obtained quarters at a very basic motel in Oceanside. After about thirty days, the Zells ran out of money, so Bernadette reluctantly agreed to return to her hometown of Jackson Heights, New York. Rick and Bernadette said their goodbyes, since Rick would not be able to take any more leave before shipping out to Vietnam. Bernadette stayed with her mother, while Rick completed his infantry training at Camp Pendleton.

Rick went overseas by ship from San Diego harbor. He joined a large group of

Marines on a converted civilian ocean liner, and nineteen days later he arrived in South Vietnam. The trans-Pacific cruise turned out to be an extension of his infantry training. "About two hundred soldiers from the US Army Signal Corps joined us aboard that ship. Most Marines stayed fairly standoffish from US Army soldiers, calling them 'doggies' and the like, but since I had spent so much time in the army, I had no such prejudices. I was one of the few Marines on board who spent time with the soldiers. My main reason for going out of my way to get to know the soldiers was because they all had the M16 rifle. I had never seen an M16 rifle, let alone fire it, but I knew that the Marines would soon be issued the M16. It just made sense to me to befriend the soldiers and to familiarize myself with the M16. I learned how to take it apart, put it back together, clean it, and fire it. Most of the Marines on board that ship just ignored the army guys, but I took advantage of the experience to learn as much as I possibly could." That experience proved most helpful to Rick Zell, who would soon take command of a platoon of Marine infantrymen. Rick also spent time with a few Marines on their way to their second tours in Southeast Asia, trying to learn from their experiences.

Rick Zell arrived in Da Nang harbor, South Vietnam, and received orders to the 1st Marine Division. He remembers his introduction to that storied division well:

> At that time, no new officer went to the field without first meeting with the division commander, Maj. Gen. Herman Nickerson, Jr. That didn't mean that a second lieutenant got a one-on-one meeting with this two-star general; it meant that you hung around until enough new officers could be herded in to meet with General Nickerson as a group. So for four days I milled around the Da Nang area waiting until a group of new officers could go see the division CG. I didn't have a weapon, and I didn't have much of anything to do except just wait. While I waited, I went over to 1st Reconnaissance Battalion headquarters and looked up a buddy of mine, Richard Johnson, the son of a Marine colonel. Richard had graduated number one in our class at the Basic School. We had graduated at the same time, but he flew to Vietnam, and I had to take the ship, so he arrived in country two or three weeks ahead of me. A good friend, Richard was the guy that everyone said would make general first; we all knew that someday this officer would become the commandant of the Marine Corps. Johnson really had his stuff together—a crack shot with rifle and pistol, and the best physically. Besides that, he was really a nice guy. He looked like a poster Marine. So I went over to recon, looking forward to seeing Johnson. I asked for Lieutenant Johnson, but the guy looked at me and shook his head. I persisted, told him that I was sure that Lt. Richard Johnson had been assigned to 1st Recon Battalion, and the Marine looked at me and

said, 'He sure was, but he died yesterday.' In my shock I told the Marine that it couldn't be, that Johnson had just arrived in Vietnam, and if anyone was going to make it through this war, it was Richard Johnson. The recon Marine confirmed that Lieutenant Johnson had just joined 1st Recon, but that he most certainly was dead. That got my attention really fast. I found myself questioning that if Johnson hadn't made it more than a few weeks, how the hell would I survive?

After four days of waiting, Rick and four other new officers gathered at the division headquarters. It was late spring, well over a hundred degrees out, so when these new officers went down into the air-conditioned command bunker, they all shivered from the cold:

> We're all freezing cold from the artificially chilled air. We finally got to a walnut-paneled office, General Nickerson's private office, and there he stood, quite an imposing figure of a man. I had learned that his nickname was Herman the German. We all stood at attention, reporting as ordered, and then he proceeded to scream at us for about thirty minutes. He screamed to the degree that I could hardly understand what he was talking about, until I finally got the gist of it. It seems the division had suffered a rash of accidental discharges, and some Marines had been accidentally shot. General Nickerson let us know that if any of our Marines got shot by means of an accidental discharge, he would personally relieve us and kick us out of the Marine Corps. Here I stood, four days in country, I don't even have a weapon yet, and here's this legendary senior officer screaming at me about accidental discharges. What an amazing welcome.
>
> Once we finally got through our "welcome" speech by the commanding general, I jumped on a truck and rode down south to Chu Lai to my new outfit, the 1st Battalion, 5th Marines, providing security for the air base there. When I reported in, in early March 1967, I joined the infantry company, Alpha 1/5. The CO of Alpha Company, 2nd Lt. Bill Vacca, was a pretty seasoned guy. Normally, company commanders were captains, or sometimes senior first lieutenants, but Bill was a second lieutenant. He was a mustang officer, though; he'd been a Marine sergeant before he got commissioned.
>
> No other commissioned officers served in Alpha Company when I joined them. All of the platoon commanders were either E-5 sergeants or E-6 staff sergeants, so they had no problem assigning me as a platoon commander. I got my wish, but it seemed a little chilling to find out about such a shortage of Marine Corps officers at that time in Vietnam.

The one great thing about having a second lieutenant company commander, from my point of view: I had no fear of him. Bill Vacca was an equal in rank; he was senior to me, but we were both brown bars. I had a chance to sit around a few nights and talk to Bill before taking command of my platoon, because the Marines in my new unit were out in the field. A very strait-laced guy, Bill Vacca was a real Marine, all Marine. You could ask any question of Bill, and he would give you a straight answer. Bill never pulled rank on me, never had to remind me that he was the company commander. He just talked to me, gave it to me straight, and I liked the fact that I could talk to him without fear or intimidation.

A staff sergeant getting ready to rotate home commanded my new platoon, 1st Platoon, Company A, 1st Battalion, 5th Marines. He was happy to get out, and from all I could gather, the Marines in the platoon were happy to get rid of him. That gave me a big advantage. The platoon wanted a new platoon commander, and they got one. They were happy to see this staff sergeant go and willing to give me the opportunity to prove myself.

Things remained relatively quiet around the Chu Lai perimeter during March and April, so that gave me a chance to get to know my men without being thrust into major combat right away. We lived in a combat zone all that time, but nothing much bad happened. I needed a chance to acclimate and get to know my guys, and I got it. When I took command, all of my squad leaders were corporals or lance corporals. During that time, 1/5 suffered with a shortage of officers, NCOs, and staff NCOs, but there wasn't much action at that time, which allowed me to gain some experience and even make some mistakes without those mistakes becoming fatal errors.

I had a lot of old salts in my platoon. Young and relatively low in rank, they possessed a great deal of experience in combat. When I did something stupid, these guys would run up to me and say, "Lieutenant, you hadn't ought to do that." At first a little bit taken aback by that—I mean, I outranked them, but they told me many times in those first few weeks, pretty bluntly, that I had just done something stupid—I quickly came to realize that they only wanted to help me and that I was very fortunate to get that experience without causing any casualties. About the worst action we saw during those first couple of months was a sniper here or there or a brief firefight with a local VC squad. I consider myself very fortunate to have had that time, because my platoon, the 1st Platoon of Alpha 1/5, ended up right in the middle of the action in Operation Union I.

When the Marines of the 1st Battalion, 5th Marines received the new M16 rifle, Rick became an instructor:

That's when my brief training aboard ship really paid off. One of very few Marines who knew anything about the new weapon, at least I knew how to field strip, clean, aim, and fire it, so I think it really helped out. It also helped my men gain some confidence in me. We set up a little rifle range in back of Hill 54 Combat Base. Right away, we knew something was wrong, bad wrong. As we test-fired the M16, we experienced failures to seat cartridges properly in the chamber and failures to extract them; the rear of the cartridge would rip off, leaving the main part of the cartridge still in the chamber. Cleaning equipment was at an absolute minimum. I think we only had one cleaning rod per squad. Cleaning rods were critical, since the only way to remove the ripped-off cartridge out of the chamber was to ram the cleaning rod down the muzzle, forcing it out of the chamber. With only one cleaning rod for every nine or ten men, we had a really bad problem on our hands. I was really shocked with the way this new weapon had been issued. First of all, none of the enlisted Marines had ever fired the M16; second, we had a woefully inadequate number of cleaning kits, the equipment we desperately needed to make sure that the weapon would function when we needed it. When we discovered these problems and reported them, they said, "Don't worry, the problems are being worked out." But they weren't. The problems persisted, the M16s continued to malfunction, and we had no choice in the matter. My Marines would carry the M16s into combat, problems or no problems.

We got into some firefights in the Chu Lai TAOR, and inside of a few minutes, almost everybody's M16 jammed. One or two M16s in a squad, for whatever reason, would continue to function, but most of them jammed right away and jammed repeatedly. My Marines had to call for the cleaning rod, forced to take their turns with the cleaning rod to clear their jam. At one point it looked almost like Revolutionary War–style combat, ramming rods down muskets, jamming the bullets down the barrels—in our case, jamming the cleaning rods down the muzzles to clear them. On a couple of occasions my men formed relay lines and passed the weapons up and down the lines to clear the jams. It became really frightening, crazy. All of my Marines knew that if we ever got into any heavy combat with these weapons, we'd be in really deep trouble. They knew the M16 would get a lot of people killed, and everybody was scared shitless. It was a nightmare.

We tried to find some M14s, and we managed to find a few. We talked to some engineers and some commo guys who still had the M14, and we managed to get our hands on a few of them. Eventually, a few weeks later, they replaced all of our M16s with an improved model, and we got some better ammo, but for a while there it was really difficult to fight this war with a very unreliable weapon. Our chain of command blamed us; they said that we were obviously not cleaning the weapon correctly, but that was all bullshit. The M16 rifle was just a bad weapon in its early days, and to make matters worse, we had some bad ammunition.

And then on 11 April 1967 the enemy shot down a CH-34 helicopter out in the Que Son Valley, and Rick Zell took command of the reaction force:

I took my platoon and a couple of squads of the 2nd Platoon out on that reaction force mission, while Bill Vacca stayed in the rear. Somebody from the S-3 section told me to get as many Marines as I could from Alpha Company together, because a helicopter had been shot down and our mission was to fly out to provide security while the recovery mission took place. I looked around and realized that Bill Vacca wasn't around. He had been sent somewhere else, and since I was the only officer in the company, I was now the acting company commander. Everybody was spread all over the place, and the lift choppers were already on their way in to pick us up, so I didn't get everyone in the company. I had most of my 1st Platoon guys with me, and some of the others from 2nd and 3rd Platoons, but not nearly all the Alpha Company Marines. This mission was shaping up as a real Chinese fire drill.

The S-3 guy told me not to worry about it. There would be a map on the lead helicopter, that it would be a fast mission in and out, that we didn't need to take any extra ammo or food, and that we would return before nightfall. So I fashioned makeshift squads, and we loaded up on the choppers. Four choppers arrived at the LZ; I put about a dozen guys on each chopper, so we probably had about fifty Marines, total. As more Alpha Company Marines reported to the company HQ, they would load up on a second wave of helicopters and would reinforce us after we had secured the site of the downed helicopter and the LZ.

I got on the lead chopper, and we took off. I had a sense of flying west, but I couldn't be certain, and I didn't have a map. I asked the pilot for the map, and he didn't have a map, so I had no idea exactly where we were going. As the first wave of CH-46s descended into the landing zone, we came under heavy enemy gunfire. This was not going according to plan. The S-3 told me that no enemy forces had been seen in the area, and just as soon as we started to land, we came under heavy small arms fire. The choppers dropped us off in the hot LZ, and we formed a hasty perimeter fairly close to the downed helicopter, which we could see not too far away in a large dry rice paddy surrounded by low hills. As we arrived in the LZ, the two pilots from the downed chopper, a captain and a major, ran from their positions in a ditch by their stricken helicopter, made it to our positions, and jumped on one of the helicopters that had brought us in. That was the last I saw of them. As the senior officers on site, they should have taken command in an emergency situation, but they just climbed on the closest chopper and took off. Two enlisted men aboard the downed chopper, a couple of Marine scouts, Cpl. Tom Manion and Lance Cpl. Jack Kennedy, stayed with us. They both had the option to leave with the pilots, but they both chose to stay out there with us. The shit was really hitting the fan, and we could use all the help we could get, so we welcomed them. They both just jumped into our positions and started fighting alongside my Marines.

The firing got so intense we never saw the second wave of helicopters that supposedly would bring in reinforcements. The battalion S-3 shop said that the LZ was now unsafe, so they couldn't land any more helicopters. We were on our own. We had to secure the downed helicopter until the next morning, when they could get help and extract it. As night fell, the darker it got, the worse the enemy firing became. We got hit by enemy mortars, rockets, machine gun fire, and semiautomatic and automatic weapons fire. I was a brand-new second lieutenant, a platoon commander and now acting company commander, with a small group of Marines that I didn't know very well, no platoon sergeant, no food, and no extra ammo, and the shit was hitting the fan, big time.

The 1/5 Battalion command chronology entries for this encounter with the enemy are very sketchy. An entry for 1810 on 11 April 1967 states, "Company A was inserted into the area [of the downed helicopter] with negative VC contact." A later entry from that day indicated that "Company A . . . observed 4 Vietnamese fleeing from the area." The Hueys strafed them, a patrol was dispatched to investigate, and the results of the engagement were four VC WIA "probable." Rick Zell's eyewitness account labels these reports as completely inaccurate:

Bottom line, it was just bullshit. We got hit from all sides and remained in a major firefight throughout most of that night. We ended up taking thousands of enemy rounds and returned fire as best we could. We didn't even have any M60 machine gun teams; scheduled to come in on the second wave, they never made it. We did remove the M60 from the downed helicopter and used it to good effect. Things got pretty chaotic, but I wasn't really worried. I knew that we had to stay put until the next morning and provide security for the downed chopper, and I didn't really know just how many of the enemy had surrounded us. Then it got really dark, and they started to really open up on us.

At one point someone in the S-3 shop decided to send Puff the Magic Dragon, a C-47 gunship loaded with flares and armed with a Gatling gun, out to help us. Puff arrived on station and started dropping flares. The next thing I know, the air controllers told the Battalion S-3 shop that Puff could see significant movement all around our positions. We had marked our positions with flares, so Puff knew our location, and they could see a large enemy force in the hills surrounding us. I requested permission to attack toward an adjacent hill, so we could take up a reasonable defensive position on some high ground, but their terse reply said, "Permission denied." We had to protect the downed chopper. If this had happened a few months later, I would have said "The hell with it" and moved anyway, but as a new guy I didn't know any better, and so we stayed put. Puff requested permission to provide us direct support with their 7.62 mm Gatling gun, and I gladly gave them permission. Until you have received close air support from Puff with its guns blazing, you have no idea the amount of devastation it can put out. That was the scariest thing I experienced during my entire tour. When Puff started firing, every Marine in that perimeter cursed me; they thought I had gone completely crazy. The horrendous volume of fire came in very close to our positions. It was a very frightening experience, but it worked, and we didn't take any friendly casualties. Puff fired at the enemy positions all around us until it ran out of ammo and flares and headed back home. As soon as it left, another Puff arrived and took up where the other one left off. I'm not sure what would have happened that night if we hadn't had the support of Puff the Magic Dragon. And if that wasn't enough, we eventually got close air support from a flight of B-52s. S-3 called in an Arc Light mission on the suspected enemy positions. That was another eye-opener. Welcome to Vietnam!

As the fighting progressed, the enemy got closer and closer to our positions. We had formed a perimeter around the downed helicopter, and since I only had about fifty Marines, my positions were spaced fairly widely apart, and some of the VC got very close to our lines. In a couple of instances, they actually penetrated our lines. We didn't get overrun that night, but it was awfully damned close.

The 1/5 command chronology states, "Company A . . . received 4 82 mm HE [mortar] rounds, 7 rifle grenades and 15 rounds of small arms fire from an undetermined number of VC in vicinity." Rick Zell's memories differ dramatically:

We took thousands of enemy small arms rounds that night. I don't know who wrote up those entries in the command chronology back in the command bunker. I've read those entries, and they read nothing like the reality of that battle. Of course, I had not experienced any heavy combat up until that night, and shortly after that we launched Operation Union I, which had a lot of heavy fighting, but the fighting on the night of 11–12 April 1967 could only be described as very heavy. I'm still amazed that we only took two Marine WIAs in that fight. After that we got heavily involved in Operation Union I, so the memories of that night faded quickly into the backs of our memories.

Sometimes really crazy or funny things happened right in the middle of a battle, and this night proved no different. Rick explains:

> One of my Marines, Carl Sulick, came over to me right in the middle of the heaviest fighting. I could see the concern on his face, as he said, "Sir, we're all going to be killed. If I get killed, who is going to make my car payment?" I looked at him in amazement. I told him to get back to his fighting position and stay down, or he surely would die. I also told him that if he did get killed, his car payment would be the least of his worries. It got so bad that night, with our positions so spread out, that I passed the word that if any of the Marines saw anyone standing up that they should assume they were the enemy and to shoot them.

At a reunion of the 1st Marine Division in the late 1990s, several of the Marines of Alpha Company reunited with one of the Marine scouts who had ended up in that firefight. Rick Zell reports, "One of the Marine scouts from the downed chopper was a corporal named Tom Manion. I hadn't thought about him for nearly thirty years when he showed up at this reunion. He walked into our hospitality room, asked for anyone from Alpha 1/5, and we told him we had served with Alpha Company. He joined us and asked us if we remembered the night of 11–12 April 1967, and when we said we did, he told us that he felt that we had saved his life that night and thanked us all." Tom Manion felt so strongly about what Rick and his Marines did that night that he led an effort to write Rick Zell up for the Silver Star for courage in the face of the enemy. In August 2000, at another 1st Marine Division reunion, Rick belatedly received the Silver Star, our nation's third highest award for gallantry, for his actions on 11–12 April 1967.

The next morning, the enemy had departed the battlefield. Rick's Marines searched the surrounding area and found two VC bodies within twenty meters of one of their positions, confirming the close nature of the fight. Shortly thereafter, a "sky hook" (CH-54 helicopter) arrived and extracted the stricken chopper, and the Marines of Alpha 1/5 finally climbed on helicopters and returned to the combat base.

Toward the middle of April, Rick Zell and the Alpha Company Marines received orders to pack up all their nonessential gear and prepare to move out of Hill 54 Combat Base. The Marines of 1/5 were headed toward the Que Son Valley, and they would not return to Chu Lai. Rick packed up all of his nonessentials in a sea bag and sent some of it home and the rest of it to Okinawa. Operation Union I was about to kick off.

On 22 April, Alpha Company helilifted into the Que Son Valley, placed under the operational control (OpCon) of 3/5. The 1/5 command chronology entry for that day indicates that Alpha Company went to the 3/5 rear area for security duty, but Rick Zell insists that they never saw any rear area after they left the Chu Lai area. Aware that they were OpCon to 3/5, Rick remembers that Alpha Company pretty much operated independently during Operation Union I, and he never really felt attached to a different battalion. Rick recalls:

> When we left Chu Lai on the 22nd of April, Bill Vacca still commanded Alpha Company. It seemed like every single day we spent in the Que Son Valley during Operation Union I, we came into fairly heavy contact with the enemy. We stepped in a bunch of shit virtually every day. Our situation stayed pretty confusing, because we weren't with our own battalion, and I got the impression from talking to Bill Vacca that 3/5 treated us like a stepchild. If they didn't want to send a company somewhere, they would send us. We stomped around the Que Son Valley, trying to figure out where we were and what the plan was, getting shot at and shit on virtually every day.
>
> The Que Son Valley definitely turned out to be enemy territory. We knew the NVA were present in large forces. They were no longer VC, taking sniper shots or hitting us with hasty ambushes. Each enemy encounter proved fierce and deadly against well-armed and well-supplied soldiers. When we killed an enemy soldier and recovered his body, we could see they wore uniforms. The pace of the war had increased significantly, to the point that we no longer felt that we had the advantage; sometimes we felt outnumbered. When we walked into one of *these* ambushes, the very well camouflaged NVA hit us hard, and we took casualties almost every time. Things had changed since we left the Chu Lai TAOR, mostly for the worst. It all became a blur, with so much heavy fighting that each day just rolled into the next, until 1 May 1967. On the 1st of May, while engaged in heavy fighting with the enemy, I got shot and was medevaced.
>
> We moved constantly, making contact, taking casualties, every single day. The day I got hit, we had a number of wounded and a couple of KIAs, and we tried to get some medevac helicopters in around 1400 or 1500 to take them

back to the rear. Every time we tried to secure an LZ to get the wounded out, we would take enemy fire. The choppers would try to come in, would come under heavy fire, and have to back off. It turned out we had enemy snipers up in the trees around us. We had stumbled into an area well prepared as an ambush zone. Spider traps in the ground, snipers in the trees. I got shot by one of the snipers, but one of my Marines took him out right away. The sniper used an SKS .30-caliber rifle, one of the weapons we captured that day. I got shot in the foot, hit pretty bad, and now needed medevac. We finally secured the area surrounding the LZ by close-in fighting and were able to get a chopper in. I was medevaced back to Da Nang. The gunshot wound hurt like hell, but mainly I found myself mad as hell. Really angry at myself for getting shot, I didn't want to leave because I knew Alpha Company was so short of officers.

I spent a week or so in the hospital and then returned to the 1/5 rear in Chu Lai on 9 May, still limping around pretty badly, but the hospital had released me so I went back to join the battalion. What they called a through and through, the bullet had nicked a bone but missed most of the important stuff, so I considered myself pretty lucky. I couldn't go back out in the field right away, but I could help out in the rear, so I found myself in the battalion S-3 shop just before Charlie Company arrived at Hill 110.

On one occasion in early May, the Marines of Charlie 1/5 detained a hard-core Viet Cong operative. Lance Cpl. Jim Coxen, the blooper man of the 2nd Squad, 2nd Platoon, and a couple other Marines took custody of this particular detainee. Jim remembers that the man refused to comply with any of the Marines' instructions, and for quite some time the Vietnamese man, who looked forty or forty-five years old, refused to speak or move and acted as though he didn't understand English. Several Marines in Jim's squad had to take turns carrying or dragging the man to an LZ so that they could send him to the rear for interrogation. He simply refused to speak or walk. Finally losing his patience with the man, Jim gave him a swift kick in the butt. When he kicked him, the man rose to his feet, looked at Jim Coxen and the other Marines with a glare of hatred in his eyes, and in very fluent English said, "Ho Chi Minh will bury you." Jim and the other Marines were quite startled and chilled by his vehemence, but the man got the point and offered no further resistance. Coxen heard later that this man confessed to being a Viet Cong artillery officer.

While Charlie Company operated with 3/5 and 1/5 in the Hiep Duc Valley, they crossed the Song Ly Ly (Ly Ly River) many times. They first crossed the Song Ly Ly after a long, hard, sweaty march in the middle of a steamy hot moonlit night. When they reached the river, Captain Caswell sent out some scouts to try to find a ford, but they couldn't find a place to wade across even though they went up and down the bank. Finally, he called for a volunteer scout/swimmer. Caswell took off all his equipment, put his pistol and hand grenades in the pockets of his jungle utilities, and took off his boots. The volunteer scout/swimmer turned out to be one of Caswell's lieutenants. Captain Caswell worried briefly about putting two of his three officers at risk but shook off the thought. He wasn't going to force anyone else to swim this deep river at night.

Before entering the deep, dark water, Caswell made sure that his platoons were deployed properly and that he had his machine guns in positions for quick support if needed. He then put the other lieutenant temporarily in charge of the company. He told them to give him covering fire if they encountered any enemy units and had to leave in a hurry, and then he swam the river with his volunteer. The two Marine officers reconnoitered the area, found no one, and swam back. The company crossed the deep river safely, without incident. Jim Caswell realized later that if anything bad had happened to him that night, but he had survived, he would have been brought up on charges in front of a general court-martial for leaving his command, but nothing bad happened. He actually enjoyed it—a nice, cool swim on a hot, sweltering night.

The long, hot days of early May stayed fairly uneventful for Charlie Company, although several of the other 1/5 companies made contact with the enemy. From 1 May through 9 May, 1/5 moved twenty kilometers from LZ Condor west to Hiep Duc and then another twenty-five kilometers northeast toward the small town of Que Son. The boredom of marching through the sweaty days and dark nights was occasionally interrupted by brief moments of violence at the hands of the Viet Cong. Sporadic sniper fire and a few booby traps, interspersed with an occasional firefight with a small enemy force, kept the Marines alert to any possibility. Charlie Company invariably came out ahead during these encounters and took very few casualties. Captain Caswell and his Charlie 1/5 Marines continued to march, and Caswell crossed off each of his operational objectives on time and with very little difficulty other than that caused by the heat and the terrain.

As they reached the hill mass north of Que Son, the 1/5 command group assigned Charlie Company the responsibility of working alone to cover Objectives H, J, M, and N. A small river north of these objectives separated Objective N, a medium-sized hill (identified as Hill 110 on their 1:50,000 terrain maps) and the TAOR of the Special Landing Force (SLF). The SLF was comprised of three infantry companies from the 1st Battalion, 3rd Marines (1/3). Caswell and his Marines, accustomed to working alone, liked it that way. They received less interference, no one second-guessed Caswell's decisions, and they got fewer edicts passed down to them. None of the Marines of Charlie 1/5 realized yet just how alone they truly would be the next day when they climbed to the top of Hill 110 and engaged a large force of NVA soldiers at point-blank range.

6: The Battle for Hill 110, 10 May 1967

Early on the morning of 10 May 1967, upon reaching Objective M, the small hamlet of Nghi Thuong (4) located about a kilometer and a half west of Hill 110,[1] Charlie Company encountered a male and a female Vietnamese of military age. Following standard operating procedures, the Charlie 1/5 Marines took these individuals as detainees because they didn't have the proper identification papers. As the company departed the village with the detainees, two Marines stepped off a small trail that led out of the hamlet and detonated a booby trap. Capt. Jim Caswell remembers that incident quite clearly because he hated mines and booby traps and took great pains to avoid them. Unfortunately, the explosion severely wounded both Marines, who now required immediate medical evacuation. Captain Caswell called in for the medevac; the choppers arrived quickly, picked them up, and flew the injured Marines to the 1st Medical Battalion in Da Nang.

One of those injured Marines, Pfc. David Babb, had joined the Marine Corps from his hometown of Brevard, North Carolina, in October 1966. The fact that David's brother, Wayne Babb, was already serving in the Marine Corps at the time didn't have anything to do with his joining up. David simply didn't want to go to college, and it seemed like the right thing to do on that day. Wayne Babb had graduated from college and then received a commission as a Marine officer. During their training at the Basic School, Wayne shared a room with another Marine officer who would go on to become the thirty-first commandant of the Marine Corps, Gen. Charles C. Krulak. Wayne served the Marine Corps for many years and honorably retired as a lieutenant colonel. But David Babb wasn't interested in walking in his older brother's footsteps.

David joined the Marine Corps to serve his country as an enlisted man and entered recruit training at Parris Island, South Carolina. He graduated from boot camp at the end of 1966, transferred to Camp Lejeune, North Carolina, and completed the three-week Infantry Training Course (ITC). After thirty days' leave, David arrived at

Camp Pendleton, California, and completed jungle warfare training. Then something unexpected happened. David Babb's MOS changed from 0311 (infantry) to office clerk; his next assignment was to work in a company office at Camp Pendleton. Under twenty-one years of age, David couldn't go to bars, so he read books, climbed up and down the mountains of Camp Pendleton, had a pretty good time, and stayed in really good shape. He and the Marines he served with lived in Quonset huts, and David remembers his eye-opening introduction to scorpions and tarantulas and the other desert creatures that dwelled in the arid hills of Camp Pendleton.

David remembers the infantry training he received as outstanding. The Marine NCOs in charge of the training had already served in Vietnam, and they worked very hard, doing their utmost to prepare the young Marines for combat. Unfortunately, even with that extraordinary training, David felt, in hindsight, that he was *not* prepared for what he was about to experience.

In early March 1967, Pfc. David Babb arrived in South Vietnam and joined Charlie 1/5. David can vividly remember a brief conversation he had during those first few days with a veteran when asked what company David had been assigned to. When David answered that he had joined Charlie 1/5, the veteran said, "Ah, Suicide Charlie." When David asked him what he meant by that, the veteran responded by saying, "Charlie 1/5 is a company of good Marines. You will like serving in Charlie Company." And that's all he would say.

David spent the next week or so going out on patrols with various units at Chu Lai Combat Base, learning the ropes. A few days later, the Marines of Charlie Company returned from an extended combat operation, and David started his job as a company clerk. He recalls:

> That didn't last very long. They came to me and said that they really didn't need another company clerk, that they needed me elsewhere. So, for a while there, I worked with different platoons and squads. It seemed like they would just assign me to a unit that needed an additional hand, so I moved around a lot. I didn't have much of a home until eventually I joined the 60 mm mortars. I kept telling people that I wouldn't stay out in the field very long because I was a company clerk, but they kept moving me from unit to unit. One day, another Marine looked at me and told me that he knew my *real* MOS. I asked him to explain, and he said that I was a 1369, that I was just an unlucky cocksucker. Momentarily confused, I quickly figured out that he had just told a bad joke. Sometimes I worked as a runner for Captain Caswell or Gunny Cruz, but if they didn't need me, they'd just send me back to a platoon that needed someone. This type of thing went on for quite some time until I got hit by a booby trap and medevaced. I never did go back to the rear as a company clerk.

During Operation Union I, Lance Cpl. David Babb worked as the company runner. Captain Caswell once told David to "take something to battalion," and David had a hard time trying to figure out what "battalion" was and where it was located. They were out in the field at the time, so there weren't any obvious buildings to go to. Finally someone clued him in that he needed to locate Lieutenant Colonel Hilgartner, the battalion commander, and deliver the message from Captain Caswell. David quickly found Lieutenant Colonel Hilgartner and delivered the message. He remembers seeing Highpockets for the first time. "I looked up at that tall guy, and he looked down at me with this look that said to me, 'What are you?' I guess it was because I was so green, or something. He gave me the orders to take back to Captain Caswell. Eventually I learned my job. That's what I did: I ran errands for Captain Caswell, walked point for him wherever we went until I got hurt. Whenever we got stuck in the thick foliage, Captain Caswell or Gunny Cruz would send me ahead to cut through the growth."

On the morning of 10 May 1967, as Charlie Company approached their objective, Hill 110, David Babb still worked as the company runner for Captain Caswell. He remembers:

> As we left the village that morning, Dewitt Price, who would later become my squad leader, unwittingly picked up a mine. Realizing his error, Dee instinctively tossed it away. The mine immediately exploded and sent a chunk of shrapnel into the left side of my chest, leaving me with a sucking chest wound. Wayne Tarr also got hit by that explosion. I never really knew what had happened, just that one minute I'm standing there on that trail, and then the explosion and I'm on my back with a sucking chest wound.
>
> Many years later, at a reunion in Orlando, Florida, Dee Price drove to the reunion, looked me up, told me what he had done, and apologized to me. Dumbfounded to learn what had actually happened, I prayed that God would grant Dee Price peace and the ability to forgive himself, as I have certainly forgiven him. Sometimes people do things without thinking, and I'm included in that. One other time, while out on a patrol, as we moved down this trail, a Marine next to me pointed down at the ground and said, "Grenade!" I looked down, saw the grenade sitting there on the ground, and without thinking stooped over and picked up the grenade. I picked up the grenade, hooked it onto my web gear, and then I looked back up at the other Marine who looked back at me with huge eyes. Then I heard Captain Caswell say, "Babb, did you pick that fucking grenade up?" And I said, "Yes, sir." And then it dawned on me what I had done, and I broke out into a god-awful cold sweat. I did stupid things like that without thinking, and that's what Dee Price did that day. When

he told me about it many years later, he told me that while talking with Corporal Punjamie, he looked down and saw the mine, and without thinking just picked it up and threw it to get it out of the way. Unfortunately the damn thing exploded, and I got hit in the chest.

With his injured Marines safely aboard the medevac chopper, Captain Caswell gave the word to move out, and they left the village and their memories of the mine incident behind, moving toward their next objective. Charlie Company arrived at the base of Objective N, Hill 110, at about 0900 that morning, slightly behind schedule but in good shape to continue the mission. Caswell said:

> We had heard small arms fire coming from the area north of the hill for some time. When we arrived at the base of Hill 110, we encountered a platoon from one of the companies of the 1st Battalion, 3rd Marines preparing to take the hill to take pressure off the other companies of 1/3. The platoon commander told me they had three companies pinned down in the hedgerows and tree lines along the river north of Hill 110. These companies were receiving heavy fire from an NVA unit on the hill and the ridgeline behind it. I told the 1/3 platoon commander to return to his company, that we would take the hill, that it was our objective in our assigned zone of action. He told me he had just called in an air strike, and then he tossed a yellow smoke grenade that would mark our friendly positions. Almost instantly, the smoke attracted enemy mortar fire, and we started taking incoming. We scattered and hit the dirt, and the platoon from 1/3 departed. The jets arrived on the scene and immediately started their bombing runs, dropping 250-pound Snake Eye bombs on the top of Hill 110.[2] When the air strikes lifted, I had my 60 mm mortars commence firing on the top of the hill, and I signaled for the assault up the hill just as my 60 mm mortar teams ceased firing.

Capt. Jim Caswell ordered a classic "two platoons up, one back" assault formation for the attack on Hill 110. The Charlie Three Platoon had the responsibility of the left side of the attack force, and Charlie Two had the right. The 1st Platoon trailed in the reserve position, responsible for security for the company CP group and rear security. The thick scrub growth covering the south side of the hill made it difficult to deploy on line in a standard frontal assault formation. Therefore, each of the attacking platoons took different paths toward the top of the hill, the 3rd Platoon on the north side of the hill and the 2nd Platoon on the south side, attacking from the west toward the east and trying to maintain some semblance of an attack formation. The company CP group and the 1st Platoon followed the 2nd Platoon. Sgt. Juan Sanchez,

Left to right: Bill Edge, Jim Reed, and Lance Cpl. John Rusth on the hill across Highway 1 from Hill 54 Combat Base. Courtesy of John Rusth.

Weapons Platoon commander, working that day as the 60 mm mortar section leader since his machine gun teams had reinforced the platoons, closely trailed the company CP group. Once the platoon commanders had their orders, the Marines of Charlie 1/5 advanced toward the sound of gunfire coming from the top of the hill.

Jim Coxen, with the 2nd Platoon, clearly recalls his first view of Objective N, Hill 110: "I can remember finally arriving at the bottom of Hill 110 on the morning of 10 May, and the villagers telling us not to go up there, because there was beaucoup VC

A Viet Cong sign left along a trail, Summer 1967, Que Son Valley. Courtesy of John Rusth.

up there. We also had some Kit Carson Scouts with us, and they told us the same thing. These Kit Carson Scouts, former NVA soldiers captured and then supposedly reindoctrinated by the ARVN, became scouts for American forces. They were also sometimes called Chieu Hois after the Vietnamese words for 'I surrender.' They refused to go with us when we started our assault on Hill 110."

Pfc. Richard Schlagel moved with the point element, the 3rd Squad of the 3rd Platoon of Charlie 1/5, as they approached Hill 110:

Cpl. Nick Tague (*left*; KIA 10 May 1967 on Hill 110) and Harvey Cunningham. Courtesy of Harvey Cunningham.

Third Squad had point as we walked up to the base of Hill 110. I walked about five or six guys back from the point. Gunnery Sergeant Rivera-Cruz, our new platoon commander, and his radio operator moved just ahead of me. As we walked on a trail at the base of Hill 110, a Vietnamese person popped up in the brush ahead of us. One of the point Marines started to shoot him, but then someone hollered at him not to shoot but to try to take him prisoner. The Vietnamese wore a gray or tan uniform. I didn't see a weapon. We didn't shoot, and the Vietnamese started running up the hill and disappeared into the thick brush. We went after him through brush so thick you could not stand up. Someone said not to follow the same path that he ran away on, so the point man stayed over maybe five feet to the right of the path. We had to crawl on our hands and knees through the brush. The sweat dripped off me in the heat and humidity. I wondered why in the hell they didn't shoot him in the leg; that way they would have had their prisoner still able to talk. The point got tired of the slow going through the brush, so he said the hell with this and went over to the path the NVA took. We never did see that enemy soldier again.

Lance Cpl. John "Rusty" Rusth, Richard's fire team leader, says:

The enemy shot at us from the top of Hill 110. Of course, we had been out on this operation for several weeks by now, and this type of thing, getting shot at by a persistent and elusive VC sniper or two who would fire off a few rounds and then run away and hide, happened all the time. We had gotten used to it. We all figured that when we chased them up and over Hill 110 that the shooting would stop again, at least for a while longer. When we first started up the hill, Tom Kintner took the point up this trail through a lot of nasty scrub trees and thick brush up on that part of the hill. Right away, a VC threw a grenade down at us at the base of Hill 110. You could see it as it tumbled through the air. Everything went into slow motion. You could see it wasn't a frag grenade; it was a concussion grenade. It exploded right over near Tom. Kintner shot at the VC, and right away we had a blood trail leading to the top of Hill 110. It seemed like this guy tried to lead us that way, up to the top. And he did. We followed that blood trail all the way up that hill. It didn't lead us right straight up the hill, but more around the left side and up over the top. The platoon commanders tried to keep us on line at that point.

I remember watching the 2nd Platoon commander at one point during our attack up that hill. He ran back and forth behind his men, smacking them on their helmets with a stick from behind to get them to move faster and to stay on line. In the thick brush you couldn't stay on line, you just had to go around things going up that hill, but he stayed right behind them, really agitated with some of the guys in his platoon, screaming at them to move faster and to stay on line.

Sgt. Hillous York, the platoon sergeant of 3rd Platoon, says,

At around 0900 or 0930 that morning, we heard some firing from the top of Hill 110, so Captain Caswell called in a fixed-wing air strike, and several F-4 Phantom jets dropped their bombs right on top of the enemy positions, on the top of Hill 110. Gunny Rivera-Cruz had rejoined us two or three days before that and had taken over as our platoon commander; I took back the responsibilities of platoon sergeant. As soon as the air strike lifted, Captain Caswell put us in an attack formation, with 2nd Platoon on the right flank, our 3rd Platoon on the left flank, and Charlie One trailing in reserve with the company CP group. We immediately started to assault the hill, going from west to east, and it wasn't very long after that that the first fight for Hill 110 started.

Jim Coxen, the blooper man, found himself in the thick of things as the battle heated up:

> About 0930 that morning I can remember being at the bottom of the hill, with Anthony Vega, Sergeant Lynch, Phil Daly, Tom Kintner, Al Chaveau, Morris, and Houser. We started up the hill and took a little enemy small arms fire. It wasn't a lot to begin with, but the enemy had dug spider holes all over Hill 110, and it proved pretty difficult to charge up that hill with our heavy loads. I can remember seeing one of those spider holes open up, and the enemy soldier hiding inside threw a hand grenade at Kintner, and it bounced off his pack but it didn't go off. Tom turned around and put a burst into him. I think that's all that guy had, just a pineapple-type grenade, and that was the end of him.

Del Best remembers those events as well: "We started receiving sniper fire from the top of the hill as we approached it from the west about mid-morning. The next thing I know, we're sweeping, attacking up the hill going after the sniper, when a VC jumped out of a hole with a hand grenade, and he threw it right at us. It bounced off Kintner's backpack and bounced away before it exploded. Another close call, but fortunately nobody got hurt."

Harold Thrasher recalls, "On the morning of 10 May 1967 we started out of our nighttime positions well before first light and continued to march. It seems like we walked for miles, and we finally arrived at the village at the foot of Hill 110 late that morning. We started taking sniper fire from the top of the hill, so the CO called in air strikes on the top of the hill. After that we assaulted the hill, and the whole world seemed to go crazy with gunfire."

As Charlie Company moved up the west slope of Hill 110, the Marines made contact with the enemy outposts and drove them back with sharp bursts of small arms fire. Unfortunately, as often happens in combat, Murphy's Law took hold at the worst possible time, and the new M16s began malfunctioning all over the hill. As Caswell started his climb up the hill, a Marine from the 3rd Platoon ran back down the hill to his position and reported that they had the enemy OPs dead to rights, but their M16s had jammed and the enemy soldiers had gotten away. This disgusted Marine saw that Caswell carried an M16 and said, "Skipper, the fucking M16s are jamming right and left, and the gooks got away. Can I borrow your rifle, sir?" Caswell quickly exchanged rifles with the frustrated Marine, who then turned around and charged back up the hill, hoping to get back into a firing position before the enemy got away. During the next few minutes, this bad situation turned very ugly as the Marines of the 2nd and 3rd Platoons crested the hill, and started down the eastern side of Hill 110. Still climbing up the west side of the hill, Caswell quickly started to receive radio reports about a huge volume of enemy small arms fire and incoming mortars and rockets.

Capt. Jim Caswell didn't need a radio report to tell him that his Marines were under enemy fire; he could hear it clearly. After eight years in the Marine Corps, this was, by far, the heaviest volume of fire he had ever heard. He had observed on several occasions a Marine infantry company as they executed a Mad Moment (every Marine in the company firing final protective fires), but what he heard just ahead of him far exceeded those Mad Moments. Jim heard no distinct individual gunshots coming from over the top of the hill, just a horribly loud, continuous roar of enemy and Marine gunfire.

The first Charlie 1/5 Marines to fall during the Battle for Hill 110 were Gunnery Sgt. Marcelino Rivera-Cruz and his radio operator, Lance Cpl. Fred Tate, both instantly killed by enemy mortar fire right at the beginning of the fight. Gunny Cruz, concentrating on his job of controlling his 3rd Platoon Marines as they attacked up the hill, never knew what hit him. The next moment a shattering explosion from an 82 mm mortar round snuffed out both their lives.

Gunny Cruz believed in leading his platoon from the forward edge of the attack formation, with only a four-man fire team ahead of him. It was his style, and it had served him well for many months. But this time he was in the wrong place at the wrong time, and the enemy gunners had gotten lucky. As soon as word reached him, Sgt. Hillous York automatically assumed command of the 3rd Platoon and continued the mission.

Warfare is a wicked taskmaster; it pays no attention to an individual's abilities to fight or to lead, but rather takes its wages and reaps its harvests of death and destruction arbitrarily. In one moment a proven combat leader's life can abruptly end; a stray sniper's round or a well-aimed artillery shell or mortar round will wantonly kill a man who has demonstrated undaunted courage on many occasions, a man who earned the right to live on, to fight and to encourage others to fight, to lead by example. In another moment, a man barely able to function, someone who has proved himself a coward, can change in an instant in the cauldron of battle into a hero who turns and runs through death unscathed to charge the enemy and kill him, to protect his buddies and to find redemption.

The life of Gunnery Sgt. Marcelino Rivera-Cruz ended abruptly, too soon, and too harshly. Universally liked and respected by his men, his peers, and his leaders,

Gunny Cruz had a presence on the battlefield that always brought great comfort and confidence to his Marines, so his Marines would greatly miss him during the remaining hours of this bloody day. Any thoughts of mourning him, however, would have to wait until later. The Marines of Charlie 1/5 had their mission, and they were engaged with the enemy. Objective N, the small mountain called Hill 110, lay right in front of them.

Pfc. Richard Schlagel's memories of the Battle for Hill 110 are of surreal, insane moments, especially those moments when he walked by the bodies of Gunny Cruz and Lance Corporal Tate:

> As we walked up Hill 110, basically in a triangular formation, because the path ran in a zigzag pattern, as I looked up the hill I could see the gunny. He was about twenty feet above me and a little to my left, moving up the hill. Lance Corporal Tate was about fifteen feet above me and to my upper right. All of a sudden all hell broke loose. As I looked up the hill at the Gunny, a mortar round came in and landed about five or six feet from the Gunny's right side. I saw the explosion throwing the earth upward, and forcing Gunny Cruz's body violently downward to the ground. As I went down, I only had dirt hit me. While staying on the ground, I tried to see if they were okay. As the dust and smoke started to settle, I first saw Tate, lying face up, motionless. I heard other explosions to my left. We started taking small arms fire. As I looked around for the enemy, I heard cries from different places on the hill. "Corpsman up! Corpsman up!" Staying low, I went up to Tate. Then I saw Gunny Rivera-Cruz. He lay face down, completely still. His backpack, torn to shreds, oozed bright white shaving cream out of the many shrapnel holes. More holes covered the back of his utility trousers, some surrounded with blood, and I could see blood on the side of his neck. Marines screamed for corpsmen all over that hill.
>
> I hollered for a corpsman as I went up to Tate. Someone ran up and said the corpsmen had their hands full tending to other wounded Marines, and it would take a while before they could help, just to do what I could. Then that Marine continued up the hill to check the Gunny. After a quick look at the Gunny, I heard him say something, shake his head, and continue on up the hill.
>
> Looking at Tate, I didn't see any blood or holes in him, but he wasn't breathing. I started mouth-to-mouth resuscitation and hoped a corpsman would get there real soon. I stayed as low as I could, because enemy small arms fire still raged. I couldn't see any of the enemy soldiers. They had to be in the brush that we had just come out of; we must have walked right over them.

> Another Marine came by and told me to take off Tate's backpack. He got out his KA-BAR knife and cut the straps and then pulled the pack out from under him. I continued the mouth-to-mouth. I glanced up the hill and saw the same Marine check out the Gunny. As he continued up the hill I heard him say, "We're not going to get out of this alive."
>
> I heard gurgling sounds coming from Tate's chest. While giving Tate mouth-to-mouth I remembered Tate telling the Gunny the day before that he was too short to go on this operation. The Gunny told Tate that he needed him, we had too many new guys, and not to worry; he would make sure Tate wouldn't miss his plane home.
>
> At this time, Rusty came up and checked out Tate. He said there wasn't anything we could do for him. They couldn't do anything for either Gunny Rivera-Cruz or Tate. They were both dead. We continued to climb up the hill.

John "Rusty" Rusth would prove his mettle that day, although he very rarely talks about his heroic deeds. Besides the fact that Lance Cpl. John Rusth personally helped saved the lives of ten Marines that day, he set a determined and courageous example to all those who witnessed what he did. Rusty says:

> At about that point it all started to happen. We had reached the top of the hill and started down the other side when we realized that the VC we chased had brought us to exactly where they wanted us, because all hell broke loose. Almost instantly, we lost our platoon commander, Gunny Rivera-Cruz, and his radio operator, Lance Cpl. Fred Tate. At that point the rockets and the mortars and a huge volume of small arms fire hit us all at once.
>
> We found ourselves on a really rough, nasty, brushy hillside, down in sort of the military crest.[3] A large bunch of enemy soldiers shot at us from the base of the hill, on the north side, and at one point it seemed like there were some behind us as well, like we had walked past them, so they just permeated the hill. We could see them all over at the base of the hill, on the north side. These guys had on khaki uniforms. For the first time I saw actual combat uniforms on the enemy, and these guys had them. These were definitely NVA, and they just swarmed around the base of that hill.
>
> We couldn't believe how many of them moved around down there, so we just started shooting at them. We understood later that the ones we could see equaled a very small part of the NVA force in that cane field at the bottom of the hill. There turned out to be thousands of them. Incoming enemy fire hit all around us. At that point, most of us just tried to find a place where we could get down, to take cover from the deadly enemy fire. Right away, we heard that

> we lost two corpsmen, and that meant that we only had one remaining corpsman. Men all over that hill screamed for a corpsman, but there weren't enough corpsmen, only the one. Quite a few Marines went down on that forward slope, many badly hurt, and those who were still alive were screaming for help.
>
> For the rest of that afternoon we spent most of the time trying to defend ourselves and some of the time trying to get help for those wounded Marines. It seemed like we always had to do both, shoot at the enemy and try to get our buddies out alive. At some point the adrenaline kicked in, and the screams got to us, and we just had to get them out. We saw them going down; we were all scared to death. In some cases we knew who was screaming, but in many cases we didn't. Because of the thick brush, we couldn't tell for sure who was screaming down there, but we knew it was a Marine and we knew we had to help him. So we did.
>
> We knew that we urgently needed to get these wounded Marines to the top of the hill, to the limited shelter behind the military crest, where they could receive medical treatment and could hopefully be medevaced. Cpl. Nick Tague, one of our best squad leaders, was really badly wounded right away and died later that afternoon, and there were a bunch more wounded Marines down. So we concentrated on getting each man back to the top of the hill, and some of them made it.

Lance Corporal Rusth received the nation's second highest medal for heroism, the Navy Cross, for his courageous actions and valiant leadership that day. Throughout that long and bloody day, Rusty fought the enemy at nearly point-blank range and set the example for many others. Rusty also took ten hazardous, arduous trips from the kill zone at the bottom of the hill to the Charlie Company CP, each time carrying a wounded Marine over his shoulder, exposing himself to the horrendous enemy gunfire and saving many Marines' lives in the process before finally being painfully wounded himself and medevaced (see the Citation, Appendix A).

The chaos that inevitably overwhelms a battlefield had taken firm hold on Hill 110 that morning, and the Marines who fought there remember snatches and pieces of hellish insanity. Harold Thrasher remembers:

> The whole rest of that day we engaged in a horrendous firefight, but I never saw any of the enemy that entire day. I heard about the huge body count later, after I got off the USS *Repose* and rejoined Charlie 1/5. I saw a lot of enemy bodies later on, but I never saw an enemy alive.
>
> Once we got over the top of Hill 110, I asked a Marine to my left if he knew the enemy's positions. He pointed out some bushes at the bottom of the hill,

so I aimed at those bushes, put my M16 on full automatic, and intended to shoot up a full magazine at those bushes, but I didn't get three rounds out of the M16 before it jammed on me. I brought it down, cleared the chamber, and started to shoot again when I heard this Marine say, "I should have known better." I looked over at him and saw his face covered with blood. Later on I heard that the enemy had shot his M16, and it had literally exploded and shrapnel had hit him in the face. I got hit at the same time, shrapnel in my left hand. I didn't even know that I was hit at first. About that time a very high volume of enemy fire started raking the hill. At first we did everything wrong. They had taught us to keep our distance from each other and to keep down as much as possible, making use of available cover and concealment. We all stood up, grouped together. It didn't take me long to realize that we no longer fought an elusive VC, but this was a determined enemy force who could really shoot. We all hit the ground, but there was no cover. Anytime anyone moved, the enemy fire would increase in volume, and rounds hit everywhere. I could feel the thuds of rounds hitting next to me and clods of dirt and bits of rocks hit me as the incoming enemy bullets hit right next to me. There for a while, since we were so exposed and under such heavy enemy gunfire, I decided to play dead. When I looked around I saw that all the Marines in that area were also playing dead. No one returned fire. That didn't last too long, though, and pretty soon the Marines on Hill 110 poured out hot lead at the enemy.

Confusion took hold; communications were bad, and it was hard to keep track of what was going on. It had been a cakewalk from the base of the hill to the top of the hill; our squad had not encountered any enemy at all. But when we got to the top of Hill 110, all heck broke out as we started down the other side. We all stood up and charged down the other side, shooting at the enemy positions; it reminded me of a turkey shoot going on. That's when the enemy opened up on us, guys started dropping like flies; calls for corpsmen came from all over the hill.

The air strike that had hit the top of the hill earlier had blown or burned away most of the brush. We didn't have any cover at all. I remember my chest being sore later from lying on the ground, on a lot of broken-up rocks all over the hill, I think from the air strike. Every time you moved, you had a volley of enemy fire coming at you. I heard later, after I recovered from my wounds and returned to the company, that an enemy soldier, down at the bottom of the hill, stood with a flag, pointing out targets. We were the targets. I never saw that NVA with the flag, but several of my buddies told me about it later.

One of our machine gunners saw the NVA who killed Gunny Cruz and Tate pick up his mortar tube and start running away with it, so he fired his

M60 and walked his rounds right up that NVA gunner's back. I don't remember taking many more incoming mortar rounds after that. It seemed like we stayed pinned down on the front of that hill for hours and hours. Later on that afternoon, the resupply and medevac choppers started coming in. We got some fixed-wing support, and I think we got some helicopter gunships as well. It took a long time to get the air support out there to help us. All we had to fight with that day were our machine guns and M16s, and the darned M16s kept jamming.

The others who fought that day on Hill 110 found themselves in equally harrowing circumstances. Sgt. Hillous York says:

We assaulted up to the top and took control of the top of Hill 110 amidst not a tremendous amount, but a lot of small arms fire. Once we got to the top of the hill, the fight really started. I didn't hear any radio traffic from the Gunny, and I thought that unusual. Of course I found out a little later that Gunnery Sgt. Rivera-Cruz and his radio operator, Tate, died almost immediately, but I didn't find out about that until I reached the bottom of the east side of Hill 110 the first time. Tate's radio had also been smashed. We had lost our platoon commander and an important piece of communications gear, but we had to continue the mission. I was now the platoon commander of the 3rd Platoon. We continued our assault down the eastern side of Hill 110. We had two or three new guys with the platoon, so I had told them to stay close to me. The fighting really picked up on our way down the eastern side of the hill. A large cane field sat at the bottom of the hill due east of us on our side of the company assault formation, just beyond a stretch of short grass. That turned out to be the enemy's "wall of steel." When we got just short of the cane field, the enemy really started to put it to us.

The big fight really started right then. We had stopped moving forward, so I moved around to my left flank to make sure that side of the platoon was secure, and I found Tate and the Gunny, both dead. I also found several other wounded Marines. By that time my men had all expended over a hundred rounds of M16 ammo each, but they all held good. Knowing that we faced a large enemy force, judging by the volume of fire, I called Captain Caswell and asked for both artillery and air support. We got no artillery support that day. We also got no air strikes to support us until much later on, after the enemy had finally broken contact with us.

No artillery, no air strikes, so I knew we could do nothing but just "bull up" and fight. That's what everyone did, we just fought. A tremendous volume of fire roared constantly. The side of Hill 110 was pretty thick and brushy, but if you stood up you could see over the brush. I can remember looking out as this battle raged and seeing so many bullets and tracers firing that it looked like sheets of red and green rain; the huge volume of incoming and outgoing small arms fire viciously distorted the air with its heat. The high-pitched noise of the horrendous firing was just unbelievable. By that point, I couldn't hear very well because of all the noise. My ears rang. Everybody still held, everyone continued to put out fire, but of course we had wounded down. Third Platoon had some KIAs, but we all just fought like hell. The fighting would go on for a little while and then it would ease off for a while; then it would ratchet back up. The intensity of the firing went up and down during that entire day, but I don't think the firing ever completely stopped until the battle finally ended, at about 1800 that evening. In the midst of all the small arms fire, I could hear enemy mortar tubes popping, and then the loud detonations of high explosives. The enemy mortars, fired at us from positions out in the cane field, sounded like the 82 mm variety.

We took a lot of casualties, but the enemy suffered a hell of a lot more casualties. I really couldn't keep up with the time. In some ways it seemed like this fight went on forever, but it would die down for a while and then come back. Later on, I found out that the NVA tried several times to break out of our trap. They would try to get away from us, but they would always run into another company, so they would come back at us. It seemed like they were trapped in a pinball machine; they'd hit one side and then bounce back right at us. We weren't maneuvering, we really didn't have anywhere to go, we just had to stand and fight.

As Marine command reacted to the situation on Hill 110, the enemy position on low ground became less tenable. Charlie Company made the most of their high-ground advantage, and other units in the surrounding area blocked the enemy's retreat.

Lt. Col. Peter Hilgartner remembers the Battle for Hill 110 vividly:

I took operational control of the 1st Battalion, 3rd Marines, on 10 May. Colonel Houghton, the regimental CO, still called all the shots, but I commanded all the troops on the battlefield. In addition to my own battalion's troops, I had three additional companies: B, C, and D Companies of 1/3. I only had one company of my own Marines with me, Delta Company; my other three companies stayed spread out in the vicinity of the fighting, but I was still several kilometers away from the fighting. I tried to get choppers in to lift us into the area, but no choppers were made available, so we had no choice but to march. We moved as fast as possible, actually running most of the time, and ultimately climbed up to the top of Hill 218, located about three clicks north of the combat base, and 1,500 meters south of Hill 110. Alpha Company approached from the east, and Charlie Company attacked from the west and had engaged the enemy in a major battle. Delta Company stayed with my battalion CP group, and Bravo Company approached from another direction. We had the enemy boxed in.

We had them boxed in, and I was certain we would slaughter them all until Alpha Company got hit with that damned air strike. I had called Colonel Houghton and requested that he get out to the battlefield just as soon as possible, because we had the enemy trapped, but we didn't have enough communications gear to handle all of the companies we had at or near the battlefield that day. We didn't have enough radios, the 1/3 companies communicated on a different frequency, and I didn't know any of the 1/3 company commanders. This is one of the problems with having other outfits attached at the drop of a hat. I now had three companies from 1/3; I had never seen them, never talked with them, and didn't know their location. Worse, neither did the 1/3 battalion commander, who, it turned out, had given me incorrect information. It was a real problem.

Sergeant York continues his narrative of the battle for Hill 110:

Early that afternoon I realized that some of our wounded were really in bad shape. For the most part they had remained where they had fallen on the side slope of the hill, and although they tried to stay hidden in the brush, in reality they remained constantly exposed to enemy gunfire. The brush did provide some concealment, but no real cover that would stop an AK-47 round. I knew I had to get them back up the hill to Captain Caswell, our anchor. I found even more wounded Marines on my way up the hill. I told Captain Caswell that I needed help getting the wounded out, since everyone down on the side of the hill was either dead, wounded, or absolutely necessary to keep fighting off the NVA. Captain Caswell gave me what he could, and we took off back down the hill. I can remember one of these Marines saying that he didn't have an M16, he only had a .45-caliber pistol. I told him that he wouldn't need a rifle, just to watch me as I pointed out the wounded that needed immediate evacuation. I pointed at those seriously wounded who needed immediate help, and I bypassed the dead bodies. They would have to wait until later.

When we started back down, of course, we came back under heavy enemy gunfire, so we had to fight our way back down the hill, shooting at the enemy as we moved back down the hill trying to get to our wounded. The sun beat down relentlessly, my wounded Marines suffered horribly, but we could do nothing for them except try to get them to the top of the hill. Roseberry had taken a bad wound to the head, and after we got him back up to the top of the hill I put his green towel over his eyes and poured some of my canteen water over the towel in an effort to save his eyes. About that time, Rusty got wounded, after he had made several trips up and down that hill carrying out wounded Marines.

Jim Coxen's squad in the 2nd Platoon advanced on the right flank. Jim remembers:

We made it up to the top of the hill, moved forward to the far side—the military crest—and everyone stopped and flopped like we were trained to do. We could clearly see NVA soldiers running down the other side of the hill and into the cane field. Our platoon commander hollered at us to go get them. We all got up immediately and started to charge in the direction of the enemy's withdrawal, but I can remember both Sergeant Lynch and Anthony Vega saying they thought it was stupid to charge down that hill. The backside of that hill had very, very little cover and concealment, virtually none. But we had our orders, so we got up and attacked down the hill. I think we all got to the bottom of the hill, maybe about twenty or thirty meters from the edge of the cane field, when the enemy opened up on us. All hell broke loose, and everything just came unglued. We got hammered from the cane field and from the ridgeline on our right-hand side. We took a high volume of small arms fire, as well as incoming rocket-propelled grenade (RPG) and recoilless rifle fire. I think they had one or more 57 mm recoilless rifles, because the high explosive rounds just screamed in on us. Because of its slower velocity, you could actually watch an RPG round as it floated by; but these damned recoilless rifle rounds just screamed in on us and blew up.

The din from all the fire nearly overwhelmed us. The lieutenant told us to fall back up the hill and to set up on the military crest. He told us to go straight back up the hill, but Sergeant Lynch said, "Bullshit," so we moved laterally around the right flank, and started to make our way back up the hill. Sergeant Lynch only got about three steps before he got hit by small arms fire in the arm, but we grabbed him and helped him get back up the hill with us.

Eventually we made it back up to the military crest. Everyone stayed spread out as much as possible, and a lot of the guys moved in short rushes from bush to bush, the way we learned in training. A few very small, scraggly bushes represented the only concealment we had. A guy would hide behind a bush and try to hold still because of our very close proximity to the enemy; if they saw any movement the enemy would immediately pour their fire on the bush. I can remember one guy, trying to get small and holding perfectly still behind a very small bush. As I moved toward him I heard him say, "If you come near my bush, you son-of-a-bitch, I'll shoot you myself." So I kept going, trying to get back up the hill without getting shot.

I don't know how long it took us to get back up to the top of the hill. It seemed like hours, but I really don't know how long it took. When the shit hits the fan, time either goes really fast or really slow. We just kept wondering if we would ever get any help. At the height of the battle, about 120 Charlie Company Marines, 2nd and 3rd Platoons, and several machine gun teams fought to hold the north and east sides of the hill, and it seemed like at least eight to ten times that many enemy soldiers fired at us constantly, at nearly point-blank range.

The combat after-action report of Operation Union I indicates that an estimated enemy strength of nearly three thousand enemy soldiers (VC and NVA) operated in the Que Son Valley TAOR. The Charlie Company Marines, who fought on Hill 110 that day, 10 May 1967, believe that they had trapped the 3rd NVA Regiment in that cane field—an estimated force of eighteen hundred NVA soldiers.

The Blooper Man had seen a lot of combat by this time in his tour, and he knew they were in dire straits. Jim Coxen said, "If the NVA had wanted us, they could have had us there, right at the start, because we didn't have any air cover or artillery support. I don't know why they didn't just come and get us, but they didn't. I guess that's why we're still alive. I think that they probably left a covering force and tried to break out three or four or five different times in various directions away from Charlie Company. The firing never completely died off, but the small arms fire would slow down and the mortar attacks would stop for a short time, and then all of a sudden it would go crazy again."

Del Best found himself right in the middle of the fight:

We continued up the hill, and when we looked down the eastern side of the hill, we saw NVA soldiers everywhere, running around like crazy. All of a sudden as we started down the hill toward them, still walking, all hell broke loose. I can't remember the name of the guy next to me, another rifleman in our squad. I remember that he hailed from Wisconsin, but I can't remember his name. He caught two rounds real quick, hit in the chest and shoulder, and the fire team leader and I grabbed him and pulled him into some cover. We put a bandage on him real quick. I grabbed him behind his back, and the fire team leader grabbed him by the feet, and as the fire team leader bent over, I just happened to look right at the top of the fire team leader's helmet. A round grazed right across the top of his helmet, and knocked the fire team leader senseless.

And from there on, the corpsmen started coming around. When we wanted to set up in a firing position, we had to crawl. I fired off about four rounds and my rifle jammed. That wasn't the first time that had happened. I cleared the jam with my cleaning rod and kept on firing. We continued to fire at the enemy hiding in the cane field at the bottom of the hill but sustaining a high rate of small arms fire at us. We just held our positions. As the corpsmen came around, they got our canteens to use for the wounded, because there wasn't any water except what we had. One of the corpsmen—it's a shame I can't remember his name—he came over into our part of the hill. As he approached, we told him not to move, because an enemy sniper had this area zeroed in. We told him not to move, but he kept moving in our direction. He went about ten yards, and then he took a round right in the head.

This kept going on all day long. I remember this one guy, I think his name was Ginn, he had an M60 machine gun, and he and I stayed together almost all day. We could see them once in a while, and we would shoot like crazy. The M60s kept up firing all day long. But sometimes we couldn't see the enemy. They continued throwing mortar fire at us on the Hill, and shooting RPGs at us, all day long. We just continued firing back and forth all day long. I remember that we always tried to get into as much cover and concealment as we could, but there wasn't much of that on Hill 110.

The initial sketchy reports coming from Captain Caswell's platoon commanders at the top of Hill 110 indicated that they were under a hail of enemy fire, on the receiving end of 82 mm mortar fire, B-40 RPG fire, 57 mm recoilless rifle fire, machine gun fire, and small arms fire from both SKS and AK-47 rifles. Not yet fully understanding what his Marines had tangled with, he thought that at least some of the firing might be coming from the 1/3 Marines to his north, who might have mistaken his Marines for an enemy force. Fearing that the 1/3 Marines had opened up on his men, Captain Caswell called those companies on their battalion tactical net and asked them to cease firing on Hill 110. All of the 1/3 companies responded quickly that they weren't firing at the hill. At that moment Caswell finally realized that the fight of his life had begun, so he quickly called in a situation report to the battalion commander and told him that Charlie Company was in heavy contact with the enemy and gave him Charlie Company's position.

At about that time, just a couple of minutes after the heavy enemy firing had broken out, Caswell received a terrible report from the 3rd Platoon: Gunny Cruz and his radio operator were both dead. Caswell knew that Gunny Cruz didn't have to die. He had done his time in the past as a platoon commander, and Caswell had "promoted" him back to company Gunny. But when Rivera-Cruz learned from some of the Charlie Three Marines that the new gunny assigned to lead them couldn't keep up, Gunny Cruz had volunteered, rather forcefully, to take over his platoon again. Caswell had approved the reassignment on a temporary basis until such time as a junior officer or another staff NCO became available.

At that moment, however, the Marines of Charlie Three had other things to worry about. The point elements had crossed over the top of Hill 110, following the fleeing enemy soldiers who had abandoned their outposts and had run down the other side of the hill. They had passed the military crest of the hill, and many of them had neared the bottom of the hill, just short of an open grassy area about fifty meters short of a large cane field, where a regiment of NVA soldiers hid. When the NVA opened up on the Marines with an ungodly volume of fire, they stood at point blank range. Terribly outnumbered, and at the risk of slaughter, the Marines of Charlie Three hit the deck and quickly tried to find some cover and concealment in the very sparse, low scrub growth on the eastern slope of Hill 110. They lay flat on a rocky surface with no holes to crawl into. For the most part, the Marines lay out in the open, with perhaps a bush to hide behind, pinned down with a horrific volume of enemy small arms, mortar, and rocket fire. Those Marines would stay there, returning the enemy's fire, for the rest of the day. They couldn't attack forward, because they knew they were overwhelmingly outnumbered. They couldn't move back up the hill, because they would have to expose themselves to the enemy gunners, and they couldn't move right or left for the same reason. So they held their ground, took advantage of what little cover and concealment the side of the hill afforded, and returned fire at the concealed enemy in the cane field.

Fortunately for the beleaguered Marines whose M16 rifles continued to jam, the M60 machine gun teams following closely behind the point elements survived the initial outburst of enemy firing and took up adequate firing positions. The M60s hosed down the cane field with a high rate of 7.62 mm machine gun fire and kept up a continuously high volume of firing throughout that long, hot day. Caswell later acknowledged that the M60 machine guns were the one positive element that kept his company from disaster, because, as he shortly learned to his great disgust, the supporting arms that he had come to rely on would completely fail him that day.

Capt. Jim Caswell realized his tough situation. But he also knew from previous experience that he could easily turn the situation around with the use of artillery and air strikes as he had so often done in the days and weeks and months leading up to the battle for Hill 110. Caswell turned to his two forward observers (FOs) to command them to call in fire missions on the enemy below the hill, but before he could open his mouth, his young FOs squeezed their radio handsets and screamed "Fire mission!" at the top of their lungs. Although Charlie Company's 81 mm mortar FO and artillery FO were both corporals (Charlie Company had not enjoyed the services of a lieutenant FO for many months), they performed very well whenever needed. Caswell had come to rely on these young NCOs, and they had never let him down. They didn't need to hear orders to realize the critical importance of their fire missions; the accurate and relentless fire of artillery and mortars would most certainly devastate the enemy soldiers who remained invisible in the cane field but who also were certainly exposed to the company's supporting arms. From his position atop Hill 110, Caswell could clearly see the green tracer rounds, so he easily pinpointed the enemy positions. Absolutely certain that he could completely destroy this enemy force, no matter how large, he planned to drop as many high explosive weapons on top of the enemy's heads as possible.

Meanwhile, the Marines of Delta 1/5 accompanied Lieutenant Colonel Hilgartner to his vantage point overlooking the Battle for Hill 110. The Delta Company commander, 1st Lt. Dave McInturff, had only recently taken command.

David Lee McInturff had joined the Marine Corps in 1962. He obtained his commission by spending two summers at the PLC and completing basic training for Marine officers at Camp Upshur and Mainside, Marine Corps Base Quantico. Upon graduating from West Texas State University in Canyon, Texas, located about fifteen miles south of Amarillo, Dave received his commission as a second lieutenant in May 1965. While attending TBS in Quantico, he also participated as a football player for the Marine Corps' team based there. Dave played varsity football in college, and this had come to the attention of the head football coach in Quantico, so even before he graduated from TBS, he received orders to play on the team.

Unfortunately, Dave broke his leg during the first game in the fall of 1965, against the University of Toledo. He recalls:

> I broke my leg, they took me to the hospital, and I'm in agony. I finally woke up the next morning with the leg straightened out and a cast on it. I shared a hospital room with an older gentleman. We got to talking, and he said to me, "I understand you're a Marine," and I said, "Yes, sir, I am." He said, "Tough game last night," and I said, "Well, I don't know because I didn't stay in the game long enough to know about that." He introduced himself as Burt Hardy. The name sounded very familiar to me, and I finally remembered why. I had just finished reading a book about Guadalcanal, and one of the main characters was a reserve company commander by the name of Burt Hardy

from Toledo, Ohio. On hearing his name, I immediately began to query him about his background. Sure enough, he proved to be the same Burt Hardy that the book described. Some coincidence! Burt gave me a first-hand account of the landing and combat on "The Canal."

After my release from the hospital, I finally graduated from the Basic School and became a football coach for the varsity team and a track coach. I stayed on restricted duty (in a long-leg walking brace) going through physical therapy, and it took quite a while to completely heal, about a year. In December 1966 I finally got orders to report to the 1st Marine Division in South Vietnam. During my assignment as a coach, I also served as an escort officer for the remains of one of my basic school classmates, a good friend who had been killed in action. I knew that things were going to be tough in Vietnam. I first reported into Camp Pendleton, California, and went through the replacement battalion training course there. We shipped over right after the first of the year, and I reported to the 1st Battalion, 5th Marines on 7 January 1967. After battalion orientation, I then joined Delta Company and became the XO and 1st Platoon commander. The battalion, at that time, stayed in the Chu Lai area on Hill 54 Combat Base, and Delta Company occupied Hill 10, a company-size outpost adjacent to and across Highway 1 from Hill 54, about fifteen clicks north of Chu Lai. Capt. John Carty commanded Delta Company at the time; he knew that I needed to spend some time as a platoon commander, so he assigned me both billets.

My first experiences in combat came during Operation Desoto/Deckhouse VI. We saw hardly any action during that operation, but it did give me some experience, for which I was grateful. Upon return to our combat base, my platoon provided security on Snaggletooth Island with a platoon of Popular Forces. This assignment lasted about one month (March '67). Lieutenant Colonel Hilgartner and Captain Carty finally concluded that I could handle the command of a rifle company. Carty and I had a change of command ceremony on Hill 10. Carty went to the S-3 shop, and I officially became CO of Delta Company.

Just before Operation Union I kicked off, battalion sent Delta Company out on a company-size search-and-destroy operation. We took off in the middle of the night and got out in the middle of this weird-ass valley before first light. We started getting shot at by VC snipers, and my radio operator had his radio practically shot off his back. We found three holes in the radio, and I had been standing right in front of him. Both of us were luckier than hell that time. We continued our search-and-destroy operation, and we crossed a fairly swift and deep river, and wouldn't you know it, we lost an M60 machine gun in the middle of that river and never found the damned thing. My tour as a company commander had not started out very well. I just knew that Lieutenant Colonel Hilgartner would fire my ass just as soon as I returned to the battalion combat base, but he didn't. I guess he figured that as a new company commander I deserved some slack, and that shit happens. I also had to medevac two guys because leeches had managed to work their way into their urethras.

A few days later, we trucked up to Tam Ky and set up a perimeter around the artillery compound up there. We slept under the muzzles of 175 mm artillery pieces, and those damned guns fired H&I fire all night long. We didn't get much sleep that night. We had an early wake-up the next morning, 29 April 1967; we had a zero dark thirty start, left the area before first light, and headed west on foot, the kickoff for Delta Company's involvement in Operation Union I.

We walked all the way from Tam Ky west to Hiep Duc over the next several days, a distance of about forty kilometers as the crow flies over a bunch of mountains. About halfway there, we got to watch the regimental commander crash in a helicopter. We had advanced up a horseshoe-shaped ridgeline, and Colonel Houghton's CH-34 planned to land in a dry rice paddy below our positions. It approached the LZ in a kind of a steep bank, and apparently the helicopter's rotor hit a paddy dike, which threw it off balance, and the son-of-a-gun just settled down and then fell over on its side. It fell over on the left side, and fortunately the door opens on the right side, and here comes Colonel Houghton, crawling out of the door, now facing straight up in the air. That was one of the most exciting things we saw all the way from Tam Ky to Hiep Duc.

We got to Hiep Duc on the 5th or 6th of May. I remember the area as, literally, the scariest place I ever spent any time in during my first tour in Vietnam. We had been briefed that it was a heavily populated area, but as we walked into Hiep Duc we didn't see hardly any people. No dogs barking, no birds chirping, and no people in the open. I said to myself, "Holy crap!" We expected the first shot to ring out from an ambush any minute, but it never did. The company walked all the way into Hiep Duc without a shot fired. We set up our defenses on the outskirts of the village, sent out patrols, and waited for resupply.

One of my security patrols ran into a small group of VC, and a pretty good firefight took place. We had one Marine sustain a minor wound, but we ended up killing five VC. More importantly, we found a big cache of brand-new Chinese medical gear, brand-new NVA uniforms, and an NVA flag. The VC had obviously been guarding this weapons cache, but we blew them away and found the cache. After things got settled down, the patrol presented me a captured NVA flag. We found about four thousand pounds of gear in that cache. We didn't find any weapons or ammo in the cache, just several tons of medical supplies and clothing. One of the weirdest things we found in that enemy supply cache was a 1967 Sears spring catalog, still in the shipping wrapper. That Sears catalog proved to be one of the strangest things I saw during my first tour. It was May of 1967, and here was this Sears spring 1967 catalog. It made me wonder if the VC and the NVA were buying stuff via mail order from Sears.

After destroying the enemy supply cache, we left the Hiep Duc area and headed north and northeast toward the Que Son Valley. Several valleys in the area comprised the Que Son Basin, but we referred to the whole area as the Que Son Valley. Delta 1/5 patrolled the mountain range that ran along the west side of the Que Son Valley for several more days before finally reaching what would soon become our new battalion combat base, the low hill that Lieutenant Colonel Hilgartner would dub Hill 51. We never ran into any enemy up in those mountains, but we came across hundreds of butterfly mines that the US Air Force had dropped in the area, the early cluster bomb units. A large canister, dropped from an aircraft, would burst in the air, and a whole bunch of these small mines would saturate an area. They had wings that popped out, which would give them a soft landing, at which time they became activated and sensitive to movement. We knew that they were sensitive to movement, and we had to take great care walking around in those mountains. That whole area, up in the mountains west of Hill 51, turned out to be just loaded with those damned things.

We finally came out of the mountains; Lieutenant Colonel Hilgartner directed us to the new combat base location, and we commenced to build our new home. It was called Hill 51, but it sure as hell wasn't 51 meters high. I don't think the hill stood more than 10 meters high, but the battalion CO called it Hill 51, so that's what we all called it.

As soon as we arrived at Hill 51, not more than a day or two later, on the morning of 10 May 1967, Hilgartner gave us orders. Delta Company and the battalion CP group moved out of the bivouac area and headed north in a big hurry. Charlie Company was in heavy contact with a large NVA force over the ridgeline to our north. The battle for Hill 110 had started. Several mountain peaks dominated a sharp ridgeline located between the Hill 51 Combat Base and Hill 110. We climbed to the top of the ridgeline and acted as a blocking force. We could see all the action between Charlie Company and the NVA.

> The bad guys ran around all over that valley below Charlie Company. From only a couple of clicks away, we had a good vantage point, but we were out of small arms range, so we couldn't fire on the enemy. Almost immediately, the 81 mm mortars fired all their ammo on the gooners' heads. The NVA hid in a deep saddle between Hill 110 and the mountains we stood on—in that saddle and also out in the cane fields below it.
>
> As we stood on the forward slope of the ridgeline, all of a sudden one of my platoon commanders, 2nd Lt. Larry Chmiel, gave out a big yelp. And I'll be damned if he didn't drop his drawers right there and found a 5.56 mm round stuck to the middle of his thigh, sticking out of his skin. He had obviously been hit by a spent round from an M16 fired by one of the Charlie Company Marines, so he was pretty lucky. I asked him, "Chmiel, do you really expect a Purple Heart for that wound? That doesn't look like it deserves a Purple Heart." I went on and on about that minor wound and how he didn't deserve the Purple Heart, you know, just giving him a hard time, harassing him. I'm sorry to say that a few days later he was killed in action.

Second Lt. Rick Zell, still recovering from the gunshot wound he had suffered in early May, also observed the battle for Hill 110 from a distance, but his observations came from listening to radio reports. He recalls:

> While on radio watch in the S-3 shack on the 10th of May, I heard some incoming situation reports stating that Charlie Company was in a major battle and that Alpha Company had been hit by an American air strike and had taken a whole bunch of casualties. We couldn't believe the reports at first, but when the reports continued to come in regarding Alpha Company's plight, it turned out to be true. Alpha Company had taken a direct hit from an air strike, and a whole bunch of the Marines had died and many more wounded. That was one of the worst things I ever heard over the radio during my tour in Vietnam. I felt awful; there was nothing that anyone could do. It had happened, and the results were terrible. We all felt so helpless in the rear. At first no one knew how it had happened, and to this day it still remains something of a mystery. I heard later that a forward air controller thought he saw an NVA force and called in Alpha Company's positions as an enemy concentration. He mistook the Marines for the enemy. Before he realized his mistake, it was too late. The fixed-wing jets had already hit the target and blown up the Alpha Company CP group. There was a lot of fighting going on right then, and the airborne observer mistook the Marines for NVA. It resulted in a tragedy.
>
> No one could believe what we had heard. I found myself in a state of shock,

because the initial reports were just horrific. First reports led us to believe that dozens of Marines had died; Alpha Company had been wiped out by air strikes. Rumors started circulating that the NVA had overrun Alpha after they had been hit by air strikes. All of this was really hard to take, because Alpha Company was *my* outfit. I had only been gone a little over a week, back just one day, and now my company's Marines, my Marines, were hurt badly by friendly fire. I knew that Bill Vacca was out of harm's way, because he had finally been replaced. Lt. Col. Hilgartner assigned Capt. G. L. McKay command of Alpha 1/5 on 8 May. Captain McKay survived the air strike, but he only stayed in command of Alpha Company for five days, so I never served under him. By the time I rejoined my Marines in the field, Captain McKay had returned to his duties as our communications officer, and we had a new company commander.

Lt. Col. Hilgartner remembers:

Jim Caswell's Marines continued fighting like hell, Alpha Company got hit by an air strike out of the blue, and I didn't know the 1/3 companies' exact locations. However, I knew we had the NVA trapped. I told the 81 mm mortar section to commence firing ASAP. They could see the enemy from their position, and those guys dropped their rounds right on top of the enemy's positions. They could see their targets clearly, and they adjusted their fire very effectively; the mortar crews kept shooting until their tubes got red hot. They could see their hits clearly and saw bodies fly into the air with nearly every explosion. With each direct hit, the mortar men cheered. From my viewing point, the mortar crews performed magnificently.

The memories of different combatants of a particular battle are understandably limited by their perspective. Two Marine riflemen, engaged in the same firefight but shooting from positions maybe fifty meters apart, very well can and often do remember things differently. Jim Caswell's perspective, as the company commander of the Marine rifle company engaged at point-blank range with a thousand or so NVA soldiers, differs from that of the battalion commander, who stood nearly a mile away from the fighting. As Caswell recalled many years later:

Over the previous five months we had been offered more fire support than we could ever use. We often heard from fixed-wing aircraft returning from missions with ordnance still on board who would offer to make runs for us at targets on our request. We had used naval gunfire from destroyers steaming

> off the coast in the South China Sea. We had used 8-inch howitzers, 155 mm guns, 105 mm howitzers, and 4.2-inch and 81 mm mortars. Whenever we called for heavy support, we had always received an adjusting round in less than five minutes. One day in early 1967 we fired sixty-seven rounds of 155 mm artillery at a VC platoon that had taken us under fire from across a rice paddy. I believed in the tremendous value of coordinated supporting arms in a combat situation, and Charlie Company had become very proficient in its usage. So at that moment when I knew that we had the enemy right where we wanted them, I fully expected that my FOs would be busy adjusting salvos of HE [high explosives] and WP [white phosphorus] within minutes, wreaking terrible damage on the NVA to our front. It never happened.
>
> First, we found out that the 81 mm mortars with the battalion command group were out of range. That was okay for the moment; I really wanted artillery. Around 1300 that afternoon, the battalion 81 mm mortars finally came into range and dumped all their mortar rounds on the NVA in the cane field in front of Charlie Company. This proved helpful, but the sum total of that fire mission was limited to the ammunition that they carried at the time, about forty to fifty rounds.

According to the command chronology for the 2nd Battalion, 11th Marines, the 105 mm artillery battery assigned to provide direct artillery support for the 1st Battalion, 5th Marines (Delta Battery, 2/11), and that had been providing such terrific heavy support for Charlie 1/5, executed a planned dislocation on the morning of 10 May 1967; they tore down their weapons and moved via truck convoy to a position much closer to the Marines of 1/5, near the town of Que Son. Delta Battery had established firing positions in a small "hasty combat base" several weeks earlier, but the route of march had brought the Marines of 1/5 nearly eleven kilometers north of the firebase and therefore in danger of getting close to the extreme edge of the range of Delta 2/11's artillery pieces, so they moved. Their timing could not have been worse. On the day Charlie Company needed heavy support the most, Delta Battery was towing their 105 mm artillery pieces behind six-by trucks to a better position. For some unexplained reason, neither Captain Caswell nor Lieutenant Colonel Hilgartner was made aware of the dislocation of Delta Battery. Neither did the 2/11 command element plan for any temporary artillery support for the Marines of 1/5 during Delta Battery's move. The tragic consequences of this decision hampered the Marines of Charlie Company as effectively as the NVA hammered them; the cause of this tragedy was one of those vagaries of war—just plain bad timing.

With no mortars or artillery available, Captain Caswell called for air strikes. Although air strikes did not have the accuracy of artillery or mortar support and proved more difficult to adjust fire across the battlefield, fixed-wing strikes would certainly be better than nothing. High explosive bombs and napalm could prove very dangerous to his Marines, who occupied fighting positions only a hundred meters or less from the closest enemy positions. But Caswell was willing to take the risk, and through battalion he requested air strikes on positions in the middle of the cane field.

Again Caswell would be frustrated:

> After we requested the air strikes, we received a response that simply said, "Wait, out." We didn't hear anything more from our FAC until many hours later. I found out later that shortly before I called for the air strikes, Alpha 1/5 was devastated by a mistaken friendly air strike about two clicks to the north east of our position. Five Alpha Company Marines died, and nearly twenty-five more were seriously wounded by the tragic mistake, so they canceled our air strike until the higher-ups could sort out what had happened. We finally got some air support late that afternoon, about 1630, but by that time the fight was nearly over.

Commissioned in 1962 from the NROTC program at the University of Kansas, Jerry McKay graduated from TBS as a reserve officer, augmenting to a regular commission out of TBS. Jerry's first choice of MOS was aviation, but his eyesight prevented that choice of career; his second choice was artillery, and his third, communications. He was made a field artillery officer. Jerry served in field artillery for the first two and one-half years of his career, including service as a battery forward observer with Golf Battery, 3rd Battalion, 11th Marines (assigned to support the 1st Battalion, 7th Marines) and as the assistant battalion S-3 officer and battalion gunnery officer with 3/11.

Jerry subsequently received assignment by Headquarters Marine Corps to the six-month-long Career Communications Officer School. He then served in a communications assignment with the 2nd Battalion, 6th Marines during the Dominican Republic crisis. It was from that training and experience that he was first assigned as the battalion communications officer when he joined the 1st Battalion, 5th Marines on 23 March 1967. When he arrived in Vietnam, he had primary artillery and secondary communications specialties. When he left Vietnam many months later, he was a primary infantry officer, with a secondary in artillery and a tertiary in communications. After Jerry's experiences during his tour with the 1st Battalion, 5th Marines in Vietnam, Lt. Col. Pete Hilgartner felt that Jerry would make an excellent career infantry officer, so he put in the papers to make that happen.

Jerry served as the battalion communications officer during a couple of smaller operations in the southern section of the battalion's TAOR during the remainder of March and April 1967. One memory Jerry has of those early days was the transition from the M14 to the M16. Jerry recalls, "We made the transition to the M16 while we were out on a sweep. I remember it clearly, because my M16 jammed."

Shortly after his arrival in Vietnam and his assignment as battalion communications officer, Jerry was assigned the responsibility to investigate an unfortunate incident that had resulted in a Marine's having been killed by another Marine. The incident had been reported as an accidental discharge, but Jerry's investigation determined that it had not been an accidental shooting. This incident could have reflected poorly upon the battalion commander, and Captain McKay knew that. However, his report indicated that charges should be made against the shooter, and Lieutenant Colonel Hilgartner subsequently and immediately reported those facts up the chain of command. Jerry McKay believes that that difficult but honest report resulted in mutual respect between himself and Highpockets, from one Marine officer to another.

A battalion communications officer had to ensure that all the communications gear and the Marines who operated that critically important equipment stayed up to snuff. The ability to communicate with units in the field and to higher headquarters created the lifeline of any combat outfit. In addition to those responsibilities, when the battalion CP group went into the field, Lieutenant Colonel Hilgartner would leave the H&S Company commander back at the combat base, and Capt. Jerry McKay assumed the duties of H&S Company commander in the field. Essentially, Jerry became responsible for the security of the battalion CP group when they moved outside the wire.

Every officer or enlisted man serving in the US Marine Corps is first an infantryman. However, many Marines develop additional occupational specialties (artillery, communications, intelligence, aviation, etc.), and much time is spent becoming proficient in those important fields. When called upon, however, those specialists understand that they need to stay ready to serve in an infantry capacity, often at a moment's notice, so Jerry McKay feels that his additional assignments as the field security commander during those early weeks helped him gain experience as an infantry officer, which helped him immeasurably when he was called upon to serve as an infantry officer during a major combat operation.

On 8 May 1967, during Operation Union I, Capt. Jerry McKay was assigned to take temporary command of Alpha Company when its CO became ill. Lieutenant Colonel Hilgartner needed someone to take command of Alpha Company, and having seen Captain McKay's ability to serve in a tactical infantry role during those small operations preceding Operation Union, he decided to assign Captain McKay to take over that responsibility. Highpockets obviously had a great deal of confidence in Captain McKay:

> About 1600 that afternoon, Lieutenant Colonel Hilgartner sent word that he wanted me to come over to his position. I went over there and found out

that Bill Vacca had become ill and was about to be medevaced. Hilgartner said, 'I want you to take command of Alpha. The battalion needs resupply, and I want you to move out at 0400 tomorrow morning, move to this position (indicating the position on the map), and secure an LZ so we can get resupplied.' You can imagine my surprise, since I knew the battalion had at that time other captains, one of whom even had some experience as a company commander, but at the same time I felt much honored that Pete Hilgartner was assigning me to command a reinforced rifle company in combat. Since the battalion CP group was traveling with Alpha Company, I was immediately available to take command, and I did.

At 0400 the next morning, Alpha Company moved out, headed for the designated LZ. The first thing that happened as we took off was we lost a machine gun team. They got separated from our column in the darkness, and we lost physical contact with them. We got the word that they weren't in the column, but fortunately they had a radio with them. Long story short, we got them back with us, but it was a challenge. I knew it was extremely important to get them back quickly, for many reasons. But my primary reason for this urgency was that as we moved toward the designated LZ location, a valley opened up on our left flank running perpendicular to our line of march. As dawn broke, we could see a bunch of people moving around down in that valley; people with uniforms, packs, and weapons, and they kept shooting their weapons in the air. Obviously they were trying to get us to come over; but when you looked at the situation, you could just see the ambush they were preparing for us. Lieutenant Colonel Hilgartner had emphasized that my primary mission was to move to the LZ and prepare it for resupply, so I called in a position report and told them of the enemy sighting; we focused first on getting my machine gun team back with the column, and then we continued to march. We reached the LZ location without further incident, the battalion CP group joined us shortly thereafter, and we affected our resupply. As soon as that was accomplished, Alpha Company received orders to move out once again, and from that moment forward we operated independently. The battalion CP group proceeded toward Que Son along with Delta Company.

Excerpts from the 1/5 combat after-action report for 8–10 May 1967 for Operation Union I describe the action as follows:

081710H Company A while searching for water vicinity coordinates AT 986340 [this location is approximately four kilometers due west of Hill 51] came upon a house which had 2 VC flags, expended ammunition cartridges,

1 canteen, and 1 North Vietnamese book. One Vietnamese male was apprehended near the house. Detainee and items found were forwarded to 5th Marines S-2.

091030H Company A in vicinity coordinates AT 984353 [this location is approximately 1.4 kilometers due north of the last position, at what appears to be a secondary road that runs west into the mountains and east to Que Son] apprehended one Vietnamese male age 40, without an ID card, dressed in black clothing. The detainee was questioned by Battalion S-2 and forwarded to 5th Marines S-2.

101200H Company A had completed a sweep of Phuoc Duc (2) vicinity coordinates BT 082365—[located approximately 7 kilometers east and two kilometers north of Hill 51; Alpha Company moved over 11 kilometers in one day, on foot.] and was deploying to vicinity coordinates BT 051385 [3 kilometers west of the above location] when it received fire from six automatic weapons and intense small arms fire from the northwest at a distance of 200–300 meters from vicinity coordinates BT 050387. The NVA wore khaki uniforms, carried packs, and were well entrenched. Company A was deployed and closing with the NVA positions when the center of the command post was marked with rockets from a Huey gunship. A flight of F-4 aircraft immediately strafed the Company A Command Post and the surrounding area. Company A sustained 5 USMC KIA and 24 USMC WIA from the airstrike. This airstrike was not requested or cleared by units of the 1st Battalion, 5th Marines. Company A broke contact with the enemy in order to establish security for an LZ so the wounded could be evacuated from the operational area. Heavy automatic weapons fire and mortar fire were received in the LZ. Company A returned fire with 8,000 rounds of small arms fire, 60 M-79 rounds and 20 3.5 inch WP rounds. The medical evacuations were completed at 101500H. Company A stayed at coordinates BT 051385 [a short distance north, out into the valley] to consolidate its forces and await an emergency re-supply; Company A moved to coordinates BT 049383 [up on higher ground]. As a result of the contact, Company A sustained 6 USMC KIA (5 from the airstrike) and 31 USMC WIA (24 from the airstrike). The NVA lost 3 NVA KIA confirmed, 30 NVA KIA probable and 50 NVA WIA probable.

On the morning of 10 May 1967, Alpha Company was located well east of 1/5's new combat base, Hill 51, continuing their mission of search and destroy. Having marched for over eleven kilometers since the previous morning, Alpha Company was now positioned approximately four kilometers east of Hill 110, moving east, when Lieutenant Colonel Hilgartner contacted Captain McKay and told him that

Charlie Company was in trouble and needed help, so Alpha Company turned around and rapidly moved west toward the sounds of gunfire. "As he gave us our marching orders," McKay recalled years later, "Pete told me that as we moved west there would be a river on our right flank, and that the river had been designated as a Fire Support Coordination Line (FSCL). He said, 'The Special Landing Force (SLF), made up of three companies from the 1st Battalion, 3rd Marines is on the other side of that line, so do not shoot at anyone on the other side of that river.'"

Alpha Company's Marines completed a sweep of the hamlet of Phuoc Duc (2), located about five kilometers southeast of Hill 110, and moved briskly toward the west to reinforce the beleaguered Marines of Charlie 1/5. Suddenly, Alpha Company received fire from six automatic weapons and intense small arms fire from their northwest at a distance of 200–300 meters. Captain McKay reported that these NVA wore khaki uniforms, carried packs, and appeared well entrenched. Alpha Company deployed and closed on the NVA positions; suddenly, the center of the Alpha Company command post was hit with rockets from a UH-1 Huey helicopter gunship that seemed to appear from out of nowhere. Only a few scattered clouds high in the sky disturbed the otherwise clear visibility, so the air strike was clearly a case of mistaken identity. The HUEY gunship thought it had just marked an enemy command post out in the open. A flight of F-4 Phantom aircraft immediately bombed the Alpha Company command post and the surrounding area. According to the 1/5 combat after-action report for Operation Union I, authored by Lieutenant Colonel Hilgartner, "This airstrike was not requested or cleared by units of the 1st Battalion, 5th Marines."

Jerry McKay remembers those last few minutes before the air strike as though they happened yesterday:

> We could hear the sounds of gunfire ahead of us, so we knew Charlie Company was in a major battle, but as we moved along toward them we began taking fire from that dry riverbed. There was a bunch of NVA down in that riverbed. We were headed due west, with a fairly steep mountain on our left flank, with an open area on our right, and the NVA were hitting us from our right flank.
>
> I had no radio communications with anyone except the 1/5 Battalion CP, so I couldn't talk directly with anyone in the SLF. I had deployed my Marines in an attack formation, two platoons abreast up front and one platoon back, in reserve, and my CP group stayed right behind the attack force. That's when my CP got marked with smoke rockets fired from a Huey gunship. We didn't even know they were there until the rockets impacted. That was a memorable moment. The rockets came in, and I saw that they were smoke rockets, so I

immediately knew what was going on. Our position had just been marked for an air strike.

I looked up, and as I looked up I saw two F-4 Phantom jets and watched as four 250-pound Snake Eye bombs dropped off those Marine jets and the fins deployed. I got the command group up and running, because I knew that if we stayed in that location we would be in a really bad situation. The Snake Eyes went over my head and got one of my lead platoons. My FAC, a corporal by the name of Madeira, was doing everything he could to get in touch with those jets, and finally he was able to get a green star cluster up above us when the jets started their second run, so they broke off their second run. I got a report from the stricken platoon that they had five Marines dead and over twenty wounded. We had our hands full. That air strike just stopped us in our tracks. My only main concern at that point was to get the company consolidated so we could protect ourselves and to get my dead and wounded out of there.

As we started the medevacs, every helicopter that came in to take out the wounded was fired upon, so we were also starting to run low on ammunition. We had to call in an emergency resupply by helicopter during the middle of the medical evacuations. As all of this went on, we continued to call in air strikes against the enemy positions in the dry riverbed.

Once able to evacuate the wounded and dead, we moved up to our left on that mountainside and established a defensive perimeter up there. We continued to call in air strikes on that dry riverbed all night long.

The next morning, after it was all over and we got ready to move out (at one point Alpha Company reestablished flank security for the battalion), I had a visit from a Marine colonel from the 1st Marine Air Wing (1st MAW). He landed in a helicopter, came over to me, and asked, "Captain, why were you out of position?" I replied, "Colonel, I was not out of position. The FSCL is right over there (pointing out the dry riverbed), I was going in that direction, and I was exactly where my battalion commander told me to be. I was not out of position." He looked at me, turned around, got on his helicopter, and flew away.

Thinking back on that day, and this is pure speculation on my part, I think the fact that the NVA were between me and the SLF, and that they were firing in both directions (at us and at the SLF), I believe that 1/3 mistook us for the enemy and called in that air strike on us. I could see the Marines of 1/3 from our position, so I know that they could see me. They were taking fire from the NVA between us, and my speculation is that they saw us come up on that high ground, assumed we were the enemy, and called in that air strike. Unfortunately, it was a very effective air strike.

Tragically, several entries in the combat after-action report for Operation Beaver Cage, dated 17 May 1967, written by the headquarters of the 1st Battalion, 3rd Marines, support Jerry McKay's contention that the headquarters group of 1st Battalion, 3rd Marines, situated a couple of kilometers to their northeast, mistook Alpha 1/5's Marines for the enemy and called in an air strike on them. According to that report, on the evening of 9 May, Battalion Landing Team 1/3 issued a frag order for a sweep operation east, toward the coast, starting early in the morning. The following are pertinent entries in the 1/3 combat after-action report:

> 100730—Co's B and C at Phase Line Alpha on north south line from 0241 through 020387 [a location about three kilometers east and slightly north of Alpha 1/5's position at the time, on the high ground on the other side of the valley] continuing sweep to the east [toward Alpha 1/5]. Co D in trace moving down center of valley.
>
> 100740—Bravo Co receiving SAF and automatic weapons fire from Hill 110 at 033386.
>
> 100750—Co C firing mortars on Hill 110, Co B returning fire on Hill 110 with 60 and 81 mm mortars, 3.5 rockets and automatic weapons. Request for UH1E gunship support.
>
> 100820—Hill 110 being worked over by Gunships and automatic fire.
>
> 100830—Co B reports one WIA. Request Med-Evac.
>
> 100848—Co B reports VC moving toward Co B from left rear. Request Co C to check it out and assist.
>
> 100849—Co D reports Co C, 1/5 is 300 meters west of Hill 110 moving east.
>
> 100853—Co B taking heavy sniper fire. Reports 20 VC moving East.
>
> 100915—Co B taking mortar fire at a rate of one round per minute.
>
> 100925—Co B pinned down by heavy fire, suffering unknown number of KIA and WIA. Requesting close air support. Co C [1/3] attempting to envelope village at 035395 [Nghi Trung (2)] with one platoon to stop enemy fire from that vicinity. Enveloping platoon receiving mortar fire.
>
> 100935—Co C, 1/5 moving toward Hill 110 sweep toward the east. Airstrike will be run on Hill 110 prior to sweep.
>
> 100949—Co B reports one company of VC wearing green uniforms and helmets, well camouflaged and entrenched on Hill 110.
>
> 100951—Co C has one platoon pinned down by heavy fire from village Nghi Trung (2) at 035395 [about one kilometer due north of Hill 110, out in the center of the valley].
>
> 101025—Airstrike run on VIC 033385 [Hill 110]. 5 VC KIA (Prob) and a

secondary explosion. Airstrike also run at coord 025384 [eastern flank of Hill 110].

101039—Co C, 1/5 sweeping Hill 110, has control of objective. Co C needs help on left flank. Withdrawing platoon from right flank to assist left flank platoon pinned down by heavy fire.

101045—One platoon of Co D moving down to left flank to assist Co C. Co B reports VC moving east away from Hill 110.

101054—Co C has VC in trench line directly in front of position delivering heavy fire. Units are pinned down.

101210—Heavy contact continuing. Airstrike run on Coord. 044387. 50% coverage of target. [This target coordinate marks a spot approximately 400–500 meters west and slightly north of Alpha 1/5's reported location, out in a low area adjacent to the hamlet of Nghi Thuong (5). This information brings in the possibility that the air strike was not targeting Alpha 1/5, but that the Huey spotted them and marked them, and the air strikes hit the marked target, Alpha Company].

111100—1/3 Casualties reported for action on 10 May 1967. Friendly: 22 KIA, 62 WIAE, 26 WIANE; Enemy: 86 KIA (Conf).

Eyewitness accounts of (then) Capt. Gerald L. McKay and Lt. Col. Peter Hilgartner, and the command chronologies and after-action reports from both 1/5 and 1/3, reveal that interbattalion communications challenges played a large part in this tragedy. Had the various company commanders, and in particular the two battalion commanders involved, been able to communicate consistently and effectively throughout this battle, this tragedy might have been avoided. Further, the NVA regiment trapped in the cane field that day could easily have been completely sealed off and then systematically destroyed in place by supporting arms.

This incident is one of those tragic examples of what can happen when communications break down in the middle of a battle and things start to go wrong. Or, as the mud Marines referred to this phenomenon frequently: "Shit happens."

The personal experiences of Capt. Jerry McKay, USMC, are also an excellent example of the importance of one of the fundamental precepts of the US Marine Corps: "Every Marine is a rifleman." Essentially, every Marine knows that he is first an infantryman, a grunt. Captain McKay was initially an artillery officer and then became proficient as a communications officer, but he never forgot the importance of his infantry training, and he knew that he might be called upon to serve as an infantry leader. His experience with Pete Hilgartner as his field commander helped him gain practical knowledge of what is expected of a Marine infantry officer in combat, and he was able to take command and to function extremely well under very adverse conditions.

By the time he left Vietnam, Capt. Jerry McKay had gained invaluable experience as an infantry company commander under fire, and this knowledge and experience served him well in his career. He retired in August 1991 as a brigadier general of Marines and went on to serve after his retirement as the chief operating officer of the Marine Corps Heritage Center, one of the key contributors in building the new National Museum of the Marine Corps in Quantico, Virginia.

At this point in the battle for Hill 110, early on the afternoon of 10 May 1967, as Alpha Company's Marines struggled to deal with the carnage wreaked by the air strike, Charlie Company had been engaged with the enemy on Hill 110 for nearly three hours. Captain Caswell felt that the enemy commander finally figured out that he had nothing to fear from American artillery, mortars, and air strikes, so he became emboldened. Shortly after that the NVA launched the first of many ground attacks on the Marine positions on Hill 110. Caswell speculates that the NVA had tried, unsuccessfully, to break out of the cane fields to the north, turned back by the other Marine companies now surrounding them, so they tried to attack Caswell's men on Hill 110. Caswell remembers:

> I radioed the 1st Platoon and ordered them to move up on line by moving to their right around the hill and linking up with the 2nd Platoon. That gave us a horseshoe-shaped defense and freed up all our firepower to the front. As the 1st Platoon accomplished this maneuver under fire, the 1st Platoon's radio operator, Pfc. Lauff, got shot and rolled all the way to the bottom of the hill. Communications with the platoons came largely by runners. At this point, the outcome of the battle rested firmly in the hands of the platoon commanders, squad leaders, and fire team leaders. Alone at the foot of the hill, Pfc. Lauff stayed in radio contact with us all day long, even though he was painfully wounded several more times. He reported on the movements of the enemy as they mounted flanking assaults and frontal assaults. We attempted to relay this information to the platoons. The three platoons began repulsing assault after assault, sometimes at point blank range.

Throughout that long and deadly afternoon, Captain Caswell called the command groups of both 1/5 and 1/3 repeatedly, begging for artillery and air strikes, but no artillery fired on the NVA that afternoon, and the air strikes arrived very late in the day. Caswell asked for the companies of 1/3 to mount some sort of attack on the enemy positions, but no attacks came. Seething with frustration and anger, Caswell recalls, "The companies of 1/3 never seemed to move, indicating that their commander had committed his reserve in the same zone of action as his engaged companies. The worst possible thing a Marine commander could do, it resulted in all his units being engaged with the same enemy force in the same terrain and left him no maneuvering element. The S-3 of 1/3, a friend of mine from Amphibious Warfare School, asked me at one point on the radio if we were in danger of being overrun. I replied that we were. He asked me how I could remain so calm."

Throughout the rest of that long afternoon, the Marines of Charlie 1/5 started passing their M16s to the top of the hill to have the jams cleared. They used all the rifles of the dead and wounded. Caswell didn't think that things could get any worse, but they *were* made worse, horribly worse, by the constant jamming of the M16 rifles. "The jams," Caswell remembered, "largely caused by double feeding, were not due to the baloney that 'the troops weren't keeping them clean,' because every Charlie 1/5 Marine cleaned his rifle several times a day. We figured out later that faulty ammunition caused the jams. The extractor ripped the base off the cartridge in the chamber, and then another round loaded inside the old cartridge, causing the jam. The Charlie Company CP group used cleaning rods to clear the jams, like in an assembly line, and then we would send them back down the hill."

Jim Caswell spent most of that day in a rage directed at battalion for giving his Marines no fire support, directed at the Fire Support Coordination Center that could not handle the situation with Alpha Company and still give them air support, and directed at the artillery crews that were not firing for them. At one point that afternoon Caswell became certain that he was witnessing the death knell of the Marine infantry company known as Charlie 1/5. He recalls his fear and frustration:

> I formed the CP group into a secondary perimeter on the reverse slope of the hill and told them if any NVA came over the top of the hill to kill them. The members of the command group included the radio operators and forward observers, the acting company gunnery sergeant, the 60 mm mortar crews, and the wounded who had been brought back to the top of the hill. They possessed hardly any rifles among them and no automatic weapons. When I told them we would hold this position, they all just nodded and checked their pistols. No one said, "We have no rifles; we have no machine guns." They had a few grenades and their M1911A1 .45-caliber pistols and two extra magazines each. They made sure they had a round in the chamber, left the pistol cocked, put on the safety, and put it back in their holster. Then they returned to their work. They knew that if the NVA had broken through and attacked our secondary perimeter, they couldn't have held the hill for ten minutes, but they just nodded, checked their pistols, and went back to work. I became absolutely determined that we would not move off the hill or leave any of our dead or wounded behind.

> I halfway expected that the NVA would penetrate our thin outer perimeter somewhere, but the troops had other ideas. In order to flank us, the NVA had to move to an assault position on the saddle to our right. The NVA couldn't try our left flank because they would expose themselves to the 1/3 Marines on the other side of the rice paddies. The noise the NVA made climbing the hill, the information we continued to receive from Pfc. Lauff, and the vigilance and determination of the Charlie 1/5 Marines demolished every one of their attempts to flank us.
>
> The NVA commander finally resorted to frontal attacks, but our machine gun fire, rifle fire, M79 rounds, and hand grenades met each attack furiously and blunted them. The enemy commander knew that we could probably bring our murderous supporting arms into play sometime soon; he knew he was running out of time.

About 1600, the enemy began to disengage, and then air support finally arrived on station over the battlefield. The fixed-wing aircraft began making runs with 250-pound general-purpose Snake Eye bombs and napalm. Under cover of the air strikes, Captain Caswell began moving his casualties to the top of the hill.

Del Best remembers those last few hours of the battle:

> Finally, orders came down that anyone who had air panels should crawl out a little ways in front of our lines and lay them out, because air strikes were on their way.[4] I had one, so I crawled out and laid my panel out the best that I could, because although it was dangerous to crawl out in the open, I'd rather do that than be hit by bombs and napalm. Not much later, the Phantoms came in right over our heads and dropped their napalm. The napalm hit the grassy area right at the bottom of the hill, just in front of the cane. I could feel the heat from it; that's how close we lay to the enemy lines. We weren't quite halfway down from the top of Hill 110, about a hundred meters from the enemy lines, where the napalm hit. I remember after the air strike, things started to settle down, and we started bringing up the wounded, and then we went back down the hill and brought up the dead.

Caswell's Marines succeeded in getting all the dead and wounded Marines up to the top of the hill, and then he called for medevacs. As soon as things calmed down and it became apparent the enemy had withdrawn, Lance Cpl. Bill Pettway, the company radio operator, and Lance Corporal Ramsey, the battalion radio operator, asked Captain Caswell if he would watch the radios. They wanted to help move the wounded up the hill, so Caswell watched the radios and the radio operators helped carry the wounded. They particularly wanted to find their friend, Private First Class Lauff. Absolutely sure Lauff was still alive, the two radio operators scrambled down the hill and quickly found their buddy, still alive, although seriously wounded. Lauff was medevaced with the others.

Two of the three US Navy corpsmen assigned to Charlie 1/5 died that afternoon, and the third corpsman gallantly and tirelessly worked to ease the suffering and save the lives of the nearly forty Charlie Company Marines wounded in action that day. HM3 John C. "Doc" Tate, from Seattle, Washington, and HN William R. "Doc" Fowler, from Rome, Georgia, both lost their lives that day trying to save the lives of US Marines. About thirty-five Charlie 1/5 Marines were wounded badly enough to require medical evacuation, which was finally completed that evening.

Harold Thrasher, one of the many wounded, remembers feeling very relieved as the battle wound down:

> They put me on the last chopper out of Hill 110 late that evening, along with a couple more wounded guys and a few dead bodies. The dead guys' bodies were pretty torn up, not a pretty sight.
>
> The thing I remember most about that day was learning how to play dead really good. We were all exposed to enemy gunfire, with no cover, and pinned down, and if we moved the enemy would open up on us. At one point, as I lay there on my face playing dead, one of the other Marines in my squad thought I really *was* dead, so he crawled over behind me, put his rifle on my body and started firing on the enemy, using me as cover. I cussed him out.
>
> I did another stupid thing. One of the guys didn't have a weapon for some reason. I saw him over there and asked him if he was in a good position to fire, and he said yes, so like a dummy I passed my M16 over to him. No sooner had I done this very stupid thing, we started to hear some guys talking about the enemy getting ready to come up to get us. I started hollering at him, "Where's my rifle, where's my rifle?" but now he wouldn't talk to me. So, I got out my grenades and straightened the pins on them and I said to myself, well, I'll use these. But, finally, he gave me my rifle back, and the NVA never did come up that hill after us. But when I thought about all this later, I knew that I had been really stupid and wondered why in the world I would do something that stupid. I found out later that this Marine's M16 had jammed, and he got so frustrated he hit a big rock with it and busted the stock off it.
>
> We trained stateside with the M14, qualified with them. During my stateside training I fired exactly ten rounds through an M16. When I arrived in Vietnam, they issued me an M16. Everyone had a lot of problems with their M16s. They had two different types of ammo—fast burn and slow burn—and

they told us not to mix them. Every time we stopped to take five, we had our toothbrushes out cleaning our weapons, because the M16 was just not very dependable.

Pfc. Harold Thrasher's painful memories of the Battle for Hill 110 remain vivid to this day:

> I was so scared I made a lot of promises to God. I know I haven't kept all those promises because there were so many of them. I was scared. When I was a kid I had liked to play war games, watch war movies. On Hill 110 I learned that kids' games are nothing like the real thing. I think everybody wants to be a hero, but when you're scared you're shaking in your boots.
>
> My wounds were really not very severe; I had some shrapnel in my hand. Some of the shrapnel had hit the ligament that connected my thumb with my hand and had swollen up about the size of a golf ball, so I had lost the use of my hand, but I wasn't really hit badly. I really didn't want to get on the medevac chopper, because the previous choppers had all received enemy fire when they left the LZ. I went up to the gunny supervising the medevacs. I told him that I didn't think I was bad enough to be medevaced. I wasn't brave. I just didn't want to get on the choppers because they were getting shot at, and I felt sure that the one I got on would get shot down. But the gunny looked at my wound and told me that I had to be medevaced because the wound was likely to get infected, and then I'd really have some trouble.

Harold Thrasher flew to the 1st Medical Battalion in Da Nang, and the following morning another chopper flew him and a few others out to the USS *Repose*. He spent eighteen days on the *Repose* and then returned to Charlie Company for duty.

Pfc. Richard Schlagel managed to avoid any wounds on Hill 110, but he carries the memories of that long, terrible day like a physical scar:

> I remember feeling terribly thirsty. I only carried one canteen at that time, and I ran out of water fairly quickly. Someone hollered for more water for the wounded, but we never got any resupply. At one point I saw a black Marine, Private First Class Washington, sitting up a few meters off to my right (as I looked down the other side of the hill), and I hollered over to him to see if he had any extra water. I couldn't figure out why he was sitting up in the midst of enemy small arms rounds coming in thick. He didn't answer me; he looked asleep or something. I couldn't believe that this Marine could sleep right in the middle of this horrendous battle, so I crawled over to him. He still didn't

respond, so I shook him, and he fell over, dead. I hollered for the corpsman, and then saw that Washington had two full canteens, so I took the water and crawled back over to my fighting position. I threw one of the canteens over to the guy on my left. We moved forward further, and I could now see that almost no cover or concealment remained on the top and the front of that hill.

I saw Rusty down below me, maybe fifteen meters down below me, trying to take cover behind some small rocks and scrub trees. Someone hollered up to me to throw some grenades out past him. I really didn't want to stand up, so I got up on my knees and threw a grenade over their heads. Evidently I hadn't thrown it far enough, because after it went off, the guys down below me hollered up to me, saying, 'What in the hell are you trying to do, kill us?' They said to throw the grenades farther down the hill and over to the left, at a tree lying down on its side. So, I threw the rest of my grenades as far down the hill as I could, and a little over to the left. I stood up and managed to throw them far enough that time.

I completely lost all track of time. New in Vietnam, I couldn't really tell the difference between enemy and friendly firing, but there was sure a hell of a lot of shooting going on throughout that day. I can remember this one Marine who had arrived in Vietnam a few weeks after I did. He was really green, and I had spoken to him briefly and he had asked me about things out in the field, and I had told him that it wasn't too bad. He got shot several times on Hill 110 and was medevaced. I think he survived his wounds, but he must have thought that the Vietnam War was extremely deadly, if this experience wasn't considered "too bad."

We made a couple of trips down the hill to pick up the dead and the wounded. I especially felt bad for Lance Cpl. Fred Tate; he had already been in Vietnam over a year and was about to rotate back home. He only had two or three days left on his tour, and he had said he was too short to be in the field. But then he died on Hill 110. They finally got some choppers in to get the wounded out late that evening, but they had to leave the dead on the hill that night. Medevacs for the wounded had a very high priority, as did resupply. But the dead guys had to wait.

John Rusth's memories of the final hours of that battle remain equally vivid:

We didn't have any communications, because the mortar round that killed Gunny and Tate had also blown up Tate's radio, so we had to rely on runners. Captain Caswell and the company CP group stayed at the top of the hill.

> Finally, after what seemed like many, many hours, we saw some Phantom jets. We hadn't received any artillery or air support all afternoon, but finally the Phantoms came in and dropped their bombs and napalm at the base of the hill. The Phantoms came in so low, and so close to us, that I can remember looking straight across as the jet went across our front and clearly seeing the pilot in his cockpit as he dropped his loads. We started carrying wounded Marines up the hill under the cover of the air strikes.
>
> As I made my last trip up the hill with a wounded Marine, I got hit by two enemy rounds, both in the legs, and my rifle got shot up. I still carried an M14 because we experienced so much trouble with the M16s, but it got shot and disabled. I think one of my wounds occurred when my M14 got hit and some of the shrapnel hit me. I was later medevaced out with some of the dead bodies.

Sgt. Hillous York felt strongly that Cpl. John Rusth had earned the Medal of Honor that day. Rusty saved many lives that afternoon and deserved as much recognition as possible: "Rusty came to my platoon as a 'peach-fuzz' greenie, but that day on Hill 110, Rusty proved himself a true hero. John Rusth gave everything that day, everything except his life. We all owe him a lot for his courageous actions."

Awarded the Navy Cross, America's second highest decoration for valor, John Rusth doesn't think of himself as a hero. He thinks of himself as a combat Marine, a Charlie 1/5 Marine, a man who somehow managed to survive a chaotic battle. "I remember the unbelievable confusion during the Battle for Hill 110, but throughout that day I also knew that all the Charlie 1/5 Marines did the best they could. Most of us stayed really scared. I just helped out like anyone else would have done, taking those guys up the hill. I don't know why I got singled out to get the Navy Cross, because a lot of other guys did the same thing I did."

To this day, John Rusth downplays what he did on 10 May 1967. He will tell you that he only did what anyone would do, that many other Marines did the same thing. In truth, many Marines of Charlie 1/5 fought like demons that day, and many of them were heroes; but the fact remains that Lance Cpl. John "Rusty" Rusth made ten rescue trips from the hell at the bottom of the hill to the relative safety of the top of the hill, saving a fellow Marine from certain death each and every time, while under hellacious enemy fire every step of the way. Rusty would have made even more trips down that damnable hill, but enemy gunfire finally stopped him. After the battle, no one had any disagreement about who should receive recognition and a citation for bravery under fire; John "Rusty" Rusth got the recognition that he richly deserved, the Navy Cross. Still, Rusty only talks about what the others did that day: "When I got hit, Private Wallace took care of me. He was a Marine who had been in the service for almost five years. Wallace was the man who dragged me up that hill so that I survived."

Rusty also blames the Marines' weapons for the number of dead and wounded that day: "We had a lot of trouble with the M16s during the Battle for Hill 110. I saw guys who threw their rifle as far as they could because it had jammed. I saw dead Marines with jammed rifles with their cleaning rod in their hands. Everybody carried their cleaning rod, extended, tied to their backpack, so that they could grab it quickly when their M16 jammed, which happened all the time. But the M14 worked flawlessly. You still had to keep it clean, but mine got wet and fired every time."

Amid the heroics exhibited on Hill 110, human frailty was also in evidence. Rusty remembers:

> For a while we couldn't get any medevac helicopters in, because of the air strikes, but finally we got the medevac choppers for the seriously wounded. Our one remaining Corpsman worked almost constantly that afternoon, patching up wounded and dying Marines. Late that afternoon, I remember looking across that hill as a helicopter got ready to lift off. I saw the new second lieutenant walk up to the helicopter. He was wounded. He had been hit in the head, but he wasn't as bad off as the guy in the door of the helicopter. He pulled that badly wounded Marine out of the helicopter and climbed on board. I guess he wanted to leave Hill 110. We never saw that lieutenant again.
>
> I left on the last CH-46 to fly out of Hill 110 that night. All the emergency medevacs had already flown out, and so I flew with some of the dead bodies. I remember making that flight with the body of Lance Cpl. David Suapaia from Honolulu, Hawaii, as well as a few of the others. I don't remember seeing Gunny Cruz's body on the helicopter, though. As we lifted off, and I could see the guys still on the hill, I remember thinking that they weren't going to make it through the night. I felt certain that Hill 110 would be overrun and that everyone left behind would die.
>
> I heard later from some of the guys that we interrogated some of the villagers and learned that the NVA had been operating in this area for several weeks, preparing for us all that time. I remembered having the distinct feelings that the VC led us into this NVA trap, and it appears as though that's what happened.
>
> I had mixed feelings when the helicopter started to land in Da Nang. I felt a sense of relief, because after sleeping on the ground for nearly four weeks, without a bath or hot food in all that time, I knew I was headed for a hospital, food, and clean sheets. At the same time I couldn't stop worrying about the

rest of the guys on Hill 110. The corpsmen joked around quite a bit. Another Marine outfit had been hit by the NVA, and the corpsmen joked that their business was booming, but they did a good job. I didn't have to wait around very long before the corpsmen started working on me.

They put me in a tent with a breeze blowing through. I had a bed with clean sheets. I felt like I had walked into a whole different world. After only a couple of days, they took me on a C-130 to Cam Ranh Bay into an Air Force hospital. I didn't get hit that badly. They had to leave my wound open for a few days, so it wasn't comfortable to walk for a couple of days, but then this doctor sewed it shut.

I ran into an Air Force chaplain there from Oregon, where I grew up. I recognized him; he had served for a while at Kingsley Field in Klamath Falls, Oregon, my hometown. A major in the Air Force, he was nice enough to show me around the base at Cam Ranh Bay, once I got up on my feet again. I spent a couple of weeks there, and when my wounds fully healed, in June, I rejoined the battalion. I went back to the 3rd Platoon of Charlie Company. I flew into Tam Ky on a helicopter. Got to Hill 51, the new 1/5 combat base at Que Son, on a Sunday morning.

Just as I arrived, I could hear people singing "Rock of Ages" in a Catholic church in the adjacent village of Que Son, and I remember feeling amazed that Vietnamese Catholics lived out here.

When I finally got back with the 3rd Platoon, I was happy to see the guys, but they had just gotten back to the compound, and they smelled really bad. I had had the luxury of taking showers every day for a few weeks and had forgotten that I had stunk like they did, but I remembered very quickly.

Sgt. Hillous York stayed so busy during that long, hot day, 10 May 1967, that events started to blend together, but his memories, forty-five years after the battle, remain excruciatingly vivid: "After we had finally gotten our badly wounded to the top of the hill, I went back down to where my men still fought, holding firm. I then went around to the right side, down the hill, and heard the crack of a rifle, and someone screamed. I figured out that shot came from an enemy sniper, but I couldn't see him. I heard him fire twice more, and then he finally moved, and I saw him. He had on a brown uniform and had a scope on his rifle. This time my M16 smoked. Scratch one NVA sniper." Sergeant York had done his duty again.

He continued:

The volume of fire from the AK-47s and M16s was tremendous, but we kept holding them. As time went on that day we took more casualties, but they took even more. Finally, around 1600 we got some fixed-wing aircraft on station. We all hoped these aircraft would hit the right target. My radio operator had one of those orange panels, and he spread it out on the ground. I called the pilot on the FAC frequency and hollered, "Do you see me, do you see me, do you see me?" The next thing I knew I saw an F-4 Phantom coming down on us. I had told him danger close, two hundred meters, but someone on the radio had said, "Negative." The damn pilot made a dry run on his first pass, and I got so frustrated I got on the radio and said a few things I probably should not have said. I got really, really mad because we had not had any support all day long, and then we finally got an air strike, and the pilot had not dropped his bombs on his first run.

He came back around, and dropped a couple of 250-pound Snake Eye bombs right on the back edge of the cane field. The NVA remained in the cane field, trying to stay hidden. The bombs detonated so close to us that a lot of the shrapnel flew over our heads. After two F-4s made bombing runs, I saw many NVA try to escape the cane field by climbing up the side of the hill on our right. Then another flight came in, this time A-4 Skyhawks. They made several strafing runs with their 20 mm cannons, and then the Crusaders came in and shot off several rockets. All of this took place under three hundred meters from our positions.

When the planes finished their bombing and strafing runs, the volume of fire started to ease up. We fought on a little while longer, and then the NVA just broke off. We finally got the rest of the wounded and the dead to the top of the hill, and a short while later some choppers arrived, medevaced our wounded, and dropped off the resupplies that we desperately needed.

During the entire fight, we fought at point-blank range, measured in feet. Charlie Company held that ground without giving an inch. A little strip of grass, like someone's front yard, maybe fifteen feet across, separated the base of the hill and the cane field. We stayed on the base of the hill, with very little concealment and no cover, and the NVA stayed right inside the cane fields. We fought the NVA from midmorning to late afternoon, continuously. My Marines didn't give in as much as an inch. They fought with courage, and they did not yield. When called on, they answered; every rifleman, every fire team leader, every squad leader, and every weapons team. They assumed responsibility and gave everything they had in them. That's what made the Marines of Charlie 1/5 win out on Hill 110.

After the battle, I asked some of my men to count the enemy bodies lying just in that narrow strip of grass in front of us, right in front of the cane field. They counted forty-four NVA bodies in that narrow strip of grass. We could see a lot more enemy bodies out in the cane fields and on the north side of Hill 110.

The enemy outnumbered us, they outgunned us, we had no artillery support, we had no air support, and our damned M16s jammed over and over again. My own M16 jammed at least twice during the fighting on Hill 110, and I know that many more of those damned things jammed that day. But despite all of that, Charlie Company held. Captain Caswell, a determined man, had the will to win, and he proved himself an exceptional company commander. Other company commanders may have been as good, but none better than Capt. R. J. Caswell. But by the same token, the Marines on Hill 110 owed a lot to Capt. Buck Darling, who had led the company for several months before Captain Caswell took over. Captain Darling was also a company commander who never backed up from the enemy, and he taught us a lot. Captain Darling taught us that we could never give an inch; that we just had to stand and fight the sons-of-bitches. Every man in Charlie Company owed a lot to both Captain Darling and Captain Caswell.

Jim Coxen's memories of 10 May 1967 still haunt him to this day:

We had a guy named Pfc. Dorian Houser who got killed there. I saw him get killed. He should never have gone in the service in the first place. It seemed like someone had to always keep an eye on him. During the peak of the battle, Dorian tried to hide behind a small bush, when he got hit dead center by a direct-fire weapon, a 57 mm recoilless rifle round. There one moment, the next moment he just completely blew up.

I remember feeling very frustrated when they ordered us to charge down Hill 110. I mean, here we go again, "Semper Fi, Do or Die," and charge down the hill. You know, some things are just dumb. After you had been in Vietnam a while, you could figure out the difference between the dumb stuff and the stuff that wasn't dumb. Everyone knew that charging down that hill was just plain dumb. The anger and frustration I felt nearly overwhelmed me, and I had a kind of fatalistic knowledge that I knew they would get us this time, but we still charged down that hill. I also remember arriving on top of the hill later on, seeing all the wounded guys lying about. It seemed like a million of them. Of course there weren't that many, but a lot of my buddies lay there, hurt really badly. I had run out of M79 rounds, scrambling around trying to find ammo for everyone. Since I had run out of ammo for the M79, I crawled around and found an M16 and scrounged magazines from dead and wounded Marines and continued to fight with the M16. I was one of the lucky few who didn't have any jams with the M16 on Hill 110. The guy I took it off of must have taken really good care of his weapon, or must have been really lucky, because it worked fine. We shot way too much at the start of the battle, but then maybe that convinced them that we outnumbered them. We all carried double and triple loads of ammo, and we still nearly ran out. Standing on top of that hill, seeing all the dead and wounded Marines, wondering if medevacs or resupply choppers would ever arrive, I got very angry and extremely frustrated.

The carnage was really hard to believe. We kept saying, "Man, are they just going to leave us out here?" We knew there were a lot of enemy soldiers, and we knew we were pretty much on our own. No one ever came to reinforce us during the battle. No one came to Hill 110 until well after the battle ended. I can remember feeling very fatalistic, wondering if, since we had survived this incredible battle, if they would let us get back into a rear area for a while. But the next day we just mounted up again and continued the mission.

The end of the Battle for Hill 110 did not mark the end, or even the beginning of the end, of this war—or even this particular combat operation, for that matter—and the Marines of Charlie 1/5 knew it. Those who had fought on Hill 110 knew that they faced many more long and difficult days in the weeks and months ahead.

Delbert Best remembers those final hours on Hill 110 and the next few days following the battle, although his memories come back to him through the thick fog of time:

I thought it would be my last day on this earth, but somehow I survived that day, 10 May 1967. I went down on the patrol the next day, the day after the big fight—the patrol that took General Walt [who had flown in on his command chopper on 11 May], Highpockets, and Captain Caswell down to the base of the hill. We found mass graves at the base of the hill, in a wide grassy area, and dug up some bodies. If these were Vietnamese, they sure were big Vietnamese. I kinda think they were Chinese, but I don't really know for sure. They seemed really big in comparison with the Vietnamese men we saw every day, the civilians, the ARVN, and the VC. The NVA had dug a bunch of holes and dumped their dead bodies in them; they weren't hard to find, since a bunch of arms and legs stuck up out of the ground. They had full combat uniforms on.

As the fight for Hill 110 ended, the platoons attempted to regain radio contact with the command group. After the loss of two radio operators and two platoon commanders, radio communications within the company suffered. As the air strikes began to come in, and the NVA began to pull back, Marines picked up radios and opened communications again to report enemy movements, casualties and so forth. The first person on the company radio net asked for Charlie Six Actual. Captain Caswell answered. The voice on the other end said, "This is Sergeant Sanchez. Please move the air strikes further out; they're hitting too close to us. Out." As usual, Sergeant Sanchez moved all over the battlefield, ending up where needed most. Jim Caswell remembers, "He wasn't tall and Anglo-Saxon, and he wasn't as big as a house. Our John Wayne was a medium-height, medium-build, Hispanic sergeant of Marines from Texas named Juan Sanchez."

Charlie 1/5 finally received resupply of food and ammo that evening, and Jim Caswell sent some of his surviving Marines back to the village they had passed through earlier that morning for water. Caswell also evacuated the two VC suspects picked up that morning, who somehow remained alive and under the control of the company CP group, on one of the medevac choppers. The Marines of Charlie 1/5 retrieved the bodies of their fallen comrades and all the weapons they could find so that they would not fall into the hands of the enemy. Caswell formed a defensive perimeter around the top of Hill 110 for the night. Patrols from other companies crossing Charlie Company's front reported "hundreds of NVA bodies and a large amount of equipment."

Suicide Charlie, with the dark nickname that other companies often used when referring to the Marines of Charlie 1/5, had somehow survived the battle for Hill 110 against huge odds and with very little heavy fire support. The two hundred or so Marines of Suicide Charlie faced and fought a force of over a thousand NVA regulars, and despite all that went wrong, the Marines prevailed, essentially destroying a key NVA regiment.

Charlie's company commander, Jim Caswell, went over the events of 10 May 1967 in his mind repeatedly during the next few days. He simply could not figure out what had gone wrong with his ability to use supporting arms. He would not find out until many years later about the relocation of Delta Battery, 2/11, which resulted in no artillery support. He learned about the unfortunate incident involving Marine air and Alpha Company quickly enough. Although Charlie Company's Marines bore the major brunt of the Battle for Hill 110, what happened to Alpha Company's Marines that day was in many ways much worse.

Jim Caswell attributes the survival of Charlie 1/5 that day to the skill of the individual Marine with his personal weapon (despite the damnable jamming that plagued them), hand grenades, and especially the crew-served weapons teams. Although they killed hundreds of NVA that day and wounded many more, Charlie 1/5 lost only ten dead, including eight US Marines and two US Navy corpsmen, and nearly forty wounded, most of them serious enough to require medical evacuation. It was a loss made small by comparison with the havoc wreaked on the NVA, but it was a huge loss for the Marines of Charlie 1/5. During seven savage hours of fighting on 10 May 1967, nearly one out of every four Marines in Charlie Company either died or received wounds bad enough to require medical evacuation. The battle for Hill 110 during Operation Union I was the deadliest single day of combat for the Marines of Charlie Company, 1st Battalion, 5th Marines during the entire Vietnam War.

Captain Caswell declared Hill 110 secure by 1830 that evening, after nearly nine hours of intense combat, and Lieutenant Colonel Hilgartner ordered Delta Company to link up with and reinforce Charlie Company. With Delta Company's assistance, Charlie Company consolidated its positions on Hill 110, evacuated its wounded and dead, and received emergency ammunition resupply.

Charlie Company conducted a thorough search of the area and initially reported sustaining eight KIA and 37 WIA, while the 3rd Platoon from Charlie Company counted more than forty enemy bodies in the open ground just in front of the cane field. From all appearances, the NVA's losses that day were high. Over the next few weeks, several hastily dug NVA mass burial sites were uncovered, indicating a much higher enemy casualty toll than initially reported.

Many years later, Col. Peter Hilgartner, USMC (Ret), stated unequivocally, "I think Hillous York, Jim Caswell, and John Rusth are real heroes. The reason that the outcome of the Battle for Hill 110 was so good was because of Jim Caswell's calm leadership under fire and because of guys like John Rusth and Hillous York."

After submitting his report of the battle up the chain of command, Lt. Col. Hilgartner received orders to stop and hold his current positions. Rapid pursuit of this very badly mauled enemy force was not to be. It turned out that when Lt. Gen. Lewis Walt, commanding general of the 3rd Marine Amphibious Force (III MAF), received 1/5s report on the battle for Hill 110, he found the high enemy casualty report difficult to believe and would not let 1/5 pursue the enemy. He wanted to see the battlefield and make his own judgments. The next day, 11 May 1967, General Walt flew by helicopter into the area and, accompanied by Lieutenant Colonel Hilgartner, Captain Caswell, and a small security force, walked the battlefield, observing first-hand the dead NVA bodies.

The official combat after-action report for Operation Union I tersely summed up the Battle for Hill 110. It said, in part, "The intense firefight taking and holding Hill 110 continued until approximately 1830, when the enemy finally began to break contact to the east. During the battle for this key terrain feature, which lasted nearly ten hours, Charlie Company returned fire with 15,000 rounds small arms fire, 200 M79 rounds, 12 3.5 inch rocket rounds, and 60 60 mm mortar rounds. Artillery and airstrikes were continuously called in while Alpha Company was deployed (into a blocking position) at approximately 1045, effectively cutting off the NVA battalion's northeastern avenue of escape."

Reflecting back on his months as a battalion commander, Peter Hilgartner states very bluntly:

> I have three main criticisms of the Marine Corps during that period of time. First, they kept moving companies back and forth between battalions all the time, which caused serious command and control problems. Second, I hated that stupid M16. I hated it because it kept getting my Marines killed. Third, it seemed like every time we got the enemy on the run, we always had to stop and count the bodies, and we couldn't pursue them. We had these NVA trapped, and I wanted to slaughter them. But they ordered us to stop and call in a body count. Charlie Company took most of the casualties. The rest of my companies stayed in pretty good shape, and the 1/3 companies were in good shape. We put ourselves in position to just nail them. But we had to stop and count the damned bodies. We should have taken umpteen jillion prisoners. The NVA should have had to surrender down there on the battlefield because we really had them trapped. But the people back in the rear really didn't understand what was going on.
>
> I think we had the better part of two NVA regiments in our trap, and they ended up squirting out of the trap. We had a regiment minus of Marines at hand surrounding them, and if we could only have gotten another battalion of Marines to seal off the trap, we would either have killed them all, or they would have had to surrender. At the very least, I should have had the three companies from 1/3 pursue them, but I couldn't even communicate with them, and regimental headquarters told me to hold up.
>
> When Colonel Houghton called in my report to Division headquarters, I don't think that General Walt believed my report. General Walt wanted to come out to see for himself, so the next day he flew in, and he and I walked the battlefield together. Dead NVA bodies lay all over the battlefield. The Marines of Charlie Company had fought like demons on Hill 110. This was the first real commitment of 1/5 troops in a large-scale combat operation. I was very proud that, while under my command, 1/5 went from having a reputation as the worst battalion in the First Marine Division to the cock of the walk.

Jim Caswell remembers the horrific enemy incoming fire and the heroism and determination of his Marines on 10 May 1967 as if it were yesterday: "About 150 of us walked off Hill 110 the next day; the rest were carried off the battlefield. We lost some great Marines, some outstanding corpsmen, and a professional gunnery sergeant. We all knew deep in our hearts that we had lost really good friends that day. But as a unit, these Marines had stood the trial by fire, and they had soundly defeated a very large force of the best fighters that North Vietnam had to put against them."

Early the next morning, Caswell found it strange and somewhat surreal when a famous Marine Corps general landed in a helicopter on top of the hill and asked to be shown the kill zone. Caswell says:

> General Walt arrived at my location by helicopter. The general told me to take him to the battlefield, so of course I obeyed. I told him that the only radios that would go would be mine, since I didn't want a forest of radio antennae walking around, making a tempting target for enemy snipers. He agreed. I found the last squad leader that had taken a patrol down the hill, Lance Cpl. Richard Holloway, and told him his exhausted men would take the general and all these other officers down the hill exactly where he had patrolled before. As we left our perimeter, General Walt reached down to the nearest rifleman, grabbed his rifle, and said he needed to borrow it for a little while. General Walt knew it was not a good idea to go on a patrol without a rifle; he could easily be singled out by an enemy observer as a leader. I watched, horrified, while this Marine held on to his rifle and said he wasn't going to give his rifle to anyone, general or otherwise. I handed this Marine my pistol and told him to give General Walt his rifle. I promised to return it in a few minutes, and he finally released his grip on it.

The NVA had policed up the battlefield by then, and although there weren't too many bodies or much equipment left lying around, enough remained to let the general know that a considerable fight had taken place there. After the senior officers looked around for a while, the impromptu patrol returned to the top of the hill. Shortly thereafter, General Walt's helicopter landed again, and the brass all departed in a cloud of dust.

As Jim Caswell thinks back on that day, he remains angry and frustrated at all the mistakes made and at the unreliable M16 ammunition that had hampered his Marines so terribly. But most of all he realizes what a missed opportunity this had been. Caswell sadly recalls, "We caught the NVA in the killing zone, and although we were seriously outnumbered, Charlie 1/5 remained clearly in control of the commanding terrain, with good visibility of the enemy's positions. The weather had been clear. A golden opportunity to destroy a large regular NVA unit had passed, while our superiors ineffectually maneuvered units around the battlefield and deprived us of our most powerful weapons: artillery fire and air support."

After the intensity of the combat for Hill 110 and the tragedy of what happened to Alpha Company, many of the Marines of 1/5 started thinking that they had had enough. But military operations don't just end when the troops are tired or pissed off. Certain objectives must be reached and secured, and Operation Union I was no different. So, the Marines of 1/5 spent another week searching and destroying and trying to forget their buddies who had died so tragically. Jim Coxen says:

> We tromped across the Que Son Valley for another week. Plenty of NVA still ran around in that area, but mostly in smaller units. I can remember that at one point, as the main column took a rest break, our acting platoon commander told three of us to drift out on the left flank a couple hundred meters, so we complied. We moved to an area of cover, but a rice paddy lay in front of the company. We snuck out to a little three-hut village a couple hundred meters away from the main column. We climbed up on a kind of high spot, right beside the hooches, watching the area. We saw a couple of Vietnamese civilians, but they acted normal. And then, all of a sudden, we could hear some NVA officer screaming at his troops just on the other side of the hooches out in the paddy. We could hear him screaming at the top of his lungs, and here we sat, several hundred meters away from the company, three of us, and an NVA unit of some size lurked just on the other side of the hooches. It sounded like a billion NVA over there, and all we could do was hope they went in the other direction. We heard a few shots, from what sounded like a Thompson submachine gun, so we snuck out of there. We reported in to the company, let them know what we had heard, but no one in the platoon had heard a thing, and we never found anything there later. The three of us really snuck up into that ville, acting jungle warfare-ish, but then when the screaming and shooting started, we decided that we weren't quite so tough, so we got the hell out of there.
>
> We continued our endless walking until we finally crossed the creek and reached Hill 51, the new battalion combat base. There was nothing there. Someone came over to us and said, "Welcome to your new home. Start digging in." The battalion had to build the combat base. There wasn't even any hot chow.
>
> Shortly after we arrived at Hill 51, my squad and a few other Marines went to Nui Lac Son [pronounced Newey Lock Sawn—an observation post and recon base on top of Hill 185, a very steep, high mountain located a little over five kilometers south of Hill 51]. I can remember becoming highly pissed off after getting there when we heard that the Marines on Hill 51 had finally gotten some hot chow, and we had nothing to eat but C-rations on Nui Lac Son.

> Actually, duty at Nui Lac Son turned out pretty good, despite the lack of hot chow, because we knew that no enemy in his right mind would attack us. I think nearly every combat force that had ever fought in Vietnam had set up a combat base at Nui Lac Son. I think Japanese forces stayed there during World War II, and the French stayed there in the late forties and early fifties. Nui Lac Son had very steep sides, many antipersonnel mines planted on the approaches, a lot of trenches and bunkers, and a lot of barbed wire. That place appeared impregnable. A reconnaissance team based itself there, a 4.2-inch mortar emplacement, and someone had built a wood platform that allowed us to get our resupplies by helicopter.

Back on 11 May, the day after the Battle for Hill 110, the Marines of Charlie 1/5 left the hill after disengaging themselves from helicopter loads of journalists, combat photographers, and other correspondents. The reporters had arrived unexpectedly, just after General Walt's departure, and they told Captain Caswell that he had to escort them around the battlefield. Caswell replied that he had received no such orders, but they could follow him if they desired. Caswell made it perfectly clear that he could not guarantee their safety. The reporters stayed with Charlie Company for a while, but then more helicopters picked them up, and they hastily departed the scene.

Charlie Company then moved to link up with a company from another battalion and colocate for the night in a nearby hamlet. They met the other company and proceeded to the hamlet. Then one of the strangest things that Jim Caswell ever witnessed during the war took place:

> I told the other company commander that I would take the northern half of the hamlet for our perimeter, and he could have the southern part of the perimeter. He said, "Fine." I then set in my machine gun teams with Sergeant Sanchez, the way I always did, told the platoon commanders to set their two-man positions about ten to twenty meters apart just as we always did, and to start digging foxholes—a normal night for us. I checked my lines after an hour or so and everything looked good. We had all routes of access to the hamlet covered in our half of the perimeter; my Marines' positions were well spaced out, and we had interlocking, grazing fields of fire in front of everyone. While I checked positions a little later, my platoon commanders at both ends of our line told me that they had seen nothing of the other company. I took my radio operators, and we went looking for the other company. We found them in the middle of the hamlet in the inhabitants' air raid trench, which most villages had. An entire Marine Corps rifle company sat in the bottom of this hundred-

meter-long trench, shoulder to shoulder. It looked like a flashback from the Civil War. I asked the company commander when he planned to take up his night defensive positions. He replied that he already had. In disgust, I departed the trench, called my company leaders together, and said, "New plan. Charlie Company will form our own 360-degree perimeter." This marked, essentially, the end of Operation Union I.

Jim Caswell reflects back on the Battle for Hill 110 with bittersweet memories. He remembers the frustration and anger, but he mostly remembers his men:

I thought we had been abandoned up there on Hill 110. That's what it felt like. We got nothing: no artillery, no air support, and we got no reinforcements that day. I know Alpha tried to get to us, but nobody ever reached us. It was a set-piece battle. I mean, how many times in a military career do you get something like this? We had a perfect situation for artillery, but all we got were some 81 mm mortar rounds. I was in a set-piece battle, and I had the terrain. Man! I had always dreamed of this, and I could get nothing. I don't know why we got, basically, stranded up there. At the time I stayed so busy that I guess that didn't go through my mind until later. When I had the time to go over this battle in my mind, I couldn't get over the sense of feeling abandoned. I wondered, "Where's my support?" And I got very upset that we lost so many casualties. For me, the toughest part of the whole battle came when they started bringing the casualties up the hill—the wounded, the guys who needed the medevacs that I couldn't get until later. Sergeant York brought up a guy, a PFC, with an eye out, and I tried to comfort him. His eye hung out on his cheek. He wasn't a model Marine, and he had gotten in trouble a few times; I told him that if he would try harder, that if he would start acting like a Marine, I would promote him to lance corporal. So he's lying there, at my feet, with an eye out, asking me if he's going to be promoted to lance corporal, and I told him yes, that he was going to be promoted to lance corporal. So they medevaced him, and several years later I got a call from a lawyer who represented this man in front of a Marine Corps retirement board or something. This lawyer says to me, "You told him he would be promoted to lance corporal," and so I said, "Yes, I'll take care of it." I called Pete Hilgartner and asked him if he would sign the warrant promoting this guy to lance corporal, and he says, "Okay. Why?" and I said, "You don't want to know. Just sign it." So Pete signed it, and the PFC got promoted to lance corporal.

The main thing I thought about that day was worrying about whether we would have enough ammunition, and whether or not we could hold our position for the whole day. I hadn't even thought about what might have happened that night. If we hadn't gotten the air strikes late that afternoon and gotten some reinforcements that evening, we might not have held that hill. But that unwelcome thought didn't cross my mind that day. I just felt that we could hold the hill, and that's what we did.

Jim Caswell continues the recollection of his sad memories: "Just before dark that night, after the battle for Hill 110 ended, I went over to the part of the hill where we had put our KIAs. I really just wanted to say goodbye to Gunnery Sgt. Marcelino Rivera-Cruz, because he was my friend. I got very angry at my new company gunny because I saw that he hadn't made sure that every one of them was inside our perimeter. I counted them. There were only nine. The next morning we found the tenth KIA close to our lines."

7: Dying Delta and the Move to Hill 51, 11-17 May 1967

As Charlie 1/5 recovered from the events of 10 May 1967, the Marines of Delta 1/5 plunged into a different, even more intense hell of their own. Company commander Dave McInturff recalls:

After the Battle for Hill 110 ended, Delta Company "chopped" to 3rd Battalion, 5th Marines. On 12 May 1967 we walked off the ridgeline, walked down the road, and now we're working for the 3rd Battalion, 5th Marines. We humped to a predesignated location and met up with the 3/5 CP group. They had stopped and had set up temporary defensive positions. The 3/5 Battalion commander tells me, "Okay, McInturff, you get your people out in front of my battalion. You're going to lead us down this trail toward this next objective." So now Delta Company went on point for 3/5, and I'm pissed, because my troops had been out in the field pretty much constantly since 1 May and were pretty much beat to crap. We had climbed up and down hills for nearly two weeks, my troops were worn out and in need of a decent resupply, and now we're on point for another battalion. I got off the 3/5 tactical radio net, got on the 1/5 tactical net, and called Lieutenant Colonel Hilgartner. I told him that I was flat pissed off and explained the situation. I didn't know much about the op order, just that I was told to get out in front of 3/5 and take point. But, being good Marines, we went ahead and did it. I just needed to vent off a little steam, and Lieutenant Colonel Hilgartner allowed me to do that.

I put out fire teams for security on both flanks and we proceeded down the trail, a pretty wide and well-used trail. We moved out at a pretty good pace. Little did I know that the 3/5 Battalion CP group and the company guarding them just stayed in place until we got about a click and a half out in front of them. Suddenly, one of my flank security fire teams gets shot at, and they see a couple of armed gooners running away. I had always made it a habit to keep my point platoon at full strength and to take two fire teams from the rear-end platoon to act as flank security, and they would move up adjacent to the point platoon. Initial reports from the fire team on our right flank indicated that these were well-armed NVA wearing khaki uniforms. Before I could do anything, my platoon commander in the rear, who handled flank security, took off with the rest of his platoon in pursuit of the NVA around our right flank. The further they got, the more intense the firing got. Before we knew it, that platoon found itself in a pile of shit.

I got the platoon commander on the radio and told him to hang tough; that we would get him some help as soon as possible. Then I reported to the 3/5 Battalion commander that we had made heavy contact with the enemy and had taken casualties and needed help immediately. Just after that, just as I started to maneuver the rest of my company toward the sounds of gunfire, the NVA attacked my right flank in force, and we came under extremely heavy enemy small arms and mortar fire all up and down my column. The main enemy force hid in camouflaged positions across a rice paddy from us, so we couldn't attack in that direction; I actually started to worry that the platoon would get cut off and overrun, but I soon found out that they weren't really that far away from us. We stayed in contact with the NVA for a really long time that day, in a heavy firefight.

We fought the NVA for the rest of that day, 12 May, pretty much by ourselves; finally, shortly after dark, we got helicopters headed in to medevac our wounded. The fighting lulled down quite a bit after dark, so we thought it safe to bring in the choppers, but I'll be damned if the enemy didn't open up on the choppers. You could see green tracer rounds going right through the hulls of those aircraft. I heard that the copilot on the first chopper died from enemy small arms fire that went right through the windshield, but the pilot still managed to land and take out some of my really badly wounded Marines.

We waited for a while longer, fired some more artillery, and then we got more choppers in and got the rest of our casualties out. That first chopper pilot was very lucky to get out of that LZ. That guy had to have balls about as big as bowling balls. Delta Company lost ten or twelve KIAs that day, and we also unfortunately lost two MIAs in that shit storm as well. Twelve May 1967—a bad day for Delta 1/5, especially because of those MIAs. Months later, in January of 1968, after the battalion had moved up north to Phu Loc 6, our guys on the perimeter of the combat base spotted a guy walking down the road from Bach Ma. They got out their binoculars and saw that he wasn't a Vietnamese, so they let him get closer. I'll be damned if it wasn't one of my MIAs from the battle on 12 May. He had gotten away from his captors somewhere to the west of Bach Ma and made his way down to Phu Loc 6 Combat Base. We never got the other MIA back, and the last I heard he is now assumed dead.

The official combat after-action report submitted by the 3rd Battalion, 5th Marines covering Operation Union I indicates that Delta 1/5 chopped to them at 0900 on 12 May 1967. At 1750 "all units moved out from the [previous] night's position toward [new] night positions," and the report places Delta about one kilometer east of the village of Phuoc Duc (2) and about six kilometers east of Hill 51 Combat Base (coordinates BT 010361). Continuing, the combat after-action report gives the following report on the battle:

> The order of march was Delta Co. 1/5 leading out, followed by India and Mike. The CP was with Mike. Kilo was not in the column but was proceeding across country direct. At approximately 1750H Delta encountered the enemy, but were stopped by intense semiautomatic, automatic weapons fire, and mortars. India, who was directly behind Delta, started to Delta's north, but on order moved around to the rear of Delta and on down to their south flank where they received intense S/A fire and a few incoming mortar rounds. India then regrouped and set up in a 360-degree (perimeter) as by this time it was dark. When Delta first encountered the enemy, Kilo continued on their compass heading until they were directly north of Delta. Kilo then on order turned south to link up with Delta at 122015H. This link up was very successfully accomplished.

McInturff's recollections of this battle remain quite different:

> The problem I have regarding that battle on 12 May 1967 is that I don't think anyone in 3/5 had a clue about what Delta Company went through because they stayed so fucking far away. All during that fight, they never caught up with us. They finally sent Mike or Kilo Company up to help us because I kept requesting them to send us some help, but they didn't get there until almost first light the next morning. The company commander finally got there and said, "We're here to help; what can we do?" I told him that it was just a little too late, that the battle was already over and that we had the gooners on the run. That really pissed me off. It took 3/5 way too long to get us some help. We needed help within the first ten minutes of the fight, and we didn't get any help until the battle ended the next morning. We chopped to 3/5 on the morning of the 12th, immediately went out on point for that battalion, got in a horrendous firefight, and didn't get a lick of help until way too late.

In the terse language typical of a Vietnam War–era unit's combat after-action report, 3/5's command group reported the results of this battle as follows: "At 122335H Company K medevaced the last of their emergency casualties and re-supply was accomplished. Results which were finally evaluated came to 15 USMC KIA, 26 USMC WIA medevaced, 18 WIANE [wounded, but not evacuated], and 2 MIA; 15 VC KIA (probables)."

Delta Company chopped back to 1/5 on 15 May 1967 and received orders to move back to Hill 51 Combat Base. Shortly afterward, Delta went up to Nui Lac Son and relieved Charlie Company, and the Marines of Delta 1/5 stayed the next month up there. Duty up on Nui Lac Son couldn't really be described as rest and recreation, because you were still in a combat zone, but bad stuff seldom happened up there. The relative security at the Nui Lac Son outpost would allow Delta Company's Marines to resupply and recover from their wounds. However, on their way to Nui Lac Son, Delta Company lost yet another Marine. Dave McInturff recalls, "We didn't get more than a couple of clicks outside Hill 51 Combat Base's defensive wire when a single sniper round hit one of my Marines right in the center of his helmet. A corpsman and a couple of his buddies immediately ran to help him, but when the Doc pulled his helmet off, the whole top of his head came off. The only good thing about that incident was that he never knew what hit him."

On 13 May 1967, another new captain joined 1/5 and immediately took command of Alpha Company. Capt. Jerry McKay resumed his duties as the battalion communications officer, and Capt. R. G. Babich became the new Alpha Six. Rick Zell remembers:

> Captain Babich was an older guy, in his early thirties, and one of those tragic stories. He had served most of his first tour as the company commander of regimental headquarters company at the 5th Marines, and I heard he extended his tour to get command of an infantry company. He had already been in Vietnam for quite some time. A nice guy, married and with two children, he was a career Marine, and he knew the importance of leading an infantry company in combat, so he extended and transferred to the 5th Marines. Unfortunately, he wasn't necessarily very combat-wise. He absolutely cared about his Marines and had actually earned a Silver Star when the 5th Marines headquarters got hit badly during a night attack on their combat base several months before this, so he was obviously very courageous. It turned out that Captain Babich just wasn't very concerned about his own personal safety; that's what I mean when I say he wasn't very combat-wise. When we made contact with the enemy, and a firefight exploded, he would get up and run around, directing fire, exposing himself when he didn't really need to. Several

One of 1/5's 81 mm mortar crews manning their weapon at Hill 51 Combat Base. Courtesy of Bill Pittman.

of us told him that he would get himself killed doing stuff like that, but he never listened to us.

On the morning of 17 May 1967 Charlie Company moved into the village of Que Son and found a new combat base under construction, the beginnings of the new permanent home of 1/5's Marines called Hill 51. As rudimentary as it was, the Hill 51 combat base provided the Marines of 1/5 some creature comforts—hot food and shelter—for the first time since 21 April. The Marines took off their packs and collapsed. They were gaunt, tired, and filthy.

Jim Caswell noticed that a 105 mm howitzer battery had moved in, and the gun emplacements were being sandbagged in. He wandered over and found the battery commander, Capt. Marty Tull, an old friend who served with Jim in the 4th Marines. "It was great to see Marty," Caswell recalls: "He said I looked terrible and he asked me to have breakfast with him. He seemed very proud of the fact that he had flown his field ranges in and that his cooks could prepare hot chow for the Marines of his

Living quarters for some of the 81 mm mortar men, Hill 51 Combat Base, taken from the 1/5 fire control center's lookout post. Courtesy of Bill Pittman.

battery. I told him that I would really like to, but that I had 150 hungry Marines who hadn't seen a hot meal in thirty days. I couldn't accept, when they would only get C-rations again. Marty just said, 'Bring them too. I'll tell the cooks we're going to feed a few more.' Marty's cooks worked in the sun all morning feeding all of us blueberry pancakes, one of the best meals I ever tasted."

The exhausted survivors of the Battle for Hill 110 and the many other shorter but still very intense firefights during Operation Union I found little rest at Hill 51 Combat Base. The war continued at a brisk pace, so they knew they must continue to take the fight to the enemy. The enemy certainly continued to do their best to do damage wherever and whenever possible. Jim Caswell remembered, "Command told us the VC mortared this base frequently and suggested we dig in. We did. A few days later we received a mortar barrage, and all of us hunkered safely down in our new holes. Meanwhile, Marty Tull's gunners had all run out to their 105s during the attack, in case they received orders to fire counterbattery fire. Seeing they would not be needed, Marty ran out of the fire control bunker to get his men off the guns and back into

Poncho Hooch on Hill 51, home sweet home for Harvey Cunningham and Ken Clark in June and July, 1967, when they were not in the field. Courtesy of Harvey Cunningham.

their holes. As he ran toward his men, Capt. Marty Tull was hit by an enemy mortar round, killing him instantly."

On 17 May 1967, Operation Union I officially ended. All told, 1st Battalion, 5th Marines lost 34 Marines or Navy corpsmen killed in action and 150 wounded in action as a result of Operation Union I. On the other side of the macabre Vietnam-style scales of warfare, the Marines involved in Operation Union I accounted for 865 enemy KIA, including a reported 486 NVA regulars of the 2nd NVA Division. The 1/5 Marines also captured tons of enemy war-fighting materials. Including all of the units involved in the twenty-seven-day operation, 110 Marines died by hostile fire, 2 were declared missing in action, and 473 were wounded in action. The mission of Operation Union I was accomplished. The area surrounding Hiep Duc and the Que Son Valley became considerably more peaceful after Operation Union I ended—at least, for a while.

One Five's new combat base sat atop a small hill located about two kilometers west of the small town of Que Son. This new combat base's purpose was to help secure Highway 534, which linked the town of Hiep Duc with Highway 1, as well as a secondary road, which linked Highway 534 with Que Son. More importantly, Hill 51 Combat Base was positioned in the center of the Que Son Valley and protected the western approaches to the vital supply line of Highway 1. The Marines of 1/5 would stay in the Que Son Valley for several more months.

Although this new combat base became known as Hill 51, the hill it sat on wasn't much more than a small bump on the landscape. On the tactical maps it didn't even have an elevation number. Located within an amoebalike circle on the 1:50,000 terrain map, Hill 51 Combat Base was situated on a low hill about three hundred meters in diameter and just slightly over thirty feet in elevation higher than the surrounding countryside. However, when asked by 5th Marines headquarters for the name of the new 1/5 combat base, Lieutenant Colonel Hilgartner unhesitatingly dubbed their new location as Hill 51. In later years, when reflecting on this decision, Colonel Hilgartner stated:

> Hill 51 was not fifty-one meters high, or fifteen meters low. When asked by Regiment for a name, I gave it the name Hill 51, which really stood for 1st Battalion, 5th Marines, backwards. They bought it hook, line, and sinker.
>
> When we occupied Hill 51, many of the men wanted to have liberty, but I would never allow any Vietnamese inside the combat base. However, I did allow the locals to set up a cottage industry a few hundred meters outside the wire. I made sure that each group of Marines who took liberty treated these activities as a combat patrol, so it really wasn't much of a liberty.

The rural South Vietnamese people were often very clever and industrious and seemed to be born capitalists. Unruly clusters of improvised shops, offering a wide range of food, drink, souvenirs, haircuts, and so on, inevitably sprang up around American combat bases. Designed to separate young Americans from their hard-earned money, these shops often represented a headache to American leaders due to intestinal sickness caused by the local food, water, and ice—or worse, venereal diseases from the "back rooms" of the shops. All too often these shops provided cover and concealment for the elusive Viet Cong who operated in the area. Lieutenant

Colonel Hilgartner's decision to prevent the South Vietnamese civilians from entering the base proper was a sound one. Many American bases did allow them to enter, only to find out the hard way that these supposedly innocent vendors were pacing off distances and providing important intelligence to enemy gunners.

Hilgartner continues:

> We conducted our briefings every night. All officers and staff NCOs who could be spared from duty attended these briefings. The leaders heard everything that we planned to do the next day. After the briefings, the officers and NCOs went back to their men and let them know what the battalion commander had planned for them and why. We had a great battalion. I mean, when I waved my arm to the right, the Marines went to the right. When I waved my arm to the left, they went left. Everybody knew what everybody was supposed to do, and everybody did what they were supposed to do. One Five was a great battalion, and I will never forget that experience. We operated like a well-oiled machine, and we didn't have any disciplinary problems. It was "All for one, and one for all." We had a great spirit in that battalion. And the men performed brilliantly; I can't praise them enough for the way they conducted themselves while I commanded the battalion, officers and enlisted alike. They are all heroes in my judgment.

That spirit and experience would pay off during the difficult weeks and months to come.

8: Operation Union II, 26 May–5 June 1967

Upon cursory examination, Operations Union I and Union II might appear as merely numeric designations of different phases of the same combat operation. Certain similarities between these operations did exist, but also many differences. Both operations took place in the same general tactical area of operations, the Que Son Valley. But while the Marines of 1/5 maneuvered in a generally western direction from their insertion at LZ Condor and then swung north during Operation Union I, during Operation Union II they maneuvered in a generally eastern direction from their insertion at LZ Robin (located about fifteen kilometers south and somewhat east of Hill 51 Combat Base) and then attacked in a northeasterly direction from the LZ into the northwestern portion of the Tam Ky district. They then swung around the eastern side of Nui Da Ngua (Hill 251, located about eight kilometers from LZ Robin across some very rugged terrain) and then attacked in a northwesterly direction through Thang Binh district of the Quang Tin province of the Republic of South Vietnam. Putting the two operations together, Marine forces operated in large, opposing circular patterns during the Union I and II operations. The Hill 51 Combat Base sat at the center of these sweeps.

In another similarity, it appears the enemy used the same strategy and tactics. Enemy tactics during Operation Union II featured small-unit actions, carried out by the Viet Cong or small NVA units, designed to draw Marine forces into killing grounds defended by large NVA forces, the same strategy they used during Union I. Individual guerilla snipers or small units of VC continuously harassed and harried the Marines, knowing that the Marines would always assault forward toward the enemy locations. The NVA would try to use the element of surprise and would hit the Marines hard, trying to inflict as much death and destruction as possible, and then they would do their best to evade the heavy firepower that the Marines would inevitably bring to bear. This pattern continued somewhat erratically, but looking at these two operations with 20/20 hindsight, there seemed to be a method to the NVA's madness.

Although the Marines and corpsmen of Charlie 1/5 took the brunt of enemy gunfire during Operation Union I, especially during the battle for Hill 110, during Operation Union II the Marines of Charlie Company watched most of the action from the lofty heights of the Nui Lac Son outpost. One platoon of Charlie Company did fight in Union II, running squad-sized patrols out of Hill 51 Combat Base during the early phases of the operation, but this time the Marines of Delta 1/5, Alpha 1/5 and Foxtrot 2/5 would take the brunt of enemy gunfire. A hamlet called Vinh Huy (2) became the main killing ground of Operation Union II. This seemingly sleepy little village became infamous to the Marines of 1/5.

After Marine commanders officially terminated Operation Union I and the Marines of 1/5 began building their new combat base at Hill 51, Charlie Company assumed the security duties at the communications outpost called Nui Lac Son. In addition to the Marine security forces, Nui Lac Son was home to a Marine reconnaissance team and a communications relay station. From Nui Lac Son the Marines had excellent views of a large section of the Que Son Valley.

On 26 May 1967, while Charlie Company enjoyed the relative safety of Nui Lac Son, the rest of the battalion received orders to commence the search-and-destroy combat operation called Operation Union II. Two 1/5 companies established blocking positions across an expanse of rice paddy lands and small hamlets stretching approximately eight hundred meters on the northeastern edge of the Que Son Valley, not far from the location of the disastrous "friendly" air strike that had crippled Alpha 1/5 on 10 May 1967. Then for the next several days, additional companies of Marines conducted sweeps and patrols designed to drive enemy units toward the blocking positions. The planners of Operation Union II intended to put enemy units between the anvil of blocking positions and the hammer of the maneuvering elements and to crush them with fire and steel. For the most part, this strategy worked, but the enemy commanders had their own strategies in play at the same time.

Sgt. Craig L. Jackson served in Delta 1/5 during Operation Union II. Craig enlisted in the US Marine Corps from his home town of Boston, Massachusetts. He graduated in 1963 from a trade high school in Boston and worked for a year as a printer. As the oldest of eight children, Craig found it difficult to raise and save money for college. One day his cousin came up with the great idea of joining the Marine Corps, so the two of them enlisted together in August 1964. Actually, Craig's cousin had a problem with "driving other people's cars." He called Craig one day and asked if he could borrow Craig's car. It turned out that he had stolen a car and had gotten caught, and the judge told him he had a choice of either jail or enlisting in the Marine Corps. So Craig went with his cousin to the US Marine Corps recruiting

Harvey Cunningham (*left*) and unidentified buddy at Hill 51 in the background.
Courtesy of Harvey Cunningham.

station in Boston, Massachusetts. Craig listened very closely to the recruiter and joined the Marine Corps with his cousin.

Recruit Pvt. Craig Jackson became the "house mouse" in Platoon 368 at MCRD Parris Island late in the summer of 1964; he managed to survive that job, which essentially meant that he acted as the gofer for the drill instructors, given all manner of odd jobs and assignments. Pronounced a US Marine upon graduation in early November 1964, Craig proceeded to Camp Geiger at Marine Corps Base Camp Lejeune, North Carolina, for his infantry training. Promoted to private first class, Craig took twenty days' leave after receiving orders to report to Henderson Hall, Headquarters Marine Corps, Arlington, Virginia.

> I thought I was going to a guard outfit, but when they got everyone together, I found out I got assigned to mess duty. That was how Henderson Hall got its people for mess duty. I suffered through mess duty for sixty-four days, and I thought it would never end. At the end of that period, they interviewed everyone, and I told them that I wanted to leave. That turned out to be the wrong thing to say. They thought I was gung ho, so they selected me to stay.

Nui Lac Son. Courtesy of Harvey Cunningham.

> Finally assigned to Guard Company, I stayed there until I got orders overseas. I made lance corporal after ten months, which at that time was considered early, and again promoted, this time to corporal, in July of 1966. Rank had started to come very fast by that point. We not only provided guard duty for Henderson Hall, but also the main US Navy facility in Washington, DC, a big responsibility. I served on a unit that provided hospital security for President Lyndon Johnson while he had his appendix removed.

Craig received orders to WestPac in January 1967. He remembers that when he joined the Marine Corps in 1964, he had never heard of Vietnam. One day in late 1965, as he and a bunch of his fellow Marines watched a ball game on TV, a news program interrupted the broadcast. It covered a big battle in the Ia Drang Valley involving the 7th Cavalry. The reporter interviewed the battalion commander as the cameraman panned around; the cameras caught many wounded soldiers lying around, and the reporter asked about the brave soldiers and the battle that had just ended. That went on for about a minute, and then they cut back to the game. Craig recalled:

Sgt. Ed Engel (*left*) and several other Charlie Company Marines in a bunker atop Nui Lac Son. Courtesy of Harvey Cunningham.

We all looked at each other, said, "Where in the hell is Vietnam?" Nobody knew. We shared a barracks with the embassy school trainees, who occupied the other end of our barracks in Henderson Hall. We went and looked at the globe in our classroom, trying to find Vietnam. We couldn't find it. Then one of the guys pointed to "French Indochina" on the globe, and another guy said, "Hey, I think that's where Vietnam is!" We found it hard to believe that none of us knew Vietnam's geographic location. We would hear a lot more about it in the near future.

In the summer of 1966, I came back from the rifle range at Quantico and became a squad leader. In August, the first sergeant called all of us corporals into the classroom and made a speech. He said that since so many of us had bitched about the chickenshit spit and polish of Guard Company, we would now have the opportunity to go fight like real Marines. He asked for a show of hands from anyone who wanted to volunteer to go to Vietnam. Guys raised their hands. My buddy, Gary Tunstall, from Providence, Rhode Island, raised his hand. So I raised my hand, and my other buddy, James Brown, from New York City, he looked at me and asked me what I thought I was doing. Both

Tunstall and Brown were team leaders in my squad, and they had both been members of my fire team before we all made corporal. I explained to him that Gary had raised his hand, and I couldn't let him go off by himself, so that was that. We all had orders to Vietnam. They were both bigger than me; I couldn't have whipped either one of them if I had tried, but for some reason I couldn't let them go off without me to take care of them.

In the meantime, my friend James told me that he wasn't raising his hand, and he actually talked me out of it also. I went in to the first sergeant, told him I'd changed my mind, and he chewed me out and chased me out of there, muttering something about wasting the Marine Corps' paper and time. When I saw Gary, I told him not to sign, but he had already signed his papers. Gary and all the rest of the guys got orders to Vietnam within two weeks. Then, in December I found out that James Brown had received orders to Vietnam. So I went back to see the first sergeant and told him I wanted to volunteer for Vietnam, and the first sergeant threw me out of the office again. I requested mast; I told the first sergeant I wanted to see our CO, Capt. Robert Johnson. So I finally went in to see the captain, and he said, "Well, you're on the sergeant's list, and I'm not going to transfer a stripe out." He said that I had plenty of time to get to Vietnam. Captain Johnson stayed in the Marine Corps and rose in rank to lieutenant general.

I had a friend who worked across the street at Headquarters, Marine Corps, Henderson Hall, an admin type named Cpl. John Chichester, so I went to see him. I told him I needed to get orders for Vietnam. He took me across the street to Henderson Hall to see this corporal in Records. He climbed this ladder to the top of a stack of records and climbed down with my fairly thick military service record. He knew at a glance that I had been there for a while. He looked at me and said, "You sure you want to do this?"

I said, "Yeah."

He said, "Okay, you're out of here."

Sure enough, I received orders by speed letter. The first sergeant had the orders, gave them to me, and asked me if I knew anything about this, obviously amazed that I had received my orders by speed letter. I told him I didn't have a clue. I actually cleared the base a couple of days before my buddy Brown and went home on leave within a few days. I then reported in to Camp Pendleton at the end of February 1967.

I reported in half a day early. I found out they put the names of corporals and sergeants with the MOS of 0311 [rifleman] on a list to go to additional training for ultimate orders to a reconnaissance battalion. When I saw my name on that list, I told the admin clerk that I had never received any recon training and that I wasn't even coming from an infantry outfit, but he just said, "Those are my instructions." So I told him to leave a spot for my buddy James Brown when he comes through. When Brown reported in, he told the admin clerk that if he put his name on the recon list, he would knock him out.

I became a squad leader during infantry training. As the senior NCO in the entire staging company he went to, Corporal Brown became the company gunnery sergeant. I had a lot of fun hazing him about being a lifer. He had always given me a hard time about being a fire team leader and then a squad leader, so I told him that now he knows how it feels.

Once the training started, the squad leaders took their squads to a simulated Vietnam village complex, down in a draw. I took my squad through, and we went through in attack formation, when all of a sudden all hell broke loose, explosions, small arms fire. I pretty much froze in place, looked left, looked right, and then the instructor ran over to me and yelled, "Where are they? Where are they?"

I said, "Who?"

He said, "The enemy."

I said, 'I don't know."

He said, "You're dead. You're dead and all your men are dead."

He had the aggressor force stand up—right next to us. That experience sobered me right up, and at that moment I started to take everything seriously. I started to pay attention and tried to learn everything I could. Something must have sunk in, because when we ran the escape and evasion course, my group didn't get caught like everyone else did.

When we finished our infantry training, just before I left for Vietnam, I got called to the battalion office. I just knew I'd get orders for recon. When I got down there, they told me I had been promoted to E-5 sergeant, with a date of rank of 1 March 1967. They took us up to El Toro to fly us out, and they held a promotion ceremony and promoted several of us to sergeant. All the other new sergeants acted very excited about it, but I wasn't. The experience of getting my squad wiped out in the Vietnamese village still bothered me, and I remained concerned about the responsibility of serving as a squad leader. More rank, more responsibility. It really bothered me; I had very little experience in the infantry, and now I had to worry about more responsibility.

The new Sergeant, Craig Jackson, boarded his plane and took off. Next stop: Okinawa.

When I arrived in Okinawa, I nearly missed a buddy from my boot camp platoon as he rotated home; he found out that I had just arrived, and somehow he found me. He had served on the Rockpile and other places up north, places I had heard about. His skin, seemingly permeated with red dirt, lurked below hair much lighter than I remembered. We talked for about fifteen minutes or so, and he told me that I would be okay, just to keep my head down, and then he took off.

I did the typical stuff in Okinawa, got drunk, chased women; as a sergeant, I got to stay out later than the other enlisted guys. I stayed in Oki for only thirty-two hours: stowed my gear, got my shots, tried to give blood. At that time, when you gave a pint of blood they would give you a little paper cup of government-issue bourbon. They put me, a brand-new sergeant, in charge of the bourbon. A bunch of Marines stood there, lined up to give blood. Quite a few of them didn't want the bourbon, so I started sipping their shots of bourbon. A while later, it became my turn to give blood, but the corpsman said, "You can't give blood. You're drunk." I didn't realize that I was, in fact, quite drunk, but when I stood up I started heading sideways. I got a good choke from this gunny hovering nearby. My experiences as a sergeant of Marines didn't start out too good.

They put me in charge of a pretty large group of Marines when we flew, in the middle of the night, on a Continental Airlines jet into Da Nang. I didn't really know what to do when we got there, so I took my group of Marines over by this big shed, out of the light. On our earlier flights, into Hawaii, and even into Okinawa, we stayed in a pretty upbeat mood. Not any longer; the ride into Da Nang became pretty somber. They put us up in a temporary receiving barracks there at the Da Nang airbase to spend the rest of the night. They had told us if we heard a loud noise something like a jet, that it could be an incoming rocket and to get out of the building and hit the deck. So, of course, the first time a jet took off after I had finally gone to sleep, I woke up running.

We flew down to Chu Lai the next night in a small transport plane, a two-engine job, like a Caribou. When the plane first tried to take off, it started backfiring, so they stopped and told us to get off. A couple of lance corporals and a PFC ran out there with a bunch of wrenches and started fooling around with the engines, and then they put us back on. Of course it started backfiring again, and they took us off again. The third time they put us back on, of course, none of us wanted to fly on the damned plane, but it finally managed to take off and we made it to Chu Lai okay. They picked us up by trucks, in the dark, and drove us over to some hardback tents. We stayed there for a day and a half and then they finally drove us up to the 5th Marines regimental headquarters north of Chu Lai. They initially put me in the sniper platoon's hardback tent for a couple of days until I received an assignment. While I waited, another sergeant asked me to go on the trash dump run, for something to do. We made the rounds of the various mess halls and took their garbage to this huge trash dump. When we arrived, a bunch of Vietnamese people greeted us, and then they went through the trash as soon as we dumped it. The sight of this made me sick, so when he asked me to go on the trash dump run the next day, I told him no, I'd rather not. I went over to the mess hall and hadn't been there very long when I heard this huge explosion off in the distance. I looked to my left, up Highway 1, and saw something very large going up in the air—the truck's engine. Word came back within the hour that when that trash dump truck got to the dump, the enemy blew it up with a command-detonated mine, killing everyone in the truck. That shook me up; all of my gung ho attitudes disappeared rapidly.

When they finally called my name for assignment, I reported in to the S-1 office and ran into a Marine I had known at Henderson Hall. Concerned about my lack of experience and knowledge of the infantry, I asked him to give me a break. I told him that I had been playing Marine for the past two years and that I didn't really know anything about the grunts. He looked through a bunch of files and noticed that I had a top secret clearance and that the 5th Marines needed someone in the S-3 shop. I didn't really know anything about S-3, but I told him that sounded just about right, so he sent me to the regimental S-3 office. I reported in to this major, who looked at my records and immediately knew that I didn't have any S-3 experience, but I rapidly told him that I had high pro and con marks, that I learned fast, and that I had a top secret clearance, so the major decided to give me a chance. When I walked out of that S-3 shop that day I must have jumped three feet in the air. I just knew that I had it made. I became the S-3 senior watch NCO, responsible for about ten or twelve enlisted Marines in the S-3 shop junior to me. I barely knew what S-3 stood for, but I found myself determined to do my best, and I quickly learned that it meant operations.

I worked from six in the morning to six in the evening, and I got the hang of it pretty quickly. I would check out a jeep and a driver, drive from combat base to combat base, picking up ambush plots and after-action reports; then I would bring them back to the regimental S-3 shop, help to plot them on the map, and pass them up to division. We had to keep track of everything. Working in the S-3 shop was okay, except when snipers shot at us while we drove up and down Highway 1. The first time that happened, I heard some cracks but

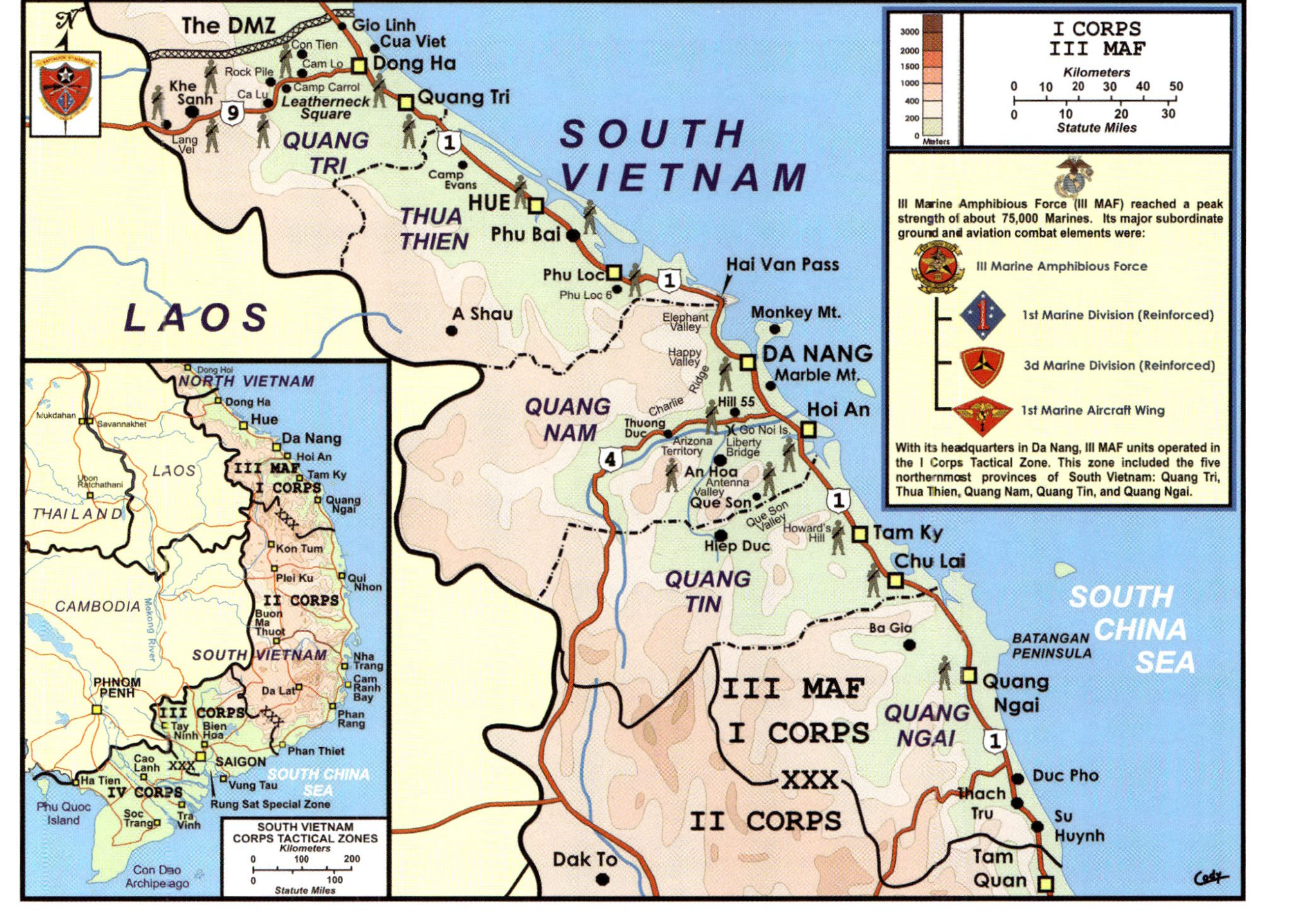

Map 1. I Corps Tactical Zone with Inset Depicting the Republic of South Vietnam and All Corps Tactical Zones

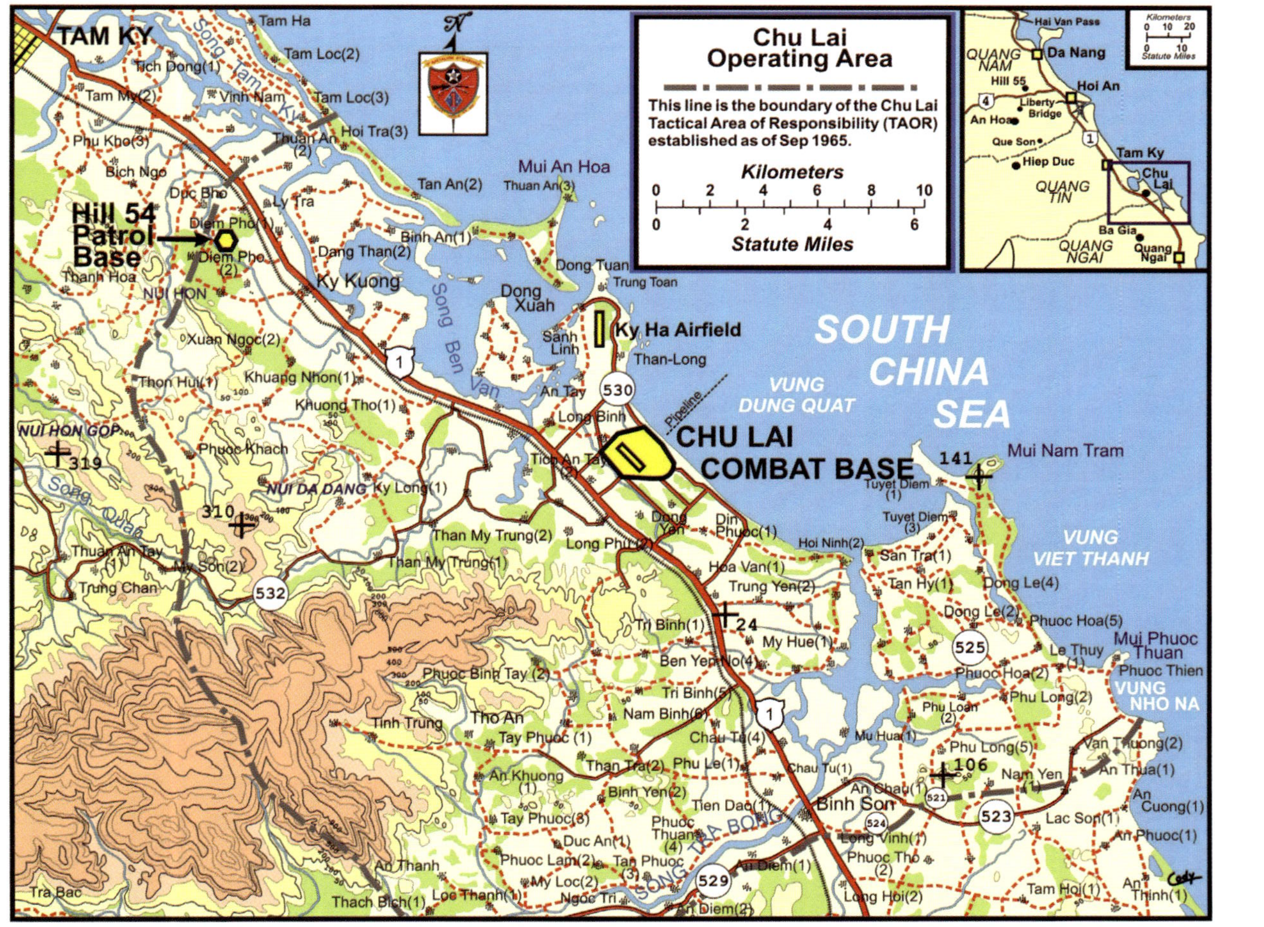

Map 2. Chu Lai TAOR, the Chu Lai Airfield and Combat Base, and Tam Ky

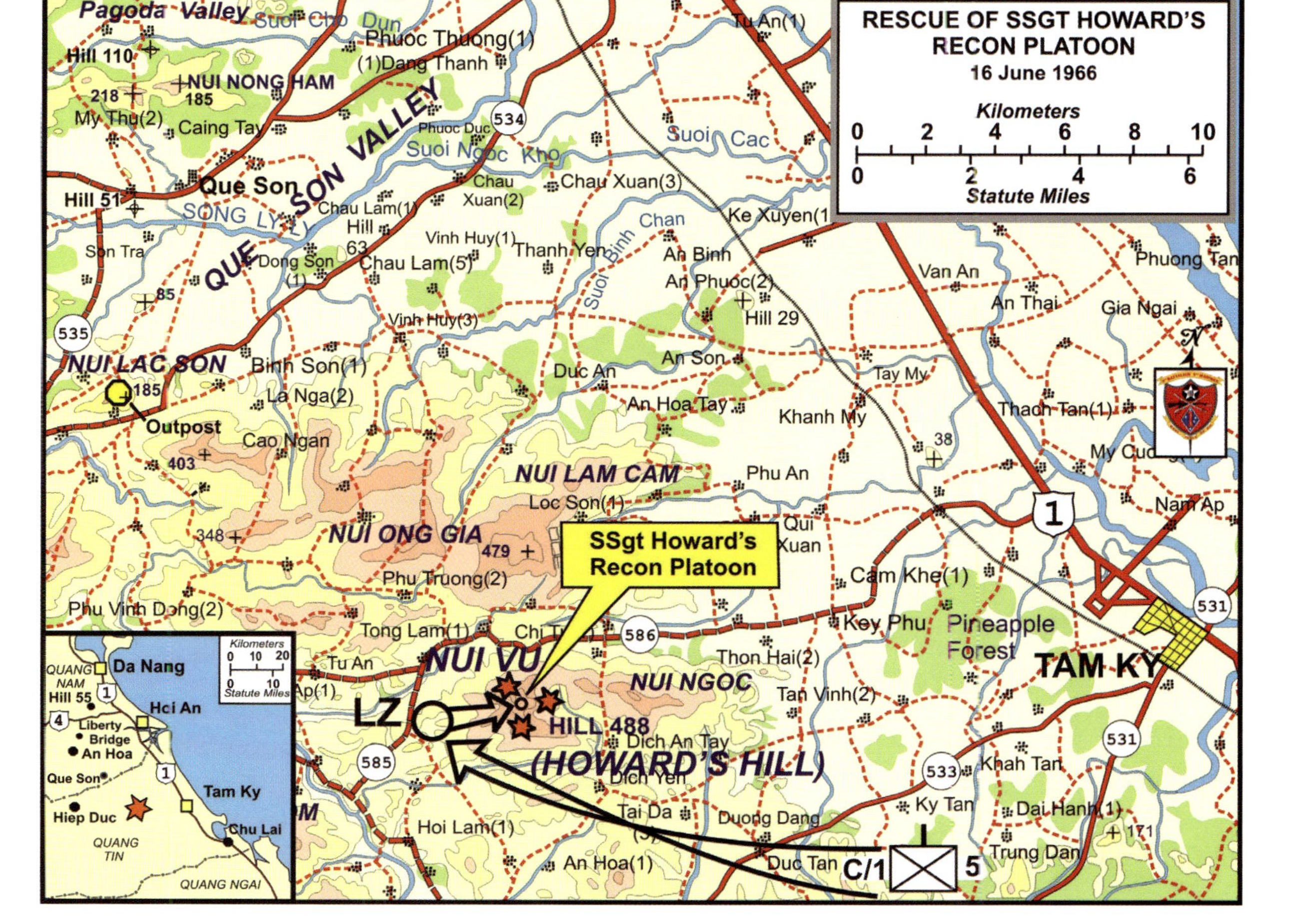

Map 3. Rescue of Staff Sgt. Jimmie Howard's Recon Team on Hill 488

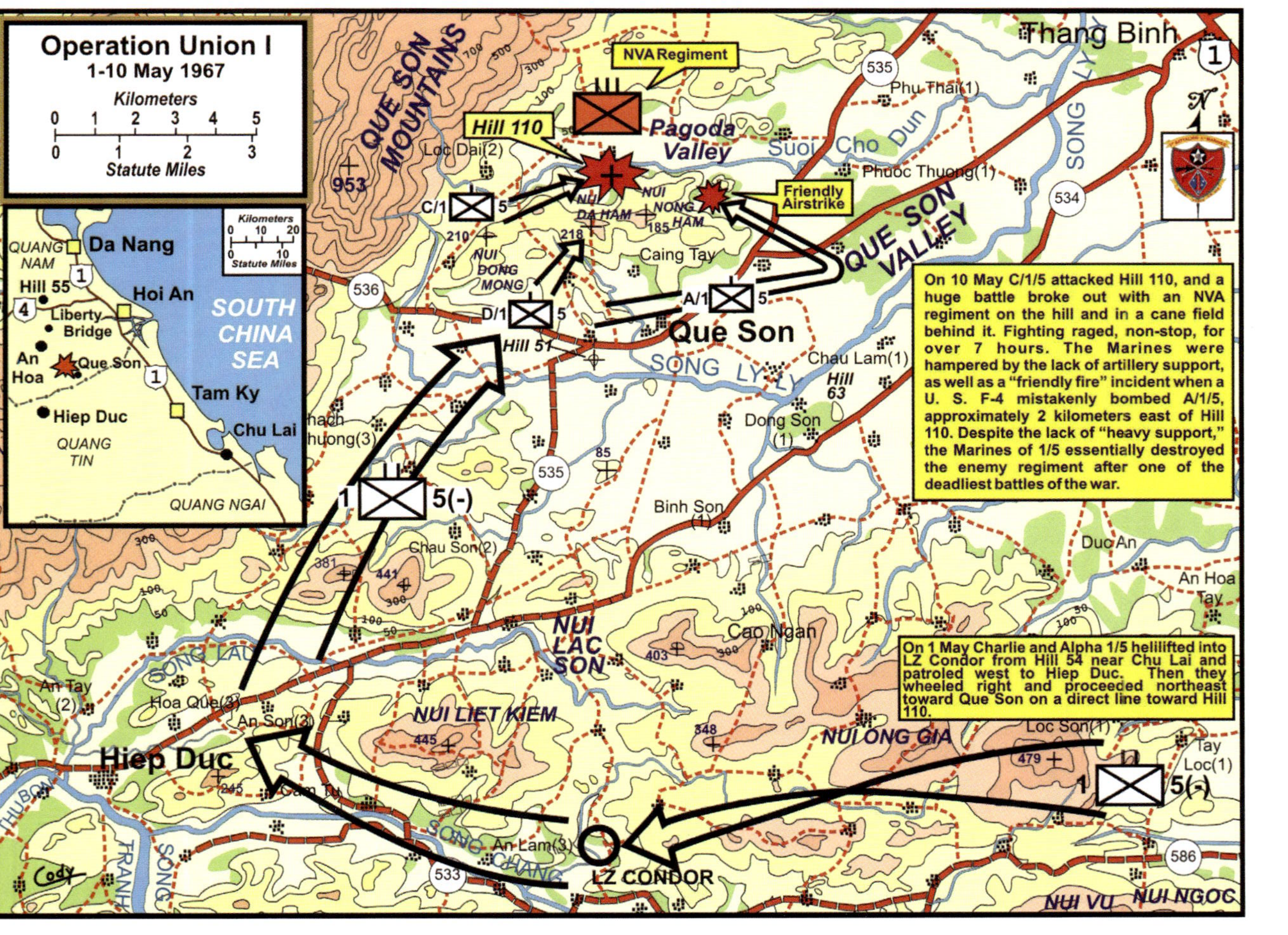

Map 4. Que Son Valley; Battle for Hill 110

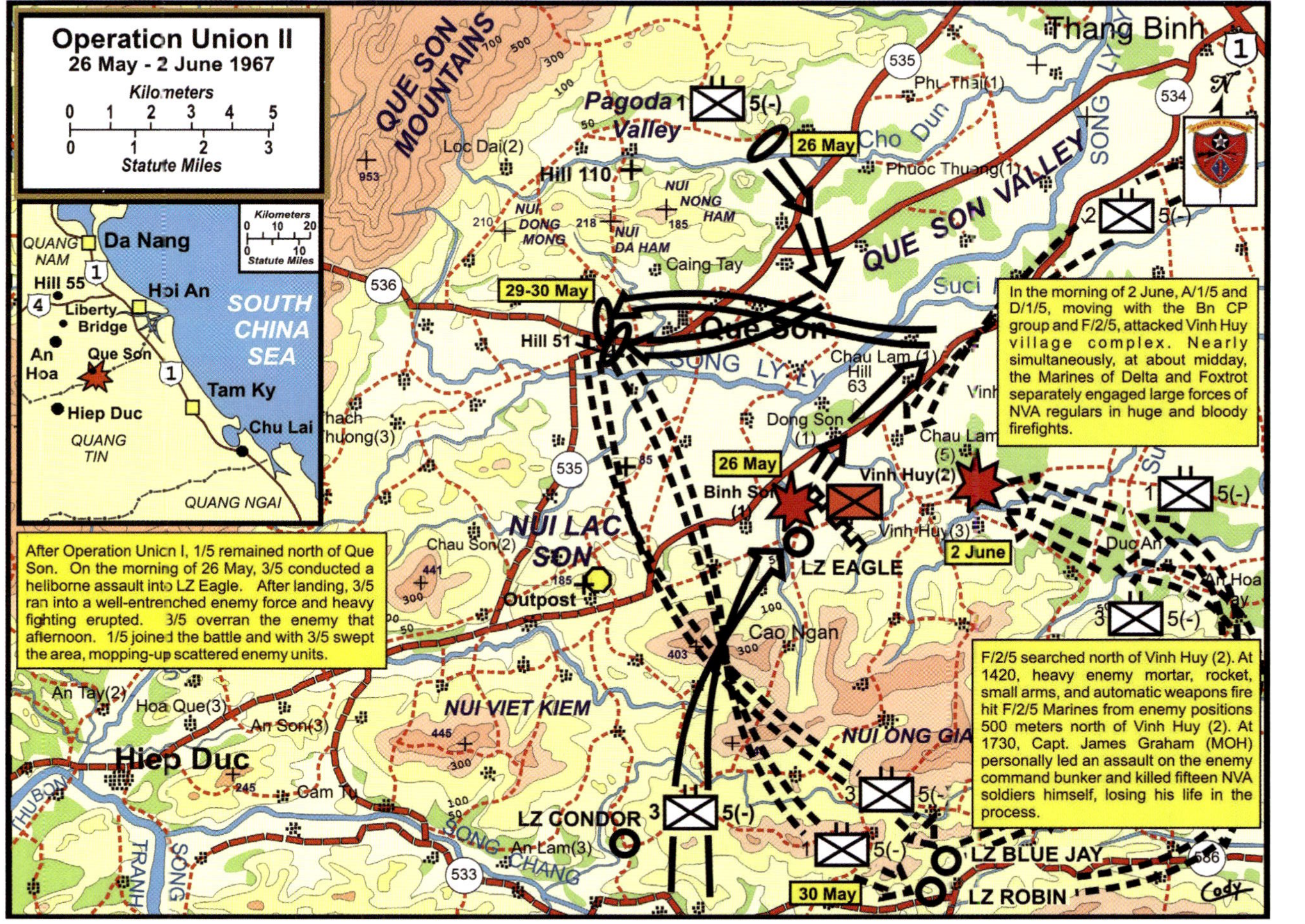

Map 5. Operation Union II

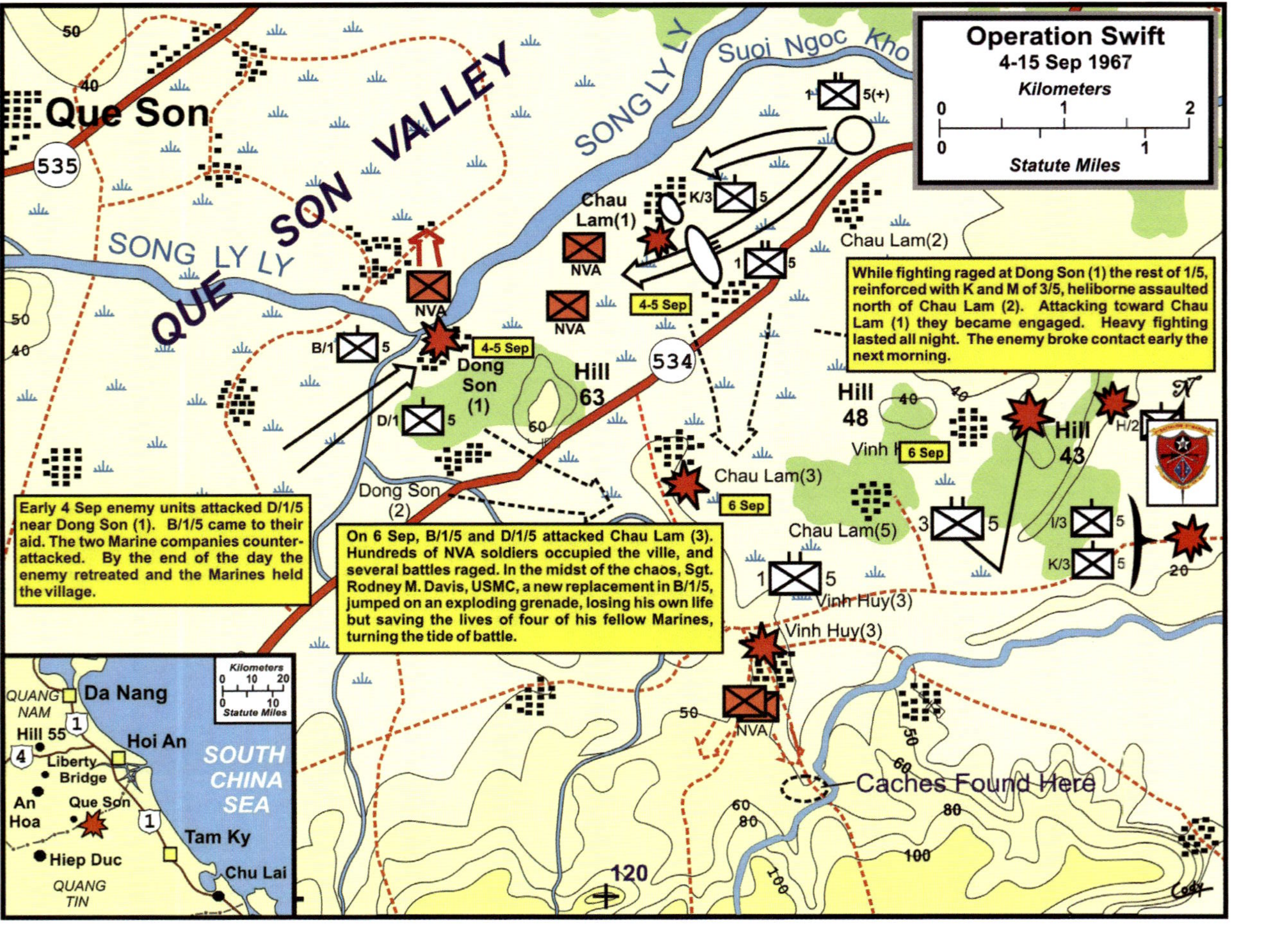

Map 6. Operation Swift

Map 7. Da Nang and Hoi An TAOR and Vicinity

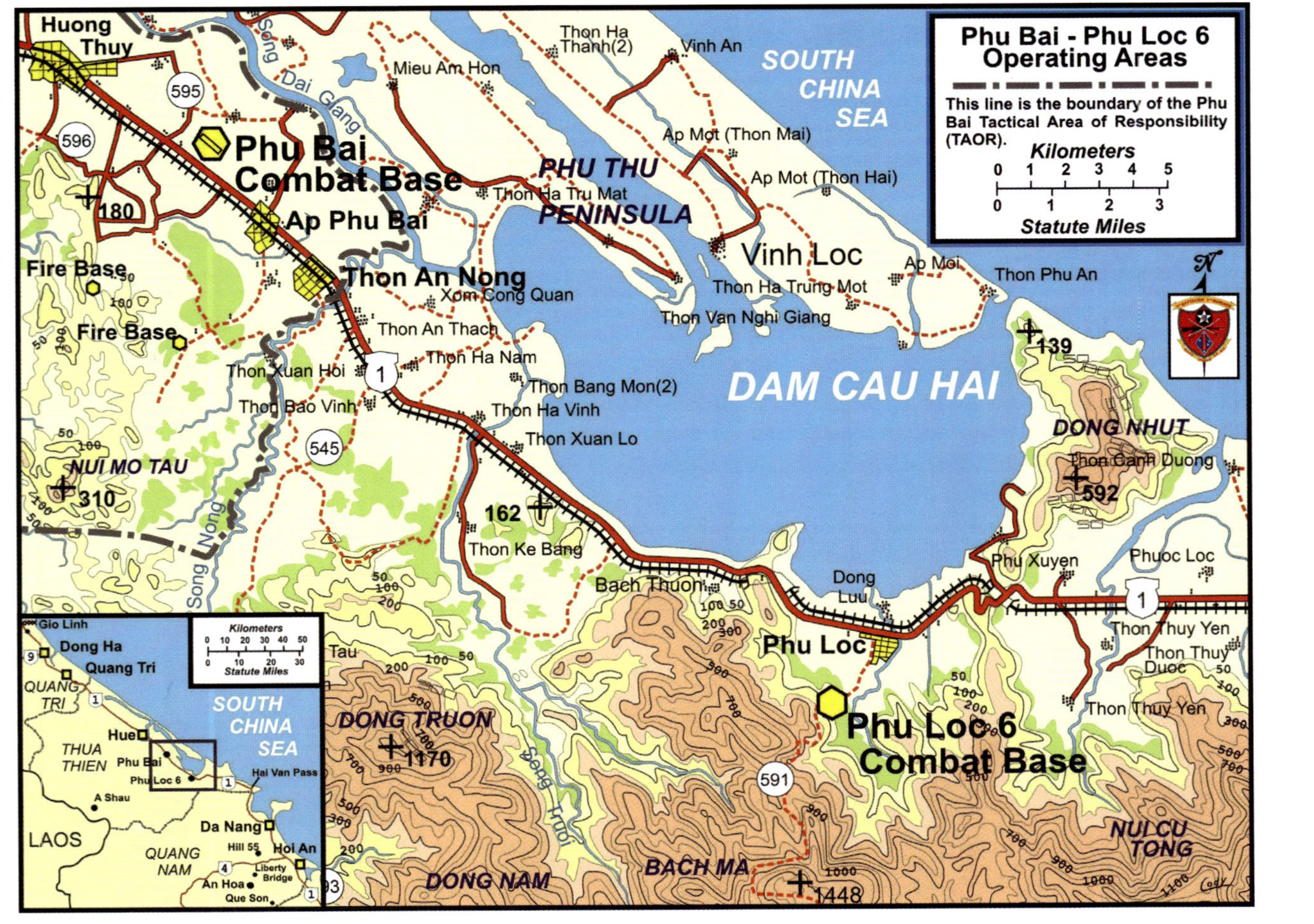

Map 8. Phu Loc 6 Combat Base TAOR and Phu Bai Combat Base

didn't even know we had been shot at until my driver told me to get my rifle ready, because those cracks were bullets cracking over our heads.

About two weeks after I arrived in Chu Lai, the 196th Light Infantry Brigade of the US Army arrived in Chu Lai to take over our TAOR. The 5th Marines headquarters prepared to head further north. We went north by convoy and set up just a little north of Tam Ky, right next to an ARVN compound; we sort of appended ourselves to the ARVN compound.

Sgt. Craig Jackson's duties included supervising all of the radio operators in the command tent from 0600 to 1800 every day, so he was in a very good position to monitor the events of Operation Union I. Craig remembers clearly the events that occurred on 10 May 1967 when Charlie 1/5 engaged an NVA regiment on Hill 110:

The word came in over the radio nets that Charlie Company was in a big battle, and a lot of discussion took place in that command tent, between the regimental S-3 officer, Maj. Dick Alger, and the regimental CO, on how units should move, who should move, how they could help each other, what units could go in as reinforcements, that kind of thing. I stayed really busy taking down the spot reports that came in that day and sending reports up to Division G-3. Colonel Houghton, the regimental commander, stayed very busy working with Major Alger, the S-3, analyzing all the reports as they came in, trying to make sense out of all of it.

I don't remember sensing a lot of anxiety coming from the radio reports from the Marines engaged in that battle, but when that air strike hit Alpha Company, before we knew how many casualties we had suffered, it got a little crazy there for a while in the 5th Marines command tent. It took a while to get that all sorted out. That battle resulted in a lot of KIAs and WIAs. A tremendous amount of radio traffic came in that day; spot reports from the various battalions engaged in the fighting, orders going out from the regimental CO, as well as our reports on the action going up to the division G-3. At the time, from my perspective in the regimental command tent, all this activity didn't really mean that much. I mean, we received a lot of information. I could certainly tell that the units in the field suffered a lot of casualties, but the names and the injuries didn't really hit home because of the overwhelming amount of information that came in over the tac net. At night we could see the fighting off in the distance; we could see the tracers and the explosions. But still, everything happened at a distance, and it didn't really hit home.

Then, two days later, Delta 1/5 got hit, and hit hard. I can remember that day, 12 May 1967, very well, because they not only suffered seventeen KIAs during that single day, but they also reported two Marines as missing in action. But the very high number of Marines killed during a single battle taking place in a single day surprised us, and the MIA reports shocked us. That very seldom happened to the Marines during the Vietnam War. That spot report got my attention. A report came in from a helicopter saying that they could see the two captured Marines being taken away by an enemy force, and it felt almost as though the NVA wanted us to see them.

I had just gotten to sleep early the next morning when someone came and woke me up. He told me to report to the first sergeant because I was headed to the grunts. I got up and reported to the Top. He said, "You're so gung ho, you can go play Marine for a while." So I caught a ride on a truck down to Tam Ky, where they brought all the KIAs in. Body bags lay in rows on the ground, seemingly everywhere. I hung out there on the defense line for the rest of the day, stayed with a corporal friend that I had known back in the States.

The next morning, while trying to find something to eat, I walked by this tent. A captain walked out, saw me, and asked me who I belonged to. I told him, "Nobody." He asked where I was headed, and I let him know that I didn't have any orders, that the Top had just told me to get on a truck, get to Tam Ky, and report to the grunts. A voice came from inside the tent, asked, "Is that a sergeant?" The captain said yes, and the voice said, "There's a resupply chopper going out to Delta Company. Put him on it." That's when I took my first helicopter ride on a CH-34.

When I got in the helicopter, it took off right away, and I almost fell out the door. I hadn't received any training on helicopters, so I had to learn on the job. Within a few minutes, we circled over an LZ next to a small village; I could see a bunch of burning hooches in the area. The helicopter landed, and they started throwing boxes of ammo off, so I figured I should get off, too. I hadn't received any training on helicopter operations, but I had seen a bunch of training films, so when I jumped off that helicopter, I started running. Gunny Fish, the Delta 1/5 company gunnery sergeant, grabbed me, and in his gravelly voice he asked, "Where you going?"

I said, "I don't know," so he said, "Get down!"

So I got down on one knee, started looking around the area, and the gunny said, "You're going to 2nd Platoon."

Before he sent me over to 2nd Platoon, the gunny called Staff Sergeant Mankowski over. Staff Sergeant Mankowski got down next to me and said, "I'm Staff Sergeant Mankowski, and I just got a battlefield promotion, and Staff Sergeant Lukenbill just got a battlefield commission." Then Lukenbill got on the helicopter that I got off of. Mankowski looked at me and said, "If you're scared, the men will know it." My body felt like jelly. I had never been in the field before, let alone in a combat zone, let alone on a battlefield. Staff Sergeant Mankowski, as the acting platoon commander, said, "Get in line; you're the new platoon guide." I got behind another buck sergeant, the acting platoon sergeant. Things started happening pretty fast out there. The platoon sergeant sent one of the Marines, a guy they called Big Campbell, over to get an NVA prisoner they had taken during the fighting. I'm not quite sure what that prisoner did, but I heard later that he kicked Big Campbell in the nuts, and Big Campbell retaliated in kind. Campbell and one other Marine were all that remained from his squad. Both of the Marines reported MIA came from Big Campbell's squad.

We moved out almost immediately, within ten minutes of my arrival in that LZ and joining Delta 1/5, and we started taking sniper fire right away. Welcome to the harsh realities of a combat zone during the Vietnam War. We spent the rest of that night and the next morning moving toward Que Son. Delta Company set up next to the artillery battery, located right next to the site where they planned to build the main combat base.

On 19 May, battalion called in an air strike targeting some enemy snipers who had harassed us. The first air strike that I ever witnessed from up close, those planes hit several locations right across the Song Ly Ly [Ly Ly River] inside half a click south of the combat base. What a great show. Second Platoon got the mission of patrolling the area of the air strikes. We went out, crossed the river, to see what we could find. I felt really nervous. I knew how to be a sergeant, but I didn't know much about the infantry. As the platoon guide, I just followed the platoon sergeant. On the other side of the river it was a good thing we had some engineers with us, because we found a dud bomb, so they blew it in place. The air strike had blown some hooches up, and at least one civilian had died. We moved out further, going along the river bank on the south side.

All of a sudden we got caught in a sniper ambush. Several snipers opened up on us in a crossfire. One of the guys in my platoon, called Little Campbell, tried to fire on the enemy positions with his 3.5-inch rocket launcher, but it misfired. Quite a few of the other Marines' rifles had jammed. I had a brand-new rifle, and it worked just fine, so I did a lot of shooting that day. I couldn't really see anything, but I kept firing. One of our corpsmen, Doc Omilion, lying behind me, started firing his .45-caliber pistol using me as cover; he fired his .45 repeatedly in the general direction of the snipers. He had just joined the platoon as well. I told him to cease firing so close to my ear. Little Campbell went further down the trail and found the place where the trail crosses the river again. He found this knoll that sat just above the trail in some shrubs and got his 3.5-inch rocket launcher ready and fired it. Again, the rocket launcher misfired, and then it misfired again, and I could see the gooks start to zero in on his position. You could see some of the shrubs around him cut down by enemy gunfire. We yelled at him to get down, and then a round hit really close to him, and he yelled, "Hey, they're really trying to ding me!" We yelled at him again to get down, but then, only about thirty meters away from me, he took a round right in the middle of his forehead, instantly blowing out the back of his head. When Little Campbell got hit, we were standing behind him, not too far away. Doc Omilion rushed to his side and tried to treat him, but you didn't have to be there for very long to know what dead looked like.

By this time, one of our machine gun teams that had been separated from us when the shooting first started caught up to us and started putting a high volume of fire on the enemy positions, which really slowed down the rate of enemy small arms fire. We worked our way up to this rice paddy dike, back down toward the river, and we could see a steel beam that crossed the river, pretty high, maybe twelve feet above the very deep water. It looked dangerous, but it provided the only fast way back across the river, and we took it. We couldn't just leave Little Campbell out there. Big Campbell wrapped him up in a poncho, and slung him over his shoulder and ran across that steel beam under fire. Everyone who crossed that beam that day got fired at; rounds hit the beam several times. We took the only way out of the trap. I was so concerned about making it across that river that when I got close to the other side I just leaped. I remember when I landed on the other side and hit the deck, I took stock of myself. I saw that I was down to three full magazines, I had lost all my grenades, and my utilities had gotten all torn up. I felt like I had been in Vietnam for about a year. The firefight had probably gone on for about an hour, and I had only been in the bush for about four days, but it already seemed like a lifetime.

At one point, maybe a week later, Staff Sergeant Mankowski had gone somewhere and left me in charge as the acting platoon sergeant. Lieutenant Lukenbill, our platoon commander, suffered from an attack of appendicitis. Obviously really sick and in a lot of pain, he had to be medevaced, but I could tell that he didn't want to go. I didn't want him to go either, because as the acting platoon sergeant, if he left I would be in charge of the platoon, and I hadn't been there for very long. As a new guy, I really didn't know what I was doing. Fortunately, one of the squad leaders, Corporal Fitzpatrick, helped me out a lot. Still out in the field, he was very short, which meant that he would return to the United States in just a few weeks. I told Fitz, "It's you and me now. You just tell me what to do."

We had *good* officers in Delta 1/5, although we didn't always have *enough* officers. Lieutenant Lukenbill and 1st Lieutenant McInturff, our CO, proved to be outstanding combat leaders. I can remember watching Lieutenant McInturff one day as he got ready to call in a situation report. He always did everything really quicklike. He quickly found his terrain features, mountaintops, and the like, that he could use to take back azimuths to determine our position exactly. I sat in some shade, next to my radio operator, watching Lieutenant McInturff go about his business. He walked back and forth, just a few feet in front of me. He pointed at a grassy spot right in front of me and said, "Gee, that ground seems soft right there. It doesn't seem right. Gunny, check that out." Gunny Fish looked at me and told me to check it out. One of my Marines got out his entrenching tool and started digging it up, and we found out that I had been sitting on a punji pit.[1] The VC had used green bamboo, so it hadn't broken. I remember I turned to my radio man, who I always thought carried bad luck anyway, and I said, "Don't ever sit near me again."

When we got back, the new Hill 51 Combat Base had been built. For the next few days we patrolled constantly around the new combat base. I can remember one patrol very clearly, because when we got back to the combat base we learned that we would have to go over by the graveyard, close to the artillery battery; worse, we couldn't stay inside the combat base, and I can remember feeling pretty pissed that we had to stay outside the wire. But, we had our orders, so we went.

We had just taken off our packs and started to dig fighting holes when I looked back over toward the combat base and watched as the VC mortared the combat base. We heard a short time later that the mortar attack wounded a bunch of Marines, and the battery commander of Delta 2/11, Capt. Marty Tull, died. We didn't complain too much after that.

Sergeant Jackson had experienced a violent baptism by fire during his early days with Delta 1/5, but worse was yet to come. From 26 May through 1 June 1967, 1/5's Marines fought several fierce skirmishes with small enemy units. These firefights resulted in several confirmed enemy KIA as well as a few probable enemy KIA and WIA and a few detainees, mostly local Vietnamese civilians without the proper identification papers, suspected Viet Cong.

On 27 May 1967, Company F, 2nd Battalion, 5th Marines, the infantry company known as Foxtrot 2/5, went under the operational control (OPCON) of the

1st Battalion, 5th Marines as one of their maneuvering forces. Another hammer had been added to Lieutenant Colonel Hilgartner's arsenal. Commanded by Capt. James A. Graham, Foxtrot 2/5's Marines moved west into the Que Son Valley from Highway 534 from an intersection about five kilometers east of Hill 51 Combat Base with the mission of seeking out and destroying any enemy positions they encountered. Foxtrot 2/5 engaged the enemy on several occasions over the next few days in a series of fierce but brief firefights while moving over fifteen kilometers cross-country, hopping from village to village through the rice paddies of the Que Son Valley. The Marines of Foxtrot 2/5 killed several VC and captured many weapons and other materials of war.

On 30 May 1967 the 1/5 battalion CP group and Delta 1/5, still under the command of 1st Lt. D. L. McInturff, helilifted from the combat base to LZ Robin, located about eight kilometers east of LZ Condor and about fifteen kilometers southeast of Hill 51 Combat Base. With the cordon forces in place, the battalion commenced a coordinated attack in a northeasterly direction from the LZ into the northwestern portion of the Tam Ky district. When they reached the eastern tip of the mountain range that defined the southern edge of the Que Son Valley, they then wheeled around the eastern side of Nui Da Ngua (Hill 251) in a northwesterly direction through Thang Binh district back toward Hill 51 Combat Base. They hoped that this enveloping movement would catch VC and NVA forces in a vice between the main force of the battalion and the companies working in the northern section of the Que Son Valley. It succeeded, but the Marines would not realize that until the bullets had already begun flying.

Late on the morning of 2 June 1967, the Marines of Alpha and Delta 1/5, moving with the battalion CP group and Foxtrot 2/5, approximately twelve hundred meters apart from each other, reached the vicinity of the Vinh Huy village complex. Nearly simultaneously, at about midday, the Marines of Delta and Foxtrot separately engaged large forces of NVA regulars in huge and bloody firefights.

The Marines of Delta 1/5 swept the paddy area east of a small hamlet called Chau Lam (5), situated about fifteen hundred meters north of Vinh Huy, in a southwesterly direction. As the Delta Marines approached Chau Lam (5), eighty to a hundred well-camouflaged NVA in heavily fortified positions suddenly opened up on them at close range. The enemy fire swept across the front and left flank of the Marines, catching the left flank platoons in a deadly crossfire. Throughout the rest of that day, and well into the night, the Marines of Delta Company fought in a life-or-death struggle at nearly point blank range with a determined force of NVA soldiers. At approximately 1445 that afternoon, after nearly three hours of deadly combat, the reserve platoon deployed to the right to roll up the enemy flank, but it also came under heavy automatic weapons fire. The Marines fired 60 mm mortars on the enemy positions, and

1st Lieutenant McInturff ordered an assault under the cover of his 60 mm mortar barrages, but the assault pulled up short after taking heavy casualties.

Alpha 1/5 also fought with large enemy forces during this major battle. Rick Zell remembers:

> Bill Vacca took command of Bravo Company for a short period of time right as Operation Union II started up. He didn't last too long. He got shot during a pretty big firefight, just as Alpha passed through Bravo's positions. I saw Bill, bleeding pretty badly, and I thought he might even die, so I went over to him and knelt down beside him and started talking softly to him, afraid that this really great guy was about to die. He looked up at me and said with a surprisingly strong voice, "Get the hell out of here, Zell. I'm not dying and I don't need you cuddling me. Get back to your Marines, goddammit!" I took off, because I could tell that although hurt pretty badly, Bill would make it and he really didn't want me worrying about him.
>
> On 2 June 1967, my platoon split off from Alpha Company to provide security for the battalion CP group. I saw Captain Babich get killed, not that far away from where I stood, and I heard it on the battalion tactical network. For a while there it seemed like Operation Union II was over. The first really big fight had died down, and not much had happened for a couple of days. We actually headed back that afternoon to Que Son Combat Base. Foxtrot 2/5 acted as point for the battalion, not too far away from us. We saw this very large rice paddy area, and to my surprise Foxtrot Company started going straight across the open paddy area, the entire company, en masse. They stayed spread out, but they didn't send a point element across to check it out. They just started walking across the open area. It struck me as odd that an entire company would walk across that huge open rice paddy area like that. I wouldn't have done it that way. It seemed as though everyone thought the operation had ended, that the fighting was over, so we just started to go straight back to the combat base, and we took the shortest route, right across that large open rice paddy area. It just felt wrong. That rice paddy stretched probably a thousand meters across, and a thick tree line dominated the other side. In broad daylight, it seemed to me as though every Marine in the rice paddy looked like a target in a shooting gallery. As Foxtrot 2/5 got close to that tree line, all hell broke loose. Not just with the Foxtrot 2/5 Marines, but with everyone out in that area. We got hit on all sides. My platoon, providing security for the battalion CP group, was in the shit, the rest of Alpha Company was in the shit, and Foxtrot 2/5 had stepped in really deep shit as well. Alpha and Delta Companies both maneuvered to support Foxtrot. My platoon stayed

with the battalion CP group, providing security. We mounted a small promontory, and I could see the battlefield really well, Captain Babich and the rest of the Marines of Alpha Company clearly visible in front of us. Although from a few hundred meters away I couldn't be certain, I just knew it *was* him. He was standing up, moving around, sort of like he was calmly directing traffic, one minute, and the next minute he fell to the ground. He had both of his radio operators with him, his company radioman and the battalion radioman. Standing up, directing traffic, Captain Babich and one of his radiomen were easily shot and killed. It was unnecessary. He just didn't have a sense of personal safety, which became his undoing. He was a great guy; I had gotten friendly with him, but I had told him repeatedly that he needed to get himself down. He died right in front of me doing what we had warned him to stop doing. What a waste. I just could never get through to him. I couldn't believe that he had been in Vietnam for a year, and he had never gotten a sense of when he could walk around and when he should have taken cover. He just kept walking around like he was still back at Camp Pendleton. I mean, sometimes as leaders, officers and senior NCOs would have to expose ourselves, be the first to go, to get our Marines moving; but most of the time I found this completely unnecessary, and it eventually caught up with him. We heard the report just a couple of minutes later coming in over the radio. Capt. R. G. Babich, USMC, Alpha Six, was dead. I couldn't worry or think about this for too long, though, because an NVA regiment was attacking us, hitting us hard, and the battle had just begun.

The battalion's combat after-action reports for Operations Union I and Union II lead the reader to believe that the Marine forces maneuvered very methodically based on detailed intelligence reports. In fact, the combat after-action report for Operation Union II indicates that "the Battalion commenced a coordinated attack," an accurate description, at least from the perspective of the battalion commander. Certainly, each maneuvering company had assigned routes of march, phase lines, specific objectives, and so forth, and each company worked in conjunction with, and in support of, the other companies. However, things look much different to a platoon commander a couple of levels down on the chain of command. Rick Zell, one of those platoon commanders, claims,

In reality, we had a bunch of Marine rifle companies, operating independently, walking around the Que Son Valley, walking down some trails, and acting as bait. Then, when one company would get hit and started taking casualties, they would send another company to reinforce them. When that larger force started getting hammered, they'd send more troops. Then, by the time enough Marines forces massed to do significant damage to the enemy, the enemy would invariably break off and disappear. That pattern repeated itself constantly. When a large battle finally took place, they would give the operation a name, and then wrote the after-action reports in such a way as to indicate that we had planned it all. In reality, from my perspective, simple luck (either good luck or bad luck depending upon how you look at these things) put us in contact with the NVA in the Que Son Valley. Luck sometimes gave us the advantage, and allowed us to fix the enemy in a disadvantageous position and bring our heavy firepower to bear, and we would win those big battles.

This was one of those battles. In this particular case, very bad luck put Foxtrot 2/5 on point to run smack into that NVA regiment. The entire lead element of Foxtrot 2/5, pinned down in that rice paddy, became the most important thing in all of our lives. From that point on, everything we did focused on trying to get the Marines of Foxtrot 2/5 out of that rice paddy. That's when Delta 1/5, under Dave McInturff, got involved. Delta tried to get into a position to flank the NVA positions, hoping to take the pressure off the Marines of Foxtrot Company.

Monitoring the battalion tac net, I heard every transmission made by Captain Graham until his last one. Captain Graham did everything possible to get his Marines out of that terrible trap. He died leading a group of his Marines as they attacked an enemy machine gun position. It seemed surreal, like watching *Apocalypse Now*. I could see the battle; I could hear it all and hear the frantic radio transmissions as this Marine rifle company was decimated. My platoon went out that night, trying to round up any survivors from Foxtrot or Delta Companies, and we did find a few other Marines who froze in position, scared shitless, hiding from the enemy, and unfortunately we found several dead Marines as well. It was just disastrous.

Col. Pete Hilgartner reported many years later that he purposely decided to put Foxtrot 2/5 on the left flank of Delta Company, in a two-up, one-back attacking formation, for a very specific reason. He had just conferred with Colonel Houghton, who indicated that he had good intelligence that a large force of NVA lurked very close by and that he should keep an eye on his left flank as he moved toward the next set of objectives. Hilgartner also moved Alpha Company, in the reserve position, left to support Foxtrot's attack position. Thus, Hilgartner placed his main strength on the left side of the battalion's formation, and that's where most of the battle took place.

On 2 June 1967, during the battle for Vinh Huy (2), Alpha Company lost five

KIA, including their company commander, and ten WIA. Delta Company lost seventeen KIA and twenty-two WIA, and one Marine later died of wounds inflicted during that terrible fight. Foxtrot Company lost thirty-two KIA, including their company commander, and thirty-nine WIA. On the other side of the macabre scales of kill ratios, Delta 1/5 reported a total of forty enemy KIA confirmed, Foxtrot 2/5 reported a total of 170 enemy bodies, and Alpha 1/5 reported an additional thirty confirmed enemy KIA. When reporting enemy casualties, most Marine Corps infantry company commanders took great care to make sure that their enemy KIA reports were based on enemy bodies that they had physically counted. Often asked to report any probable enemy KIA as well, many did, and they often reported probable enemy WIA. These probable counts were mostly guesses and not really relied upon at the company or battalion levels, but the confirmed body counts usually proved very accurate. In addition to those enemy KIA confirmed and reported by Alpha, Delta, and Foxtrot Companies, they collectively reported more than five hundred additional probable enemy KIA as a result of the battle for Vinh Huy (2).

Rick Zell remembers the battle for Vinh Huy (2) as a gruesome bloodbath:

> My platoon went out to try to find any survivors from Delta and Foxtrot. The guys we found from Foxtrot who had managed to live through that holocaust acted pretty upset. They had either hid or played dead until it got dark, and many of them obviously suffered from battle fatigue. Sporadic firefights continued to break out. Delta's Marines still fought for their lives to our west, and it started getting dark as hell, but we went out into the battlefield to see if we could find them and bring them back in. We walked around in the rice paddy, blind as hell at first and yelled, "Anyone from Foxtrot Company? Anyone hear us?" I could hear McInturff on the battalion tac net, and I could see the firefights, and then battalion sent up illumination flares over our heads to help us search for survivors. We spent the rest of that night walking and crawling around on that battlefield looking for Marines, and we did find a few and brought them back in with us. Then we'd go back out to look some more, and that went on all night.
>
> That day, 2 June, turned out to be a really wild day. It seemed like every Marine in the Que Son Valley fought the enemy that day. At one point the Marines got mixed in with the NVA, and the battalion CP group came under direct attack. We tried to use artillery to support Foxtrot Company, since they had been hit hardest, but since the point element of Foxtrot 2/5 went down so close to the main enemy positions, the artillery could have easily blown the Foxtrot Marines away. So artillery was of minimal use to us during that battle because the enemy stayed so close to our positions.

Marine commanders officially terminated Operation Union II on 5 June 1967. Rick Zell's oldest child was born on 2 June 1967, but through some mix-up Rick never received his Red Cross notification, so he remained unaware of that fact until nearly a month later, when a letter from his wife, Bernadette, finally caught up with him. "I remember feeling pretty mad at the time, because the Red Cross had not done its job, but these days it's kind of a blessing, because I will never forget my daughter's birthday: 2 June 1967, the date of the battle for Vinh Huy (2)."

Sgt. Craig Jackson found himself right in the middle of the fighting during Operation Union II:

> During the last week of May, we got choppered out on Operation Union II. Alpha and Delta Companies went out together, and Foxtrot 2/5 joined us. Three Five stayed up on a ridge overlooking our area of operations. When we landed in the LZ, we took incoming enemy small arms fire—not particularly heavy at first, but definitely a hot LZ. Enemy ground fire hit an American Phantom jet, which crashed into the side of a mountain near our LZ. These fast movers made a lot of runs, dropping bombs, strafing, shooting rockets, and one of them got hit and crashed into the side of the mountain. It went up in a big ball of flame. Boom!
>
> We got out of that rice paddy LZ just as soon as we could and started patrolling. We got in a few firefights over the next couple of days. On the 2nd of June, early in the morning, we headed down out of the hills. Second Platoon brought up the rear of Delta Company. By now, Staff Sergeant Mankowski had returned and was acting platoon commander; I was the acting platoon sergeant. I can remember the word coming back that they had seen a bunch of stuff up ahead of us. We moved into a village area; we saw packs lying around, fires still burning, clothing, and all kinds of stuff. One of the guys said, "This is some bad shit right here." We moved through that area. One of the other companies had gotten in a small firefight in this area, but it just looked like a whole bunch of gooks had bivouacked there and had just taken off.
>
> We had come out of some hills; the company was down and to the left of my position, and I could see them moving through the village. We began to see folks running from that village, across an open area and into a tree line that fronted an adjacent village. I asked the squad leader, Fitzpatrick, what was going on. He said, "Those are gooks. Open up on them." We started firing down in front of the company, but we got a radio call right away from Lieutenant McInturff to cease firing, that we were shooting at civilians. So we stopped shooting, but by the time we caught up with the company, we could see a couple of them down in that open area. They were definitely NVA soldiers,

wearing camouflage uniforms. The Marines of Delta Company curved around in front of me. As the platoon sergeant of the trail platoon, I traveled with the last squad, back at the end of the company column. All of a sudden I could hear firing off to the left and well ahead of us. We found out that the Marines of Foxtrot 2/5 had been hit, and we could hear the firing really ramp up. Then, suddenly, some gooks took off across the rice paddy right in front of us, maybe ten or fifteen of them. They all had uniforms and camouflage, pieces of shrubbery on them. We opened up on them and nailed every one of them.

Then battalion called in an air strike on the area just to our right front, across the open area and in and around the tree line and small village. After the air strike, we formed up on line, and we got orders to "recon by fire." I stayed on the extreme right flank of the company, trying to keep my Marines on line and moving forward and shooting from the hip. Since we were on the right flank, and the village sort of swung to the left, we had to also swing left, and we had to move pretty fast to stay up and to keep on line with the rest of the company. We ended up going into that tree line. When we came out of that tree line, we started across another big rice paddy, still on line. That's when the gooks opened up on us.

At that moment our battle formation had Foxtrot 2/5 on the left and Delta 1/5 on the right. Second Platoon was all the way on the right side of the attacking formation, and 3rd Platoon was on the left, with 1st Platoon in trail. 3rd Platoon was more in front of the village, taking most of the enemy fire. When I went to the ground and started firing back, my rifle jammed. I lay behind a low rice paddy dike, and every time I tried to move, a bunch of enemy small arms fire would hit the paddy dike, which was only about a foot and a half high. Fortunately, that paddy dike angled away from the village, off to the left. People were getting hit. The Marines looked back at me, yelled at me to ask if I was okay. I let them know I was okay, and then they told me that they were planning to assault a knoll right up ahead of them. When they assaulted that knoll, and everybody started firing, I caught up with them; actually, I passed them. Later on, Fred Scott told me that I was one of the fastest guys he'd ever seen. I started out somewhat behind them, so I had to move pretty fast to catch up with them, and when you're under fire you do move pretty quick. I came up from the ground running and passed those guys as they attacked toward that knoll, which had a big tree on it. When we made it to the top of the knoll, we spread out around it and took up firing positions but started taking casualties. We had a red-headed kid from Philadelphia, named McNally, who had received the Silver Star for his actions during Operation Union I. He was a fire team leader, a little guy. He had gone up on the other side of this knoll and said he could see the enemy positions and hollered at us to send over an M79 grenade launcher. A couple of guys crawled over to him with the M79, but they all came back a few minutes later. McNally had taken a round through his elbow. Actually, an enemy round had lodged in the breech of the M79 he had slung over his shoulder, which had saved his life. I remember helping the corpsman treat him. We weren't able to get any medevac choppers in, so we just had to treat the wounded and protect them the best we could.

From our position on that knoll we looked across this rocky area right at the village, so we had front row seats for some air strikes that battalion called in on that village. The jets came in from our right to the left, right over our heads. When they dropped those bombs they looked like they would land on us; some of them went over our heads by no more than forty or fifty feet, but they all hit the enemy positions in that village. One bomb blew a gook up in the air about thirty feet; he flew up into the air, still in a firing position. The jets fired rockets, they fired cannons, and they dropped bombs. I can remember that when they fired the cannons, the spent shells rained right down on our heads. Then they dropped napalm, and those canisters went right over our heads, but they hit the enemy positions in the village, right on top of them. It seemed like those napalm bombs would kill everyone in the village, but the enemy kept firing at us, and the situation was still very dangerous. This went on all afternoon. One of our Marines got hit by shrapnel in his hip from one of the bombs. I knew all about close air support, but this was really close.

Orders came down for us to assault the enemy positions in the village. So we left the knoll and went through this rocky area a little out in front of our positions. An M60 machine gun position, manned by a Marine named Lance Corporal Pennington, had set up in those rocks; as we moved through the rocks we all dropped off our extra machine gun ammo. He had given the enemy positions fits all afternoon. We got right up next to that village, but we couldn't get any further because of heavy enemy fire. It got dark fast; they threw grenades at us, and we threw grenades back at them. We realized that the gooks had mounted a counterattack to try to flank our attacking positions. The company command group didn't know our exact position, so we popped a flare so the CO could see us. Once they knew where we were, and realized that it was getting dark and we were still taking heavy enemy fire, they told us to pull back. There were two problems with that: one, the enemy also now knew our exact position, and two, we would have to move back across that dry rice paddy while exposed to enemy fire. We couldn't stay put; we knew we had to move back, but it proved very tough to move across that open ground. Night rapidly fell so that the red and green tracers that crisscrossed that dry rice paddy gave pretty dramatic evidence that we would have to move across a heavy kill zone. Our movement back away from the village and across that big rice paddy towards the safety of that knoll turned into a situation where it became every man for himself. Just before I got ready to make my move, a Huey gunship moved in to fire on the village with both rockets and machine guns. Unfortunately, we lay on the ground so close to the enemy positions that the chopper's door gunner shot my radio man in the arm and the thigh. As I got ready to make my move across that dry rice paddy, something lit up the dusk. I looked back to my left rear and saw a group of soldiers, some of them no more than fifteen feet away from me. One of my squad leaders, Corporal Fitzpatrick, lay close by and I asked him if they were Marines. He said they were gooks and to open up on them. By that time the first one stood less than fifteen feet away from me, so I shot him, and then I went to automatic and shot two or three of the others, and then my weapon's magazine ran out of ammo and I thought I was about to die. My mind seemed calm, and I knew I had to change magazines, but I couldn't get my hands to cooperate, so by the time I got a new magazine in my rifle, the other Marines in the area had shot all the other enemy soldiers. We started moving much quicker to get out of that area. I don't know how long it took to crawl out of there. Before we made it, I hit Fred Scott in the rump with my helmet as he crawled over one of the paddy dikes. I just crawled right over him and kept going. Later on, Fred claimed that I was not only the fastest runner, but I was also the fastest crawler in Delta Company.

When we finally got back in that night, around midnight, as we approached the platoon CP, one of the Marines, a kid named Cherry, manning the radio, asked me for the password. I told him I didn't know anything about any goddamned password. I guess he figured that I wasn't a threat, because he told me to come on in. We stayed there for the rest of the night, the night of 2 June 1967. The next morning we could see all the carnage out in that rice paddy. We finally got medevac choppers in and got out all of our casualties, and that was pretty much the end of Delta Company's involvement in Operation Union II.

We stayed out in that area for a few more days, but that marked the end of the fighting. Still, it seemed pretty strange out there. We looked out across that big rice paddy the next morning, amazed that any of us made it across that paddy. We had lost seventeen KIAs and a lot of wounded, and two more of Delta's Marines had gone missing. Fortunately, the two MIAs ran into another company the next day and made it back. On the other hand, we had killed a whole bunch of NVA. The next day I had to make a head call, so I went into this small garden and started to dig a latrine. My e-tool hit a hastily buried NVA body. We found bodies buried all over the place out there.

Delta 1/5 company commander 1st Lt. Dave McInturff had a first-hand view of the action. At 0805 on the morning of 2 June 1967, Delta Company traveled once again with Lieutenant Colonel Hilgartner and the 1/5 Battalion CP group. McInturff recalls:

> We had stopped for a break, setting up on a low rise, and we came very close to where Alpha Company and Foxtrot 2/5 fought the NVA that day. Operation Union II was based on some good, strong intelligence reports, which didn't happen very often, but this time the intelligence guys got it right. They had determined that elements of the 2nd NVA Division operated in our area, and Union II was designed to find and destroy them. That morning we came really close to where Foxtrot 2/5 had advanced, and we saw a couple of NVA close to our positions running away from us; one of my machine gun teams took them out, killing them both immediately. It turned out to be an enemy observation post (OP). They had been watching us, and then they ran, trying to get back to their main force to report our movements. Early that afternoon, Lieutenant Colonel Hilgartner told us to attack that village area, which he suspected to be the location of the main enemy force. I put two platoons up on line in attack formation and had one platoon back in rear security, a two up, one back formation. Lt. Bill Link's platoon had rear security. I had my CP group in the middle and began crossing the rice paddies. At about that time, Capt. Ron Babich, the Alpha Company commander, was killed by an NVA who jumped up out of a spider hole and shot him. Foxtrot 2/5 stayed to the left, Delta Company to the right. We were attacking side-by-side across those rice paddies, and all of a sudden all hell broke loose. My two attacking platoons had moved about halfway across the rice paddies, completely out in the open, before they opened up on us. We found out later that the NVA had cut firing ports in the side of a ditch, and fired at us at paddy dike level, cutting the legs out from under my men. I had stayed in contact with Captain Graham, the CO of Foxtrot 2/5, because we covered each other's flanks. We coordinated movement on the battalion tactical net to make sure that either of us didn't get out in front of the other. Then, all of a sudden, the shit broke loose. My radio operator told me that Foxtrot was getting the shit kicked out of them, but Delta was stuck in the middle of a firestorm as well, so I didn't have much time to worry about Foxtrot Company. I realized that with all the enemy firing going on, and our two companies so close to each other,

we needed to make sure of our exact locations. So I popped a smoke grenade. I called Captain Graham and told him that I was right behind the red smoke grenade. I asked him if he saw our smoke, and he said, "No, I don't see your smoke." So I said, "Okay, here's my coordinates," and gave them to him. We never really established exactly where we were in relationship to one another. He couldn't see my smoke, and I couldn't figure out exactly where he was, either. We were supposed to tie together, with his right flank in contact with my left flank, as we moved across that area. Of course, I had the most wide open area, and he had some high ground he had to go across, and that's where he ran into the shit, on that high ground. Delta Company didn't run into the enemy until we had proceeded quite a ways further across those dry rice paddies. Captain Graham went on to do just a fabulous job commanding Foxtrot Company in the middle of that battle, but, unfortunately, he was killed in action.

Finally, during a little bit of a lull, I took my radio operator and moved my CP group to the left, running out of the rice paddies, and got into the area where Bill Link and his Marines were fighting, linked up with them. We set up a defensive perimeter there in some trenches. The fighting went on, hot and heavy, but we got our 60 mm and 81 mm mortars firing, and we called in artillery and air strikes on the enemy positions. My AO worked with my FO, and they called in continuous heavy support, alternating back and forth between air and artillery support. We really had continuous heavy support until well into the night on the area around the Vinh Huy (2) village complex, where a lot of the enemy forces concentrated. That's when I tried to send Bill Link and his platoon around the right flank, and they ran into a lot of shit as well.

We policed the battlefield up. We didn't find a lot of equipment, but we found something that I thought really interesting. We discovered a couple of shallow graves, so we dug them up and found two Chinese soldiers. At least, that's what I thought at the time. I sent in a spot report that stated that we had found two dead Chinese soldiers, and I got a reply back from Lieutenant Colonel Hilgartner that said, "Delta Six, do not repeat what you said earlier in your spot report. Out." At that time we were still trying to get our casualties out, like the remainder of Foxtrot Company, and here comes a helicopter filled with a bunch of goddamned press guys; it dropped them off right in the middle of the battlefield. Worse, the helicopter refused to take any of our casualties out. I started to get really pissed off. Here comes a helicopter bringing in reporters, I couldn't get my casualties out, and I'm told to keep my damned mouth shut about what I had found in those shallow graves. All of this happened because of "higher-level priorities." They didn't want me to say anything about Chinese advisors on the ground, but they sure looked like Chinese to me, and that's what I reported. But then I later found out that they might not have been Chinese advisors, but rather North Vietnamese from the far north of Vietnam, up by their border with China. But let me tell you, these guys were big. They didn't look anything like any NVA from the 2nd NVA Division that I ever saw. They also had the facial features that made them look more like Chinese than Vietnamese.

The 2nd NVA Division operated throughout the whole Que Son Valley, and we had just walked into a headquarters group, a pretty large contingent. We stayed hot on their trail for several days after that. They headed to the northwest, and we chased them all the way up into the mountains. We found another big supply cache in some tunnels on a hillside. This time it included weapons and ammunition. We found ammo of all types, a big ammo dump. We destroyed it and continued to patrol around the area for a few more days, and then we eventually went back to Hill 51 Combat Base.

Delta Company consolidated its positions at approximately 1940 that evening, 2 June 1967, and continued to engage the enemy through the night with small arms, automatic weapons, artillery, and air strikes. They observed several secondary explosions following both artillery and air strikes.

About half an hour after Delta 1/5 made their initial contact with the enemy in Chau Lam village, the Marines of Foxtrot 2/5 stepped into their own hellish battle. A few minutes after noon that day, as they searched the area north of Vinh Huy (2), they encountered resistance from the NVA, resulting in a brief but fierce firefight. Foxtrot 2/5 Marines killed five NVA without any casualties in that initial skirmish. As they continued down into the flat paddy land, a Kit Carson scout started shooting at flat mats of hay lying in the paddy. The NVA had concealed themselves under the hay mats, and thirty-one more not so cleverly hidden NVA died while Foxtrot advanced. At approximately 1420 that afternoon, heavy enemy mortar, rocket, small arms, and automatic weapons fire tore up the Foxtrot 2/5 Marines from a heavily fortified enemy trench position located about five hundred meters north of Vinh Huy (2). Based upon the high volume of fire, an estimated three hundred to five hundred NVA fired on them from their well-prepared, heavily camouflaged trench positions. All hell had truly broken loose.

The heavy enemy fire stopped the Foxtrot 2/5 advance cold. The well-trained Marines consolidated their positions and brought heavy return fire on the enemy positions. Within a few minutes Captain Graham ordered his reserve platoon to maneuver to secure the high ground to their south, which would allow him to mount an assault on the main enemy positions. As soon as they approached the high ground, the reserve platoon encountered another enemy force of approximately forty NVA or VC, and another big firefight broke out. The reserve platoon of Foxtrot 2/5 assaulted the enemy positions on the high ground and killed thirty-five more of the enemy. This bold action took some of the pressure off of the rest of Captain Graham's Marines, pinned down in the rice paddies, but they were still under heavy fire and had taken many casualties. The Marines of Foxtrot 2/5 had hurt the enemy badly, but the NVA continued to pour fire on the Marines, and more men died as that terrible afternoon wore on.

At approximately 1730 that evening, Capt. James Graham personally led an assault on the enemy command bunker and killed fifteen NVA soldiers himself. Although this courageous action bought his Marines some time and put a serious dent in the enemy's firepower, the enemy heavily outnumbered the Marines of Foxtrot 2/5, and Captain Graham knew it. One of his Marines was wounded so severely that he could not be moved. In an act of indomitable courage, Captain Graham bravely ordered the remainder of his Marines to withdraw from the killing ground while he remained behind, putting fire on the enemy positions so that his beleaguered Marines could withdraw to positions of relative safety. During his last radio transmission, Captain Graham reported that a large force of NVA was assaulting his position. Captain Graham and the Marine that he stayed behind to protect both died at the hands of the attacking NVA soldiers.

Capt. James A. Graham, USMC, was posthumously awarded the Medal of Honor for his gallant acts of courage in the face of horrific enemy fire on 2 June 1967 (see citation, Appendix B). Second Lt. W. A. Tight, as the next senior officer in the chain of command, assumed command of Foxtrot 2/5 and consolidated his positions, calling in artillery and air strikes on the enemy positions throughout the remainder of the night. Early the next morning, after the enemy had broken off, the Foxtrot 2/5 Marines counted 170 NVA bodies and estimated that another 300 NVA had probably died or been wounded. Thirty-two US Marines of Foxtrot 2/5 died that day, and another thirty-nine Marines were wounded and medevaced.

In an effort to completely cut off and destroy the NVA forces deployed against his Marines, Lieutenant Colonel Hilgartner committed his reserve company, Alpha Company, at 1400 that afternoon. This maneuver also aided in taking some of the pressure off both Delta and Foxtrot. As the Marines of Alpha 1/5 deployed to engage the enemy, they came under sniper fire and enemy recoilless rifle fire. The Marines of Alpha returned fire, resulting in four NVA KIA confirmed, two KIA probable, and the capture of a Chinese rocket launcher.

At 1700, the Alpha 1/5 Marines linked up with some of the Marines of Foxtrot 2/5 and began to assist them in taking control of the battlefield. Just as the Marines thought the battle was dying down and that they had the upper hand, they encountered heavy fire from a large group of NVA soldiers entrenched in an area covered with heavy underbrush. The Marines of Alpha and Foxtrot returned fire and assaulted the enemy position. The company commander of Alpha 1/5, Capt. R. G. Babich (just finishing his first month in command) was killed during this firefight. At approximately 1900 the enemy fire started to die down, and the Marines carried their dead and wounded out of the area as they moved into night security positions. Results of this action were thirty NVA confirmed killed, thirty-three enemy probably killed, and twenty-seven enemy probably wounded, while Company A lost five Marines KIA and ten WIA requiring medical evacuation.

The infantry companies were not the only ones to feel the wrath of their enemy. The battalion command group, after moving close to the battlefield while Delta, Foxtrot, and Alpha Companies engaged the enemy, came under enemy sniper fire and received mortar and rocket attacks throughout the night. The 81 mm mortar platoon fired missions all night long, and a landing zone was set up and secured so that the Marines could evacuate the dead and wounded and receive emergency ammunition and other supplies. Late that night, enemy forces broke off their attacks and withdrew from the area under cover of darkness.

The battle of Vinh Huy (2) was over, but Operation Union II continued. The Marines of 1/5 consolidated their positions; regrouped, reorganized, and searched the area for equipment and enemy dead and wounded; and evacuated their own dead and wounded. At about 0815 the next morning, Colonel Houghton, the regimental commander, arrived via helicopter at a location just a few hundred meters north of Vinh Huy (2) and received a briefing on the battle by Lieutenant Colonel Hilgartner. During that visit, Colonel Houghton and Lieutenant Colonel Hilgartner faced the grim task of assigning a new commanding officer to replace Captain Babich at Alpha 1/5. Capt. B. K. Brodie, a new arrival, received the assignment and took command of his Marines that same morning. Captain Brodie would serve as the Alpha 1/5 CO for nearly three months before Capt. Floyd S. Giordani replaced him on 27 August 1967.

With the major fighting during Operation Union II now behind them, the Marines of Delta 1/5 still operated out in a very dangerous combat zone. Craig Jackson had survived, but he knew that much more combat faced them in the days and weeks ahead. He recalls:

> On 3 June, night fell pitch black. I mean, you could hold your hand out a foot in front of your face, and you couldn't see it. I went to check the lines, responsible to make sure that the lines stayed secure and that each Marine in his fighting position was well prepared and alert. I found the first position after a while, although I could hardly see a thing. I tried to be very careful, because we had set up on the edge of the village that had been occupied by

enemy forces the previous day. We were surrounded by rice paddies a good three or four feet below the height of the village ground, and I didn't want to fall off the edge into that dry rice paddy. I felt my way along and finally found the second position. I had walked right up on them, thinking that they should be there, but I couldn't see them. I stopped, and after a few seconds I could barely make them out. Two Marines vigilantly manned the second position, down in their fighting hole, and they let me know through hand signals that I could barely see that I should get down and stay quiet. I got down and eased into their position and, whispering in one of the Marines' ear, quietly asked him what was going on. One of the Marines whispered, "They're throwing dirt. They're probing our lines by throwing clods of dirt." So I stayed down and stayed quiet, and the next thing I know I got hit right in the face by a handful of dirt. So I took out a couple of grenades that I had, handed them to the Marines in the second position, and whispered to them, "Whatever you do, don't fire your rifles. If they throw any more dirt your way, give 'em these grenades." I went out the back of that hole and went back to the platoon CP. I decided that I wasn't checking any more positions that night. It was just too dark.

Later on that night I heard a couple of explosions, and it turned out that the Marines in the second position had thrown my grenades. They got one of 'em. We found his body the next morning. Those NVA crept in very close to our positions, threw dirt at us, probed us, and tried to draw fire. If we had fired at them, the gooks would have easily thrown grenades in on us. We held our fire and turned the tables on the enemy, and that was that. So many enemy bodies lay buried in that village that by the time we left the village it really stunk.

When Delta Company left that village, we humped to Nui Lac Son, about eight or nine clicks to our west and a little south. I ended up spending my twenty-first birthday climbing Hill 441, a pretty big mountain located a few clicks further southwest of Nui Lac Son, that battalion suspected was home to an enemy radio relay station, so we got the job to climb it and check it out. Our orders were to go up and come back on the same day, but we couldn't make it up to the top that first day because the enemy sniped at us all the way. We called in some air strikes and eventually got to the top the next day. Once we got on top of Hill 441, we could see gooks all over the place on the other side, the south side of the mountain. We called in more air strikes and artillery, but since we had planned to be gone for only a day, and had only enough supplies for a one-day patrol, we got called back to Nui Lac Son. Right after that patrol, 2nd Platoon got assigned the responsibility of providing security

> for the battalion CP group, so we left Nui Lac Son. We had to walk cross-country to find the battalion CP group. We walked off that hill, back through that village, the site of the big battle during Operation Union II on 2 June 1967, and stayed with the battalion CP group on a small operation for a while.

Late on the afternoon of 3 June 1967, the 1/5 command group occupied the NVA positions they had captured, and they remained in that area until 5 June 1967, at which time Operation Union II officially ended and the battalion moved back to Hill 51 Combat Base. On 4 June operational control of Foxtrot 2/5 passed back from 1/5 to 2/5. Operation Union II was over. In eleven days of intense patrolling and major combat, the Marines of 1/5 accounted for approximately seven hundred enemy dead, with 258 of those confirmed. They also captured many tons of enemy supplies and ammunition and totally denied the Vinh Huy village complex to the enemy. A total of 55 Marines lost their lives during Operation Union II, and more than seventy Marines were wounded seriously enough to require medical evacuation. This became known as another one of those numerical victories.

I believe that Vietnam veterans have developed a love-hate relationship with casualty counts. I think most combat veterans of the Vietnam War loathed the McNamara policy of reporting actual and probable enemy KIA, and we especially detested the resulting kill ratios. One learns that body counts or kill ratios can actually be quite meaningless in combat, especially to those who die and those who receive wounds, both mental and physical. What did have meaning was the fact that after Operation Union II ended, enemy activity in the Que Son Valley died off to a very low level, and the low American casualties during the months of July and August 1967 reflected that.

In stark contrast to the months of May and June of 1967, 1/5 casualties during July included only eleven KIA, and only seven 1/5 Marines lost their lives during the long, hot month of August 1967. During those same two months the Marines of 1/5 accounted for nearly three hundred enemy soldiers killed. Enemy activity in the Que Son Valley TAOR plunged to a very low level, but the VC and NVA were still out there. The Marines of 1/5 could sense them out there during their incessant patrols, but a new combat operation launched on 4 September 1967 would prove—the hard way—that they were still there. The next search-and-destroy operation for the Marines of 1/5 was dubbed Operation Swift. It was aptly named.

9: Operation Swift, 4-15 September 1967

During the next two months, the Marines of 1/5 mounted two more relatively small combat operations out in the Que Son Valley—Operation Cochise and Operation Adair.

First Lt. Dave McInturff had taken command of Delta 1/5 in March of 1967, just as the battalion mounted up for some of their toughest combat operations during the entire Vietnam War. During the long, hot months of the summer of 1967, Dave led his Marines during both Operations Union I and Union II under some extremely adverse conditions. He had proved to be an outstanding leader in many battles as the Marines of 1/5 moved around the Que Son Valley. But on 4 July 1967, Dave was reassigned as 1/5's H&S Company commander. The Marines of Delta 1/5 came briefly under the command of Capt. Ferdinand Jennings, and on 2 August, Capt. Ronald F. Morgan replaced Captain Jennings.

On 27 August 1967, Capt. Floyd Giordani took command of Alpha 1/5 from Capt. B. K. Brodie. At that time, Capt. T. D. Reese commanded Bravo Company, and Capt. H. C. Johnston commanded Charlie Company. Each company continued to operate somewhat independently, supporting each other as they humped around the countryside in the Que Son Valley. Suddenly, in early September events escalated once again and rose to a scale that would erupt into another major battle. Early on the morning of 4 September 1967, a large force of NVA regulars savagely attacked the Marines and corpsmen of Delta 1/5, still under the command of Captain Morgan. Sgt. Craig Jackson recalls:

> The summer of 1967 turned out to be a long, tough summer for the 2nd Platoon of Delta 1/5, because we kept getting screwed. We would have to go out on company- and battalion-sized operations with the rest of Delta Company, and then when it became our turn to provide security for the combat base, duty that would typically mean that we could eat hot chow and get some

rest, the battalion would go out on an operation and we would have to go out again as the security force for the battalion CP group. We went out on both Operation Adair and Operation Cochise that way. We had gotten a bunch of replacements to make up for our losses during Operation Union II, and one of my jobs as platoon guide was to make sure that these new greenies came up to speed as quickly as possible. I remember these two replacements in particular, a couple of Mexican [American] kids. They both had MOSs that indicated they knew crew-served weapons—I think they were rocket men—but they both had decided that they wanted to be grunts, so they got assigned to 2nd Platoon. These guys got excited about becoming regular grunts. I thought that was downright stupid, so I took them back to Gunny Fish and told him that I didn't want them in 2nd Platoon. They both acted like good Marines, but they had been trained as weapons guys, and I thought that's what they should do. I didn't win that argument, though, and they ended up staying with 2nd Platoon as grunts. A few days later I got to go on R&R. When I got back, I found out that they had both died violently in a firefight on the 24th of July. The Marines of Delta 1/5 went out on a company-sized sweep and ended up getting hit hard; eight Marines died that day, including my two wannabe grunts. Pfc. Richard Lopez, from San Antonio, Texas, and Pfc. Antonio Salinas, from Douglas, Arizona, lost their lives that day, doing what they wanted to do most, be grunts.

When I returned from R&R, I landed in Da Nang. I got on this truck convoy headed south, down Highway 1, to the 5th Marines combat base around Tam Ky. I asked where I could get a weapon, and they said I wouldn't need a weapon. A bunch of Marines were told to get on that truck convoy, and they weren't going to issue any of us weapons. I told the rest of them that I didn't know what they planned to do, but I would not get on any convoy without a weapon. Not to be difficult, I just thought it was absolutely crazy to send us out on that convoy unarmed. So, when I got back late on the 4th of August, I got in trouble for returning late from R&R. First I got company office hours, and then I received battalion office hours in front of Stretch for being late, missing movement, or something like that. Most of the guys called Lieutenant Colonel Hilgartner Highpockets, but some of us called him Stretch. It took a while for the office hours to get organized, and I didn't even think that Lieutenant Colonel Hilgartner knew who I was, but when I finally reported in to him, he asked me, "Sergeant Jackson, what are you doing here?"

I told him, "I dunno."

He said, "Well, I gotta do something, since this went through Division."

He gave me fifteen days' restriction and forfeiture of two months' pay. At that time that added up to about $225.00 or so. I asked him if that meant restriction to the Hill 51 combat base, and he said, "Hell no. This is just for the record."

Sergeant Jackson went back to his platoon, and he and his Marines spent the remainder of August and early September in and around Hill 51 Combat Base in the Que Son Valley.

Suddenly, at 0430 on the morning of 4 September 1967, an enemy force of unknown size violently attacked the Marines of Delta 1/5 on two sides. Fortunately, the initial enemy gunfire wasn't very accurate, wounding only four Marines during the first engagement. Based on the sheer volume of fire, the initial situation could have been much worse. Unfortunately, things did get worse—much, much worse.

Enemy gunfire continued to escalate rapidly, and by 0830 that morning Delta Company reported a cumulative total of fourteen Marines killed in action and another fifteen seriously wounded. The company commander of Delta 1/5, Capt. R. F. Morgan, one of the early casualties, sustained serious wounds as a result of hostile gunfire at 0620 that morning and urgently required medevac.

Operation Swift started swiftly and escalated swiftly and violently, and it worsened over the next two days. On that dark morning of 4 September 1967 (which would ultimately become the bloodiest day in 1/5's combat history during the entire Vietnam War), Delta Company's situation deteriorated rapidly. Immediately after the company commander went down, the XO, Lt. Carl Fulford, took command. He reported heavy contact with an enemy force of approximately a company of NVA, reported several WIA and KIA, and requested immediate assistance.

Under orders from Lieutenant Colonel Hilgartner, and reacting rapidly to the very fluid and dangerous situation, Bravo Company mounted up and moved toward Delta's positions to assist them. Hilgartner requested several medevac helicopters, ordering them to proceed as quickly as possible to the scene. The Marines of Delta 1/5, those sometimes unlucky Marines darkly referred to as Dying Delta, had already taken a shocking number of casualties, and they needed a lot of help.

The Marines of Bravo Company, commanded by Capt. Tom Reese, departed Hill 51 Combat Base at 0655 that morning. Bravo Company's Marines arrived in the vicinity of the battle at about 0820, near the hamlet of Dong Son (1), about five kilometers east and a little south of the combat base. Dong Son (1) was really just a cluster of hooches that sat on a low, tree-lined rise close by and just south of the Song Ly Ly. Dong Son (1) sat adjacent to a huge rice paddy complex that included several square kilometers of active rice paddies and dikes on the north side of the village. Low foothills dotted the landscape to the south, but the predominant terrain features in that area were the villages of Dong Son (1) and Chau Lam (4), the two small hills that separated the villages (the tallest of which was labeled Hill 63 on the 1:50,000 terrain map), and the surrounding rice paddies.

At 0700 that morning, shortly after Bravo Company departed the combat base, armed Huey gunships (UH-1E helicopters with deadly 40 mm rocket pods attached) arrived and delivered air strikes within fifty meters of the beleaguered Delta Company Marines' positions. A few minutes later, an aerial observer (AO) in an O-1 aircraft directed an artillery attack against the enemy positions with good results. Enemy firing slackened for a few minutes after the air and artillery strikes, but the NVA forces came back quickly, attacking again in force. The NVA attacked the Marines again and again that day, repeatedly and relentlessly, and they attacked with ferocity every time. The 1st NVA Regiment's soldiers seemed determined to wipe out the Marines where they stood.

Arriving in the vicinity of Delta's positions, Captain Reese's Bravo Company Marines started a sweep of the village of Dong Son (1), looking for the main NVA forces, initially estimated by Delta Company as an NVA company. Usually about a hundred NVA soldiers served in an NVA infantry company, and usually double that number of Marines served in a Marine Corps rifle company.

The Marines of Bravo 1/5 kicked off the sweep within a couple of minutes of receiving their orders, ready to fight and very determined to find the NVA soldiers shooting up their buddies over in Delta Company; they wanted to destroy them. Then they heard an ungodly roar of gunfire erupt to their southeast, a few hundred meters away.

No one heard from Delta Company for the next several minutes over the tactical radio network. The Delta Company Marines were in serious trouble, evident from the loud, grinding noise of a steady and heavy volume of enemy and friendly gunfire. Fifteen minutes later, 1/5's battalion command group received a message from Delta Company letting them know that two of their medevac helicopters had been shot down. The NVA, seeing the helicopters approach the area, had thrown out several smoke grenades, misleading the chopper crew, luring them into a vulnerable position. The NVA waited until the life-saving helicopters flew very close, and then they sprung their ambush, killing the flying Marines instantly from a few meters away. The choppers crashed in a fiery cauldron of chaos, gunfire, and exploding aviation fuel. A bad situation rapidly got much worse.

A few minutes later, the Marines of Bravo Company, as they swept the village, received a hail of enemy gunfire and returned fire immediately, killing two enemy soldiers and sustaining seven WIA of their own. At about the same time, some of the Bravo Company Marines observed a large enemy force a few hundred meters away maneuvering toward the rear of Delta Company's position, where the Marines fought viciously, at nearly point-blank range, with the NVA in front of them. Bravo reported the situation immediately, likely saving Delta Company from becoming outflanked and badly hurt.

Delta Company's Marines shifted some of their defensive positions and opened up on the NVA soldiers trying to get behind them, while Bravo Company requested that Huey gunships fire on the village using CS gas prior to their assault. The noxious gas hit the village at 0914 that morning. Enemy gunfire erupted briefly from the enemy positions threatening Delta Company's rear, but the Bravo Company Marines then observed an undetermined number of enemy fleeing to the north across the river. The accurate deployment of four hundred pounds of CS gas had done its job. Delta Company's rear and flanks became secure once again, but it was unclear just how long they would remain that way.

By mid-morning on the 4th, the Marines of both Bravo Company and Delta Company 1/5 had their hands full, totally engaged and fighting for their lives with large groups of NVA regulars within a few hundred meters of each other. The NVA had dug extensive trenches and other fighting positions in these villages. The area had obviously been used as a base camp for some time; the fighting positions and trenches were very well prepared and cleverly camouflaged.

One Five's command group requested reinforcements from the regimental commander. The 5th Marines command group responded by sending both Kilo and Mike Companies of the 3rd Battalion, 5th Marines to support the now-dubbed Operation Swift. Those two companies arrived at the battlefield before the end of that long and deadly day. Once again, the Marines had the enemy soldiers of the 1st NVA Regiment in a stranglehold, and every Marine in the Fighting Fifth worked urgently to make sure that the hard-fighting but slippery NVA soldiers wouldn't get out of the trap this time. Most of them didn't. Before Operation Swift ended, the 1st NVA Regiment would effectively cease to exist as a fighting unit. But that would take a while longer; exactly twelve days longer.

During Bravo Company's assault on the hamlet of Dong Son (1), one of several main enemy positions, twenty-six Marines died and another thirty-three Marines were wounded seriously enough to require medical evacuation. But the enemy had fled the village, and Delta Company's position was secured.

A situation report (SitRep) entry in the combat after-action report covering Operation Swift states, "At 1043, Captain Heinz assumed command of Company D." This entry included a typo. The new skipper of Dying Delta was Capt. D. W. Hinz. Captain Hinz would continue to command Delta 1/5 until 12 October 1967.

Although Dave McInturff no longer commanded an infantry company, he was not done with the hazards of life in a combat zone. During Operation Swift he and his H&S Company Marines provided security for the battalion CP group as well as the 81 mm Mortar Platoon, which traveled with them. Mike and Kilo Companies, from 3rd Battalion, 5th Marines, chopped to 1/5 after Lieutenant Colonel Hilgartner and the CP group left Que Son Combat Base to set up a forward command post. Dave recalls:

> After Mike and Kilo linked up with 1/5, the shit really hit the fan. Bravo Company went out in reaction to support Delta Company's fight, and then the battalion CP group went out on helicopters to an LZ. We left Charlie Company back at the combat base for security. Mike and Lima Companies went out right in front of us, and they got hit almost immediately after landing in the LZ. We got hit pretty hard that day. Then another couple of days went by, and then we got hit again, very hard. Those bastards weren't more than thirty meters away from us when they opened up on us, and the NVA used CS gas on us. We ended up dropping gas on the NVA from air strikes, and one of the companies, India 3/1, hadn't brought gas masks with them, so they found themselves in deep shit.

Before the end of that terrible and confusing day, 4 September 1967, many 1/5 Marines would lose their lives. Other units rushed to the battlefield to support and reinforce the struggling Marines. One of those units, Company M, 3rd Battalion, 5th Marines, included a very well known face to the Marines of 1/5: Lt. Vincent R. Capodanno, Chaplain Corps, United States Naval Reserve, formerly the 1/5 chaplain but now the chaplain of 3rd Battalion, 5th Marines. Although under strict orders to stay in the rear area, Father Capodanno hurried forward to be with his Marines.

At about midday on the 4th of September, the Marines of Mike and Kilo Companies landed in an LZ located only a kilometer from the fighting, with Father Capodanno in the vanguard. Late that afternoon, learning that one platoon of Mike Company was in a desperate fight and in danger of being overrun and wiped out, he left the relative safety of the company command post and rushed to the aid of his grunts. Seeing a seriously wounded corpsman in dire circumstances, his body exposed to enemy machine gun fire, the Grunt Padre unhesitatingly rushed to his side, screening the stricken corpsman's body from enemy fire. Father Capodanno died giving aid and comfort to his Marines and was posthumously awarded the Medal of Honor for his gallantry (see citation, Appendix C).

Stunned by the news of the Grunt Padre's death, Dave McInturff remembers, "Chaplain Capodanno served as the 1/5 chaplain for a couple of months earlier in the year, but I hadn't paid a lot of attention to the fact that he got transferred over to 3/5. When he died, I thought he still served as the 1/5 chaplain. We were all shocked by his death."

Rick Zell still served as the platoon commander of the 1st Platoon of Alpha 1/5.

When the fighting broke out on 4 September, Alpha Company stayed in the rear, at Que Son (Hill 51) Combat Base. Alpha didn't get directly involved in this fight for several days, but they knew that 1/5 was in a huge fight. Terrible casualty reports mounted up. The Alpha 1/5 Marines heard that their buddies in Delta and Bravo Companies got hit by incoming gas shells, and then they got orders to make sure they had their gas masks when they left the combat base. Other companies from 3/5 had responded to the fight, so when Alpha finally joined the fighting about five days into Operation Swift, they weren't quite sure what they faced, other than a very fierce and bloody combat operation. Rick recalls, "A lot of extraneous bullshit floated around. We couldn't get a straight story and weren't quite sure what to expect. But our briefing informed us that a really vicious battle raged out there. That part turned out absolutely true. Just about the same time we got into it, Charlie Company got into it."

Sgt. Craig Jackson remembers the early hours of Operation Swift as if they happened yesterday:

> At one point in early September, 2nd Platoon provided security for their sector of Hill 51 Combat Base, and the rest of Delta Company went out on a sweep. I monitored the battalion radio net on the afternoon of 3 September; Delta Company had planned to return to the combat base, but then received orders to stay out one more night in place and to come back in the next day. I had radio watch early the next morning, and I heard all this firing and listened to all the radio traffic. I walked out of the hooch and could easily hear the firing and see the tracers off in the distance. At that time, 2nd Lieutenant Strickland commanded 2nd Platoon, and Staff Sergeant Demory served as the platoon sergeant. We had recently gotten a new company commander, Captain Morgan. I could tell that Delta Company was really in a big fight over there. Word came down almost immediately for Bravo Company to saddle up. I remember telling my Marines to check their ammo and to get ready, because there was no way that Bravo Company would go out there to help Delta Company without the 2nd Platoon of Delta 1/5. A few minutes later, the word came over to get saddled up and join Bravo Company.

Bravo Company and the 2nd Platoon of Delta 1/5 arrived on the battlefield at 0820 that morning and immediately engaged the enemy.

Yet another outstanding Marine had joined the ranks of 1/5 just as Operation Swift ramped up. Dale Hatten enlisted in the Marine Corps in 1955. After eight years of service, in 1963 Dale served his first tour in the escalating conflict in South Vietnam. Dale served during those early days as a member of Battalion Landing Team

3/3 (BLT 3/3) operating afloat off Cap Saint Jacques on the coast of South Vietnam. In 1964, after many months afloat, Dale received orders to return to the United States for a three-year tour as a drill instructor at MCRD San Diego.

In early 1967, now Gunnery Sgt. Dale Hatten received orders for his second tour in South Vietnam, assigned to Shore Party. Dale had graduated from aerial and naval gunfire school, so his assignment made sense; he had the responsibility for coordinating all supporting arms for various infantry outfits, including army gunships, naval gunfire, artillery, and heavy mortars. In that role, Gunny Hatten fought with the Marines of 1/5 during Operations Union I and Union II. Gunny Hatten then transferred to 1/5 in late August 1967 and initially served as the assistant platoon commander of the battalion's 81 mm Mortar Platoon.

The 1/5 battalion sergeant major knew Gunny Hatten from previous duty stations, and he knew that Dale possessed a great deal of experience and skill, including extensive training in supporting arms, so he made sure that Dale received orders to 1/5. The sergeant major saw Dale in Tam Ky one afternoon, came up to him, and asked, "What are you doing?"

Dale immediately said, "I've already got a good job."

The Sergeant Major replied, "I've got a better one for you." And the next thing Dale knew, he received orders to 1/5:

> When I got my orders to 1/5, I was back at Hill 54. I had supported 1/5 during both Unions so I knew I was headed for a combat outfit. Assigned a jeep driver to take me out to Hill 51, we headed west for the forty or so kilometer trip to Que Son Combat Base. Unfortunately, we missed the turn-off for the combat base, and before we realized it we were headed for Que Son City. All of a sudden, I realized we're driving by an NVA taxing position. Here I am with one Marine driver, and there stood several NVA soldiers dressed in gray uniforms, the full bit, armed with AK-47s and deadly looking, and we're driving right by them. I tried to pull my .45-caliber pistol out but couldn't get it out. It was supposed to be a cease fire day, and the NVA knew it, so they had very boldly come out of the woods, and here they stood, blatantly taxing the local civilians. The driver made a hasty U turn after driving past the NVA checkpoint and drove right back past the NVA. Just as surprised as us, they had their mouths wide open. Fortunately for us, they didn't get a shot off either. Somehow we made it safely to Hill 51.
>
> I immediately checked in with the S-2 shop and told them about those NVA right down the road, and the S-2 said, "We'll get 'em tomorrow." The cease fire remained in effect, so we couldn't go after them.
>
> It wasn't but a couple of days later, in early September, when Hill 51 Combat

Base got hit hard by an enemy mortar attack. Incoming enemy mortar rounds scored a direct hit on the artillery ammo storage area, and it started blowing up. The damned thing exploded all night long; unexploded artillery rounds flew around everywhere as others exploded. The 55-gallon drums of powder bags in that dump burned like roaring tornadoes of fire. This engineering kid got on a Caterpillar, and he actually saved the day. With that bulldozer he buried the burning ammo and pretty much saved our butts. If he hadn't done what he did, I'm positive we'd have had a lot more casualties. That was a pretty exciting evening and one hell of a welcome to my new battalion.

On the morning of 4 September 1967 the 81 mm mortar platoon remained dug in at Hill 51. As the information about Delta Company started coming in, we had heard that one of the Delta Marines had stepped out of his position to make a head call and ran into an NVA soldier making a head call, and they started shooting at each other. That's what started Swift. Delta got in a huge battle, and then they sent Bravo out and they got into it with another large force of NVA fairly close by where Delta fought. The fight just kept getting bigger and bigger and bigger. We received a warning order to go on standby to take a section of two 81 mm mortar tubes out with Lieutenant Colonel Hilgartner as a relief force. A group of army CH-47 dual-rotor helicopters landed and took us out to the fight in the early afternoon. We got out there and immediately came under enemy fire. We only had the mortar ammo we had carried and two tubes, so we set those up in the middle of the firefight and started shooting them the best we could. Limited in what we could shoot—we only had what we carried out there—we tried to conserve ammunition. We had set up our tubes out in the middle of this dry rice paddy, and right away we started taking fire from an enemy sniper firing a .50-caliber weapon. I can't understand how we managed to avoid taking casualties by that sniper. That sniper got really close, and our tubes and Marines stayed really exposed. At one point, a corpsman stood behind me; I turned around and stepped off a paddy dike to say something to the corpsman, and a round struck right where I had stood a moment before, just missing the corpsman.

We set the base plates by shooting an illumination round straight up in the air, standard procedure. As soon as we had the base plates set, the platoon commander wanted me to go out to check our perimeter. I took a few Marines, and we went out and crossed two or three dry rice paddy areas as a crackle of gunfire continued all around us. All of a sudden a spider trap opened up, and an AK-47 opened up and he got three Marines in his first burst, probably within twenty meters of where I stood. All three Marines went down, badly wounded and in shock. Two of them had arterial bleeding and needed emergency medevac. Somehow we managed to get them back to the CP for medevac, and I went back to my mortar tubes.

We fired in direct support of Delta and Bravo the rest of that day. We had tried to get some medevacs in, but the fighting just stayed too intense; the first helicopter just got the hell shot out of it, so we couldn't get the choppers in. That night the platoon commander came back in with the body of one of his Marines who had died earlier in the fighting. I will never forget his face.

Then something very strange and disturbing happened the following morning, 5 September 1967. We had fought all through the previous afternoon, with really intensive fighting throughout the night. It had been very confusing and pretty much all-out combat since the moment we had arrived in the LZ. Just after first light, Colonel Hilgartner—he had been awake for a while, but not too long—saw Capt. W. R. Tenny, the CO of Kilo 3/5, not too far away, and Highpockets hollered at him and said, "What are you doing back here?"

Captain Tenny hollered back to Colonel Hilgartner and said, "This is the front line!"

The battalion CP group's position sat right in the middle of the fighting. We all probably sat within 300 meters of the fighting going on with all the letter companies.

Before Operation Swift ended, all of the infantry companies of 1/5 and three more infantry companies from 3/5 would join the fight. Those included India 3/5, under Capt. E. M. Burke; Kilo 3/5, under Capt. W. R. Tenny; and Mike Company 3/5, under the command of 1st Lt. D. Murray. These combined Marine infantry forces received heavy support from units of the 1st Support Battalion, 1st Engineer Battalion, 1st Tank Battalion, and 1st Anti-Tank (Ontos) Battalion and the artillerymen of the 2nd Battalion, 11th Marines. The pilots and FACs of the 1st Marine Air Wing (1MAW) provided air support, which proved readily available and was deployed in abundance. In addition, the usual gaggle of supporting Marines, including several scout/snipers and teams of Kit Carson Scouts, reinforced 1/5's ranks, and Gunny Hatten's Marines of the 81 mm mortar platoon fought in direct support.

The Marines of Delta 1/5, the Marines who all the other companies darkly referred to as Dying Delta, became the first to fight and die during Operation Swift. Sgt. Craig Jackson, having led his 2nd Platoon Delta Company Marines to the battlefield with Bravo Company, found himself in the middle of hell:

Shortly after first light, we started out. Second Platoon of Delta Company took point for Bravo Company. We got out there pretty fast, because the fighting wasn't very far from the combat base, just a few clicks away. Most of the fight took place just on the other side of the Song Ly Ly. We started to cross the river when the enemy opened up on us. I'm only about 5 foot 7 inches tall, so I had to walk under water for a short distance. I got across the river and took cover behind some rocks, and all this fire poured down on us. Staff Sgt. Demory crouched over behind another rock, and I looked over toward him and asked him if he had a cigarette. I always had a cigarette in my mouth, but mine had all gotten wet crossing the river. He looked at me like he thought I had gone crazy.

We eventually got up the bank and started to move through this village to the site of where our buddies got pinned down. We had to clean out the village. I moved through this area, sort of like a water runoff area, not so much like a defined trench but maybe a shallow ditch about three feet deep, walking next to this hedgerow, when some of the Marines from Corporal Hartman's squad went around me. Corporal Hartman walked by me, and then another Marine walked around me. The sounds of shooting erupted all over the place, and I just stood there in the middle of it all, and I hadn't really thought about getting down, but for some reason I decided that I should get down. I had just squatted down when a rifle went off and shot the Marine that had just walked by me in the side. He fell back against the side of the depression, and I heard another rifle go off and heard some Marines yelling that Corporal Hartman had been hit. An enemy round had hit him in the throat and killed him outright. Another Marine, a different Campbell, got hit four or five times in the same leg, and a bunch of other guys got hit as well. A high volume of enemy automatic and semiautomatic rifle fire roared from all over the place. I heard some M16 fire, pop, pop, and heard Fred Scott yell that he got 'em. A trench sat just on the other side of the ditch, filled with NVA soldiers. We didn't even see the trench; we had walked right in front of it in that depression, and I'd never seen it. The NVA soldier had intended to shoot me in the head, but I just dropped down and he shot the other guy in the side instead.

We moved around and spread out and returned fire the best we could. I tried to help our corpsmen treat our casualties. We had a lot of casualties and started moving them back to a somewhat safe area so the docs could do their work. Battalion had called in a medevac, and a CH-34 came in and tried to land, but unbelievably it got shot down by enemy gunfire right over our heads. That helicopter came in and crash-landed right in the middle of our perimeter. A short time later a Huey helicopter came in, and the enemy shot him down, too. That one crashed inside our perimeter, too.

We fought all day long and into the night, a nonstop, all-out battle. A couple

> of our air strikes dropped tear gas on the enemy positions, which I think helped to get them off of us. When we finally set up a little perimeter, we could see that the enemy occupied the high ground. I don't know why the company hadn't taken that high ground any earlier. They had the river to their back, this little village on their right, and this little piece of high ground over to the left, which didn't make a lot of sense. I can remember one officer who received orders to get his platoon and assault that high ground. I don't remember who they were, but they assaulted. Unfortunately, every time that platoon got up to assault, they would immediately take casualties, and they couldn't make any advances on that high ground. They had us hemmed in up there until the next day, 5 September 1967. I don't remember much about the 5th of September except for the fact that we couldn't get out of there. We seemed to be stuck.

The Marines of Bravo and Delta Companies continued to clash with large groups of North Vietnamese soldiers, who delivered heavy automatic and semiautomatic small arms fire with terrible accuracy against the Leathernecks. Shortly after noon that day, the Marines of Mike and Kilo Companies, along with the medium command group of the 1st Battalion, 5th Marines, landed in an LZ located about two and one-half kilometers east of the fighting along a country road (Highway 534), in a fairly dry rice paddy complex.

As they approached the scene of the fighting, the new task force command group and both Kilo and Mike Companies began apprehending detainees and gathering intelligence from the local villagers as they moved forward. Then the world exploded once again with enemy gunfire. A ferocious volume of enemy small arms fire chewed up the Marines of Kilo Company, and then, just a few minutes later, Mike Company made contact. Kilo had moved west, a few hundred meters north of the road, advancing toward the village of Chau Lam. One of the main battlefields of Operation Swift sat in the midst of a cluster of hamlets, all named Chau Lam. Situated a little over a kilometer east of Dong Son (1), where Delta Company still fought, Chau Lam (4) took the brunt of the battle damage. A small hill separated the two villages, and large forces of NVA soldiers occupied both villages and the hill.

For the next several hours Kilo and Mike fought "an undetermined number" of camouflaged NVA, receiving an estimated thirty-five thousand rounds of enemy small arms fire. One Kilo Company Marine died, and thirteen more wounded Marines required medevac after the melee. Mike Company's Marines suffered a worse fate. Before the shooting died down that evening, seventeen Marines from Mike Company lost their lives, and another thirty-eight received Purple Hearts. The fighting during the first day of Operation Swift, 4 September 1967, was reported to be so ferocious and continuous that even the 1/5 command group got into the fighting when they received a hail of gunfire while crossing an open rice paddy. As they called for more air strikes and artillery support, the command group began to realize that they faced a much larger enemy force than initially estimated. They now reported that they were squared off against two NVA battalions, meaning that over one thousand enemy soldiers attacked their forces. This equated to about a one-to-one ratio between the NVA forces there in abundance, waiting in well-prepared and camouflaged defensive bunkers and apparently planning to stay, and the total number of Marines in the area. The Marines of Bravo and Delta Companies could not mount an attack; they fought defensively, and they fought for their lives.

About that time, Hilgartner made the decision to attack with Kilo and Mike Companies. According to the tactical manuals, this did not necessarily represent a favorable ratio of fighting men for an attacking force against a well-entrenched and camouflaged force of defenders. Standard tactical theory indicated that a three to one ratio, with attackers outnumbering defenders, was desirable when on the attack. The combined forces of Kilo and Mike Companies amounted to about 350 Marines, and they were ordered to attack an estimated force of one thousand or more NVA. The three to one ratio against them meant that the Marines had to execute their attacks with lightning speed and maximum destructive force to expect to win this battle. Attack they did, many times that day, and many of them died. Hilgartner ordered Mike and Kilo Companies to fix bayonets and attack in a V formation, followed closely by the battalion CP group. The attack proved bloody, but successful, taking the pressure off both Bravo and Delta Companies.

As in every war and in every major battle in 5th Marines history, the Mud Marines of the Fighting Fifth ultimately prevailed, virtually destroying the 1st NVA Regiment in the process. The NVA made the mistake of standing and fighting in the hamlets of Chau Lam (4) and Dong Son (1), and the 5th Marines made them pay dearly.

But the victory came at a steep price. Of the eighty-nine Marines who died during Operation Swift, fifty-four died during that first day of terrible fighting. The Marines found and counted 150 NVA bodies, and from eyewitness reports of the Marines who fought that day, another 200 or more enemy soldiers probably died. By the end of that day, four full companies of Marines and the command group of the 1st Battalion, 5th Marines converged on the battlefield and took part in the fighting. Large groups of NVA heavily and repeatedly attacked the Marines that day, but the Marines always managed to counterattack, and each time the Marines overwhelmed the NVA with their superior firepower.

Finally, the afternoon sunlight of 4 September 1967 dimmed. Soon after, the sun went down, and the firing died off somewhat. But the fighting did not completely stop, as the Marines of 1/5 and 3/5 maintained contact with the enemy throughout the night.

Gunny Hatten remembered:

Everywhere we went, we found well-constructed, neat and orderly enemy foxholes and other enemy fighting positions. We started to move across the rice paddy, and we could see a large group of vehicles and well-armed troops in uniforms not too far in the distance. We all wondered, "Who are those guys?" We had heard that the NVA may have had some armored vehicles with them, and we worried that this was another NVA force. Then the S-3 passed the word that the outfit moving parallel to us was an ARVN outfit. As we moved along, we immediately started this big firefight. We brought the two mortars up the trail, under fire, but we managed to set the mortars up. Then we set up the FDC [fire direction center] in this pigpen. We took intensive fire; the enemy small arms fire cracked over our heads and ricocheted off the tubes, so I was amazed that we didn't take any casualties while we set up the tubes, but we got them up and started to fire. As we set up the tubes, an enemy bullet hit one of the 81 mm mortar rounds that I had strapped to my back, but fortunately for me and everyone else in the area, it didn't explode. Just one hell of a lot of firing continued throughout that day.

We stayed somewhat limited by where we could fire because of the presence of the ARVN, but we fired and fired all throughout that day. And then, in midafternoon I heard someone holler, "Fix bayonets!" Amazed, of course, to hear this, I came out of the pigpen FDC and looked around and asked, "Who the hell ordered fix bayonets?"

Colonel Hilgartner stood just across the way, and he said, "I did, Gunny. These damned guys are close!"

I turned around and saw them and they really *were* close. Too damned close. Then I looked over at my two tubes and saw that they pointed almost straight up in the air. Having had my head down in the FDC, I hadn't noticed how close the targets had gotten, but we were firing a "charge two," and the tubes had climbed nearly vertical, so I understood immediately that we were in very close combat.

About that time we started getting air support from a group of A-4s off of an aircraft carrier. Diverted from a mission up north, they had a full load of ordnance, and our FAC brought them around. The pilots of these aircraft let our FAC know that they had never provided close air support before, so they wanted to do a fly-by before they made a bombing run. As they flew over our heads, an amazingly huge volume of enemy gunfire greeted them, but they steadfastly swooped around and headed back to make their bombing run. We threw out smoke grenades to mark our positions. The four jets came in wing-tip to wing-tip and dropped off all their ordnance in one pass. I remember that the concussion of all those bombs exploding at the same time picked me up and threw me down onto the ground. I remember thinking, at that moment, that this was really a big operation.

That evening, a Puff the Magic Dragon arrived on station in the skies above us, and he fired all evening long. Some of the enemy returned fire from several locations, but no reaction whatsoever, nothing but dead quiet, came from the area that that air strike hit. The next morning, we acquired a couple more rifle companies from another battalion, and we continued to sweep the area that next day. By that time it seemed as though Operation Swift had pretty much ended, and we returned to Hill 51 Combat Base.

Early the following morning, 5 September 1967, the Marines of Mike 3/5 conducted a thorough search of the battle area. They found enemy equipment strewn all over the place, including Russian carbines, Chinese Communist light assault rifles, AK-47 assault rifles, a B-40 rocket launcher, a 60 mm mortar tube still complete with its sight assembly, and an assortment of high explosive devices and small arms ammunition. Throughout the remainder of September 5, the Marines of the task force found fresh graves with bodies in them in several locations, along with other hastily cached military gear. It looked as though the main force of the enemy had fled the area, as no firefights occurred that afternoon or evening.

But on the morning of the 6th, both Kilo and Mike Companies chopped back to their parent battalion, 3/5, leaving Bravo and Delta 1/5 and Delta 1/1 attached to 1st Battalion, 5th Marines. The Marines of Delta 1/1 had arrived on the battlefield early that morning, and they also made contact with the enemy, this time in the form of several enemy snipers, who wounded two Marines. Heavy return fire suppressed the sniper fire, at least for a while.

Later on that morning, a 105 mm short round wounded two Bravo Company Marines; both required emergency medical evacuation.[1] At about the same time, the Mud Marines of 1/5 and 1/1 had sharp but brief firefights, culminating in the discovery of a bunker complex and three Vietnamese hiding in one of the bunkers. The Marines yelled at the Vietnamese to come out with their hands up, but they refused. The Marines threw a hand grenade into the bunker, and the three Vietnamese males, armed with an AK-47 and an AK-44, all died in the blast. Things started to heat up again.

At 1500 on 6 September 1967 the 1/5 task force commander issued a frag order ordering the Marines to attack to Objective 6, the village of Chau Lam (3), located about two kilometers east of the initial battlefield on the 4th, a few hundred meters south of Highway 534.[2] The Marines of Bravo 1/5 and Delta 1/1 attacked the village of Chau Lam (3) on line in a frontal assault formation, with the Bravo Company

Marines on the right, or south, flank. They attacked right into the well-prepared positions of the enemy soldiers and immediately came under heavy sniper fire, which became more and more intense as the Bravo Company Marines advanced towards the village. As Bravo Company assaulted forward, their casualties mounted. The Marines of Delta 1/1 saw an opportunity to outflank the enemy forces, firmly lodged in the village of Chau Lam (3) and still locked in deadly combat with the Bravo 1/5 Leathernecks. As the Delta 1/1 Marines approached the line of departure for their flanking movement, the task force commander reported heavy combat with an estimated battalion of NVA soldiers. With the realization that night approached rapidly, and that the Marines of 1/5 had trapped another NVA battalion, orders went out to the field commander to consolidate their positions in a cluster of hooches at a bend in the highway a few hundred meters north. As they moved toward the hooches, 1/5 began to receive intense mortar and small arms fire. The enemy fire and consequent casualties hampered their efforts to consolidate. To make matters worse, as they tried to regain control, the enemy attempted to infiltrate. At one point in the confusion of close battle, five to fifteen NVA had managed to move within ten meters of the perimeter before the Marines' defensive fires killed them all.

Sgt. Craig Jackson had survived the ferocious fighting on 4 September but found himself right in the thick of things once again:

> On the morning of the 6th of September, we started moving out, both Bravo Company and Delta Company. We kind of had a sort of change of command; Delta 1/1 joined us along with Stretch Hilgartner and the 1/5 battalion CP group. Stretch hooked up with us, and we started moving out. Along with the battalion CP group, we had Bravo Company, Delta 1/1, and what was left of Delta 1/5. Bravo Company moved out in front, and they got into some firefights that day, along with snipers and all that stuff. Colonel Hilgartner had told Delta Company to take over security for the battalion CP group. As I recall it, at that point only forty-two Marines remained in Delta Company. We got sort of pissed that we didn't get pulled out and sent back to Nui Lac Son. We knew that Charlie Company still remained in Nui Lac Son, and they hadn't seen any action for a while, and we felt that Charlie Company should have come out to replace us, but it didn't happen. We came up on this hill and set up hasty defensive positions on this knoll. We got resupplied and grabbed a little rest. I can remember that the Marines from Delta 1/1 and the battalion CP group looked at us like we were crazy. When that resupply chopper came in, those of us in Delta 1/5 who had survived grabbed all the ammo we could carry. I even grabbed a box of machine gun ammo, and I never carried machine gun ammo.

I sent a patrol down to a small village, about a hundred meters in front of that knoll, to get water. A bunch of guys collected all the spare canteens, and went on that water run. They got back okay, and then we moved out again. I wasn't more than about ten feet from Stretch, so I could hear him clearly talking on the radio. He told whoever listened on the other end that he thought the enemy was just trying to hold us up. He used the word outguards and said that we were going to push on. So we started moving out. Bravo Company took point with Delta 1/1 following them. I followed right behind Delta 1/1 and right in front of the colonel. One of the Delta 1/1 Marines, a young sergeant who I had served with at Henderson Hall, kept calling me Corporal Jackson, and he told me all kinds of things that had happened at Henderson Hall since I had left. I called him Shinola. He seemed really squared away, and he shined his shoes so much I nicknamed him Shinola. He came from Alabama, and his name was actually Brown.

When we got down to where my Marines had gone on the water run, all hell broke loose. I yelled at Brown and told him he'd better get back with his squad, so he took off, saying that he'd talk to me later. I never talked with him again. The firing became incredibly intense. I yelled for Fred Scott, one of my flanks, at the top of my lungs, and I couldn't hear myself yelling because of the huge volume of noise caused by enemy gunfire. Most of the firing came from the left flank of our column. Then mortars came in, and I ran and jumped into this water buffalo pit. An enemy mortar round hit this hooch that I had just moved past and blew it away. A stand of bamboo stood between that water buffalo pit and the rice paddy next to it. When the enemy gunfire finally started dying down, that bamboo had been cut down. That's how heavy the firing got. It stayed really chaotic there for a while, and I thought that this was it; this time I wasn't going to make it. I saw a bunch of gooks running right through our column. I can remember one radio man running around, with his pistol in one hand and his radio handset in the other, screaming, "We're gonna die! We're gonna die!" I yelled for my flanks; I couldn't see them. Major Black, the S-3 officer, grabbed me and said, 'We've got to get some kind of order here, Sergeant. Come with me; we've got to put together some kind of semblance of a perimeter, set up a defense." He had a .45 in his hand and shot a gook who came up right behind me. He stayed amazingly cool under the circumstances. We later wrote him up for a citation for bravery.[3]

Fred Scott and his Marines crouched in a small ditch. I saw him fire his M79 at a gook as he ran into a hooch, and the round exploded right next to the doorway of the hooch and blew that gook's head off. Trying to set up a defensive position of some sort, a bunch of us got in that ditch, and a bunch of gooks jumped right over us. We're trying to get back to the main body of the battalion, so I sent a couple of Marines up around me and then sent another one around me. I had my bayonet on my rifle at the time. Just as I started to run, I looked around to my left just before I took off running, and I almost got bayoneted. An NVA soldier had jumped in that ditch with me; he could easily have shot me, but he wanted to bayonet me. He also had his bayonet fixed, and he tried to kill me with it. I just happened to turn around, real quick like, before I took off running. He charged me, and he just ran into my bayonet. I couldn't get my rifle out of him; the bayonet got stuck in his body, and so I just took off and left it there. His bayonet had just barely scraped my left side, so I was pretty lucky. At that moment, I had thought that was it. I remember feeling absolutely sure I was about to die right then and there. In that fraction of a second, somehow I survived. He missed, and I didn't miss. I was the lucky one. I was alive, but without a weapon for a few moments. Plenty of M16s lay about, available, so I just picked up another one. I felt so bad about leaving my rifle behind that I didn't tell anyone about that incident. I mean, as a sergeant I should be setting examples, and here I go and leave my rifle sticking out of that dead NVA's body. I should have planted my foot on the body and yanked the rifle out, but I just couldn't do it. I took off, left my rifle behind and didn't tell a soul.

When we finally rejoined the main body of the company, we eventually got a defensive perimeter going. We found out that the back end of the battalion CP group got cut off by the enemy, and we took a lot of casualties there. The NVA actually got one of our mortar tubes and fired at us with our own mortar rounds. Sergeant Demory and I set up a platoon CP; I had the radio. I took that radio from our radio operator, Rich Morris, and sent him up on the line because we needed more riflemen. The platoon CP stayed up near the line anyway. Rich Morris got promoted to sergeant a few months later and became the platoon guide.

Delta Company lost another six KIAs that day, 6 September 1967, and a lot more wounded. I can remember a helicopter came in; that pilot seemed determined to land to take out some of our more serious casualties. The enemy really lit up that CH-34 helicopter; I don't know why that helicopter didn't crash, killing everyone inside, but they made it in and took out some of our wounded. I heard later that some of the chopper crew got wounded. He kept trying to come in despite our people telling him that there was no way he would make it in. One of my friends, another sergeant, a guy named Henderson, was in charge of the tear gas launcher and traveled with the CP group, one of those who had gotten cut off. I saw him on the morning of the 7th and

> told him how glad I was that he had made it. He didn't even recognize me—I was covered in filth from several days of close combat.
>
> One Five finally consolidated the perimeter but continued to receive incoming small arms fire and mortar fire throughout the night. Corpsmen treated our casualties, and we established our night defense perimeter as the enemy ceased activity except for some sporadic small arms fire aimed at the medical evacuation helicopters coming into the LZ.

While the Marines of Delta Company were fighting for their lives, Bravo Company had their own fight. On 6 September, Sgt. Rodney M. Davis, from Macon, Georgia, a Marine who had been with 1/5 for less than a month, also earned the Medal of Honor. Sergeant Davis was married and had two young children. He had been serving as a Marine security guard at the American embassy in London, England, and could have avoided combat in Vietnam altogether because his enlistment was nearly at an end. But Rodney had several friends serving in Vietnam, and he felt a calling to join the fight. He volunteered for combat duty and was assigned to Bravo Company, 1st Battalion, 5th Marines.

Sergeant Davis had only been in South Vietnam for about three weeks, serving as a platoon guide. Shortly after dawn that morning, in the midst of hellacious fighting all around them, the Bravo Company Marines found themselves outnumbered and nearly surrounded. The enemy's positions were close—too close—and Bravo Company quickly found itself fighting for its life. Suddenly, an enemy hand grenade was thrown into one of the Marines' hasty defensive positions, a muddy trench, and Sergeant Davis, without hesitation and with no thought of his own self-preservation, leaped forward and covered the grenade with his body, saving many lives but losing his own in the process.

Gary Petrous enlisted in the Marine Corps shortly after graduating from high school. Gary recalls:

> I was living with my parents in Detroit after my high school graduation in 1965. I had received my draft notice and would have been drafted into the army in the coming year. College was not a financial option at that time, and I had an older brother who had gotten out of the Corps in the fall of 1964. I fell in love with the Corps, so it was an easy decision. I pretty much knew that it meant a trip to Vietnam, but the real question was two years in the army or three in the Corps. I met with a recruiter and he told me that there was a voluntary draft provision where I could get into the Corps for two years active and six years reserve. The reserve was merely a formality, because they assigned a duty station over five hundred miles from my house, so I didn't have

> to do summer camp or weekends. I was thrilled, and so I signed the paper. That turned out to be the best decision I ever made in my life. I entered the Corps in August of 1966, trained, and had leave and shipped overseas in January of 1967. I was immediately assigned to Bravo Company, 1st Battalion, 5th Marines and stayed with them until March of 1968.

Gary Petrous is a very rare combat veteran, in that he survived thirteen months of heavy combat with 1/5, fighting in Operations Union I and Union II, Operation Swift, and what he jokingly describes as a "farewell tour through Hue City" during the Tet Offensive of 1968. During all four of those major combat operations, Gary fought with Bravo Company, on the "tip of the spear." Of all those fierce battles, Operation Swift stands out in Gary's mind:

> Operation Swift—that name brings to my mind the worst three days of my tour of duty in Vietnam. The operation started on the morning of September 4, 1967. We were at the mess hall straggling in and out after a rare night on our home hill known as Hill 51. Someone yelled "Bravo Company, saddle up." We all sprinted back to our platoon area and started putting on our gear. I remember thinking that there was a real sense of urgency that I had not seen before even when we served as a reaction force.
>
> The word came down that Delta 1/5 had set in the night before on the same hill that the NVA occupied, and when the sun set the NVA came out of their holes and were right among them. We were told they were still involved in a desperate fight, and we were to go out and relieve them. We had assembled quickly and, I thought, a little too haphazardly for my liking. This sounded anything but good, and the whole company looked a little edgy to me.
>
> We first encountered the enemy as we were crossing a small river and got into a short but spirited firefight. When we continued toward our objective there was sporadic action that appeared to be an attempt to slow us down more than an attempt to engage us on a large scale. Then all of the fire ceased, and we continued, wary but unmolested. We got close to our objective and feared the worst, because we could not hear any gunfire from the supposed direction of Delta Company. In fact we were surrounded by palpable silence. We heard nothing. It was eerie. We got in radio contact with Delta Company, and we were told we could come on in but to watch our step because the area was full of the enemy and they were a large, well-equipped, and determined force. As we eased our way forward, we were all on a razorlike alert. I swear I could feel the menace. It was like being watched by many eyes from hidden

places. I had to constantly fight the desire to find cover. Once we made contact with Delta Company, we moved quickly into the positions they had manned through the night and relieved their people.

I was acting as A-gunner [assistant machine gunner] for a Marine named Gustafson, who was acting as a machine gunner in the absence of a real machine gunner. This was not unusual in the summer and fall of 1967. We were still on a high state of alert, but we adjusted the makeshift perimeter and expanded it out to create a more secure landing zone to medevac the dead and wounded. I was pretty keyed up and watched with a greater than usual intensity, but I snuck an occasional peek back to see what was going on behind us within the perimeter. It was a scene I will never get over. The dead were laid in a long row, some covered with ponchos, some not. Visible faces were twisted in grimaces and the worst of all were the ones frozen in expressions of surprise and horror. It was ghastly. It seemed like there were none from Delta who weren't wearing at least one battle dressing. It looked like every single one of them was wounded and terrified. There were some that sat and shook. Some that sat and stared. Some that smoked cigarettes with shaky fingers and some that cried silently. Collectively they wore an air of stunned disbelief. Mercifully for them and for us, the choppers came in and took them back. First they took the seriously wounded, then the less serious, then the dead, and finally the able. The last group was very small.

After Delta Company had been withdrawn completely, we had choppers come in and bring more ammo and food. We were supplied and armed to the max, and so we knew that we were going to pursue the enemy. Delta's personal hell had ended, but Bravo's was still to come.

We were encouraged that we had gotten all the choppers in and out without a shot fired and took that to mean that the enemy had fled the area. Even the bush seemed less hostile. We passed the rest of that day in minor skirmishes and passed a relatively quiet night.

We moved out again on the 5th and ran into a small group or two and did very well against them, counting a few kills and in fact taking out a group of about a dozen without taking a casualty. We took the small groups to mean that the large group was splitting up and giving up the ghost, and so we were gaining a little confidence that Delta had borne the brunt and we were just going to mop up. We know now that we were just encountering outposts and listening posts, and that the main enemy force was using the small groups as an early warning system. We wouldn't know this for another day, but the knowledge would come with a vengeance.

We moved out again on the 6th of September. We had approximately two hundred troops. That was a good-sized force for us, and we were feeling pretty good with the way things were going. We didn't see any action that morning, and we even started to relax a little, if that is possible under those circumstances. I am not sure of the time we were hit, but it seems to have been around 1300. We were in a column stretched over a couple hundred yards. I was with Gustafson, around twenty people back from the head of the column. We had just come through a small deserted village that had been heavily bombed very recently. The grass huts still stood, but the surrounding area was riddled with bomb craters. We came to an area that was more open. The trail skirted a very low line of some kind of sickly looking shrubs, and there was a little tall grass along the right side between the trees, lousy concealment and no cover.

The entire column came under a barrage of fire at once, casualties and fatalities were immediate. In my position we were in a terrible spot: no cover, very little concealment, and a volume of fire I had never experienced before. Rounds were zipping everywhere. Dirt was kicking up everywhere, wounded were hollering, and people were trying to shout orders above the din. We returned fire for all we were worth and tried to get fire superiority, but we were seriously outmanned, and the enemy fire just accelerated when we rose out of the dirt to return fire. Gustafson went through several belts of ammo quickly, and I was firing my rifle full auto between feeding belts into the M60. Still the fire lashed at us. I felt that some of the enemy fire was coming from behind us and said so to Gus. Just then a round clipped the edge of Gus's boot heel—in the bottom and out the side—missing his flesh but burning him a little. He looked back, quickly saw what had happened, and turned back to the front, raking the tree line some more. I was fixing another belt for the gun when Gus hit me with his hand and pointed to a brushy side trail that intersected our trail at a right angle.

We had passed it a few moments before the ambush, and now we were about thirty yards past it. Behind the screen of brush, we could see five or six enemy soldiers sneaking up the trail trying to get in hand grenade range. I said, "Burn 'em," and Gus did, dropping all of them in a long scattered burst. I could see the bodies jumping and flailing as the rounds tore through the brush. They looked like weird puppets being bounced around. Finally the intensity of the fire slackened, but it seemed to get more effective. The firing was zinging very close overhead, and I was thinking a sniper had picked us out.

I was just beginning to really feel sick to my stomach when the word was passed up from behind that we were going to pull back. We would start with the head of the column and peel off and run back the way we had come. The first guys ran by behind us; most were helping the wounded and going as fast as possible with the burden. We laid down covering fire as best we could, but when the enemy saw our movement, they immediately ramped back up to high volume.

The Marine next to me was a lance corporal named Costillo. I would leave after him along with Gus. We would go together to protect the machine gun. Costillo looked at me when the man before him left as if to ask if he should go. I looked to the front and yelled, "Go!" I heard a short grunt and looked back at him. He was dead. He was shot right through the front of the helmet and through the forehead. I turned to Gus and said, "Go with the gun. I'll get Costillo's weapon." I emptied my rifle to cover the start of Gus's run and quickly crawled to Costillo about ten feet away. I slung my rifle, grabbed Costillo's rifle, flipped off his safety, and got up to run in the direction we had come. The intense gunfire had slacked to almost nothing when I turned and started to run. A few rounds zipped overhead, but I ignored them. I took several steps and realized that I couldn't see anyone. They were gone. I was alone.

Panic choked me as I ran as fast as I could, hoping to see some friendlies on the other side of the hedgerow I was heading toward. I could see the trail make a narrow opening, but couldn't see anything on the other side. I was running all out when I came to the small trail that Gus had shot up. I didn't slow but swung my rifle barrel in that direction. As I flashed past, I saw NVA troops in the hedgerow. I pulled the trigger, and nothing! Costillo's weapon was empty, too. A burst of fire went past me, some in front and some behind. It was so close I could feel the heat. I veered off the trail, running for all I had. I was expecting to get one in the back any second when I got to the tree line. I leaped at the brush and luckily crashed through to the other side, landing on my chest and scrambling to my feet. If any shots were fired at me from behind, I didn't hear them. I still couldn't see any Marines, but after I took a few more steps I heard someone yell, "Over here." I looked up and saw a guy I didn't know waving me in. He stood up to give me cover, and I ran to his position and dove into the bomb crater he and about five other Marines were manning. He kept yelling, "Are you the last one? Are you the last one?" I kept gasping, "I don't know. I don't know."

My heart was pounding so bad I could feel it in my eyes and see stars with every pulse beat. There was sporadic fire, I think, but that time was sort of a blur. I don't know how long I sat in the bottom of the hole. I remember smoking a cigarette, then putting on my helmet and filling all my magazines and loading both rifles. I remember peeking up over the top of the crater to see who else was around and seeing crater after crater filled with Marines shoulder to shoulder. I remember thinking, "Let's see them crack this line."

We had a kind of lull. During that time, Sergeant Davis appeared at our position and gave us instructions about fire discipline, distributed more ammo, and assigned us fields of fire. He told us we would be moving people around into better defensive positions shortly, and then he moved on to the next position. I didn't envy him his task, but I have to say that his visit was hugely reassuring. Sergeant Davis returned to give us the word on the move, and we reluctantly left the deep crater we had been in, but we favored the new spot over the old when we saw that our position had improved dramatically. Sergeant Davis went off to another position. I thought he appeared visibly shaken by the fury of the attack and the peril of our situation, but he had mastered his feelings; his voice was anxious but even, and he performed his duties in the finest traditions of a sergeant in the United States Marine Corps. We were now in as good a position as possible and ready to respond like Marines.

The enemy had seen our action and prepared their reaction. They tried to get close and engage us, but we beat them back a couple times. They resorted to slinking through the ground cover and attempting to soften us up with a grenade attack. Sergeant Davis, Staff Sgt. Ron Posey, Lance Cpl. Don Connors, Lance Cpl. Randy Leedom, and a Marine named Hinshaw had gathered in a trench line that had been dug around a very large water-filled bomb crater a few dozen feet away from where I lay with 2nd Lt. John Brackeen (our platoon commander), his radioman, Greg Crandall, and the second machine gun team. A grenade came out of the area where the huts were and landed in their section of the trench. All of them dived out, and the grenade went off harmlessly. A second grenade came in and landed outside the trench, and they all dived back into the trench in what Brackeen later described as a wordless but perfectly choreographed ballet. That grenade went off harmlessly also. Then several grenades came in at once, some outside and one inside the trench. Those men in that part of the trench froze in the paralyzing shock and fear that happens only in combat. Sergeant Davis did not. He threw himself on top of the grenade, saving the lives of the other men at the expense of his own.

Sgt. Rodney M. Davis, USMC, was posthumously awarded our nation's highest award for courage in battle, the Medal of Honor (see citation, Appendix D). Rodney bravely acted without hesitation, saving many of his fellow Marines, and the Marines he saved were inspired and able to continue the fight, and soon the tide turned. One of those Rodney saved, Marine Randy Leedom, said, "I remember that day clearly. There were four or five of us in that muddy trench, and the NVA were right next to us. I didn't even really know Sergeant Davis, and I don't know why he did what he did, but I know if it wasn't for him, I would not be here today. He jumped on that enemy grenade, and when it exploded it drove his body straight up in the air. He was killed instantly, but all of the rest of us were saved by his heroic act."

There were forty-eight Marines assigned to 2nd Platoon when it left Hill 51 early on the morning of 4 September, including a two-man sniper team, two machine gunners, and an artillery observer. By the time the chewed-up platoon managed to return on 8 September, that number had dwindled to a mere eleven. The rest had been either killed or wounded seriously enough to warrant immediate evacuation to a hospital. Of the eleven remaining platoon members still capable of fighting, eight would later receive Purple Hearts for bullet and grenade fragment wounds suffered during combat in Operation Swift.

According to the investigation conducted to confirm the facts of his Medal of Honor citation, eyewitnesses stated that Sergeant Davis lunged on the grenade, then used both hands to stuff it completely underneath his body as to make sure he took the entire blast. Davis is among just eighty-seven African Americans ever to have been awarded the Medal of Honor.

Bravo and Delta 1/5 were badly hurt during the fighting on 6 September 1967, but the enemy forces they fought were nearly destroyed. As a result of the fighting in the village of Chau Lam (3) and the surrounding area, thirty-five Marines died and ninety-two of their comrades received wounds and required medical evacuation. One Five's Marines counted and reported 61 NVA bodies and reported 106 more NVA as probable KIA.

By the end of the next day, 7 September 1967, the Marines had policed up most of the previous day's battle detritus, and the Marines of Delta 1/5, the guys who had started all this fighting three long days before, climbed aboard helicopters and flew to Nui Lac Son. At that point of Operation Swift, the Marines of both Charlie and Alpha Companies had not gotten directly involved. Most of the Charlie Company Marines stayed at Nui Lac Son or went out on patrols around Hill 51 Combat Base at Que Son. Alpha Company had stayed pretty much on its own for several weeks, conducting combat operations up north. That was about to change. Before the end of that morning, Charlie Company went to the field again, a main maneuvering element of Operation Swift's commander. They made contact with the enemy at 0820 on the morning of 8 September. The brief but fierce clash resulted in one suspected enemy KIA and no harm to the men of Charlie Company. In addition, India 3/1, also attached to 1/5, commenced an attack on another objective in that vicinity after preparation of the objective with air strikes.

More chaos and confusion invaded the battlefield when Delta 1/1 reported that one of their medevac choppers had gone down in a rice paddy just south of the road

Sgt. Rodney M. Davis, USMC (Medal of Honor, Operation Swift; KIA 6 September 1967). Courtesy of the Davis family.

1/5 Vietnam Veterans gather at Sgt. Rodney M. Davis's gravesite at Linwood Cemetery in Macon, Georgia, to plan the building of a granite memorial monument to honor Sergeant Davis's courage and sacrifice. Courtesy of Kevin Johnson.

and west of Chau Lam (3). No one aboard suffered injuries, but the helicopter sustained serious damage when it struck a tree.

At 1025 that morning the Marines of Bravo 1/5 started humping toward the rear for rest, reorganization, and recuperation. A patrol from Delta 1/1 encountered two VC, exchanged a short but ferocious burst of small arms fire, and then called in artillery on the enemy position. The enemy probably fled to the southwest, back into the village of Chau Lam (5). At the end of that day, upper echelons decided to destroy the damaged helicopter in place.

On 9 September 1967, Alpha 1/5's Marines took the lead. Along with the Marines from Charlie 1/5, Alpha moved into the vicinity of the village of Dong Tiem, located about three kilometers south of the battlefields of Operation Swift's early stages. They found a cave with a significant cache of small arms ammunition and 82 mm mortar shells and discovered a tunnel complex and another cave containing even more high explosives and ammunition. The Marines of Alpha 1/5 did an inventory and then blew all the ammunition in place. From that point forward, both Alpha and Charlie

From the 2012 dedication ceremony for the completed Sgt. Rodney M. Davis, USMC (MOH) Memorial Monument in Linwood Cemetary, Macon Georgia.
Author's personal collection.

Company made constant contact with the enemy in that area of the Que Son Valley. Rick Zell recalled:

> All of this happened within easy walking distance of Que Son Combat Base. Some of those fights got pretty bad, but the day that Father Capodanno got killed was definitely remembered as the worst day of Operation Swift. With still a lot of fighting going on, Alpha came pretty close to the place where 3/5 got torn up. But when we heard that radio message, indicating that the Grunt Padre had been killed, it took our breath away. I mean, no one thought that could ever happen. Everybody got really angry at that point, and we all wanted some payback, so the tempo of our combat operations really ramped up after that. We all wanted to exact a toll for Father Capodanno's death. He probably wore the same set of jungle utilities since the day he arrived in Vietnam. He looked grungy, like a combat Marine, and if you didn't know him, you would never have guessed that he was a priest. Thin, wiry, and hard-looking, Father Capodanno had that haunted look in his eyes that many of the grunts had. He stayed constantly out in the field. I never saw another chaplain do that. So everybody who spent any time at all with the 5th Marines that summer were just devastated when we heard that news. A lot of Marines died in action during Operation Swift, but when I think about Swift I immediately think about Father Capodanno and how mad I got when he died.

Rick Zell contracted malaria and was medevaced a couple of days before the end of Operation Swift. Ironically, Rick took his malaria pills faithfully, every week (not every Marine did), but he still contracted malaria. While in the throes of malaria, Rick's temperature spiked to 106 degrees, and he was flown out. He eventually ended up at the 7th US Air Force Hospital at Cam Ranh Bay for recovery. Through one of those strange quirks of fate, while recovering from malaria at this rear-area hospital, Rick earned another Purple Heart during a rare mortar attack. Rick had just been promoted to first lieutenant and wanted to get back to his battalion, thinking that he might get command of a rifle company. But late one night a VC sapper squad hit the wire at Cam Ranh Bay, and another enemy squad mortared them, and Rick got hit by shrapnel; surgeons operated on him in the hospital there, and he returned to the United States in December 1967.

Rick Zell spent six additional weeks at Bethesda Naval Hospital recovering from multiple shrapnel wounds on his left leg and knee and ultimately returned to duty. Transferred to the Marine Barracks at the US Naval Base, Long Beach, California, Rick subsequently received Vietnamese language training at Monterey, California. Upon graduation from language school, he went to Army Intelligence School at Fort

Haliburton, Maryland. Surgeons at Bethesda Naval Hospital operated on Rick again for reconstruction of the damage caused by the shrapnel. Capt. Rick Zell, USMC, was released from active duty in 1973.

Sgt. Craig Jackson, one of the few Delta Company Marines who survived Operation Swift intact, looks back on that operation as the most severe combat he experienced during his entire tour in South Vietnam.

> When I think back on Operation Swift, I was scared from the time the shooting first started and stayed scared the whole time. The fighting got just so damned close, and we took horrendous casualties. When I got into the bayonet fight with that NVA, I was super scared but somehow still able to function. I also remember the calming influence that I felt when Major Black took charge; he just seemed ice cold under fire. At one point I remember Stretch running past me toward the front of the battalion formation, where most of the fighting took place. He ran bent over. I can remember thinking that he was still tall, even though he ran bent over. Both Lieutenant Colonel Hilgartner and Major Black proved very cool under fire, a tremendously calming influence on the Marines of 1/5.
>
> The US Army Air Cav relieved 1/5 on the morning of the 8th of September. I've never seen that many helicopters in my life. They helilifted the remainder of Delta Company out that day, and we went back to Nui Lac Son.

Late that next evening, 9 September 1967, Charlie Company got into the act, running across a VC in the vicinity of Dien An (2). The Marines shot at the enemy soldier with about seventy rounds of M16 fire and seven M79 rounds. Attacking into the enemy's position while firing these suppressive fires, the Marines discovered that in the enemy soldier's hasty departure, he had dropped his pack, which they recovered. They found several riggers for electrical blasting caps and a friction-type blasting cap as well. The elusive enemy had escaped, but the Marines had captured some of his deadly tools.

The final skirmish of that day took place at 2120 that evening, when some of the Charlie 1/5 Marines observed three VC in the vicinity and hosed down the area with several bursts of M16 fire. When two 60 mm illumination rounds burst overhead, the Marines saw no one, but the 1/5 task force commander ordered night patrols and ambushes around the Marines' positions to keep the enemy at bay.

The remaining few days of Operation Swift mostly repeated the previous couple of days: Marine units continued to sweep the villages and foothills south of the early fighting, having received fairly good intelligence that those NVA units had pulled back into the hills. Occasionally a patrol from the various companies would see a VC or small group of VC in the distance, shoot at them, and give careful but deliberate chase. The Marines set up night ambushes at likely avenues of egress and approach, some of which they executed, but for the most part the fighting had died down to a distant echo of the fighting on 4 and 6 September. The Marines captured or killed a handful of VC during the last few days of the operation.

Operation Swift officially ended at 1600 on 15 September 1967. During the operation, this reinforced Marine battalion had engaged in a deadly struggle with the NVA soldiers of the 1st NVA Regiment as well as elements of the 3rd and 21st NVA Regiments. The combat after-action report from Operation Swift estimates that nearly one thousand enemy soldiers had fought in Swift's battles; nearly six hundred of those NVA soldiers had died. On the negative side of the equation, Operation Swift resulted in the deaths of eighty-nine US Marines.

Dave McInturff has had many years to think about and assess the enemy's strategy during Operation Swift:

> In looking back on Operation Swift, we missed certain indicators—things I didn't pick up on at the time. Once, a fire team of NVA followed us, but we didn't register on them for a while. Then we spotted them in a rice paddy following us. Lt. Bruce Heinz, the 81 mm mortar platoon commander, asked me what we should do about them, so I told him to put out a rear security team and keep an eye on them. Less than thirty or forty minutes later, we met with the enemy's main body as they sprung an ambush on us. The CP group took a lot of casualties during Operation Swift, but I am still amazed that we didn't take more KIAs that day, 6 September 1967.

Lieutenant Colonel Hilgartner relinquished command of the 1st Battalion, 5th Marines on 20 September 1967, and Lt. Col. Oliver W. Van Den Berg, Jr., took command. On 30 September an army brigade took charge of Que Son Combat Base. The Marines of 1/5 left Hill 51 and headed north.

10: Hoi An Days, 1 October–25 December 1967

Hoi An, one of the largest cities in central Vietnam, is also one of the oldest cities in the entire region. Settled by ethnic Chinese and other East Asian seafarers, Hoi An thrived as a population center three hundred years ago. It was Vietnam's most important international seaport from the sixteenth century to the late nineteenth century. Hoi An residents interacted with merchants from both Asia and Europe, trading all sorts of goods, from spices to gold. Located on the bank of the Song Thu Bon (Thu Bon River) thirty kilometers south of Da Nang, Hoi An seems a very quiet riverside town dotted with temples, shrines, and Chinese-style tile-roofed wooden houses along a long, narrow road. Behind the beautiful scenic facades, however, the Hoi An TAOR also served as the home of one of the most active, experienced, and skilled groups of guerrilla fighters the Marines ever faced: the Hoi An "chapter" of the elusive and deadly Viet Cong.

The 1st Battalion, 5th Marines relocated from Hill 51 Combat Base in the Que Son Valley to the Hoi An area in early October 1967. Second Battalion, 12th Cavalry Regiment, 1st Air Cavalry Division relieved 1/5 of the responsibility for Hill 51 and the Que Son Valley TAOR. The turnover of responsibilities commenced on 2 October 1967; however, completion of the equipment helilift and forward displacement of the rear echelon was not accomplished until 12 October because of restrictive weather conditions. The annual monsoon season had arrived in I Corps, during which time huge, drenching downpours regularly swamped the countryside.

One Five relieved 1st Battalion, 1st Marines of the responsibility of Triem Trung (2) Combat Base, located approximately 4.5 kilometers west of downtown Hoi An, and the TAOR around Hoi An. The Hoi An TAOR covered the Hieu Nhon district and a portion of the Dien Ban district. One Five assumed the responsibility for this large and challenging chunk of real estate on 2 October upon the arrival of the 1/5 command group and the Marines of Alpha and Bravo Companies.

As the constant ebb and flow of Marines, created by the individual rotation system adopted early on during the Vietnam War, continued to impact 1/5, another combat veteran left Vietnam and eventually arrived home, but this time his rotation back to "the world" proved anything but routine. Sgt. Craig Jackson of Delta Company had a run-in with another of the hazards of life in Southeast Asia, a microscopic organism called an amoeba. He remembered:

> As the battalion packed up on Hill 51, I got sick. I felt like someone had punched me in the stomach. It actually started right before we left Nui Lac Son; since the battalion was headed north, some Huey helicopters picked us up and flew us to the combat base. I was already sick to my stomach, and then the enemy fired at us all the way over there. Once I got to Hill 51, a corpsman took my temperature, and it was really high, like 102 or 103, and I felt like I had been kicked in the gut. The monsoon season had started, and the weather had turned nasty and cold. I got so that I couldn't drink any water, and I coughed a lot. I couldn't smoke a cigarette or eat anything without throwing up. I made the movement north with Delta Company, as the last 1/5 company to move to Hoi An. I stayed in a tent at Hoi An Combat Base. Lieutenant Strickland sent me to the battalion aid station. They couldn't get my temperature down. A bunch of the Delta 1/5 Marines came to visit me over there and let me know that they didn't like this area; they talked about a lot of mines and booby traps, and they had to ride around a lot on amtracs. One morning the docs told me to go out to the road and hitch a ride to Da Nang and to report in to 1st Medical Battalion for treatment. I went to the main gate of Hoi An, and the only ride I could get was on the back of a six-by truck. No tarp covered the back of that truck, and it rained like hell. The truck driver put the pedal to the metal all the way, while I got tossed around back there, wet and miserable. By the time I got up to Da Nang, I couldn't get myself off the truck. Some guys helped me off the truck, and they helped me inside the 1st Medical Battalion. A doctor examined me; you know, he took his fingers and bounced them around my back. When he got down to a certain part of my back it felt like someone stuck an ice pick through me: incredible pain shot through my body. He went outside and ordered an ambulance to take me right over to the hospital; I had an inflamed liver.
>
> I stayed in the hospital in Da Nang for a couple of weeks and then flew on a medevac plane to the hospital at the Air Force base at Guam. They still didn't really know what I had. I heard some theories that I had hepatitis and others said malaria. I lost a lot of weight. About the third week there at Guam, I got down to about 128 pounds and felt really sick. I felt really happy out of the bush, but my situation got pretty serious. They finally figured out that I had

amoebiasis combined with dysentery, when amoebas attack your liver. My liver had become seriously enlarged. Once they figured out my problem and started treating the disease, I recovered pretty fast. The only problem I had after that came at the hands of some insensitive hospital corpsmen who thought it funny to say that they were "fattening me up to send me back to Vietnam." I didn't think that was funny at all.

While sick, I wasn't able to sleep. I didn't have anything to do at night, because I couldn't sleep, so I would go in the showers, take several showers, shave, and comb my hair. One night I took a shower and started singing, and this big corpsman came in and told me to shut up. I reminded him that I was a sergeant and that he couldn't tell me to shut up. He reminded me of my status as a patient and that he would come in the showers and make me shut up. So I told him to come on ahead and try to make me shut up. So he reached in the shower stall and grabbed my arm, and I hit him in the head with a can of Barbasol shaving cream. It gave him a concussion and cut his ear open. They actually wrapped him up and put him on our ward.

Many combat veterans suffered a significant psychological toll from the stress of combat, oftentimes without really realizing it. Sergeant Jackson had been right in the middle of horrendous and bloody combat for a long period of time. He had lost many friends and seen and done horrible things. When he and those others found themselves abruptly in a rear area, it is understandable that they might overreact in situations like this. Jackson continues:

A couple other corpsmen there initially thought they could jerk my chain. They gave us some limited liberty, after I could start walking around on my own. I went out of the ward for a few hours, off the base on liberty. It felt really good to walk around some, but when I got back to the ward, my pajamas had disappeared. I went to the corpsman in charge, and asked for some pajamas, but he told me that the linen closet only stayed open during certain hours, so I had run out of luck. Then, a couple of days later, it happened again, the same thing. The corpsmen stole my pajamas and then laughed behind my back at my plight. Finally, I just went up to the corpsmen's station and reached over and grabbed the keys to the linen locker. This corpsman grabbed my hand, so I punched him in the face a couple of times. I took the keys and went and got some pajamas. A couple of days later, it happened again, but this time a bunch of the corpsmen banded together. They had hidden the keys to the linen closet. Finally, out of frustration, I just left the hospital. The guard on duty asked me where I thought I was going, and I said, "Fuck it! I'm going home."

> They sent the MP truck to get me and took me back. The next day they sent me over to talk to the psychiatrist, and he diagnosed me as having "acute anxiety."
>
> I stayed there at the hospital for a couple of weeks more and then returned back to the States, diagnosed as having acute anxiety. Initially they sent me to Chelsea Naval Hospital in Boston for observation, and after about six weeks I transferred to Camp Lejeune, North Carolina, and joined Foxtrot Company, 2nd Battalion, 6th Marines, where I spent my last seven months in the United States Marine Corps.

John Rusth rejoined Charlie 1/5 in mid-June 1967 and spent the rest of June, July, and August with the 3rd Platoon. Rusty received a promotion to corporal during the summer of 1967, and a recommendation for the Medal of Honor for his many acts of heroism on Hill 110 had been submitted to higher command. Lieutenant Colonel Hilgartner didn't want John out in the field, because he had already seen more than his fair share of combat action and had been recommended for the Medal of Honor, so he assigned him to 1st Lt. Jack Jewell, the battalion S-5 officer, in September. John had a problem with that, but the battalion commander had his way. He remembers,

> I stayed in the hospital all the time that Union II took place. When I got back and they eventually assigned me to the rear at Hill 51, Operation Swift kicked off. We could see some of it happening, the air strikes and such, because it happened so close to the combat base. Another helicopter went down during the middle of the battle. We knew that the Marines of Dying Delta were in big trouble all the time during Swift.
>
> I stayed back in the rear all during Swift and after we moved to Hoi An. I found it really hard staying in the rear area while everyone else went out on listening posts, patrols, and ambushes. They had assigned me this nothing job when I should have stayed out there with the rest of the guys. And the award thing just continued. They brought everyone back in from the field for interviews all over again. I remember that a Major White and a Major Black conducted the interviews. In many ways I felt very guilty about it, because guys stayed out there getting hurt, and I got to stay safe in the rear area. I have definitely felt guilty over that.

From 15 to 17 October 1967 the Marines of 1/5 conducted Operation Onslow in the Hoi An TAOR. Despite a lack of enemy contact, the new battalion commander, Lieutenant Colonel Van Den Berg, felt that the operation provided valuable experience in that it gave the Marines an opportunity to become acquainted with the oper-

1/5 Marines prepare to go on patrol, Hoi An Combat Base. The battalion chapel is in the background. Courtesy of Rich Lowder.

ating area and to gain an appreciation of the difficulties of maneuvering through flooded rice paddies, the dominant terrain feature of this TAOR. In fact, the entire Hoi An TAOR seemed to be one vast rice paddy, with a few meandering rivers and streams and scattered villages strewn randomly around the countryside. The 1:50,000 terrain maps of this area showed very few contour lines that would indicate high ground. This represented an entirely new type of terrain, and the Marines of 1/5 would have to adjust their tactics and strategies to take this into account.

The Marines of 1/5 spent the remainder of October conducting squad, platoon, and company-sized operations designed to keep the enemy off balance and to familiarize the Marines with their new area of responsibility. In addition to these combat operations, they conducted programs designed to win the hearts and minds of the local populace, including the Med Cap programs, which treated a total of 821 Vietnamese civilians, mostly children, for a variety of maladies. The battalion presented several General Walt Scholarships to needy students living in the area in a ceremony at Cam Ha School on 27 October 1967. Also, the Marines of 1/5 donated two hundred canisters from expended 81 mm mortar rounds to the Quang Nam province chief for use as rat traps and built twelve cribs for the Catholic orphanage in Hoi An.

Sand berm and concertina wire perimeter of 1/5's battalion combat base at Hoi An. Courtesy of Rich Lowder.

As always, the Marines got very creative with methods to win the local populace over. Battalion leadership considered this kind of activity critical, feeling that if we helped the locals, they would help us detect the presence of Viet Cong and NVA and let us know about potential dangers.

Although the month of October proved relatively calm, especially in comparison to the summer months spent in the Que Son Valley, plenty of danger remained. During that month a total of eleven Marines died, and thirty-six sustained wounds serious enough to require medical evacuation. During the brief but violent confrontations that caused these casualties, the Marines saw very few enemy soldiers.

The weapons of choice of the Viet Cong operating in the Hoi An TAOR included sniper rifles, booby traps, and command-detonated mines. Approximately forty Viet Cong soldiers lost their lives in Hoi An during the month of October using those weapons while trying to kill Marines.

That trend continued during the month of November. On two occasions, vehicles moving along Route 538 (the east-west secondary paved road that connected Hoi An with Highway 1) were destroyed by command-detonated mines, resulting in Marine casualties. To add insult to injury, the Marines of Alpha 1/5 celebrated the Marine

Hard point bunkers on the perimeter of the Hoi An Combat Base. Courtesy of Rich Lowder.

Corps' birthday on 10 November 1967 by detecting mines, "improvised explosive devices," wired in series at two different locations in the vicinity of their small combat base located near the South China Sea about six kilometers east of the battalion combat base. The mines were constructed of 105 mm artillery rounds and other assorted high explosives.

The policy of individual personnel rotations continued. New Marines arrived and joined 1/5 in a steady stream, and a fewer number of very lucky short-timers left Vietnam every day. When the Marines of 1/5 landed to stay in the Chu Lai area in December 1965, they felt as close as a family; they had lived and trained together constantly for many months and in some cases several years. Leaders knew the strengths and weaknesses of their Marines; the chain of command became second nature to them. Unit cohesiveness reached a very high level, and the leaders at every level knew what to expect from their men. Nearly two years after the ground war began in Vietnam, the individual rotation system represented a constant challenge to that unit cohesiveness. By mid-November of 1967, virtually no Marines of that original family remained in 1/5. The challenges that the rotation system presented did not, however, change the facts and realities of their mission.

Village adjacent to the Charlie Company compound east of Hoi An. Courtesy of Rich Lowder.

Another new Marine arrived in South Vietnam in November 1967—a young second lieutenant by the name of Roger Nicholas Warr (myself). Called Nick from a very early age by family and friends, I grew up on the southern Oregon coast, graduating from high school from Marshfield High School in Coos Bay, Oregon, in 1963. The first of my family of five boys to attend college, I quickly became bored with school and dropped out of college in 1965, taking a job in a plywood mill in Eugene, Oregon, where my folks had moved. The mindless hard work and abject boredom of working graveyard shift took its toll, and I found myself in a Marine Corps recruiting office in Eugene in February 1966.

Reporting to boot camp in June 1966, I managed to excel, and my senior drill instructor recommended me for the Enlisted Commissioning Program, which took me to Officer Candidate School (OCS) in January 1967 in Quantico, Virginia. Upon graduation from OCS, I received a commission as a second lieutenant, and it was on to the Basic Officer Course at TBS.

I completed Basic School in August 1967, and I had graduated high enough in my class rankings to receive my first choice of military occupational specialty (MOS): supply/logistics. I always thought it smart, for many reasons, to serve in the rear with the gear. Then Capt. Jack Kelly, my Basic School platoon commander, made a significant impact on my life. He made me a deal that I couldn't refuse, using a very effective guilt trip. Captain Kelly reminded me that I had buddies from my enlisted days serving in the infantry in Vietnam. Further, he felt that I had what it takes to become an infantry officer, and he expressed concern that some of the others didn't. One of *them* should go into supply, and I should request infantry. If I did so, he would recommend me for a regular commission, which would put me at an advantage for promotions during my career. This man, Capt. Jack Kelly, was a great Marine and an outstanding infantry leader and teacher; he was also persuasive and charismatic. I would have followed him anywhere. I accepted.

The next day I requested an infantry MOS, and, true to his word, Captain Kelly recommended me for a regular commission. A ground-pounder, headed for WestPac, I had one more stop before I left Quantico: a six-week high-intensity Vietnamese language course.

I graduated from the language school, took my thirty-day leave, and flew to South Vietnam in November 1967. I went through processing in Da Nang at the 1st Marine Division headquarters, and got orders to the 5th Marines. They assigned me to Charlie Company of the 1st Battalion as the platoon commander of the 1st Platoon. Just like that, 2nd Lt. Nick Warr became Charlie One Actual.

Hoi An looked very much like any area surrounding the Da Nang complex: a lot of flimsy Vietnamese hooches scattered about, a large population of water buffalo, old Vietnamese men and women, a bunch of very young kids, and an enormous number of rice paddies, all flung about with no evident rhyme or reason. Much of my ignorance of the historic nature of Hoi An was due to the fact that the city center was designated off-limits to US Marines, and I believe very few of us ever set foot in the city proper during the war.

In November 1967, Charlie Company made its home in a small outpost about five kilometers east of the 1/5 battalion combat base. Located a couple of kilometers east and slightly north of Hoi An's main marketplace, this dreary little company compound sat a few hundred meters north of the Song Thu Bon. Almost all of Charlie Company's squad- and platoon-sized patrols run out of this compound headed either to the east toward the coastline or north toward Da Nang, with an occasional hazardous foray south across the Song Thu Bon.

The remainder of the battalion worked out of the battalion combat base, about four kilometers west of Hoi An, sitting astride Route 538. Although I spent very little time there, I remember the 1/5 combat base at Hoi An seemed to be made up entirely of sand. A typical Marine defensive structure, this combat base measured several hundred meters on each side, shaped like an imperfect square. Bulldozers had created a high berm of sand that surrounded the entire complex, with fighting positions established on the crest of the berm and hard-point bunkers dominating the perimeter at strategic locations. Hard-backed tents and a few wooden buildings, the mess hall and chapel, filled the interior of the structure. The 5th Marines combat base, located further west, sat near the intersection of Route 538 and Highway 1. Route 538, a narrow, old, and crumbling paved road, carried the main flow of military and civilian traffic between Highway 1 and the city of Hoi An; it was the primary supply route for the Marines of 1/5.

Command stayed stable during the months of October, November, and December, with Lt. Col. O. W. Van Den Berg, Jr., remaining at the battalion helm after taking command from Highpockets in late September. Charlie Company, however, got a new leader when 1st Lt. E. B. Burrow assumed command on 12 October 1967. Ed Burrow, promoted to captain a few days later, remained in command for several months.

Quite small by Marine standards, the Charlie Company compound itself measured well less than a hundred meters in diameter. Charlie Company had replaced the Marines of Bravo 1/5 at this compound just a couple of days before I arrived. We shared the compound with an ARVN unit. As at most static fortifications in South Vietnam, many strands of tangle-foot wire and concertina wire surrounded our compound. Tangle-foot, comprised of many taut strands of barbed wire, was always staked low to the ground and augmented by several rolls of razor-sharp concertina wire, stretched out and also staked, making a nasty barrier about three feet high surrounding the combat base. Never once during my short stay in Hoi An did our enemy, the elusive Viet Cong, attempt a ground assault on this compound. In fact, the worst attack on the Charlie Company combat base came at the hands (we found out later) of our supposed allies, a different ARVN outfit based a few kilometers away, who mistakenly dropped several 81 mm mortar rounds on our position.

I passed through the 1st Marine Division and the 5th Marines very rapidly. One Five clearly needed junior officers. I don't remember getting any briefings from any generals or high-ranking officers at the regiment or battalion level, but that may be due to the fact that I felt pretty overwhelmed by my new situation. Immediately after arriving at the Charlie Company compound in Hoi An, I got settled into my new quarters, which consisted of a canvas cot sitting on a small area of plywood-covered floor space in a Marine Corps green general-purpose tent shared by all the Charlie Company officers and staff NCOs. I was now secretly going through an on-the-job training program conducted by Staff Sgt. John "Mother" Mullan, my platoon sergeant.

I had arrived in South Vietnam with many nagging doubts about my own training and about my ability to lead a platoon of Marines in combat, despite almost a year of intensive and effective training. I decided that since Mother Mullan had been the acting platoon commander and combat leader of my new platoon for the past couple of months, it made sense to me to ask him to secretly complete my training based on his experience on the ground. Since unit morale would have been severely impacted if I had confessed my misgivings out loud, I felt it important to keep this training program strictly between me and Mother. So, for nearly four weeks, although from all appearances I ran the platoon, in fact, Mother Mullan called the shots. Either late at night or early each morning, Staff Sergeant Mullan would outline my script for the day, then I would give the orders. These actions would be considered as heresy by the higher-ups, and an extremely unconventional approach to taking command of a Marine rifle platoon, but I believe that this turned out to be one of the smartest decisions I made during my thirteen-month tour in Vietnam.

During those first few weeks, Mother Mullan suggested that I participate in daytime patrols and night ambushes as a rifleman, which is where I spent most of my time. The squad leaders ignored the gold bars I wore hidden under my utility jacket collar and treated me like one of their privates. Thus, I spent a lot of time with my squad leaders and fire team leaders, and I learned the ropes from the perspective of the Marine infantryman and from their small-unit leaders.

One of the more interesting things I learned from them during those first few days and weeks of on-the-job training was the origin of Staff Sergeant Mullan's rather interesting nickname. As one of the squad leaders put it, Staff Sgt. John Mullan cared a great deal about his young Marines and had often demonstrated a "mother-like" love toward them. At other times, however, especially when a Marine would do something stupid or otherwise incur Staff Sergeant Mullan's wrath, the other aspect of his nickname, more often pronounced "Mutha," would become immediately apparent. Although I don't remember ever addressing Staff Sergeant Mullan as Mother during the long months that we served together in Charlie Company, I have always remembered him as Mother Mullan, as both sides of that particular coin demonstrated themselves on many different occasions.

Staff Sergeant Mullan, a career Marine of Irish decent, spent his youth with his family who had settled in the Detroit, Michigan, area. Married to wife Catherine, John had two young children at home when he arrived in South Vietnam. He had served honorably and with great distinction for over ten years, and his long-term goal was someday to become the Sergeant Major of the United States Marine Corps. A big man, at least six feet, three inches tall, John stayed in outstanding physical condition. He carried himself with confidence and always seemed eager to get at the enemy, although that often proved very difficult in the Hoi An TAOR. During those long three months of Hoi An days, the Marines of 1/5 never once made contact with an NVA unit. The major set-piece battles with large NVA units that had defined the summer of 1967 would not occur in the Hoi An TAOR. Our enemy in Hoi An, almost exclusively the elusive Viet Cong, had a different agenda; their mission was to try to hurt us without being detected, and they used different weapons against us. The weapons of choice for the Viet Cong located in the Hoi An TAOR consisted mainly of command-detonated mines and booby traps. When the 1/5 Vietnam Veterans gather at reunions today, great debates spring up about which was worse: confronting large NVA forces in all-out battles or getting hit randomly and unexpectedly by a command-detonated mine. There is no clear answer to that question; both scenarios happened frequently, and both were bad news.

During those first few weeks in the Hoi An area, I was assigned many responsibilities. I would be ostensibly in charge of the company compound security one night; thus, the Marines of Charlie One would occupy all of the trench line defensive positions that night. On other days I would be in charge of assigning squad-sized daytime patrols and night ambush patrols. Normal staffing in a Marine Corps infantry unit placed four Marines in a fire team, the basic maneuvering element of Marine infantry tactics; three fire teams, a grenadier (armed with an M79 grenade launcher), a radio operator, and a squad leader comprised a squad; and a platoon was formed with three squads plus corpsmen, radio operators, and attached weapons units (machine guns, rockets, and so on). However, during much of the Vietnam War manpower shortages sometimes left three-man fire teams, and squads were too often manned with nine or ten or even fewer Marines. Regardless of their unit size, the Marines of Charlie One would break down into squad-sized and sometimes fire team–sized patrols and ambush teams.

On other nights they put me in charge of the reaction force, a designated platoon that would stay ready to move out on a moment's notice and to react quickly in the event that another unit got into serious trouble. Since three infantry platoons formed a Marine rifle company, a rotation system was established to keep all of the tactical concerns of the company commander in balance and provide each platoon with at least a few nights of relative rest and relaxation in the company compound, if nothing bad happened on those nights. On a few occasions in early and mid-December, Charlie One left the relative safety of the Charlie Company compound and spent several days on extended platoon-sized patrols.

In the Hoi An TAOR the VC forces we faced were experienced experts in the use of weapons of terror, including snipers, mines, booby traps, and the occasional mortar attack. Without question, however, the VC's weapon of choice, and the one most feared by Marines who spent any time in the Hoi An TAOR, was the command-detonated mine. Even with the best possible quality in weapons and ammunition, which America most decidedly possessed (with a few dramatic exceptions, such as the M16 when it was first introduced to combat), an occasional 105 mm artillery round or an 81 mm mortar round, or worse, a 250-pound or heavier bomb, initially directed at our enemy, turned out to be a dud. The Hoi An area Viet Cong seemed especially adept at finding these dud rounds and turning them against us with a passion unmatched in most of the other regions in Vietnam's I Corps.

One of my tent mates, 2nd Lt. Pat Polk, the platoon commander of 3rd Platoon, had already spent several months in Vietnam and had earned a reputation as a very effective and much-respected combat leader. He had gotten to know the strengths and weaknesses of his Marines, and it readily became apparent to me that he cared about them greatly. One of my first and most memorable learning experiences, and one of the most terrible, came when I was assigned to help Pat Polk's Marines one night soon after arriving in Hoi An.

Like many of the lessons I learned in Vietnam, this one proved multifaceted. It reinforced much of the tactical training I had received stateside and via Mother Mullan's on-the-job training program. It also taught me about the terribly effective use of the Viet Cong's most favored weapon, the command-detonated mine. Unfortunately, it also began to teach me, most forcefully and with bitter sadness, how much it hurts to lose a Marine, especially one who you had come to know and love through serving in combat together.

On the night of 10 December 1967, the Marines of Charlie One sat gloomily in their muddy trench positions as the rain poured steadily down on us. We had drawn compound security for the night's mission, and all the Charlie One Marines were deployed in their assigned fighting holes and bunkers around the company compound. Mother Mullan and I had just completed our rounds, which required that we check out every fighting hole and bunker on the Marine side of the compound at irregular intervals every hour. Fatigue and boredom conspired to make even the best-trained and motivated Marine sleepy, and our job included ensuring that no one fell asleep.

Charlie Two's Marines, out on an extended three-day platoon patrol, were currently located many kilometers to our north, and Pat Polk's Marines, the guys from Charlie Three, had thus gotten the assignment for night ambush patrols. Two separate squads left the compound shortly after full darkness and slowly and carefully made their way toward predesignated ambush sites located northeast and northwest of the company combat base. Both ambush sites were no more than two kilometers away from our compound, and they had both been selected carefully by Pat Polk and our company commander, Capt. Ed Burrow, as the most likely avenues of approach that our enemy might choose if they attacked our compound. Pat Polk himself remained in the compound, fighting a recurring bout of malaria. Covered in sheets of sweat, Pat stayed bundled up in his poncho liner, shivering intermittently and trying to get some sleep.

The squad leader from Charlie Three, the squad proceeding to the northeast, was Lance Cpl. Larry L. Boice, from Bryant, Indiana. From everything I had heard about this young lance corporal, he was very good at leading troops in combat, and the experienced Marines in Charlie Company respected him. One of my squad leaders, when I asked about this Marine, said that Lance Corporal Boice "really had his shit together." This was about the highest praise you could give to a Marine infantry leader at any level in the chain of command during the Vietnam War.

Just after dark, Pat Polk and his platoon sergeant, along with our company commander, conducted a thorough briefing on the ambush patrols. Although each squad took a different route to their individual ambush site location, they were briefed together to make absolutely sure that they knew each other's locations. There had been more than one instance of Marine squads firing on each other because they didn't know the other unit's location. Casualties in war under any circumstances are always terrible and nearly intolerable, but casualties taken at the hands of friendly fire are without a doubt the most horrible imaginable.

After making sure that his Marines had been thoroughly briefed and were well armed and adequately camouflaged, both squad leaders took each of his men through the somewhat strange looking but necessary noise abatement procedure, accomplished by requiring each man to jump up and down a few times and then tightening straps and placing padding in strategic locations to make sure that their rifles, ammunition, and other equipment made as little noise as possible.

Both squads left the compound at about 2100 that night. The 2nd Squad, led by Lance Corporal Boice, comprised of nine Marines and a navy corpsman, was assigned to the northwest ambush position. As they carefully threaded their way through the myriad strands of trip wire and concertina wire, they all managed to avoid the embarrassment of tripping over one of several trip flares that we placed nightly to help warn us about an attacking enemy force that might sneak in close. In reasonable silence they gradually disappeared into the damp, gloomy night.

Following proper procedures, both Charlie Three squads radioed in as they slowly moved away from the compound and worked their way through several checkpoints, well-known locations marked on our 1:50,000 terrain maps used to assist small unit leaders with navigation. As they proceeded, they made regular progress reports so that the company commander knew each unit's exact location to make sure no friendly units might accidentally fire on them and in the event they might need heavy support. Since each ambush site was over two kilometers away from the compound, we did not expect to hear that the squads had reached their assigned ambush sites until nearly 2200 that evening. Great care was taken to eliminate any unnecessary noise, so any movement during the hours of darkness was always, out of necessity, very slow and deliberate. The grunts also knew they should try to avoid the roads and trails that were heavily used by Vietnamese civilians and daytime Marine patrols and, therefore, were primary targets for Viet Cong bent on planting command-detonated mines and other nasty surprises at night.

The quiet but persistent murmuring of Marines in night defensive positions around the compound and the hushed conversations between the officers and staff NCOs in our tent were shattered into shocked stillness when the loud Wham! of a 155 mm artillery round exploded at about 2125 that evening. The squads had been on patrol for somewhat less than an hour and had just about reached their ambush sites when the explosion occurred. Someone in our tent cursed tensely under his breath; another muttered something about harassment and interdiction (H&I) fires, but it was too early for the H&I fire missions that typically disturbed the early morning hours. Plus, this was a single explosion and just too damned close to our combat base. Pat Polk sat bolt upright on his cot and immediately broke out into uncontrolled shivering, and his utility blouse became completely saturated with sweat. He knew something bad had happened, probably a command-detonated mine, and most likely the targets were the nine Marines and one navy corpsman of his 2nd Squad, the squad led by Lance Cpl. Larry L. Boice.

Before anyone spoke, our company radio man's Prick-25 radio provided us with a terrible affirmation of the worst possible scenario. In a shattered voice just barely managing to maintain control, the 2nd Squad's radio operator screamed out their situation and called for help: "Millbrook Charlie, Millbrook Charlie, this is Charlie Three Bravo. Command detonated mine; command detonated mine. We see movement to our north about two hundred meters and we are taking those gooks under fire." Sporadic small arms fire to our north confirmed what the radio operator had told us. "We have several casualties. We need medevacs, *now*! Repeat, we have several casualties and we need a medevac at our location, now!" The squad radio operator was screaming into the radio, and it sounded like he might lose control at any moment, but it was more likely that he could barely hear after being close to the explosion.

The company radio operator, always on duty at night in the company's headquarters tent, handled the situation in as calm and dispassionate a way as possible, under the circumstances. He had served with Charlie Company for over ten months, and many of the guys in the 2nd Squad of Charlie Three were friends of his as well. The squad radio operator and the company radio operator had gone to communications school together and were very close buddies.

"Charlie Three Bravo, this is Millbrook Charlie. We need you to give us an accurate situation report. What is your location? Give us your casualty reports, over." Procedure required that someone in the squad, preferably the squad leader, would take control of the situation, act without passion, and quickly and professionally provide the critically important information so that we could send a medevac chopper and possibly a reaction force, if needed. We needed accurate information, and we needed it immediately. The company radio operator asked the squad radio operator to put the squad leader on the radio.

The squad radio operator's reply was the most chilling thing we heard that night. He said, "This is Charlie Three Bravo; Three Bravo Actual is hit bad; he was standing right on top of the damned mine when it went off. Not sure he's going to make it. The doc's trying to save him now. We have two more emergency whiskey's. We need a medevac, and we need it *right now*! Get us some help, *please*!"

The company radio operator responded quickly and professionally, saying, "Roger, understand, Three Bravo. Three whiskey's, one critical. Put your next in command on the line, as soon as possible. We're calling in the medevac and will get you help out there as soon as possible. We need to know your exact location and your current situation, over."

After a few moments of static hissing, another voice came on the radio. This Marine appeared to know very little about radio procedure, identifying himself by rank and name instead of using proper codes. He was a private first class, the squad's 1st Fire Team leader and the next in command after the squad leader. The very experienced company radio operator spoke the necessary words methodically and calmly coaxed the vital information out of the young private. The new squad leader reported that the 2nd Squad had been about two-thirds of the way to their designated ambush site when the command-detonated mine went off. It appeared to be a 155 mm artillery round. They had three casualties that needed medevac immediately; Doc didn't think the squad leader, Lance Corporal Boice, would survive. Two other Marines were badly wounded and needed medical attention as soon as possible, but given a quick evacuation, they would probably survive their wounds. A couple of guys would receive purple hearts for small shrapnel wounds and rattled cages from the huge explosion, but they didn't require medevac. Their location, to the best reckoning of this young private first class, was reported to be map coordinates 164587, a spot about two kilometers northeast of Hoi An City and a little over a kilometer north of the Charlie Company combat base. Since the VC had not returned any of the squad's small arms fire, it appeared unlikely that the enemy would attack again that night, but you never knew for sure.

Captain Burrow took one quick look at Pat Polk and knew immediately that he could not lead the reaction force that night. Visibly shaken from the report about his Marines, Pat struggled in the grip of a serious recurrence of malaria. His pale face saturated with sweat, Pat shook visibly. Obviously, our CO wanted Pat to go, because these were Pat's Marines and because he had the most experience, but he sent me instead.

The CO said, "Lieutenant Warr, you will lead the reaction force. Get one of your squads, an M60 machine gun team, and get out there as fast as possible. That young PFC doesn't sound like he's capable of handling a medevac. Any questions?"

I was still very new in country and only about three weeks into my secret on-the-job training program conducted by Mother Mullan. Further, I still privately nursed doubts as to my ability to lead Marines in combat. Still worse, this situation required a fast movement into a known enemy location in the middle of a pitch black, sodden night—not a situation designed to boost my confidence. I didn't even know what questions to ask, other than, "Can I get someone from the company who knows that area, so we can cover the ground as quickly as possible, sir?"

The CO then looked over at Staff Sergeant Mullan and indicated with a nod of his head that Mother Mullan would go along for the ride. During the past several months, Mullan, as the acting platoon commander of the 1st Platoon, and his Marines of Charlie One had thoroughly covered virtually every trail, village, and rice paddy within ten clicks of the Charlie Company compound in all directions.

Mother Mullan and I quickly mustered the reaction force, assigning the squad of Charlie One's Cpl. John Sawaya as the reaction force and navy corpsman John "Doc" Loudermilk to assist the corpsman already on site. Sawaya's Marines, Doc Loudermilk, Mother Mullan, and my platoon radio operator, Benny Benware, mounted up, and we quickly headed out of the wire. It was unlikely that we needed to worry about another command-detonated mine between us and the beleaguered squad, so we moved fast to their location. It seemed like we got there in just a few minutes. The CO had called in the medevac as we moved toward the stricken squad, so there was very little for me to do on the way.

Once we arrived at the scene, a vision of madness and chaos overtook my senses and threatened to strip me of my focus on this mission. In the dark gloom I could smell something nasty, I could hear moaning from the stricken Marines, and I could hear the sharp comments and orders coming from the corpsman on the scene. One of the Marines from the 2nd Squad stood over his shattered squad leader, holding up an IV bag.

My stateside and Mother Mullan training kicked in. Our priority was to secure this location, because there was still a chance that the enemy might double back and hit us again. Corporal Sawaya, Staff Sergeant Mullan, and I took command of the situation, determining what members of the Charlie Three squad remained fit for combat. We integrated them with our Marines and formed a tight 360-degree perimeter about fifty meters in diameter. We did this by establishing several strong points of two or three Marines each at about seven points around us and about twenty-five meters away from the location where the docs frantically tried to save the squad leader's life.

Our next priority was to locate a suitable LZ for the medevac helicopter and make sure it would be secure when the chopper arrived. Many of the rice paddies in that area were currently unproductive due to the elusive although constant presence of the VC and were therefore dry. Most of the productive rice paddies around Hoi An lay fairly close to the city, and we were almost two kilometers outside the city. Dry rice paddies, although still very muddy, especially on a night like this one, were not under a foot or more of water, so a helicopter could land here without sinking into the mud and becoming stuck. Within fifty meters we found a location suitable for any type of helicopter to land. We had to stay somewhat flexible in our choice, because we would not know what type of helicopter would come until just a few minutes before it arrived overhead. Typically, either Hueys or the older CH-34s, relatively small by comparison to the other rotary-winged aircraft assigned to the Marine Corps, flew medevac missions. Sometimes the much larger dual-rotor CH-46, and even possibly one of the huge CH-53s, might be diverted to medevac duty. The location we chose had to be suitable for any of these aircraft. I had to make a professional decision that would cover all bets while under great stress. This young squad leader was dying, and we all wanted to save him.

Once I made these decisions, we moved our defensive positions so that we could protect the LZ. Once that was done (all of this took just a very few moments), there was nothing else to do until the medevac choppers arrived. So, without thinking too much about it, I gravitated back toward the center of the perimeter, where the 2nd Squad's corpsman and Doc Loudermilk struggled frantically to keep Lance Cpl. Larry Boice alive.

Someone had taken a small but necessary risk and had turned on a flashlight so the docs could work more effectively. What I saw in that dim and inconsistent light will remain with me until the end of my days. Lance Corporal Boice had no left arm. Blood had saturated his utility shirt. His legs, while less bloody, were just not right. They seemed broken in many places, twisted around like the straw legs of a scarecrow. Lance Corporal Boice struggled fiercely to remain alive. It was heartbreakingly obvious to me from first glance at his terrible wounds that the young Marine would die despite the docs who worked frantically, like men possessed, to save his ebbing life. The worst problem that the corpsmen fought was that his left arm had been severed so closely to his shoulder that there was no stump to tie a tourniquet around. Bright red blood ceaselessly spilled this Marine's life upon the muddy ground with every heartbeat. Direct compresses slowed the leaks, but the blood was simply everywhere but in the right place, inside his dying body.

After I had looked at this grisly scene only a few moments, Benny Benware, my radio man, diverted my attention by telling me that the medevac choppers were inbound. We had a Huey gunship supporting a CH-34, which would actually serve as the medevac chopper. We talked with the Huey pilot, the medevac mission commander, and let him know that we would pop a flare when we saw their running lights. When he saw the flare, he would contact us and let us know what color flare he saw, and we would acknowledge if he was correct. The Marines had learned not to give away smoke or flare colors over the radio nets; some VC and most NVA units had radios as well, and they had become adept at monitoring our tactical nets. More than one American helicopter got shot down because an enterprising enemy unit was able to learn the smoke or flare color we intended to use to mark our locations, luring the helicopter into the wrong landing zone. We could now hear the whop, whop, whop noise, the very distinctive sound made by a Huey, and then we heard the different racket made by the reciprocating engine of the CH-34 as well, now less than thirty seconds away.

As these birds of mercy approached our position, I began to worry about those elusive Viet Cong returning and perhaps taking a few pot shots at our medevac choppers. So without consulting with Staff Sergeant Mullan or Corporal Sawaya, I went to the two positions on our eastern flank, one of which was manned by the M60 machine gun team, and told them to shoot suppressing fire on my command. I had noticed a tree line about two hundred meters to our east, and I thought that this would be the most likely avenue of attack if our enemy decided to return. My theory for firing the suppressive fire was that the Viet Cong would think twice about taking up positions in this tree line if an M60 and four or five M16s hosed down the area.

When the CH-34 was about ten seconds from touchdown, I hollered orders at the Marines in these two positions, ordering them to open up, and they were very happy to obey. I had issued the order, and it was their duty to obey. Besides, most Marines would gladly fire their weapons at a suspected enemy location whether or not they had a clear target to shoot at. On my command a high volume of outgoing fire shattered the night, and many red tracers flew outward from our position and hosed down the tree line. Immediately, the CH-34 "put on the brakes," so to speak, and aborted his approach into the LZ. The chopper pilot started hollering at anyone who would listen to tell him what the hell was going on. "Millbrook Charlie, this is Dust-off Zero Four Four. What the hell's going on? Are you receiving incoming fire? Over?" Benny Benware stayed one giant step ahead of me and immediately answered, "Negative, Dust-off Zero Four Four. That is all outgoing fire. We are firing suppressive fire into the tree line to discourage any VC from taking up firing positions. Over."

The disgust in the CH-34 pilot's voice was unmistakable as he replied, "Well, stop your fun. Do not, repeat, do not open fire unless you see enemy forces or start receiving incoming fire. Out!"

As I sheepishly realized my mistake, the CH-34 recovered smoothly from his aborted approach and dropped to the ground within thirty more seconds. With the assistance of several Marines using a poncho as a litter, the two docs loaded their precious cargo into the CH-34's side door; several other Marines helped the other two casualties limp into the helicopter. Then, with a great rush of wind and noise, the medevac chopper quickly rose into the sky and headed north to Da Nang.

Without consulting me, Staff Sergeant Mullan and Corporal Sawaya took charge of the remaining Marines and formed them up in a spread file formation, and we headed back to the company compound. Our return trip proved much slower and more cautious than our run out to the site of the command-detonated bomb, so it was about an hour later when we finally reached the safety of the compound.

On the way back in, I had quite a bit of time to think about what I had done. I was somewhat heartsick to think that I had been the cause of a one-minute delay in getting the dying squad leader to the medical help that he needed. This one-minute delay would bother me immensely for several days, until another command-detonated mine wrenched my mind away from that particular night in hell and forced the memory into a back corner of my mind. The memory of that night would remain a small but significant part of all the damnable memories I have of combat in Vietnam.

When we reached the company compound, we received the sad news that Lance Corporal Boice had died en route to Da Nang. He made it about five more minutes, but the corpsmen couldn't keep him alive for the other ten minutes it took him to arrive at 1st Medical Battalion. Lance Cpl. Larry Boice, of Bryant, Indiana, was killed in action during the night of 10 December 1967, just six days short of his twentieth birthday. Like so many other young Americans, this Marine went home inside the dark shroud of a somber gray metal casket in the cargo hold of a C-141. The timing of his death and the fact that the one extra minute could not have made any difference in saving his life gave me no comfort. I would never forget the mistake I made that night.

I spent the next few days completing my on-the-job training, participating in many squad patrols and night ambushes. I also led the platoon on several long-range patrols that took us many clicks outside the company compound. Some of those patrols lasted for several wet and soggy days, as the annual monsoon rains were in full swing.

Although Charlie One did not experience any significant skirmishes with the enemy during the remainder of early December, the dangers of combat lurked all around us. Snipers could shoot at us at any moment; we needed to be constantly wary of potential enemy ambushes. But our main worry continued to be mines and booby traps.

A few days later, during one of those extended platoon patrols, the Marines of Charlie One stopped on a muddy trail to take a few minutes' rest. The Marines stayed spread out, and they took up firing positions, facing outboard, without having to be told. The constant rain was not coming down with full force, but a thick, gray overcast blocked the afternoon sun, and the persistent drizzle dampened everything, including our attitudes. Most of my Marines wore the standard-issue poncho, the six-foot-square rubberized piece of canvas with a hole and hood in the center. I had arrived in Vietnam with my own rain gear (pants and jacket), and they had not yet succumbed to the constant shredding affect of the local vegetation's thorns. Benny Benware, my trusty radio operator from Chicago, wore the standard-issue Marine Corps poncho. Since he didn't have any tactical responsibilities, and since we had announced that the smoking lamp was lit, Benny sat down on a low bank beside the trail, scrunched down inside his poncho, pulled out a somewhat soggy cigarette, flipped open his Zippo lighter, and struck it. As he lit his cigarette, the darkness inside his poncho was lit up for a moment, and he looked down and saw his death. Right between his legs, no more than six inches below his scrotum, Benny saw the three wire prongs of a detonator from a Bouncing Betty mine. Had he sat down six inches left, right, or down from where he did, he would have died a horrible death.

Seemingly as calm as a flat sea, Benny poked his head out of his poncho and announced in his Midwestern twang, "Ah'm sittin' on a mine." He was afraid to move or try to stand up, for fear that his poncho would snag on the prongs. Staff Sergeant Mullan looked down Benny's poncho with his flashlight, made a decision, and then just grabbed Benny's hands and pulled him straight up without disturbing the deadly mine. Corporal Sawaya then set up a small C-4 charge close to the prongs, with a couple of minutes' worth of time delay fuse, and we evacuated the area. We were all happy to hear the two nearly simultaneous blasts of the C-4 charge and the Bouncing Betty explosion about a minute later. The patrol continued to march.

Shortly before Staff Sergeant Mullan "graduated" me to full command of Charlie One, while on a long-range patrol several kilometers north of the Charlie Company compound, I learned another very important lesson. I learned that we could not trust the accuracy of the 1:50,000 terrain maps that we had been issued. I thought it somewhat ironic that the richest nation on earth could not give accurate maps to men in combat on the Asian mainland. Although the development of terrain maps using aerial photography was an old science by 1967, the maps we used did not have the benefit of this technology, and oftentimes what our maps indicated was dangerously different from reality on the ground.

In all fairness to our map providers, the countryside surrounding Hoi An was very difficult terrain to map. To our east lay the South China Sea, the dominant terrain feature. On the coast, about four kilometers east of the Charlie Company compound, a small, very sleepy fishing village was the eastern terminus of the dirt road that connected the compound with the battalion combat base west of us.

A small tributary of the Song Thu Bon, called the Song De Vong, separated a long strip of sandy soil from the mainland for many kilometers to our north. Although most of South Vietnam's rivers flowed from the mountains to the sea, generally west to east, as did the Song Thu Bon, this tributary ran perpendicular to the Song Thu Bon, parallel to the South China Sea. This tidal river separated us from the coastal fishing villages, many of which were fairly remote and thus suspected VC strongpoints.

There was only one bridge that we could use to get from the Charlie Company compound to the sea. A Combined Action Platoon (CAP) outpost was located just past this bridge in the center of the largest fishing village. The terrain to our north was dominated by rice paddies, many of which were, mercifully, dry and therefore passable. Occasional thin tree lines outlined a few small and primitive villages scattered around. Most important, this area contained virtually no hills of any consequence that could be used as reference points. Our maps had been made many years before we arrived, and we learned very quickly that we could not trust the trail markings and the river courses denoted on the maps as dashed and solid lines. All of the map reading techniques I had learned in Quantico, except one, proved totally useless in this situation, because they required one to find a dominant terrain feature, a hill or a mountain or two, and then take a compass reading or two, thereby determining our location geometrically. There simply were no visible terrain features except the villages and trails, and their locations, as denoted on the maps, were completely unreliable.

So there we were, out in the middle of this flat, sandy terrain. After being on the move for a day or so, I became a little uneasy because I wasn't a hundred percent sure of my exact location. If we got hit by the enemy, and I had to call in artillery or fixed-wing support, I could easily find myself in the bad position of a commander who called in supporting arms ineffectively or, much worse, on his own position. So I remembered one lesson we learned in Quantico about calling in an air burst artillery smoke round and then taking a back azimuth from that location, estimating the distance to our location by "mark one eyeball." Thus, knowing the location of the detonation of the smoke round, an estimate of our distance from it, and the azimuth or direction we were from it, I could pretty closely estimate our current position—at least within a hundred meters or so, close enough to keep us out of trouble.

I called a halt, and Staff Sergeant Mullan very quickly and effectively placed our Marines, about forty strong at that point, in a hasty defensive perimeter about two hundred meters in diameter. As he handled the job of setting up our defensive perimeter, I started working on calling in an air burst smoke round from the 1/5 combat base, located about five kilometers west of us. Several artillery batteries from the 11th Marines were located there, including at least one 105 mm artillery battery, a 155 mm artillery battery, and a battery of 8-inch guns; we were well within the range of all of them. I called in a fire mission, requesting one round of 105 mm, smoke, air burst, asking for them to time it so that it detonated about a hundred meters before it impacted the earth. I needed to target a location far enough away to keep my Marines out of harm's way, and yet it needed to be close enough so that I could easily see it when it detonated. This was very important, because although a smoke round itself could do very little damage, the steel canister it arrived in was very heavy and could easily injure or even kill someone it hit on the ground.

I looked carefully at my 1:50,000 terrain map and decided on a target location about a kilometer away—far enough away for safety, but close enough to see. Once I had determined my target location, I called in the fire mission: "Millbrook, Millbrook, this is Millbrook Charlie One Actual. Fire Mission, over."

Within a few seconds I had the 105 mm artillery battery on the radio and completed the necessary instructions. I concluded by asking for them to let me know when they fired the mission by radioing, "Shot, out." About two minutes later, I received the very brief radio message, "Shot, out." The artillery smoke round was in the air.

It doesn't take very long for a high-velocity artillery shell to travel a few kilometers. In fact, we had our evidence and our target smoke round detonation, a heartbeat or two before we heard the thump of the artillery piece's deliverance of that shell. It also didn't take my Marines very long to find out just how lost their platoon commander was. I had my compass ready, stood looking off to the north toward the target location that I thought was a kilometer away, when the smoke round burst about one hundred meters above my head. No one moved for a few more seconds. We all cringed instinctively as the heavy, potentially deadly canister whooped through the rest of its trajectory and impacted with a heavy thud about twenty meters behind me, right smack in the middle of my perimeter.

Happily for all of us, the Marines of my platoon CP group—Staff Sergeant Mullan, Doc Loudermilk and my radio operator, Benny Benware—were all clustered around me on the north side of our perimeter. Everyone else crouched around the edge where they belonged. No one was hurt. Nothing was hurt but my pride. I now knew my exact location, but I really didn't want to find out quite that way. A few sidelong glances glared in my direction over the next few hours, but like many other nonlethal events in the Vietnam War, this one was rapidly erased from everyone's memories, because a terrible and deadly event took its place. On the night of 15 December 1967, Cpl. John Sawaya's squad was destroyed by another command-detonated bomb.

In a scenario uncannily similar to that of the command-detonated mine that had killed Pat Polk's squad leader, this time the Viet Cong had gotten very ambitious. They decided that two would be better than one. Our enemy daisy-chained two 105 mm artillery rounds, two more of our duds turned against us with a violence that bespeaks mankind's potential for viciousness. The VC in the Hoi An area knew how to connect two or more high explosive rounds together with detonation cord, a long, thin rope made of plastic explosive, in a way that both rounds would detonate simultaneously from a single hand-held detonator. They had planted these connected 105 mm artillery rounds in the side of the road that led to the fishing village, just a few meters outside the supposedly friendly village that lay just outside our company compound, within seven hundred meters of our compound. The VC must have done their terrible work shortly after dusk, because Sawaya's squad left the compound before 2000 that evening, and it took them only a few minutes to reach the site. The squad that had responded to assist Lance Cpl. Larry Boice, led by Cpl. John Sawaya, one of the most experienced and savvy squad leaders in 1/5, marched into harm's way.

With one simple squeeze of a detonator, a single Viet Cong guerrilla killed Corporal Sawaya and two more of his Marines, Lance Cpl. William E. Pierson of Brookfield, Wisconsin, and Pfc. Eddie L. Jackson of Jacksonville, Florida. In addition, every other man on that patrol was severely wounded except the corpsman, John Loudermilk. Doc Loudermilk, positioned as the middle man in the nine-man patrol, stood in the exact middle of the kill zone when that VC bastard squeezed his detonator. Doc Loudermilk was instantly knocked flat by the concussion of the combined explosions of the two 105 mm artillery rounds, which had been placed about forty meters apart. He was probably unconscious for a few moments. The next thing he knew, he was sitting in the middle of hell, surrounded by carnage. For a few moments more he thought he was dead and that this really *was* hell. The next thought that passed through his mind was that he was alive, but everyone else in the squad was dead. But then one of the badly wounded Marines started to regain consciousness and moaned in pain. In that moment, Doc Loudermilk's training took over, and with the detached professionalism demonstrated by the typical US Navy corpsmen who served with US Marines in combat, he responded to this horrible challenge immediately, and despite the incredible stress of that moment, he methodically started to save Marines' lives.

For all of the rest of us, sitting in a secure location in the Charlie Company headquarters tent, the sound of a huge explosion within minutes of Sawaya's departure, from an obviously very close position, brought back the memories of the night Pat Polk's squad leader, Lance Corporal Boice, died. For a few brief moments I denied my ears and my senses and tried to ignore what I had heard. But it was no use. Immediately certain that something very bad had happened to Sawaya's squad, to my Marines, I began shaking and went into a catatonic state. In that one moment of remembering what had happened to Pat's squad leader, then a nameless, faceless lance corporal whose body had been shredded to pieces and whose blood I had watched as it had spilled onto the muddy ground, I was undone. These were not nameless Marines; they were flesh and blood; they had names and faces. They were my Marines.

I had never had malaria, and managed to avoid that malady during my thirteen-month Vietnam tour, but I immediately took on the symptoms of a malaria victim and became useless. Pat Polk, who had recovered from his very real bout of malarial fever, immediately volunteered to take out the reaction force. He and Staff Sergeant Mullan reached the site within minutes of the explosion, providing Doc Loudermilk with the help and support that he so desperately needed. I sat for several hours in one place, on my cot, listening to the radio communications and hearing in bits and snatches the fate of an entire Marine rifle squad.

Cpl. John Sawaya, originally from Orem, Utah, was a rare breed—a very experienced, very savvy squad leader who chose also to carry his squad's M79 grenade launcher. He voluntarily, and very forcefully, insisted on carrying the M79 *and* his M16 rifle, along with an average of about sixty rounds of 40 mm M79 high explosive ammunition. On several occasions this heavy combat load served his squad well when his Marines made contact with the enemy and Sawaya put out the firepower. John Sawaya was an effective combination of heavy firepower and leadership savvy. On this particular night, his combat load betrayed him. Many of the 40 mm high explosive rounds strapped to his body detonated because of the terrible explosions of the 105 mm artillery rounds. The explosion of the 105 rounds alone would probably have killed him, but the secondary explosions from the M79 rounds literally tore him to shreds. His flak jacket proved no match for this devastation, and although Doc Loudermilk valiantly kept Sawaya alive for a few minutes, he died shortly after he was placed on the medevac chopper. Two more Marines of his squad, Lance Corporal Pierson and Private First Class Jackson, were killed outright by the command-detonated daisy-chain. Their shattered bodies were put aboard a later, routine medevac flight, the saddest of all medevacs. All of the rest of Sawaya's squad, including Doc Loudermilk, who insisted on staying with his squad, were put on Sawaya's emergency medevac flight, as they were very badly wounded and would need serious medical attention. Priority medevacs—the middle classification—were those where the aircrew is asked to press, but not as hard as they would for an emergency. A priority medevac patient would most likely live through the night, so the flight crew shouldn't die coming in for him.

Pat Polk and Mother Mullan handled the reaction force and medevacs like the experienced combat professionals they were, and the reaction force Marines were all back inside the company compound before midnight that night. No one ever said anything to me about my "malaria attack." I think Pat Polk was happy that he could return the favor I had done him a few days before. Mother Mullan didn't say a word; he understood that I had already become attached to my men, and I felt then, and I feel still today, that it would have been an unspeakably shattering experience to face the reality of their shredded and mangled bodies lying there in the mud.

Doc Loudermilk returned to Charlie Company the next day and continued to help his Marines for many more months after that. He acted like it was just his job, that it hadn't bothered him much. He continued to provide a competent, extremely professional brand of emergency medical care, commonplace amongst the US Navy corpsmen I met in Vietnam. I found out thirty years later that that terrible night, along with the many other long and challenging days and nights during which Doc cared for us, remain etched in Doc Loudermilk's soul forever. The memories of that night are undiminished by time and distance. Still, to this day, John Loudermilk remembers the names and faces of those who were killed and wounded that night. He remembers, in very unnecessary but damnably persistent detail, the nature of their wounds, the looks on their faces, and the treatment he provided them. He remembers them all, but he mostly remembers the haunting faces of those who died: Cpl. John Sawaya, Lance Cpl. William E. Pierson, and Pfc. Eddie Jackson.

Somehow Charlie One continued our mission in the Hoi An TAOR. Despite our losses, and despite the persistent visions of blood, gore, and destruction that clouded our everyday thoughts, the Marines of Charlie One continued our mission. Through long daytime patrols, night ambushes, and extended platoon patrols, we managed to avoid any other nights like that of 15 December 1967, when we lost so much. We did experience the terror and anger of being tormented by ARVN 81 mm mortars, but we had very few serious casualties from those errant rounds, and that incident quickly was pushed back in our minds, dredged up later and talked about as one of the many gut-wrenching things that happened during the Vietnam War. As a group, we filed those incidents under the heading of "shit happens."

There was one more night in Hoi An, however, that contained so much terror for me that I can hardly think about it now, forty-five years later, without physically cringing. Charlie One was assigned another long-range patrol, but this one had a couple of twists. Our mission was much more specific this time. In all of the extended three-day patrols we had conducted up until that point, we were simply given a patrol route and sent off to see if we could find the enemy. This time our mission was to be the cordon force in a cordon and search operation, targeting a small village on the coast about five kilometers north of the small fishing village directly east of us. In order to be in position to cordon off that village so another Marine unit from 1/5 could conduct the search effectively, we would have to arrive in our cordon positions well before first light. Thus, we would have to leave the company compound at about midnight the night before. We would leave the Charlie Company combat base late that evening and then move east and through the Combined Action Platoon (CAP) located in the fishing village to our east. The CAP program placed a squad of Marines and one Navy corpsman in villages from Chu Lai to the DMZ in South Vietnam from 1965 to 1971. Most CAP units were reinforced by a varying number of Vietnamese soldiers, either ARVN soldiers or the citizen soldiers of the Vietnamese

Regional Forces (RF) or Popular Forces (PF), sometimes referred to as Ruff-Puffs. Those native reinforcements were often perceived as mixed blessings.

Once we passed through the CAP unit, we would then move five more kilometers north along the coast and set up our cordon positions before first light. That meant that we had to move about eight kilometers in about five hours, which we figured was doable, given adequate coordination with the CAP unit commander.

Just to be on the safe side, Mother Mullan and I visited the CAP unit the morning before our planned departure. We spent about an hour with the CAP commander, a Marine staff sergeant, going over our plans and coordinating with the CAP unit Marines. Whichever Vietnamese force they pulled from, the CAP units were a combined force and always commanded by a Marine NCO. The group we visited late that morning seemed to be, from our perspective, pretty squared away, so we had no inkling of what was to come.

It was extremely important for us to coordinate our movement with this CAP unit, since we had no other route to use to get to our destination and since we would pass through their position in the early morning darkness. The CAP unit's main defensive position was an old concrete bunker left over from the French occupation, and the fighting holes in the bunker had an extremely good view of the bridge that separated the CAP unit's position from the mainland. We were informed that the CAP unit Marines strung many strands of concertina barbed wire across this bridge every night, but that it would be possible to weave our way through the wire without getting entangled. Once we made contact with the CAP unit by radio, they would send a man over to our side of the bridge who would guide us through the wire.

The CAP commander gave us their radio frequencies and their passwords and assured us that he would have his men on full alert until we were safely through their outpost and well away from their positions. The worst thing that could happen to any Marine outfit was to accidentally get into a firefight with a friendly unit. It had happened before, and it would happen again before US forces departed from Vietnam. However, both Mother Mullan and I had a great deal of confidence that passing through this CAP unit's positions would be the least of our worries. We had been told that the village we would be surrounding early the following morning was a Viet Cong stronghold and that we could expect some serious contact with the enemy when the search force arrived.

We departed on schedule from the Charlie Company compound at midnight that night and proceeded east down Route 538 cautiously but safely to a position about a hundred meters short of the bridge that would lead us into the CAP unit compound. There we stopped to establish radio contact with the CAP unit commander. My radio operator, Lance Cpl. Benny Benware, who was extremely good at his job, took too long to make that critical contact, so I grabbed the Prick-25 handset away from him and took over.

At first, my radio calling was very calm, very professional. "CAP Five, CAP Five, this is Millbrook Charlie One Actual. Do you read me, over?" After several repeated attempts at establishing contact, I asked Benny if he was sure that he had the right frequency, and he replied in a sullen affirmative. As I stated, Benny was very good at his job, and he didn't take kindly to any talk that indicated that he didn't know what he was doing. Unfortunately, nothing that either Benny or I did could get those clowns on the radio.

Staff Sergeant Mullan joined us a few minutes later and very respectfully but somewhat forcefully reminded me that we had a mission timetable that was critical and that we needed to move out. At that point I made a command decision. We would move across the bridge and into the CAP compound. I hoped we would be halted verbally, would be able to give them the password, and would then be allowed to pass through their positions and be on our way. The previous morning the CAP commander had showed Mother and me how every night they strung several coils of concertina wire across the bridge in several spots, and I felt that my night vision was pretty good and I could follow the winding trail across the bridge. Part of my command decision, therefore, was that I would be walking point for a few hundred meters. We moved out. As we started moving, Benny continued to try to make radio contact, with no success.

We reached the bridge and came into contact with the first coil of concertina wire; my night vision had developed to the degree that I could dimly see the winding path through the coils of sharp concertina wire. So I started to cross the seventy-foot-long bridge. I got about one-third of the way across when I tripped on a trip flare wire, and the whole world instantly became a painfully bright white glare. Completely blinded for a couple of seconds by the unexpected light, I slowly recovered my vision, and my stomach lurched and knotted up tight with the view that my eyes beheld. I was staring at the business end of five Claymore mines, aimed right at me and my men, lit up like broad daylight. I knew, most certainly, that I was about to die. Time slowed unmercifully, and everything went into slow motion.

Across the bridge, the old French-built, two-story concrete bunker stared me in the face. The CAP commander, during our visit on the previous morning, had showed us this fortification with pride. He told us that he felt his guys could hold off a much larger force from this one position alone. He felt that any attacking enemy must attack this position across the confining bridge, and that his guys could tear them all apart from their firing portals in the French bunker. Now all I could think about was my certainty that tripping the trip flare would wake up everyone in the bunker and that they would see armed soldiers on their bridge and would shoot first and ask questions later. They would first start squeezing the detonators attached to the Claymores, one of the most deadly and effective antipersonnel devices known to man, and then they would stick their M16s out of their firing ports and start shooting the shit out of whoever remained on the bridge, namely 2nd Lieutenant Warr and his Marines of Charlie One, every last one an easy shot.

Using an inner force that I had no idea I possessed, I took one small step. Nothing happened, so I stepped forward for one more pace. Finding that I had not been killed yet, I took a third trembling step. Nothing happened. Now I started moving as quickly as possible, hoping to make it into the compound while the flare still provided illumination. Again, I found that I had not died, and I made it into the CAP compound, crossing the entire bridge without a scratch. I was all in one piece and damned glad to be that way. Not one of my men, trailing rapidly in my footsteps, had made an unnecessary sound.

I quickly entered the back door of the French bunker and could not believe my eyes. Five US Marines occupied that concrete bunker, every one of them sleeping like a baby. Not one of them had been disturbed by a major military force crossing their bridge; not one of them had had their sleep disturbed even with the sudden bright light of their trip flare. If we had been their enemy, we would be slitting their throats right now, and then we could take our time killing every man in the compound. As it turned out, I thought Mother Mullan was going to do just that. Mother had been with the last squad to cross the bridge, but when he reached the French bunker and saw what had happened, he had a very scary look on his face. I thought he was going to strangle the Marine NCO in charge of the bunker.

When, a few minutes later, a very sheepish, very sleepy CAP commander joined us from his comfortable hooch in the middle of the fishing village, his "headquarters," I decided that the best course for us was to get the hell out of there, and just as quickly as possible. I wanted to avoid any unnecessary bloodshed, so I reminded Mother Mullan of our mission, and we took off. Mother did let off one volley of verbal abuse on the CAP unit, calling them, among other things, "dead men walking," as we left the compound from the east gate. He also, very forcefully, suggested that they stay well away from the Charlie Company compound, because he couldn't be responsible for what might happen when word of this got around.

So we left, and we made it to the cordon target village, and just after first light the other outfit from 1/5 conducted their search. I felt it a very fitting thing that the only shot fired in anger that day was a single M79 round directed toward a close but safe target near an old Vietnamese mama-san who had left the village in our direction. This old mama-san had left the village against strict orders from the search force's interpreter because she had to take her morning crap. As she left the village, my Marines yelled at her, warning her repeatedly to go back into the village. But her necessity proved too powerful, so she found her regular bush, dropped her drawers in our direction, and took her crap despite the high explosive round that went off about twenty meters away from her. When she finished her business, and not a moment before, she scurried back into the so-called Viet Cong stronghold, where, I am sure, she was found to be the ringleader of a bunch of dastardly crappers. We found no other evidence of Viet Cong presence in that particular village on that particular day.

Hoi An days were long, cold, wet, and filthy, often uneventful, even downright boring. Some Hoi An days, however, overflowed with blood, terror, and death, and so we were very happy to learn, in late December 1967, that 1/5 would soon move north. During the monsoon months of October, November, and December 1967, a total of twenty-three Marines serving in 1/5 lost their lives; twelve of them were Charlie 1/5 Marines. Well over a hundred 1/5 Marines sustained serious wounds requiring medical evacuation. Most of the wounds came at the hands of booby traps, mines, and the VC's weapon of choice, the command-detonated bomb. Although that was a much lower casualty rate than the one 1/5 had endured during the summer months in the Que Son Valley, our Marines were all happy to leave the Hoi An TAOR. We had been forced to fight a very frustrating war against an enemy who had no face. Their hit-and-run tactics discouraged us, and our quick reactions and firepower accounted for only about fifty confirmed enemy KIA during our entire stay in the Hoi An TAOR.

On the day before Christmas 1967, the Marines of the First Battalion, Fifth Marines started moving north. With the exception of a small advance party who had left several days before, about half of the Marines of 1/5 flew in several waves of the giant CH-53 helicopters. In one smooth and easy flight, we moved north of Da Nang, over the treacherous Hai Van Pass, and arrived at our new home, the combat base at Phu Loc 6. The other half of the battalion had to endure the long and dangerous ride over the Hai Van Pass on a truck convoy.

11: Incoming! Phu Loc 6 Combat Base, December 1967–March 1968

Incoming! *Incoming!* The frantic screams came from several Marines manning a bunker about one hundred meters to our right. Dozens of other Marines echoed the shouts as they scrambled desperately toward trenches and other bunkers surrounding Phu Loc 6 Combat Base. My heart in my mouth, I willed my adrenaline-pumped and shaking legs to move me toward the nearest trench; my mind raced with wild and fearful thoughts, my vision kicked into agonizing slow motion, and then my ears picked up the dreaded hollow thunks of several more enemy mortar rounds hitting their tubes. Only a few seconds, that's all the time I had to get to the trench. How long since the first enemy mortar round left its tube? How much time left? Not enough time. Hit the dirt!

Infantrymen dread the sounds of incoming enemy mortar, rocket, and artillery fire and have since the dawn of modern warfare. Those who lived in Phu Loc 6 Combat Base in early 1968 learned that the hard way. All of the terrible sounds of combat proved hard to live with, but the random nature of a mortar attack was the worst part. You just never knew where a mortar round would explode, and you never felt totally secure no matter how extensive your trenches, no matter how deep your hole.

When Phu Loc 6 Combat Base, situated on a big lump of red dirt, became strategically important to the 1st Marine Division's planners, they ordered it built, occupied, and defended by the First Battalion, Fifth Marines. Actually, the Marines of 1st Platoon, Company B, 1st Engineer Battalion accomplished most of the initial construction of the combat base. The engineers first dug a deep trench around what would become the perimeter of the combat base, and then they erected extensive concertina and tangle-foot barbed wire defenses just outside the main trench line. As a result, the 1/5 combat base at Phu Loc 6, even in its very early stages, proved to be a very rugged and defendable home for 1/5's Marines.

At first the NVA and VC left us alone in our new combat base. We enjoyed a period of about two weeks of relative peace and quiet. It seemed to us as though our

M109A2 155 mm self-propelled medium howitzer at the Delta Company combat base located atop the Phu Gia Pass. Courtesy of Rich Lowder.

enemy stayed completely ignorant of our location. As with many of the better things that happened during the Vietnam War, these peaceful days proved too good to last.

In early January 1968 the shit hit the fan, really hard. Enemy units began to fire on Phu Loc 6 Combat Base with mortar, rocket, and recoilless rifle fire as well as small arms fire, all of which conspired to make our lives miserable. At the height of this engagement, in late January and early February 1968, more than a thousand rounds of enemy high-explosive mortar and artillery shells hit that lump of dirt every single day. Then, after the initial tide of the enemy's Tet Offensive began to ebb, in late February and early March the enemy faded away from the area, and in mid-March of 1968 American forces dismantled the combat base and abandoned it. Phu Loc 6 Combat Base had a very short but terribly bloody history.

Situated about two kilometers south of a cluster of villages in the heart of Quan Phu Loc, the Phu Loc district, the combat base sat at the foot of a range of very steep, severely rugged, and extremely hostile looking jungle-covered mountains. Route 591, a narrow and roughly paved road, terminated at its intersection with Highway 1 in the center of the main village. The narrow road wound tightly through approximately two kilometers of the sleepy villages of the Phu Loc district before the village

2nd Lt. Rich Lowder walking beside a truck convoy on the Hai Van Pass. Courtesy of Rich Lowder.

hooches petered out. The combat base location started a kilometer past the last village hooches astride Route 591, and then the old, crumbling highway departed the combat base and began to climb up into the mountains toward a complex at the top of a mountain called Bach Ma.

We had learned that this complex on Bach Ma had been built by the French during their occupation of Vietnam, originally as a resort. As we occupied our new combat base home in late 1967, Bach Ma, designated by a cluster of small, square dots on our 1:50,000 terrain maps and serviced by a significant road complex at the top of the mountains, proved to be a Viet Cong headquarters and stronghold. According to division intelligence gatherers, Route 591 served as a major enemy supply route from the Ho Chi Minh Trail to the Viet Cong hiding out in villages along the coastline. In its short ten kilometers, Route 591's elevation rose from nearly sea level at its departure from Highway 1 to over two thousand meters (over 6,500 feet) at the Bach Ma complex, attesting to its steepness and ruggedness.

Increasing enemy activity in late 1967 led 1st Marine Division planners to initiate combat operations that would result in strongholds for Marine forces blocking the enemy's supply routes. One of these strongholds, Phu Loc 6 Combat Base, was built

Severe switchback on the treacherous Hai Van Pass on Highway 1. Courtesy of Rich Lowder.

to cut off the enemy from his source of rice and arms and to provide an enticing target for the enemy that would require them to mass their forces before striking. Enemy attacks would then key our subsequent reaction force counterattacks using our superior firepower, netting almost certain battle victories and the continued denial to the Viet Cong of their bullets, rice, and Band-Aids. In 1967 we continued to concentrate our forces along the coast primarily to protect the civilian population. Lacking combat power and intelligence to go after the NVA, we let the NVA decide when and where battles would be fought, using essentially the same strategies that the French had used, albeit unsuccessfully, in the early 1950s. We still hoped to use technology and firepower to beat our enemy in set-piece battles. Because of our overwhelming advantages in technology and firepower, this strategy should have worked. It didn't; not quite. Fortunately for those of us who spent time at Phu Loc 6 Combat Base, it didn't completely fail, either.

Cpl. John Rusth finished his tour with Charlie 1/5 at the combat base at Phu Loc 6. He remembered, "We dug those bunkers, and those trenches, and we looked up at that mountain called Bach Ma, and built the combat base called Phu Loc 6. The rains came down hard, so it quickly became a very muddy and dreary place." Rusty de-

Marines of Charlie 1/5 prepare for patrol, Phu Loc 6 Combat Base, late December 1967. Courtesy of Rich Lowder.

parted Vietnam in mid-January 1968, just before the NVA began their violent and sustained mortar and rocket attacks on the combat base. It was a very timely departure, and very well deserved for this young Marine, a true hero of the battle for Hill 110.

The Marines of 1/5 started moving into Phu Loc 6 Combat Base in mid-December. After the advance party, and the company of Marines from the 1st Engineer Battalion who had arrived with their heavy equipment on the lump of dirt a few days before us, the main force of 1/5 followed on the day before Christmas 1967. Half of the Marines of Charlie One, including myself, were among the lucky ones who got to avoid the long, dirty, and dangerous road trip and made the move via helicopter; the other half, led by Mother Mullan, got the short end of the straw and had to endure the dangers of a truck convoy over the treacherous Hai Van Pass. I never heard the end of that one from Mother Mullan, who bitched about it constantly.

Although never very comfortable flying in any helicopter during my tour in Vietnam, I was happy to have avoided that seventy-kilometer road trip. Although seventy clicks doesn't sound like a very long trip by American standards, these particular forty-five or so miles took many, many hours to travel, and every click, every mile,

An M50 Ontos in a defensive posture at Phu Loc 6 Combat Base. Courtesy of Rich Lowder.

posed extreme hazards and the possibility of death. Mother Mullan, and the Charlie One Marines who also got the short end of this deal had to travel through the traffic-clogged roadways of Hoi An and Da Nang and then negotiate the terrifying climb over the notorious Hai Van Pass before they passed through the reasonably safe Lang Co village area. Then they had to make a mad dash across the Bowling Alley, a long, straight stretch of highway infamous for enemy mortar attacks, before reaching the turnoff on Route 591 that would take them the last two clicks from the Phu Loc 6 district headquarters to the combat base. It took them nearly an entire day to reach our new combat base; fortunately for them, only one breakdown occurred when one of the accompanying Ontos antitank vehicles broke a track; Lt. Bruce Morton and seven other Marines had to wait for a tank wrecker, but they still managed to make it to the new combat base before dark. Fortunately, no ambushes or mortar attacks took place, and no command-detonated mine attacks, even worse and fairly commonplace along Highway 1, occurred. However we traveled, we were all glad to leave Hoi An.

Still, in the back of our minds we started asking ourselves what lay ahead. Our destination was about a third of the way to the DMZ. The further north we would go, the fewer mines and booby traps we would have to deal with—at least that's what the rumor mill said. We had a different challenge ahead of us, though, a challenge called the NVA. At last we would see the regular enemy; no more disappearing black pajamas. That's what went through my hopeful mind on that CH-53 ride on 24 December 1967.

Our first few days in the new TAOR passed calmly and peacefully. The last days of December and the first days of January 1968 provided no portent of things to come. The local rice farmers were actively cultivating portions of the nearby land, yet many of the rice paddies in the area lay dormant. The structure of the combat base, defined by the perimeter trench and barbed wire, was almost completed when we arrived. We knew we'd have to dig our own trenches and holes, of course, but digging had become second nature to us by now. Whenever we stopped for any length of time around Hoi An, we dug, and we dug deep. Unfortunately, the dirt at Phu Loc 6 proved harder than the sandy soil of Hoi An; it contained a lot more red clay in the laterite soil, but Marine muscle power and the trusty entrenching tool could still get four or five feet deep quickly enough. The 105 mm artillery battery from the 2nd Battalion, 11th Marines was already installed and operational when we arrived, our Christmas present. The hill was covered with tents—a mess tent, the battalion CP tent row, the company GP tents in Charlie Company's assigned area—and several sturdy bunkers. Thanks to the major efforts of the advanced party and the engineers, we had all the comforts of home.

The most unsettling feelings about my stay at Phu Loc 6 during those last few days of 1967 and the first few days of 1968 came from the book I happened to be reading at the time. An avid reader, I would try to read whenever I had a few minutes of spare time. Truthfully, spare time didn't happen a lot, but *The Battle for Dien Bien Phu*, written by Jules Roy, stayed in the top of my pack in case I could grab a few minutes. I had learned about this famous battle while attending the Basic School back in Quantico and thought that it wouldn't hurt to know something about the history of the so-called French Indochinese War, our predecessor. The historic battle for Dien Bien Phu proved to be the last major battle of the war between the Vietnamese nationalists, or Viet Minh, led by Ho Chi Minh, and their French conquerors.

The Battle of Dien Bien Phu marked the beginning of the end of France's annexation of Vietnam. During that historic battle, the French massed their main fighting forces on several fortified hills down in a valley called Dien Bien Phu, located about two hundred kilometers west of Hanoi. I read with great fascination as well as a growing sense of unease that the French wanted the Viet Minh to come down from the higher hills in force so they could engage the enemy in large numbers in the classic set-piece battle. The French fully expected inevitably to win through the use of superior firepower. The primary American advisor to the French ground commander at Dien Bien Phu, Lt. Gen. John "Iron Mike" O'Daniel, laughed at the idea that the Viet Minh could bring artillery through the jungle. He was not alone. In fact, an American mission of antiaircraft experts familiar with the Russian antiaircraft artillery used in Korea had inspected Dien Bien Phu to advise the French and had assured the French that the enemy could never bring their artillery pieces to bear on the French airfield. All the experts said that the French had nothing to worry about, but the experts and the French woefully underestimated Viet Minh abilities and determination. The Viet Minh quietly moved in large numbers of artillery pieces under the cover of the jungle canopy, massed large infantry units quickly, and overwhelmed and destroyed the finest French fighting forces in just a few days of horrific fighting.

Looking around Phu Loc 6 Combat Base at the surrounding terrain in late 1967, the very disturbing thought occurred to me that the lessons of the Battle of Dien Bien Phu had obviously not been learned by the planners of Phu Loc 6 Combat Base. The only thing we had going for us that the French didn't have was that we weren't two hundred kilometers from our main resupply point. The major American combat base in Phu Bai, only a few kilometers to the northwest, would supply us by road convoy and air. Helicopter technology had advanced significantly over that available to the French in 1954. Our main resupply route, Highway 1, would easily provide us with plenty of food and ammo. Supplies and reinforcements would make it in, if needed, no matter what. But to me, fresh from the rice paddies of Hoi An and pulling my nose out of Monsieur Roy's excellent book, Phu Loc 6 Combat Base appeared to hold the potential for a repeat of Dien Bien Phu: a disaster looking for the right time and circumstances to happen.

Delta Company got the task of manning a company-sized combat base, located at an old French outpost, complete with a couple of concrete bunkers, to provide security for a battery of 105 mm artillery pieces and a couple of 155 mm "toads" (self-propelled artillery pieces). The Delta Company combat base dominated a steep, winding pass called the Phu Gia Pass, located on Highway 1 about sixteen kilometers east of Phu Loc 6 Combat Base. This artillery base became critical, because the Marines who currently protected the Lang Co Bridge and the Hai Van Pass operated too far away to receive support from the artillery units based at Phu Loc 6 or Da Nang to the south. The rest of the infantry companies, H&S Company, and a detachment of engineers and other supporting units manned Phu Loc 6 Combat Base.

Even though things stayed peaceful for the first few days, from the first moment I spent there I felt as though the enemy lurked all around us. On patrols the surrounding countryside stayed too quiet. The villagers seemed not as friendly as those in the Hoi An area. The villagers in this new area lived more remote from the major population center of Da Nang and had probably had much more contact with the shadowy, but always present, Viet Cong. Our early patrols in the surrounding jungle-covered foothills sitting below the towering mountains of Bach Ma did nothing to ease my discomfort; it seemed deathly still on the mountainsides. This was not normal; the unnatural quietness proved unsettling, but nothing much happened during those first few days. Our daily routine, when we patrolled or dug trenches or strung wire or constructed bunkers, seemed almost tolerable. A fair-sized mountain stream flowed not far from the east side of the wire-enclosed combat base, and we took advantage of its cool, refreshing water during the unseasonably hot afternoons by taking a welcome, if wary, dip with a few buddies. Charlie One never got into the villages; someone else got that responsibility. Our patrol routes focused on trails through the jungle canopy on the mountainous side of the combat base.

I did experience one terrible moment of abject terror during those early days, but it didn't have anything to do with my unwelcome thoughts caused by reading a book. Assigned by our company commander to take Charlie One out on an extensive combat patrol, I reported to battalion headquarters at the top of the hill late one afternoon just a couple of days after our arrival. Night descended on the combat base as I entered the dimly lit general purpose tent that served as the battalion command post. After a short but thorough briefing by the battalion S-3 shop, I exited the CP tent to discover that night had fallen, and it had fallen hard. The term *pitch black* failed to describe it. When I emerged from that dimly lit tent totally night-blind, I couldn't see a thing. Worse, I really didn't know the exact route I should take to get back to my company area. I waited for a few moments to recover what night vision I could, but I remained, literally, blind. However, I wasn't willing to go back inside the battalion CP tent to see if someone could please act as my seeing-eye dog. I knew that I would have been laughed out of the place.

So, knowing that I should take a right turn outside the tent and that I only had to negotiate a couple hundred meters to get to our company area, and thinking that I would see obstacles as I approached them and maybe even be able to hear my way along, I cautiously set off in the general direction of the Charlie Company area. After a few stumbles along the uneven dirt road that traveled down the middle of the combat base complex, I gained some confidence. After all, what was there to worry about? I was inside the perimeter, surrounded by nearly a thousand armed Marines. About the worst thing that could happen to me would be to trip over a tent rope and stave in a rib or two on a steel tent stake.

The sounds of the combat base remained muted that night. There was noise, but not much of it. Marines are well trained and disciplined, and we all knew that darkness seems to amplify sound, which carries long distances after dark. Battalion command rigidly enforced light discipline, so the night remained dark and very, very quiet as I moved forward.

Suddenly, without warning, a Marine guard dog, restrained only by a stout chain staked to the ground with a heavy steel tent stake, took offense at my stumbling approach and attacked. I heard the loud clank of his chain as he reached its end, about a foot from my face, and then a terrifying, sustained, roaring bark. This huge dog sounded like a hound from hell. Fortunately I had the presence of mind to stop immediately in my tracks and to back away slowly. Very ferocious and very big, the German shepherds that serve as Marine guard dogs have a bite much worse than their bark. Loyal to only one man, their Marine handler, they believe that anyone approaching them in the night is the enemy, and they will attack without mercy until their handler calls them off. Fortunately for me that night, this dog had miscalculated his attack by a foot or two, and his handler called him off almost immediately. I didn't stick around long enough to register any complaints or to hear any muttered comments about stupid second lieutenants who couldn't find their way in the dark. I just thanked my lucky stars that this particular dog, on this particular night, had attacked just a moment prematurely. Somehow I managed to make my way to the Charlie Company area without further incident.

The 1/5 command group began to understand that our stay in the Phu Loc 6 area was not going to be a picnic. On the morning of 5 January 1968, an engineer road sweep team, protected by a squad of Marines from Delta Company, triggered a VC ambush up on the Hai Van Pass. A six-by truck, hauling some of the security force, was attacked, receiving six incoming grenades, two of which landed in the bed of the truck, and heavy automatic weapons fire from an estimated enemy force of twenty-five VC. The truck driver accelerated to reach a safer position but was killed by enemy fire, causing the truck to run off a steep incline. Additional casualties were sustained in the crash at the bottom of the hill. The remaining Marines regrouped and fought off the enemy attack, and battalion dispatched a reaction force of two more squads of Delta 1/5 Marines and two Ontos vehicles. One Marine died, and nineteen sustained wounds, sixteen of them serious enough to require medical evacuation.

The next morning, a command-detonated mine destroyed an Ontos traveling with a convoy just a few hundred meters from the ambush site of the previous day, killing the driver and seriously wounding a crew member. Later that afternoon, another Delta 1/5 Marine died from enemy fire in the same general vicinity.

The real nastiness at Phu Loc 6 Combat Base started abruptly early on the morning of 7 January, the day after Charlie Company left the combat base on a reconnaissance in force. It turns out that our company commander volunteered for this hazardous mission, designed to find a Viet Cong hospital complex reported to be in the vicinity. No one in Charlie Company complained, because that's what we were being paid to do: find the enemy and destroy them. Some of us got just a little annoyed, though, because life at Phu Loc 6 Combat Base seemed quiet, and now we knew we would find some trouble. It turned out that trouble found the rest of the battalion when a huge volume of incoming enemy mortar and rocket fire impacted on the base early the morning after we had departed.

At 0335 that morning, the 1/5 command post received an urgent radio message from the 5th Marines Liaison Team, based at Phu Loc 6 District Headquarters, stating that their position was receiving mortar fire. Combined Action Group (CAG) headquarters also reported that CAP H5, located near the district HQ, was under mortar attack and that they had lost communications with CAPs H6 and H7, two more Combined Action Platoons in the area. At 0340 the enemy hit the 1/5 assembly area (Phu Loc 6 Combat Base) hard with an initial volley of at least sixty rounds of enemy mortar fire and a dozen or so rounds of 57 mm recoilless rifle fire, along with sporadic enemy small arms fire. That first volley of incoming mortar and reckless rifle fire impacted in and around the main trench line that served the battalion CP group, seriously wounding Lieutenant Colonel Van Den Berg, our CO, and killing the battalion's Sgt. Major Lawrence K. Sepulveda. During that single day of fighting, a total of twenty Marines died in the 1/5 TAOR as well as one US Army soldier serving with Phu Loc 6 District Headquarters. Ninety-four Marines and soldiers sustained wounds, with seventy-one of them requiring emergency medical evacuation. In that one day of brutal fighting, the Marines of 1/5 lost more casualties than we did during the three previous months combined. Those of us in Charlie Company could hear the distant explosions, but we didn't suffer a scratch. For all the Marines occupying it, Phu Loc 6 Combat Base quickly became a recurring nightmare.

Although those of us in Charlie 1/5 weren't around to see the action first-hand, we heard it all as it unfolded across the battalion tactical radio network. The next few days and nights became a blur of high explosive rounds, both incoming and outgoing. Numerous air strikes hit the mountainside, and our supporting arms fired uncounted counter-mortar missions of artillery and 81 mm mortars in support of the Marines at Phu Loc 6 Combat Base.

The Marines of Charlie 1/5 patrolled around our TAOR for several days before returning to the combat base. When we finally returned, we were amazed at the changes, the result of significant enemy mortar fire. The Marines had vastly expanded the trench complex; many more bunkers had been built. The Marines who had stayed behind at the combat based had a haunted look about them; they continuously looked over their shoulders and walked slightly hunched, ready to run toward the nearest trench or bunker at full speed, appearing ready for just about anything. They had been forcefully conditioned to this new environment of random, sporadic, but constant shelling by our enemy.

Charlie Company cautiously conducted platoon- and squad-sized patrols in our TAOR over the next few days. Charlie One had just returned from an extensive daytime patrol, having humped several kilometers to our east around the rice paddies and through a wasteland of thick brush with no enemy contact, when, just as I had dismissed the men to hit their tents, clean weapons, and get their orders for night duty, the first mortar barrage of the day thunked out of the tubes. The enemy mortar position seemed close, no more than a kilometer to our south, behind the first jungle-covered hill up Route 591. Hit the dirt! Not enough time to get to the main trench. Hit the dirt! A few 82 mm mortar rounds impacted the combat base at random locations.

Although I got dirt in my mouth and red clay mud all over the front of my already filthy utilities, the first enemy mortar barrage that Charlie One experienced at Phu Loc 6 Combat Base hurt no one. First Lt. Bruce Morton's civilian radio, which was stored under his cot, took a direct hit and was blown away, but those items were nonessential, and he could replace them quickly.

Bruce Morton had been my next-door neighbor for a while at Quantico during our training at the Basic School. We were both married, definitely in the minority during this stage in our careers, and we had enjoyed the use of married officers' quarters. Although Bruce was one Basic School class ahead of me, my first wife, Penny, and I had gotten to know Bruce and Pam Morton quite well, and his dog Lieutenant and my dog Bull were best friends. I had bumped into him shortly after arriving at Phu Loc 6 Combat Base on Christmas Day. I was happy to see him again, since we had been good friends at Quantico, but more importantly because of what he represented. Bruce led the platoon of M50 Ontos tracked vehicles, the squat, rather ugly, but extremely effective armored vehicles that each lugged six 106 mm recoilless rifles along with one .30-caliber machine gun. Morton's Ontos platoon had reached Phu Loc 6 a couple of days behind us, in late December. They were welcome, very welcome. An Ontos could put out one hell of a lot of firepower when needed. Bruce had just had a close call when this particular enemy mortar barrage wrecked his personal living space, but fortunately he was not hurt.

Battalion S-3 sent out a combat patrol to look for the enemy mortar squad. They found nothing. Then, suddenly, about two hours later another, this time larger, enemy mortar barrage shattered Phu Loc 6 Combat Base. This time 1/5 suffered more casualties. Medevac helicopters landed to take out our casualties; our artillery counterfire poured out their hot shrapnel on suspected enemy positions on the side of the mountain to our south; fixed-wing jet aircraft arrived later that afternoon, and a series of air strikes devastated the same positions repeatedly with Delta-8 250-pound Snake Eye bombs and Delta-9 napalm canisters. Then nothing. Quiet descended on Phu Loc 6 Combat Base once again.

We dug. Although the rest of the battalion had already developed this digging ethic, the Marines of Charlie Company had just received our first dose of incoming. No further orders were necessary. Every man not on duty manning the trenches and bunkers or out on patrol dug, and no one bitched about the extra work. The main zigzag trench line surrounding the combat base ran over a kilometer in circumference, and if you stood at the top of the hill, in the center of the combat base, you probably would not make the main trench line before the first rounds hit. Arterial trenches sprang up, running up the hill in every direction, ultimately connecting with the main perimeter trench. We burrowed rough sleeping holes into the sides of the trenches from the bottom of the trenches. Sandbag and pallet roofs covered sections of the trench.

"Stand-to" is a long-time Marine Corps tradition for those manning fixed defensive positions. Every night just before sunset, and every morning just before first light, battalion would call stand-to. This meant that every Marine on the hill, no matter what he might be doing, would go immediately to his assigned fighting position, don his helmet and flak jacket, wield his weapon, and with a ferocious expression on his face look outward toward the enemy. During stand-to we looked our enemy in the eye and challenged him to attack, to do his worst. We would stay in stand-to formation until after full nightfall. Then, before first light each morning, we would once again man the trenches in stand-to formation. We wanted to give the enemy within sight of our combat base the impression that we would all stay awake, all night long, defending our lump of dirt. I'm sure that over eight hundred Marines bristling with arms and surrounding this strategic piece of real estate looked awesome and intimidating from our enemy's perspective. During the first few days at Phu Loc 6 Combat Base, the grunts quietly complained about stand-tos, but no one complained after the first few mortar attacks.

In spite of the tension caused by the mortar attacks, it proved difficult to stay serious after the incident involving the outhouse door. We were taking hundreds of rounds of 60 mm and 82 mm mortars a day at that point, not to mention rocket and recoilless rifle fire. Most of us slept in a hole or a section of the trench when we could grab a little sleep, abandoning the tents at night. Every Marine on that hill in mid-January had already become tuned in to the sound of the first enemy round hitting its tube. We had all learned that if you could hear the first round hitting its tube, you had about twenty seconds to get underground and therefore stood a pretty good chance of surviving the first round's shattering impact. The enemy surrounding Phu Loc 6 Combat Base stayed within a kilometer or two of the wire most of the time. We were pretty tense that evening and very, very alert. I stood on the back side of the trench, boldly standing in an exposed position (we hadn't taken much in the way of small arms fire yet), slowly surveying the jungle line to our south. My Marines were spread out in front of me, either up on the back bank of the trench line like me, or up in fighting positions in the trench itself. Their rifles pointed ominously toward our invisible enemy.

And then the guy in the four-holer outhouse located out in front of our section of the trench got done with his business. Now, in order to appreciate this story, it's important to understand that an outhouse door in Vietnam, ingeniously engineered to keep out flies and other unwanted insects, came equipped with plenty of lengths of inner tube rubber. When one opened the door, the inner tube rubber stretched out nicely; when one released the door, it sprang back, shutting itself with a distinctive pop. This poor guy did not know that he was supposed to be at stand-to, having been inside this outhouse for several minutes. He got done, exited the outhouse, and the door popped shut. Someone close by, thinking that this pop was the sound of an enemy mortar round being fired, screamed, "Incoming!"

Pandemonium broke out across the entire combat base. Every one of us, incredibly attentive to the potential sound of a mortar round hitting its tube, mistook the sound of the outhouse door popping shut for that first mortar round. Acting as one organism bent on survival, all eight hundred or so Marines hit the bottom of the trenches. I always amazed myself at times like this; I could move so quickly. I dove to the very bottom of the trench and was immediately covered up by several of my Marines. Some of them had already been inside the trench, in their fighting positions, and yet there I was, lying underneath them all. I would have given anything to have had the courage to stay upright for just a moment, just long enough to see the expression on the face of the Marine from the outhouse. He had innocently caused every man on the hill to hit the dirt and the artillery battery to open up in counter-fire. Sporadic outgoing small-arms fire broke out at several points along the perimeter wire.

Slowly, sheepishly, several long seconds after the "first mortar round" failed to explode, the Marines of 1/5 began to emerge to confront their "enemy," the scared-to-hell Marine coming quickly into the trench from the outhouse.

The humor in the moment quickly dissipated, and life on the hill slowly returned to normal, if you could call it that. Most of us had learned that you couldn't afford to laugh too long in Vietnam. The outhouse door mortar attack incident affected me, though. I couldn't get over the sheepish feeling I had trying to push my way out from under seven Marines in the bottom of the trench. I was tired of sleeping in mud, and those of us in Charlie Company hadn't experienced any incoming during the night. What the hell. I would sleep in the company supply tent that night.

Actually, the supply tent was fairly safe, since it was nearly full of pallets of C-rations and other nonexplosive supplies. Although I knew the supplies wouldn't protect me from a direct hit, the cot I had picked out looked safe enough. After ensuring that the night's duties were well attended, and letting Staff Sergeant Mullan know where I could be found at 0300 the next morning for the early morning radio watch, I fell asleep within seconds of lying down.

The first round of the next enemy mortar attack came shortly before midnight that night. I heard it. From the middle of a dead sleep, I heard the first round hitting its tube. The trench! I had to get to the trench. I bounded out of the cot, sprang blindly in the direction of the tent's rear canvas opening, and ran smack into the four-inch-thick tent pole that supported that end of the GP tent. The force of my collision knocked me nearly unconscious; my forehead instantly swelled into a large lump. Out of another, more conscious part of my mind, I could hear the 82 mm mortar rounds exploding up by the artillery battery's emplacements, around the battalion CP. I knew I should get to the trench, but I just didn't give a damn. Sleep, that was the cure. If I could just find that cot in the dark and go back to sleep, everything would be okay. Phu Loc 6 Combat Base took over one hundred incoming mortar rounds that night; I heard maybe two or three of them, but I stupidly stayed in that cot until one of my Marines woke me up at 0300. I never slept in the supply tent again.

The worst thing that happened at Phu Loc 6 Combat Base occurred that next morning. Six members of a squad of Marines from one of the other companies, and two men from the Charlie Company Weapons Platoon, decided to go have breakfast at the mess tent. The battalion mess sergeant, despite the increasing incoming enemy fires, continued to make sure that hot food, including breakfast, lunch, and dinner, was available at the mess tent, but lately most of us had made a silent vow to enjoy C-rations for a while. You see, the mess tent stood out like an aiming stake just below the top of the hill. Anyone who had spent any time at all inside Phu Loc 6 Combat Base knew to avoid the mess tent.

I don't know why those Marines decided to go to the mess tent that morning; if they had been at Phu Loc 6 Combat Base for any length of time, they must have known better. I can only imagine that their distaste for a constant C-ration diet got the better of them. As a breed, Marines could do some pretty strange and risky things for food.

Just a couple of minutes after receiving their hot chow, and after having seated themselves at a table for eight, a single 82 mm enemy mortar round tore through the roof of the canvas mess tent and exploded in the center of the table. Seven of the eight men, including the two Charlie Company Marines, died instantly. The eighth Marine, although physically unharmed, would certainly never forget that moment. That marked the end of hot meals at Phu Loc 6 Combat Base.

Charlie One went out on endless, frighteningly quiet daytime patrols experiencing no real contact with the enemy. All of the 1/5 Marines rotated the necessary evils of nighttime ambush patrols and listening posts to guard the approaches to the combat base. And then, of course, the rain returned. Literally overnight we went from being dirty all the time to being muddy all the time. Although it never really got bitterly cold in South Vietnam, the dampness and chill of a steady rain could seep into your bones. As the rain increased in its steady dreariness, immersion foot became a concern. We forced the wet and weary Marines to change their socks daily and told the corpsmen to check everyone's feet at least every other day. Worse, we had to choose between sleeping in a dry tent with no protection from the steadily increasing enemy mortar and rocket attacks or sleeping in a muddy hole or trench. Every one of us chose to stay wet and muddy.

To add insult to injury, on two separate occasions after a full day of patrolling, Charlie One returned to Phu Loc 6 Combat Base to discover that the main rotor of a CH-53 helicopter on a resupply or medevac mission had sucked all of our possessions up into the sky. We weren't sleeping in the tents at this point, but we still stored most of our gear in them, and our tents sat next to the helicopter LZ. Medevacs and resupply missions had a much higher priority than any of our personal gear.

We spent many long and miserable nights in the bottom of a muddy trench. At the worst possible time, it would rain—not enough to really screw up the enemy gunners, but just enough to muck up the bottom of the trench. Once a torrential downpour filled the trenches to the brim, but fortunately the water soaked away in a few hours.

One night, toward the end of Charlie Company's stay at Phu Loc 6 Combat Base, I thought my end had come. Several of us huddled together in one muddy section of the trench looking up at the clearing sky. The moon, about three-quarters full, tried with limited success to shred the rain clouds. Sporadic incoming mortar rounds exploded across the combat base, and some rocket duels took place between Marines shooting recoilless rifles at the enemy gunners and enemy rocket men aiming at the corner hard point bunkers of our defenses at very close range. Most of this action took place a few hundred meters away, a relatively safe distance from our location. We could see the dark outline of the mountains close by in the sporadic moonlight, the enemy's positions just behind the first peaks. The counter-mortar fire from our artillery battery stayed constant, providing our only comfort.

Suddenly, the side of the mountain erupted in flame and shattering light, and shortly afterward an incredibly loud explosion battered our eardrums from above. It seemed as though our enemy had unleashed all of their firepower at once. The deafening noise sprang back at us, and as I sank down into the bottom of the trench, I prayed for no direct hits. I knew we were about to get clobbered. It sounded like a high-speed freight train screamed by within inches of our heads. But whatever made the freight train noise somehow missed us and shot out harmlessly to the northeast, toward the South China Sea.

After several seconds with no major explosions close by our positions, we began to breathe again, to relax somewhat, and to "crouch" up (I had stopped my stupid practice of loitering on the edge of the trench long ago). The side of the mountain where the sound had originated still burned, with what sounded like secondary explosions steadily erupting. The word filtered down a few minutes later. We had just witnessed a broadside from several warships—a time-on-target, a supporting arms technique that concentrated a large number of shells onto a single target in a very short period of time. The high-speed shells had exploded on the mountainside before the sound of their transit reached our ears, and the doppler effect of the sound of those shells passing over our heads fooled us into thinking that this awesome display of firepower came from our enemy. The naval gunners had obviously hit a major enemy firing position or ammo dump. After calming my nerves a bit, I felt glad I was not a VC that night.

During the rest of January 1968 Phu Loc 6 Combat Base took hundreds of rounds of enemy mortar and rocket fire a day. Intense duels between the 106 mm recoilless rifle teams of 1/5 and the 57 mm and 75 mm recoilless rifle teams of our enemy took place at several points around the perimeter. Ground assaults hit the combat base on three occasions. All of the enemy fire and the enemy assaults met with failure. Although 1/5's casualty rate mounted, the Marines withstood the pounding, which climaxed early on the morning of 31 January 1968, the kickoff of the North Vietnamese Army's infamous Tet Offensive.

Events outside Phu Loc 6 Combat Base continued to escalate. On 12 January 1968, about mid-afternoon, the enemy hit a four-vehicle convoy racing across the infamous stretch of Highway 1 that we referred to as the Bowling Alley. The Marines received one rocket round and four 60 mm mortar rounds as the convoy slowed to negotiate a bridge. Two US Marines died and three were wounded and evacuated. The M35 truck they rode in sustained serious damage. Over the next few days, the enemy hit road security patrols and other combat patrols with regularity. On 15 January a mine sweeping team took a barrage of thirty rounds of 82 mm mortar fire over a period of two and one-half hours at a different stretch of the Bowling Alley; four more Marines died, and five were wounded and evacuated.

In the midst of all this mayhem, at 1330 on 16 January 1968 the Marines of Charlie 1/5 left Phu Loc 6 Combat Base again, this time for good. During the last two weeks of January, Charlie Company trudged around the South Vietnamese countryside from Phu Loc 6 south along Highway 1 to Lang Co village and the Hai Van Pass area, chasing our elusive enemy. And with the exception of one long, very tense night at the Delta Company combat base, we made no major contact with the enemy.

Later on the evening of 16 January a squad-sized ambush patrol from Bravo 1/5 observed a small VC unit near a bridge along Highway 1. The Marines took the VC under fire, killing at least four of the enemy soldiers and capturing assorted weapons and ammunition as well as five blocks of explosive demolitions. Another Marine lost his life in that battle, and four others were wounded. The next night, 17 January, proved deadly for a Charlie Company fire team when they took a small unit of VC under fire. The small enemy unit acted as the point element of a larger force, and a major firefight broke out. Seriously outnumbered, the Charlie Company Marines broke contact with the enemy and moved to a relatively safe location so that they could call in a medevac chopper. The chopper arrived within an hour, but unfortunately for those on board, it crashed as a result of engine failure while attempting to effect the medevac. Two more Marines died as a result of the helicopter crash, and four others were wounded by fire. Violent confrontations with the enemy continued at this brisk pace throughout the remainder of January 1968.

From Charlie Company's relatively safe position at the beginning of the Tet Offensive, in the eye of the hurricane at Lang Co Bridge, we monitored the radio conversations going into and coming out of battalion headquarters at Phu Loc 6. At approximately 0200 on the morning of 1 February 1968, the 1/5 combat base once again came under heavy enemy mortar and rocket attack, and the H5 CAP Unit, located at the intersection of Highway 1 and Route 591, got hit hard with mortars, rockets, and ground forces. A relief force from Phu Loc 6 District Headquarters moved towards CAP H5 at first light, but they could not reach the beleaguered Marines there. A second relief force moved toward the CAP unit from the battalion command post, but they were also unsuccessful, so Alpha Company received orders to move to the area of CAP H5 to reinforce them. On their way there, Alpha Company came under heavy attack by an enemy force of undetermined size.

Throughout that day it seemed as if the entire TAOR in Phu Loc 6 came under enemy attack, except for those of us in Charlie 1/5 at Lang Co. A squad from Bravo 1/5 made contact with the enemy in the area just west of the Phu Loc 6 village complex. The remainder of Bravo Company remained well to the east, trying to attack toward that squad, but they didn't make much progress. Later on that morning the Bravo squad scrambled aboard a Junk Force patrol boat in the Dam Cau Hai Bay, just to their north, and were evacuated to the Junk Force base located on the southern bank of the peninsula separating the bay from the South China Sea.[1] Three days later, the Bravo Company Marines flew by helicopter back to the 1/5 combat base at Phu Loc 6.

Just before Christmas of 1967, Gunnery Sgt. Dale Hatten had reenlisted and received compensation in the form of leave to go home for Christmas. When he returned from leave, the battalion had relocated to Phu Loc 6. He recalls:

> I got back to Da Nang on the 5th or 6th of January 1968. I knew that the battalion had moved, so I called an old friend of mine, Gunnery Sgt. Gene Jensen, USMC, the 1/5 H&S Company gunnery sergeant. Gene said, "You've

gotta get up here right away. They're mortaring us really heavy, and we really need you here right away." So I went down and got a helicopter ride and landed in a very hot LZ at Phu Loc 6 Combat Base. I ran up to the fire direction center (FDC) at the top of the hill to see what was going on. That evening, we had two sets of sandbags over the FDC. It rained hard. The FDC had just enough room so that the eight people critical to the FDC could sleep inside of it. We had a scratch board for our mortar missions and a little Honda generator that gave us enough electricity to light up the interior of the FDC bunker.

The following day I found out that while I was on leave, just before the battalion left Hoi An Combat Base, we had had the worst experience that a supporting arms Marine could ever have. We had an 81 mm mortar short round one night. The round came down on top of a tent near the mortar pits and exploded, wounding twenty-seven mortar men in a tent area close by the mortar pits. Each of the infantry companies had to give up two or three of their 60 mm mortar men to replace these guys, so I saw a lot of new faces in my command when I got back. Several of those kids who had been hurt served with the 81 mm mortar platoon for nearly a year. I remember my shock at hearing about that short round, but there was just so much going on at Phu Loc 6 Combat Base that I had to push it out of my mind.

My platoon sergeant at the time, Staff Sgt. Frank Moak, served as the interim Mortar Platoon commander in my absence. Absolutely the best mortarman I ever knew, Frank served as a mortarman his whole life; that's all he had ever done. He acted as my general coordinator in the FDC. Either Frank or I would review every single mortar mission we ever fired, and we would review them with our Whiskey FO as well. We had this operation down really smooth. We had damned good FOs at the time. These kids understood the strengths and limitations of the weapons and how to call in fire missions, how to place the rounds. I always told my FOs that when they got assigned to a rifle company, they should never do anything except their job as a mortar forward observer. Some of these rifle companies stayed chronically short of Marines, and I'd send an FO out to help them, and the next thing I knew they had been assigned the duties of riflemen. So I told them to resist that tendency and to let me know if they weren't being properly used.

We took thirteen direct hits from enemy mortar fire on the Phu Loc 6 FDC bunker during that time. Then a helicopter dropped off a counter-mortar radar unit. We had never seen one of these things before, but I knew its capabilities. Constantly under heavy mortar fire, we needed all the help we could get, so we set it up right away, and the accompanying radar Marines fired it up. Unfortunately, we made the mistake of setting the radar unit up near the FDC.

We got this call at about 1000 this one morning from the radar operators letting us know that there were forty-five incoming enemy mortar rounds in the air. Using the data from the radar, we immediately started firing counter-fire and had sixty 81 mm mortar rounds in the air within a few minutes. We ended up taking twenty-three direct hits on the FDC, and that radar unit got hit so many times it looked just like a sieve. The enemy obviously knew about that radar unit, and they tried to take it out as fast as possible. We got hit really hard, but we hit back hard, and our counter-mortar fire accounted for a bunch of secondary explosions. We took a direct hit in mortar pit no. 1 which destroyed the mortar tube, and four white phosphorus rounds exploded in the pit. I went around the pit and asked if everyone was okay, and they said they were all okay. But we had these Willy Peter rounds smoking, so I picked them up by the tail fins, one at a time, and carried them up to the pit we used to destroy faulty rounds and threw them in. I look back on that day and I can never understand why I picked those smoking WP rounds up, but I did. Later that afternoon, one of the rifle companies went out and swept toward the suspected enemy mortar positions and found a lot of blood trails and destruction.

I could never figure out why we went to Phu Loc 6. The damned place looked like Dien Bien Phu, the place where the French got wiped out in 1954, but the higher-ups wanted us there, and we did the best we could. Phu Loc 6 Combat Base was really pretty defensible, because of all the supporting machine guns we had; the M60 machine guns had really good firing positions, so any enemy force that tried to attack Phu Loc 6 on the ground would get torn apart. But the combat base, surrounded on three sides by jungle-covered mountains, was very exposed to enemy mortars. Despite that, we had our mortars set up in really good positions, and our counter-mortar fire proved very effective.

During Operation Swift back in September we had captured an enemy 82 mm mortar sight. This Chinese mortar sight was significantly different from an American mortar sight. After we had occupied Phu Loc 6 Combat Base for a few days, after we started taking incoming mortars in earnest, I took a look through that Chinese mortar sight. I suddenly realized that the NVA used direct sighting methods to shoot their mortars at us. We had initially thought that the enemy mortar positions were most likely quite a ways away, maybe at the far reach of their range [about 6,500 yards], but now I could see that their tubes probably sat pretty close to us, maybe just behind the first hill to our southwest. I went to the S-3 shop and told them what I had discovered and asked them if we could change our counter-mortar firing methods. Under normal conditions, we would fire our counter-mortar fire by starting at a registration point quite a ways out and then walking the rounds in toward us. But because I had discovered that the enemy mortar positions threatened us from very close range, I wanted to start our counter-mortar fire by shooting at a target just outside our wire and then walking the adjusted fire out, toward the suspected enemy mortar positions. I just knew that they were shooting at us via direct sighting methods, because those NVA mortar men could walk their rounds right down our trenches. From that time on, after we adopted that counter-fire method, we fared much better. At night we would have one Marine in each mortar pit on watch. The NVA gunners stayed so close to us, probably within three or four hundred meters, that we could easily see their muzzle flashes. The man on watch would see the flashes, and he'd point our tubes in that direction, and we'd start shooting a couple of hundred meters outside our wire and walk the rounds out, and fairly quickly we'd hit right in their positions. We had secondary explosions on several occasions using that technique. It took somewhere between forty-three and sixty-eight seconds' flying time between the time when we fired a round until the time it hit and detonated. The flying time depended upon how many powder increments remained on the round when we fired it. With only one increment of powder, the flying time was about forty-three seconds; with the maximum number of eight powder bags, or increments, it took about sixty-eight seconds. Since the NVA's 82 mm tubes were almost identical to our 81 mm tubes, we knew that we had nearly a minute from the time we heard their first round hitting their tube until the round exploded somewhere in our combat base. We had plenty of time to start firing counter-mortar fire, and we used it to good advantage. We fired a lot of variable time (VT) fuses while at Phu Loc 6, but we had to be very careful with those fuses because of low clouds. VT fuses send out a radio signal, so that when they get close to their target, at a set distance above the ground, the radio signal would fire the detonator, resulting in an air burst. This technique devastated enemy troops in the open. Unfortunately, sometimes that radio signal would bounce off a thick, low cloud and detonate the round not too far above our heads, so we had to be very careful not to use VT fuses when covered by a thick overcast with a low ceiling.

During the battles at Phu Loc 6 Combat Base, the NVA used everything they had at their disposal against us. They used 60 mm and 82 mm mortars, 120 mm and 140 mm rockets, RPGs and B-40 rockets, and they also used 57 mm recoilless rifles. I had received training several years before on the 57 mm recoilless rifle, so I recognized that weapon when they first used it against us. It has a very distinctive, somewhat terrifying sound to it, a high-pitched shriek. No one knew what it was at first, but I recognized the sound and was able to identify it. It was actually made in the US. We had provided the 57 mm recoilless rifle to the French many years before, so that's where the VC and NVA got them. They captured them from the French during the earlier war back in the fifties.

I drilled into my people, over and over again, the critical importance of checking and double-checking their settings and targets before firing. All crew-served weapons people, regardless of the weapons they fired—mortars, rockets, machine guns—all of us had this mortal fear of hurting one of our own Marines. You just don't have to serve in a crew-served weapons team for any length of time to develop this fear in the back of your mind. We emphasized this constantly, made it a moral obligation, to check and double-check our settings before firing. Five seconds one way, ten seconds another way; the extra time it took to double-check everything, nine times out of ten it didn't matter, although the grunts in the field always yelled at us to fire immediately. I felt it much better to take that extra time to be sure rather than to hurry the situation and take the risk of hitting your own people. It was just the absolute worst thing that could happen to you, a short round or a bad target with Marines getting hurt from friendly fire. So we took the extra time to make sure of the accuracy of our fire missions.

When we lost Colonel Van Den Berg, we got a new battalion commander, Lieutenant Colonel Whalen. He had just arrived and had only been there a couple of weeks. Most of our infantry companies stayed strung out up and down Highway 1 in squad ambushes, securing the road. On the morning of 1 February 1968, Alpha Company, under the command of 1st Lt. Frank Wilbourne, operated east of Phu Loc 6 along Highway 1, and we needed them to get back to the combat base. As they moved west, just as they got to the intersection of Highway 1 and Route 591, the small dirt road that took you south to the combat base, they got hit hard by NVA in that village. The FO with Alpha Company called in a mortar mission. Two Alpha Company Marines went down in the road, wounded and exposed to enemy gunfire. Without any hesitation, I authorized the fire mission, and my men started firing at the requested target. I knew Frank Wilbourne well; he had served in Vietnam for nearly a year now, and he had spent nearly all that time in the field as either a platoon commander or company commander. Frank really knew his job. So since Frank had requested and authorized the fire mission, I didn't hesitate for even a second; I just approved it and my guys started shooting. Within just a few seconds I got a message coming over the Whiskey net, asking me why I was shooting. So I replied that I was firing in support of Alpha Company, that they were in contact with the enemy and that they had a couple of WIAs down in the road and they needed support. Whoever was on the radio ordered me to report to battalion headquarters immediately. So I left Staff Sergeant Moak in charge, went right up to battalion headquarters on top of the hill, and Lieutenant Colonel Whalen was just beside himself. He seemed really mad, obviously, and he asked me, "Who authorized that fire mission?" I told him that I had authorized the fire mission and tried to explain what was going on and why we were firing the mortars. He looked at me and said, "You don't authorize fire missions. You don't *ever* authorize fire missions. *I* authorize fire missions. Do you understand me, Gunny?" I told him, "Colonel, you haven't been here very long, but Lieutenant Wilbourne has been here almost a full tour, my FO who is out there with him has been here almost a full tour, and yes, sir, I *do* authorize fire missions, sir! Those Marines know their jobs, and they have wounded Marines down on the ground out there, and we are firing in direct support of them, and so I authorized the fire mission." Lieutenant Colonel Whalen then gave me a direct order. He told me, "You will not fire any fire missions without my approval." I told him, "Sir, you will have to relieve me, because I *am* going to fire in support of good Marines who know what they are doing." I also told him that I was the only Marine in this combat base who knew anything about firing and controlling the 81 mm mortars, so I told him, "With all due respect, Colonel, you have no one here who knows my job, so I don't think it would be very smart of you to relieve me." Obviously upset, Lieutenant Colonel Whalen gave me the direct order once again, that I could not fire any fire missions without his personal approval, and he stormed out of there. He went out, got his jeep driver and a couple of riflemen, got in his Mighty-Mite jeep, and drove out of the combat base to go see what was happening to Alpha Company.

Lieutenant Colonel Whalen had become rather famous, very quickly, as a fearless leader. He would frequently jump on his Mighty-Mite and tear down Highway 1 with no more than a few riflemen on a couple of jeeps. Some of the Marines started referring to these forays as rat patrols, comparing them to the desert tactics of World War II. For the most part, these comments stayed very respectful; certainly our new battalion commander wasn't afraid of anything, but some were concerned that he might stick his head way too far out. That concern proved portentous. Gunny Hatten continues:

A few minutes later, the NVA ambushed Lieutenant Colonel Whalen's jeep, and he got hit pretty badly. He went charging down that road to try to help the

Marines of Alpha Company, but now *he* went down, making a bad situation much worse. So Capt. Gene Duncan, our communications officer, took out a reaction team in a PC [small truck] to go to the assistance of our battalion commander, and *they* got ambushed. So we have Alpha Company under fire, and we have the battalion commander and his jeep driver down, and now we have our communications officer and his reaction team also down. What a mess.

Finally, 1st Lt. Bruce Morton, the Ontos Platoon commander, took another reaction team out to help out our stricken Marines and finally got the situation under control. I fired mortar support for that reaction team, walking my rounds down the road on both sides of the road, supporting that reaction team. Ironically, here I was, under direct orders not to fire any mortar missions without the personal approval of the battalion commander, but there he was, badly wounded and down in the middle of a shit storm. I had no choice. I fired the mortar mission. We got the colonel back and medevaced him and Capt. Gene Duncan and several other wounded Marines and a few KIAs, thanks in large part to Lieutenant Morton's reaction team and my mortar crews. All I can say is that it's a damn good thing that I decided to violate Lieutenant Colonel Whalen's direct order not to fire any mortar missions without his personal approval, or he might still be out there, pinned down in the middle of that road.

Bruce Morton remembers that day, 1 February 1968, as if it was yesterday:

All of my functional Ontoses were stationed out at various CAP units and bridge security, providing them some heavy support, and the three that remained at Phu Loc 6 Combat Base were down, broken. So when that reaction force mission came up, I didn't have any tracks to take with us. The situation called for a purely infantry mission, but we took the three .30-caliber machine guns, along with their tripods and extra barrels, off the Ontoses and took them with us. Some of my guys also grabbed the .45-caliber grease-guns, standard equipment with the Ontos, because they had practiced with them.

I quickly recognized that we faced a large, L-shaped enemy ambush. I set up my base of fire with the .30-caliber machine guns, and just then an enemy sniper round went right by my head, pretty close. Lying down on the rough pavement of the road, I looked down the road toward the enemy positions and tried to figure out the best way to attack them, and all of a sudden someone hollers something from back behind us, and here comes this mechanical mule, just bouncing down the road toward us from the combat base. I knew this mule was really going fast, because it was really bouncing; not all of the wheels stayed on the road at the same time. It came barreling right through our position and kept going down the road a ways. The mule had a 106 mm recoilless rifle mounted on it and a couple of Marines. These guys stopped just out in front of us, got off, and started firing the damned recoilless rifle. The back blast from the first round they fired knocked me out, knocked me totally unconscious for a few moments. We all knew that the back blast from a 106 mm recoilless rifle was deadly within forty meters behind the weapon, and they were closer than that to my position, lying on the road.

Gunny Hatten remarked on the same incident:

I'm not sure who drove that mule, but Master Sergeant Nuanez, the Battalion S-3 chief, and one of my FOs manned the gun. We fired an 81 mm mortar mission in their support, walking the rounds along the south side of the road, protecting their right flank just ahead of the attacking Marines riding that mule. I had two sections, four tubes firing mortars as fast as they could. They planned to run down that road, fire off a few 106 rounds, and then bring back as many of the casualties as they could on the mule. From my position in the FDC listening to the action on the radio, I heard Nuanez's radio operator communicating on my Whiskey net, so I stayed in contact with him all the time. I had no idea, at the time, that the mule had that 106 mm recoilless rifle on it. I thought it was just a bare mule, going out to try to bring some of the casualties back. It's amazing that that mule crew all made it back to the combat base unscathed.

During this impromptu operation to try to rescue our battalion commander, I had all eight tubes firing as fast as possible. Alpha Company had called in the original fire mission, which we adjusted to firing right on the wire around the perimeter of the CAP unit down by the intersection; I had two tubes in support of them. I had two tubes in support of Lieutenant Morton's reaction force as they tried to flank the enemy positions, and the other four tubes covered 1st Sergeant Nuanez and that mule as they made their mad dash down the road. Those fire missions lasted a good forty-five minutes

Bruce Morton recovered from the back blast effects of the 106 and quickly took charge of the situation:

After all that death and dying and horror out there, with Alpha Company getting hit, and then Lieutenant Colonel Whalen getting hit, and then Capt. Gene Duncan getting hit after his reaction force tried to go to their rescue, I got the job of reinforcing our fellow Marines under heavy enemy fire. When I left the battalion command post I had fourteen Marines. That's all the Marines left who weren't absolutely necessary to man the defensive positions around Phu Loc 6 Combat Base. Most of the Marines in my reaction force came from my Ontos crews. After we left the combat base and headed north adjacent to Highway 591, we moved a few hundred meters to a place next to a dam, or dike, and set up there. I set up my base of fire there, because all the dead and wounded Marines lay just ahead, out in this dry rice paddy and along the road. The outskirts of the village started just past the rice paddy, and that's where one side of the L-shaped enemy ambush was located, in the southern edge of the village. The other side of the ambush was to the left, in a substantial cemetery that lined the west side of the road. Vietnamese cemeteries always provided plenty of cover and concealment, and the enemy had taken good advantage of that. I didn't really know how many enemy soldiers manned that ambush, but obviously there were a lot of them. This was a hot, hot, hot L-shaped ambush, a classic infantry setup, and it had done a lot of damage to our Marines. A schoolhouse sat right next to the cemetery where the village started, and I figured that the enemy had concentrated their forces around that schoolhouse, so I started calling in mortar fire on that schoolhouse. I sent one fire team to the right, to cover my east flank, because I figured that no matter how big this enemy force was, that would be their likely escape route, through another cemetery up into the jungle to our southeast. Plus, my right flank remained badly exposed, so I needed some firepower over there. I also quickly preplotted mortar targets in that area in case we saw them trying to escape. Then we started rolling up the left flank of the ambush. As we began to reach the dead and wounded Marines, my Marines started to pick up radios. It seemed like radios lay all over the place, and we didn't want to leave them out there, so after a while just about every other Marine in my reaction force had a PRC-25 radio on his back. We had lots and lots of communications, so we had great communications with the battalion CP and with the mortars. I heard all kinds of crazy stuff over those radios, like, "We're kicking their asses, we're kicking their asses, Lieutenant." Then all of a sudden I heard, "Lieutenant, Lieutenant, they're coming through the graveyard." Things happened so fast that no one used proper radio protocols, with call signs and codes; they just yelled stuff, in the clear. Then I heard, "Lieutenant, Lieutenant, here they come!" That's when I called in requests for all the heavy support I could get. Major Wunderlich, the battalion S-3, came on the radio and said that he would give me artillery support, and almost immediately the 105s started firing at those preregistered targets I had plotted a few minutes before, at the cemetery and the edge of the jungle. For a little while there, all hell broke loose; mortars fired and then the arty started pounding those targets. And then everything went quiet. Just all of a sudden, all the noise died down and a silent pall fell over the area.

At that point we finally got to the wounded and recovered the dead Marines. No helicopters landed out there on the battlefield that day; we had to take everyone back in to the combat base so the medevac choppers could land relatively safely and take our critically wounded and dead south to Da Nang or up to Phu Bai. The next day my Ontos platoon left Phu Loc 6 Combat Base, and we headed north to Phu Bai. By 3 February we arrived on the outskirts of Hue, now attached to the 2nd Battalion, 5th Marines, who were heavily engaged with the NVA forces who had seized that city during the Tet Offensive.

Eventually, late in the day on 1 February, the Marines of Bravo 1/5 reached the Phu Loc 6 District Headquarters and CAP H5 and reinforced those positions. CAP H5 reported four Marines MIA. At least one hundred enemy soldiers died during the various battles that day, and an untold number were wounded. One Five lost another battalion commander badly wounded and medevaced. Lieutenant Colonel Whalen would not return.

Although the war continued to escalate, the gunfire at Phu Loc 6 Combat Base slacked off shortly after the Tet Offensive started. The main forces of the enemy were now engaged in heavy fighting in and around the major cities of South Vietnam. The enemy having finally bypassed it, Phu Loc 6 Combat Base became less and less strategically important to both sides in the overall scheme of things.

One day, in mid-February, the incoming mortar fire at Phu Loc 6 stopped altogether. The enemy simply left. At the end of March 1968, another squadron of bulldozers arrived at Phu Loc 6 Combat Base. We vacated the combat base, and everything of value was stripped from the hill. The rest was simply bulldozed under. Within a few hours all signs of the presence of the war, save the red, scarred laterite soil, were obliterated. Phu Loc 6 Combat Base, that pain-filled, blood-drenched, and tear-stained place, reverted once again into what it had been all along—a lump of dirt.

The Marines of 1/5 were not there to witness this transformation of their temporary home from combat base to clay dirt. In early February 1968, an army outfit relieved 1/5; most of us went north to prepare to attack the citadel fortress of Hue City, which had been overrun by substantial NVA forces during the initial attacks of the Tet Offensive and was now completely under their control. On 13 February 1968, the Marines of 1st Battalion, 5th Marines commenced their historic attack against the NVA who occupied the citadel in force. But for the Marines of Charlie Company, one more chapter occurred in our story before we arrived in Hue.

12: Lang Co Village and the Phantom Mortar Crew, 16 January-10 February 1968

I believe that every single Marine of Charlie 1/5 was happy to leave the damnable hell-hole of Phu Loc 6 Combat Base. Speaking for myself, I was ecstatic. We had experienced heavy enemy mortar fire for only a few days, but that was plenty. We were happy to leave, but that doesn't mean that we had it easy. On foot, we eventually moved nearly fifty kilometers over some of the most rugged terrain in I Corps before reaching our final objective, the Lang Co village and bridge.

Over a period of several days we climbed hills and mountains, and we spent one sleepless night at the Delta Company combat base at the top of the Phu Gia Pass while under heavy enemy mortar fire. Here they were once again, Dying Delta, getting the short end of the stick. It was a bad time for a visit. Departing early the next morning, we gladly left the mayhem of the Delta Company combat base, moved down the pass on Highway 1, and then struck northeast toward the South China Sea, out into an area of seemingly endless sand dunes covered by hellishly thick snarls of brush.

We could see on our 1:50,000 terrain maps that a long, narrow spit of land ran southeast from the cluster of mountains that rambled down to the sea northeast of the Delta Company combat base. This peninsula ran six or seven kilometers south before being cut off by the inlet of the Dam Lap An (Lap An Bay). Lang Co, a fairly large village for this part of I Corps, occupied the southern tip of the peninsula and a small area on the opposite shore situated on the south side of the bay's inlet. A very long bridge, one of the longest in I Corps, the Lang Co Bridge, crossed the tidal inlet, linking the northern and southern stretches of Highway 1.

At our earliest opportunity, after hiking southeast a couple of kilometers down from the Phu Gia Pass on Highway 1, we left the easy footing of the highway and moved northeast toward the South China Sea. Initially, we made reasonable progress, but we soon reached the brush-covered sand dunes, which proved treacherous for the few vehicles that accompanied us. Two of the lightly armored, wickedly armed Ontos vehicles had crawled down the pass and turned into the dunes along with us. We felt confident having the Ontoses along with their six 106 mm recoilless rifles each, our own personal, mobile artillery battery.

Once we hit the brush-covered dunes, however, the Ontoses bogged down quickly in the loose sand, and both became hopelessly stuck. We had to call for a heavy tow truck, and we couldn't slow down our reconnaissance in force mission, so we left a squad behind as security for the Ontoses and continued to plod through the sand. We ended up spending the better part of two days futilely looking for the VC hospital, the primary objective of our mission, before we ended the search and moved along the beach toward Lang Co village.

As soon as we arrived in the center of the village, we met the village chief. Actually an ARVN first lieutenant, the village chief spoke passable English. He let us know right away that he had experienced very few problems with the Viet Cong. "We're a Christian village," he insisted. "There is nothing here to fear from the Viet Cong. My villagers don't want anything to do with the VC; we won't feed them or give them shelter. We are just a peaceful fishing village. You Marines are welcome here."

Although we had heard this before, many times, and in some cases had found out the hard way that the peacefulness and friendliness disappeared in the night, in the case of Lang Co it turned out to be true. Although it lay adjacent to Highway 1, the main north-south supply route, Lang Co seemed remote and quiet. Our enemy most likely realized that if they got caught in Lang Co, we could easily cut them off and either capture or annihilate them. A small, sleepy town of several hundred souls, mostly Catholics, Lang Co was nearly surrounded by water and only accessible via the bridge from the south and Highway 1 from the north. The Delta Company combat base, with a reinforced rifle company and its artillery batteries, effectively blocked Viet Cong access from the north, and the bridge blocked it from the south. The only other approach was by water.

It was also easy to believe that most, if not all, of the residents of Lang Co were fishermen. Teeming with sea life, the open expanse of the South China Sea framed the long white beach of the Lang Co shore. Dozens of boats lay idle on the beach, and the nets drying on racks beside nearly every hooch bore testimony to a thriving fishing industry. Many of the homes in this small town were substantial, constructed of plaster-covered concrete, with only a few of the more familiar thatch hooches scattered about; many had wood floors and tin or tile roofs. A large stucco Catholic church with a high steeple stood in the center of the town square. Small children abounded, running around and among the Marines, yelling amazingly cheerful and profane insults and begging for candy.

2nd Lt. Rich Lowder in front of the Lang Co Bridge, January 1968. Courtesy of Rich Lowder.

Once certain that we had little to fear from the villagers themselves, we set about planning how to accomplish our new mission, to protect Highway 1 on the Hai Van Pass south of us and the bridge at the village. Captain Burrow developed a fairly basic but sound plan of daytime patrols, and nighttime ambush missions covering the obvious approaches to the Lang Co Bridge and the other smaller bridges and culverts that dotted Highway 1 up on the Hai Van Pass.

In comparison with our harried existence at the hellhole called Phu Loc 6 Combat Base, our lives at Lang Co became nearly idyllic. A good-sized mountain stream ran close by our daytime positions, which were shallow foxholes dug into the hard ground to protect the southern approaches to the Lang Co Bridge. At one point a few hundred meters upstream, a waterfall fell from a rock shelf about seven feet high, so we took showers in the stream at least once a day. One platoon conducted daytime patrols up and down the Hai Van Pass as well as night ambush patrols in that vicinity. A second platoon ran patrols and ambushes out on the deserted railroad tracks that ran westward around Lap An Bay. The third platoon stayed close to the bridge, running patrols north along the peninsula on the other side of Lang Co (just in case), and manned the bridge defenses at night. Every third day or so we would rotate those duties.

Left to right: 2nd Lt. Nick Warr and 1st Lt. Scott Nelson. Author's personal collection.

When my platoon conducted patrols up in the Hai Van Pass, I made it a point to move constantly and to stay in a different location every night. We would always move until well after dark and then find some piece of defensible terrain and set up for the night. We religiously dug foxholes when we stayed anywhere out in the bush, even for a short time; the loose, loamy soil on the side of the mountain made it easy. Huge, ancient trees and several layers of jungle vegetation covered the terrain. When assigned to the south end of the bridge down at the bottom of the pass, we found it much more difficult to find cover and concealment. The hard dirt atop the bluff that sat above the bridge had been baked to a nearly rocklike texture. The typical jungle vegetation that we normally dealt with was virtually nonexistent; what plant growth there was consisted of unhealthy-looking scrub and brush.

A few hundred meters above us, on the lower slopes of the mountain, the single-, double-, and triple-canopy jungle thrived. Although our government and the chain of command told us that no chemical defoliants were used anywhere close to populated areas, I believe that this area had been liberally sprayed with what would eventually become infamously known as Agent Orange. We didn't think anything of it at

Left to right: Nicholas Warr; Maj. Gen. John H. Admire, commanding general, 1st Marine Division; and Staff Sgt. John "Mother" Mullan, USMC (Ret), taken on the occasion of the 1st Marine Division Anniversary, February 1998. Courtesy of Travis Curd.

the time, because we weren't aware of its long-term adverse effects, and it certainly made it easier for us to defend the road and the bridge, because the defoliant ensured that the enemy had very few positions of cover and concealment close to the road and the all-important bridge.

When we first arrived in the Lang Co area, we had little motivation to dig in because it seemed like nothing ever happened there. Besides, digging foxholes in the hard-baked clay dirt wasn't easy. Therefore, our daytime defensive positions were little more than shallow depressions hacked out of the hard ground with our entrenching tools. We experienced a mostly peaceful existence at Lang Co despite the hard ground and the long hours.

On two occasions we received invitations to join the local villagers for dinner. The first dinner, hosted by the ARVN first lieutenant village chief and his family, represented a typical Lang Co meal. It consisted entirely of a heap of freshly cooked crab legs, some very hot sauces, and a bottle of whiskey. Delicious! The second dinner celebrated Tet, the Vietnamese holiday that, from an American's point of view, combines the Thanksgiving, Christmas, and New Year's holidays together.

Tet is the Vietnamese celebration of the lunar new year. The Tet holiday traditions call for family gatherings, with the exchange of gifts and best wishes for a healthy and happy new year, and for a lot of eating and drinking. This meal, billed as a traditional Tet dinner, gave us some insight into this important holiday, celebrated by all Vietnamese families, both North and South. Tet was so important to the Vietnamese people that the combatants always called a truce during this time of the year so that everyone could enjoy the Tet festivities. American troops became very suspicious of any truce during the Vietnam War because our enemy consistently violated those truces and used them against us. The Tet truce of 1968 proved no different: the Marines at the Delta Company combat base and Phu Loc Combat Base came under constant enemy fire as if no truce had ever been agreed upon. However, those of us in Charlie Company began to believe that the truce had taken affect in our area of operations. It was so peaceful at Lang Co that the sounds of gunfire across the Dam Lap An seemed somehow like someone else's war.

I don't know if any of the other Marines liked that meal, but with the exception of a dish of very sticky rice and pork, most of the dishes served during that Tet celebration meal seemed very strange to me. The very strong smell of *nuoc mam* (pronounced "nook mom"), a pungent fish sauce that accompanied all Vietnamese meals, nearly overpowered my sense of smell. With my Americanized sense of food aromas, the smell of *nuoc mam* repulsed me. To be polite, I picked at the food placed in front of me. But when I started to eat what I thought was some kind of Jell-O salad and was told by a translator that it was blood pudding (he said it with a big smile on his face, as if this was the greatest thing since sliced cheese), my appetite completely deserted me. Having eaten nothing but a steady diet of C-rations since arriving in Vietnam, I had hoped that this change in diet would be welcome, but I just couldn't bring myself to eat congealed water buffalo blood.

During the daytime if we weren't on patrol, when there wasn't much to do except sit in our daytime positions, we played "back alley bridge" games almost around the clock. We had plenty of C-rations, enough to last two or three days, and the usually bland C-rations were nicely augmented by fresh tomatoes, onions, rice, and rice bread, plentifully available in the village market, as well as a few dashes of hot sauce from our Tabasco bottles. No self-respecting combat Marine would ever be found without his own personal bottle of Tabasco sauce.

The net effect of all of this was that, except when we ran patrols up on the Hai Van Pass (during which time we occasionally ran into the VC and had brief but violent firefights), we almost felt like the war was somewhere else. We didn't even worry about conserving food or ammo, because the constant streams of US Army and Marine Corps truck convoys that came through Lang Co on a regular basis would regularly drop off supplies. Overall, we pretty much had it made.

But on two occasions that idyllic life was seriously disrupted. One incident involved an enemy ambush against a truck convoy that resulted in a fairly large battle with our enemy, and the other involved the hazards of the terrain we operated in.

On 19 January 1968 my platoon had the assignment of patrolling and protecting the upper reaches of the Hai Van Pass. We had patrolled and set night ambushes over the past couple of days at different points along the steep and twisting road, so when we heard the explosions and the roar of gunfire of the ambushed truck convoy, we were located about seven kilometers up the pass from the Lang Co Bridge and about a kilometer below the old French fort manned by a small unit of ARVN soldiers. When the enemy struck, the point truck of this unfortunate convoy was about a kilometer below us. At about 1345 that afternoon, the quiet drizzle was shattered by several explosions and the discordant sounds of a large volume of automatic and semiautomatic fire. We understood immediately what was happening, because our company CP group had regularly radioed us with the convoy's progress up the steep pass. We could also differentiate the sounds of AK-47 fire from M16s, so we knew that the first burst of firing came from the enemy. From the sounds of it, we knew that a pretty large force of VC, just a kilometer below us, was tearing up that convoy.

In order to cover more ground during daylight, we had split the platoon. I led half of the Charlie One Marines, and Mother Mullan led the other half; they were located about two kilometers farther above us. My Marines just happened to be located at the intersection of Highway 1 and a narrow, steep dirt logging road. I had sent a fire team up that logging road a few hours before to check it out, so I knew that it ran straight up the mountain for a few hundred meters, but then it crossed a saddle and headed due west. Judging the location of the ambush site from the sounds of gunfire, I quickly figured out that if I took my Marines up this road about a kilometer, we could quickly move above the VC ambush positions, and we could easily cut them off and ambush the enemy ambush force as they withdrew. VC ambushes took their toll, but they usually hit hard and then pulled out, so they were somewhat predictable. I made the decision, gave the orders, and we took off at a brisk trot up the logging road. As we moved up the road, I told Benny Benware to call the company CP and let them know our plan. I completely understood the necessity of making sure that our CO knew our exact location, but in the excitement of seeing an opportunity to do serious damage to our enemy by acting immediately, I had forgotten to call in to request permission to move up the mountain to cut off the enemy force. Understanding the situation on the ground, the rare opportunity to hit our enemy hard just made sense to me, and I decided to go for it.

Within thirty seconds of sending in our report, Captain Burrow came on the radio asking to speak to me personally: "Charlie One Actual, this is Six. Give me your exact location. Position report, immediately. Over."

I could tell by the urgent tone of his voice that he was very concerned about something, so I called a quick halt, estimated my distance up the logging road, and returned his call: "Six, this is One Actual. Position: from thrust point Beans and Weenies, right three point three, down zero point four. We are moving up the logging road, and will be in a position to ambush Victor Charles within five mikes. Over."

Captain Burrows changed our plan urgently: "Negative. I repeat, negative. Get the hell out of there, Charlie One. Fast movers are inbound. Air strikes are on their way, over."

My mind raced a thousand miles per hour. I could still hear the roar of enemy and friendly gunfire below us, so I knew the enemy was still engaged below us, and I was absolutely positive that I could destroy the enemy if given a chance to get into a good ambush position. We had a classic opportunity to turn the tables on our enemy and to kill them up close and personal. I called Captain Burrow back and tried to convince him that we had the upper hand: "Six Actual, this is One Actual. We can be in position to nail them in just a couple of minutes. Requesting permission to continue our mission, over."

I didn't have to wait more than a heartbeat for his reply: "I said *negative*, dammit! Fixed wing is inbound and will be dropping their ordnance, HE and nape, within two minutes. Get the hell out of there. *Now! Out!*"

That was it. There was no question that I wanted my Marines out of harm's way of a fixed-wing attack, so we turned around and ran down the road to our original position and listened to the air strike. The VC broke off their attack, and the convoy security force called in a medevac for their wounded. The bombs dropped and the napalm burnt a big hole in the jungle. An hour later, Charlie One went back up the logging road to conduct a bomb damage assessment. We found the craters and the burnt area, but nothing else. The VC had fled, and it looked to us as though they had escaped unharmed. There was no evidence of enemy casualties, no blood trails, no equipment left behind. The only casualties that day were two Marines killed riding security on the convoy and six seriously wounded. We had missed another opportunity to inflict damage on our too-elusive enemy.

Two days later, Charlie Company was nearly swallowed up by a rice paddy. This time we patrolled up the Hai Van Pass for several kilometers, and then we left the roadway and made our way down the steep hillside toward a small cluster of hooches that we could see below us sitting close to the old railroad tracks. Our mission was to check out this hamlet to see if we could find any evidence of recent use. After a couple of hours of struggling down the steep, jungle-covered mountain, we cautiously approached the hooches and searched them. Nothing. Obviously, no one had set foot in that ville in years. Since the railroads no longer ran in that part of South Vietnam, the hamlet wasn't strategic to either side; it had been just a suspected enemy harbor site. We called in the report and continued our patrol route, which would take us along the railroad tracks and then down to the coastline.

At one point I realized that this patrol had accomplished absolutely nothing. No one had been anywhere near this area in years. I saw that if I could divert slightly from my planned route and cut across a very large dry rice paddy, I could save my Marines about an hour of humping. We had accomplished our mission, and now it was time to return to our base. I called in the request, got permission to change our patrol route, and we cut across the rice paddy. A large triangular area, this paddy had not been cultivated in many years. When we stepped off the railroad tracks into the paddy, the ground was dry and firm. As usual, I positioned myself behind the point fire team, so I stood fifth in the spread-out column of Marines. When on the move, my Marines always kept a ten-meter interval, and the point team did a great job of watching the front. I had two fire teams out—one on each flank watching our flank security. Everything proceeded as planned.

I didn't notice it right away, but then I began to get the feeling that something was wrong. There were no enemy threats in sight, but something just didn't feel right. I kept going, as did my point fire team. Then, just as my point man approached the other side of the rice paddy about fifty meters from the main paddy dike, I realized what was wrong. The ground bounced. Every time I took a step, the area right around my boot would squash down a bit, and then a little wave would spread out. The ground bounced, as though we were walking on a bowl of Jell-O with a thick skin. The old rice grass was matted and still looked solid, and I couldn't see any mud, but the hair on the back of my neck stood up, and I began to understand that something really was wrong. Just then, my point man broke through the skin and sank to his crotch in a soupy mud. His Marines, seeing the point man sink and understanding the situation we had all marched into, forgot all about patrol discipline and took off at a dead run straight ahead. It reminded me of walking across a pond upon a raft of very small logs; if you could run fast and keep going until you got to firm ground, you could make it to the other side without getting wet—or, in our case, muddy. I took off running as well and got across okay. The point fire team, minus their leader, automatically took positions of cover and concealment on the other side of the paddy dike, and I turned around to see the fate of my platoon. The fire team leader struggled, waist deep in soupy mud. A few more Marines made the mad dash without breaking through the skin, but anyone who stepped where another Marine had stepped just a moment before was doomed. Before I knew it, I had several Marines, including an entire M60 machine gun team, stuck in the mud. Staff Sergeant Mullan growled at me over the radio, cussing me out for getting them stuck in this muddy hellhole. I think it took us over an hour to get everyone across the muck hole, but we finally all made it. Then, of course, we found out that the soupy mud was filled with leeches, so anyone who had gotten muddy above their trouser flies had to take them off and take care of the leeches. We laughed about this incident later, because fortunately no enemy unit was within range to do us any harm, so no one ended up getting hurt, but I had just learned another lesson that I would always remember: stay away from shortcuts.

On the afternoon of 3 February 1968, amidst the chaos of the newly launched Tet Offensive, Capt. Ed Burrow returned to the 1/5 combat base at Phu Loc 6 and received a new assignment as the commanding officer of H&S Company. His replacement, a first lieutenant named Scott Nelson, having just arrived in Vietnam, climbed off the same helicopter that Captain Burrow used to return to Phu Loc. Scott Nelson took command of Charlie Company after a cursory briefing from Captain Burrow, and with no fanfare. From all appearances, Scott, a big man exuding a great deal of confidence, looked forward to the challenges inherent in leading a Marine infantry company in combat.

Along with the change of command came a dramatic change in our war. The relative peace around Lang Co had ended abruptly during the long night of 31 January 1968, the night the North Vietnamese Army launched their infamous Tet Offensive.

Tens of thousands of NVA soldiers, accompanied by their Viet Cong allies, descended from the highlands and jungles of Vietnam and invaded all of the cities and towns of South Vietnam. In some cases, notably Saigon and Hue, the NVA invaders captured huge chunks of real estate. Many small American and ARVN outposts came under attack; most were overrun, and some of them were wiped out. Certainly, from that morning forward and for the next few weeks, virtually everyone, American and ARVN, fought for their lives.

When I woke up at zero dark thirty that morning, 1 February 1968, the war that raged all around us had never been more evident. Huge explosions were heard coming from the Hai Van Pass south of us, auditory evidence of the destruction of virtually every bridge and culvert on the north side of the Hai Van Pass by the Viet Cong. The visual evidence of the fighting at the Delta Company combat base was dramatic, and if not for the fact that we knew that Delta Company was fighting for its life, it would have been very entertaining. A huge battle was being fought over there. We could see the explosions and the incoming greenish white and outgoing red tracer rounds that spelled a very tough time for the Delta Company Marines. But, strangely, we did not come under attack at the Lang Co village and bridge.

The next morning took on a surreal quality because the constant and sometime colorful road traffic that had always passed us in both directions on Highway 1 disappeared. No one, nothing, traveled the highway from that day forward until well after we left ten days later. But the Lang Co Bridge remained intact, and our bridge security mission remained in effect. It made no sense to continue patrolling up the Hai Van Pass, because Highway 1 was clearly out of commission, and all the bridges and culverts had already been destroyed, so there was nothing up there to secure. Second Platoon had patrolled up on the pass the previous night, and they had inspected every bridge and culvert at first light. Their brief, grim report stated that every bridge and culvert had been completely destroyed, so Highway 1 was out of commission until the Seabees could get back up there; it didn't look like that would happen anytime soon. Monitoring the battalion radio net, we also heard that every bridge north of us, except the Troui River Bridge, had also been destroyed, so no vehicles could move south from Phu Bai or Phu Loc 6, either. We were stuck on the bridge, and the area surrounding us got deathly quiet except for the continuing battle for the Delta Company firebase eight kilometers northwest of us.

Still, we knew the importance of protecting the Lang Co Bridge, because we knew that when the fighting died down and we inevitably pushed the enemy back into the mountains, work would immediately start to reopen the highway. Once that happened, the Lang Co Bridge would become extremely important again. The bridge, over five hundred meters long, was one of the largest bridges between the Demilitarized Zone (DMZ) and Da Nang. We could not have replaced the bridge with a pontoon bridge, because it spanned strong tidal currents from the sea. The center of the bridge looked like something built with an erector set, consisting of two spans of interlocking steel girders mounted on three large concrete piers, and it spanned a deep channel carved by tidal flows; much of the remaining structure of the bridge covered mud flats during low tide. During high tide the entire half kilometer of the bridge spanned another ten or more feet of water. Although the destruction of the bridge would have dealt a severe blow to US and ARVN supply lines, it was one of only two bridges that the enemy left alone during the long night of 31 January 1968; the other was the Troui River bridge located about twenty kilometers to our north. On 3 February the NVA and Viet Cong attacked the Troui River bridge in force and destroyed the bridge in the middle of a hellacious firefight. But for some reason they left Lang Co Bridge alone.

Late on the afternoon of 3 February, a lone helicopter landed on the south side of Lang Co Bridge, and one Marine, our new company commander, Lieutenant Nelson, climbed off. After a brief discussion with his replacement, Captain Burrow climbed on, and the helicopter departed. We had a new company commander. As it turned out, that would be the last helicopter we would see for the next nine days.

First Lieutenant Nelson pulled all the platoons in, and we set up the company CP in the abandoned railroad station on the south side of the inlet. Patrols and night ambushes continued up on the side of the mountain and to our west, along the avenues of approach to the bridge. Several of the officers of Charlie 1/5 would also make a point of visiting the village chief, the ARVN first lieutenant, on a daily basis to see what he knew. Every day we talked to him, he became more and more agitated and concerned about our situation. Each day, with increasing intensity, the young officer said to us, "Beaucoup VC come to the bridge tonight, shoot the bridge, bang-bang the bridge." We would act accordingly and set up a series of night ambushes in randomly selected locations that seemed likely avenues of approach. Since we had all three platoons near the bridge, we also heavily manned the bridge defensive positions at night. But nothing happened. The following day the village chief would insist more than ever that the enemy would come that next night. After a few nights of dire warnings and no action, we began to ignore the "village chief who cried wolf" and had almost convinced ourselves that the enemy must have forgotten about the Lang Co Bridge.

After one of these discussions with the village chief, I returned to my Marines, currently occupying our shallow foxhole positions on the naked bluff overlooking the bridge from the south, and then I went with some of my men up to the stream waterfall for a shower. I had convinced myself that the village chief was telling us stories designed to make sure that we stayed put. He didn't want the Marines to leave Lang Co. I think I became more relaxed that afternoon than at any previous time during my two-plus-month stay in South Vietnam, despite knowing that the war raged at unprecedented levels all around us. And then it started.

At about 1600 that afternoon, right in the middle of a back-alley bridge game, we heard the unmistakable, paralyzing blooping sound of a mortar round hitting its tube, launched in our direction. And then another round was fired, and within a few more seconds, a third. I found the ground. Several of us yelled, "Incoming!" and we all hit the dirt. I dove into my now obviously inadequate foxhole and made love with the hard dirt.

The first mortar round exploded several hundred meters short and to the left of our positions, its shrapnel and flame hurling away harmlessly. The second and third rounds also hit well off their intended targets—us. They sounded like sixty mike-mikes, the slang term for a 60 mm mortar round.

The effects of an enemy mortar attack, whether or not we took casualties, are the same: a welling of deep fear filled our guts, surrounded by frustration and anger. When the sound of the third round's explosion died off and no other loud noises followed, I willed myself to crawl out of my shallow shelter and started to do my job. I could easily pinpoint the location where the VC had launched the mortars from the sound of them leaving the tube. We thought we could see a spot in the jungle about two kilometers south of us up on the mountainside that we suspected had been cleared for a launch site. After one of my men retrieved one of the mortar round's tail fins, we confirmed that they were sixty mike-mikes. They had probably been fired from a hand-held mortar tube. It had to be hand-held; they had missed us too far to have been launched with the aid of a tripod and aiming mechanism like we used on our mortar tubes.

Lieutenant Nelson called in a belated fire mission to the Delta Company firebase, and a few minutes later several salvos of 105 mm and 155 mm artillery screamed over our heads and erupted on the side of the mountain, right where we thought they had been. We called in more fire missions that evening, having the artillery crawl up and down the side of the mountain above the suspected enemy mortar position and in the most likely direction that the VC would have gone. I suspected that those VC lived way up on the top of these mountains, so they would most likely have gone straight up the hill. The artillery counter-fire did make me feel a little better, but I noticed that the fun had gone out of the back-alley bridge games. Some of my men had taken again to the habit of scrunching their heads down into their shoulders in an unconscious effort to make maximum use of their flak jackets and helmets and started looking over their shoulders from time to time. These were the unconscious habits of combat Marines under mortar fire, acts of self-defense that became normal posture in a combat zone. We had stayed pretty relaxed and walked around mostly upright of late, but that had disappeared abruptly with the arrival of three 60 mm high explosive mortar rounds.

The foxholes went deeper and deeper. I didn't have to order any of my Marines to dig, they just did it. We all got out our entrenching tools and chipped through the hard ground with the pick end, deeper and deeper into the hardpan. The Marines of Charlie Company didn't rest well that night. We were too exposed, and we couldn't move very far; we had to defend the Lang Co Bridge.

That night was like the rest, dark and unnaturally quiet, but nothing happened. No VC. No "bang-bang on the bridge." We had moved shortly after dark a few hundred meters away from our daytime positions into the scattered scrub brush and formed a platoon perimeter, sending out listening posts (LPs) in three directions, but nothing happened that night. By daybreak, when we moved back into our daytime positions, we had relaxed somewhat, and I prepared to go across the bridge to talk to the village chief. Suddenly, another 60 mm mortar round hit its tube, coming from the same suspected launch site. And another. And a third and a fourth, each round a few seconds apart, and all headed our way. The Marines of Charlie Company hit the ground, deeper in our holes this time but feeling just as exposed. In moments like this I always had the distinct and terrifying feeling that one of those damned rounds would surely drop right inside my foxhole. The odds against that happening were huge, but I couldn't prevent that thought from dominating my mind.

After a wait of a few seconds, which seemed like hours, the four rounds exploded, one after the other. The first hit close to where the others had landed the day before, but the second landed on the other side of our positions, about a hundred meters from my right flank. The third and fourth came dangerously close to a couple of my Marines' foxholes, only fifty meters outside Charlie One's right-most position.

We had been bracketed. The VC had landed mortars on either side of us. I knew the significance of being bracketed by enemy mortar fire, and it wasn't a pleasant situation to contemplate. Even with their rudimentary aiming system, which most likely featured a few sticks stuck in the ground with a string hanging from the mortar tube, it was only a matter of time before the VC would lob them right in on us. This time, however, we were prepared with an artillery target registration that the batteries at the Delta Company firebase had already hit, so we only had to wait a couple of minutes before they opened up on the target area. Delta's artillery batteries fired more than fifty rounds of high explosives and Willy Peter on the area of the VC's launch site and the jungles above it. The result of this barrage: silence. A few of the jungle's tall trees in the area smoldered from the spreading fire started by the white phosphorus rounds.

The rest of that day dragged by; we had taken to wearing our flak jackets, completely buttoned up, and helmets with our chin straps fastened all the time again. These were precautions usually reserved for patrols and combat bases taking incoming. And, despite the hard ground, the foxholes went deeper still.

The third enemy mortar attack came at around 1700 that afternoon, and only luck saved us from casualties. The three 60 mm mortar rounds from this attack exploded very close, with one of them hitting the ground just a few feet from one of my Marines' fighting holes. Fortunately, the Delta Company firebase started firing at the "phantom mortar crew," as my men had started calling them, almost immediately. A 105 mm artillery high explosive round struck close to the VC mortar position just as they lobbed their fourth round. It must have done some damage, or at least rattled their cages, because it caused the VC mortar crew to launch their last round off line, and it struck a tree right above their heads and exploded. Once again, the silence that followed this attack was profound and very disturbing.

Tangible tension around Charlie One's dug-in positions permeated the air, surrounding us like a shroud. We had been bracketed, and the rounds were coming uncomfortably close. The artillery counter-fire didn't seem to intimidate the phantom mortar crew in the least. Quite the contrary, they were becoming habitually prompt.

I called for all of the squad leaders and Staff Sergeant Mullan to assemble to receive orders for the night patrols and defensive ambushes we always set up on the approaches to the Lang Co Bridge. Once that was taken care of, I asked for comments on the mortar attacks. The small group of Marines huddled around the rim of my foxhole agreed completely that a pattern had been established and that the phantom mortar crew had definitely bracketed us. We would certainly take casualties if the VC returned the next morning. Lance Cpl. Ed Estes, who had taken command of Charlie One's 1st Squad after Sawaya died, came up with the solution: "Shoot, Lieutenant," drawled Estes in his distinctive Texas accent, "Let me take an early morning patrol up the mountain well before dawn and set up an ambush for them when they come down. They've come down to the same place each time, and at the same time every morning and evening. We know their exact location. If we take off about 0300 we should be in position before first light. It's only a couple of clicks up the side of the mountain."

While the others discussed Estes's idea, I thought it over in my mind. The suggestion was a bit hairy, because while the VC had been firing from a location only two kilometers up on the side of the mountain as the crow flies, the patrol would have to move about four kilometers to get there on foot, and our daytime patrols had usually stopped well short of that distance. Further up the trail, the VC might have prepared booby traps or mines to guard the approaches to the enemy's positions. It would be dark as hell under the triple-canopy jungle, making progress difficult. But it also made sense. It was risky, but we would likely take casualties anyway if we didn't do something pretty quick.

I talked the plan over with Lieutenant Nelson, and he agreed that the effort was worth the risk and it might just work. Estes would take his squad, but they would leave by 0230. The trail followed a steep, winding route, and I didn't want them to get there too late and I didn't want them to have to hurry. I assigned the night LPs and squad ambushes to the other two squads and then got to work setting up the plan.

Lieutenant Nelson got on the radio with the Delta Company firebase to establish our supporting arms plan for Estes's squad. He ordered a time-on-target (TOT), a massive artillery barrage of one hundred or more rounds from as many artillery pieces as possible, firing all at the same time at the same target. A TOT would virtually saturate the target area, which I designated as the area a hundred meters above the phantom mortar crew's position. The impact zone would be about two hundred meters square. We planned to order the TOT on command, asking that they be available and ready right after first light. We would wait until we heard Estes's Marines firing, wait about a minute, and then call for the TOT. If Estes didn't get all of the VC, they would run right into this hell of explosive fire and steel.

At 0200, Benny Benware woke me up as instructed. I found Estes and his squad in the gloomy darkness. I inspected each of the thirteen members of Estes's squad, which included an M60 machine gun team, had them each jump up and down a couple of times, and then helped them tighten down straps or anything else that could make noise. Silence on this particular night was critical. I then took Estes aside and asked if he had any last-minute questions or concerns. When he shook his head no, I said, "Look, Estes, I want to make damned sure that this VC mortar crew doesn't ever come back. If you see them when they start shooting at us, and you aren't in a good position to take them completely out, let them shoot at us until you can get into a good position and then hit them with everything you've got. Don't worry about casualties down here; that's my responsibility. Your job is the phantom mortar crew. Don't let them know where you are until you're sure you can blow them away for good. And for God's sake, don't pursue them up the mountain if any of them get away. You know I've called in a TOT just above their position. If any of them get away, they'll run right into it. You do your job, and let the artillery do their job."

Estes gave me the hurt look I had become accustomed to when I overmanaged his squad, muttered something under his breath, and said, "Aye, aye, sir." The 1st Squad, Charlie One, departed, quickly disappearing into the darkness.

The dark shroud of night closed back in around me as I crawled back into my foxhole. Thinking that it would be a couple of hours before anything would happen, I tried to get another hour's sleep. But sleep wouldn't come in any form. I couldn't close my eyes. Just before first light we left our nighttime positions and moved back to our daytime positions, the target for the phantom mortar crew.

Finally, dawn broke. I slowly struggled partially erect and looked around my defensive positions at the other Marines of Charlie One. Everyone stayed on one hundred percent alert. Every Marine crouched in his foxhole with his buddy, helmet on, flak jacket buttoned tight, with his own thoughts raging through his mind.

The sun appeared and began to warm the bare earth around our positions. The daylight was intolerable. I felt more exposed than ever before in my life. The sound of a 60 mm mortar round hitting its tube abruptly interrupted my thoughts. The phantom mortar crew kept a strict schedule. A heartbeat later a single burst of semiautomatic rifle fire erupted on the side of the mountain, an M16 from the sound of it. Then, after a brief pause, the whole side of the mountain exploded in small arms fire, mostly from M16s and the M60 machine gun. Estes's squad had initiated their ambush. I got on the tactical net and called for the TOT, and just a few seconds later the Delta Company firebase responded with all of their 105 mm and 155 mm artillery pieces. The rounds screamed over our heads, and the area just above the phantom mortar crew's position erupted in flame and black smoke. The pounding seemed to go on for hours. The trees and vegetation in the TOT target area constantly moved in a shattering dance. In our positions down below, we couldn't tell if the small arms fire continued, due to the continuous explosions of the TOT.

Then, after about fifteen minutes, the artillery barrage lifted, and silence descended on the side of the mountain. The TOT had hit its target, with no stray rounds. I thought it would have been impossible to survive that holocaust above ground. The one round that the phantom mortar crew managed to launch hit right in the middle of our positions, fortunately causing no injuries, and went almost unnoticed because our attention stayed focused on the sounds of Estes's ambush and the awesome display of the TOT.

About an hour later, Estes's squad returned to Charlie One's position. The mischievously impish smile on Estes's face told me that they had succeeded. Seldom seen in Vietnam, elation was a welcome expression on the faces of his Marines.

"One of my new dudes got antsy and blew off a burst from his M16 when they lobbed their first round. We were still about fifty meters away and below them, trying to work up through the bush and flank them. But when he fired, it was too late, so we all blew off our weapons. I think we hit a couple of them, but they all got away. Yeah, they got away from us, all right, right into the damned TOT." Estes's grin widened at the memory of the phantom mortar crew running into the death trap. "We surprised the shit out of them and they just dropped everything and di-di'd up the mountain. Even if they got away, which I seriously doubt from that hellacious TOT, they ain't gonna be bothering us for quite a while."

We celebrated that day. There were so few times in Vietnam when we had a complete victory, because our enemy was very good at hitting us and then disappearing. We knew we had completely outfoxed the Viet Cong. But celebration in Vietnam was relative, subdued by normal standards, highlighted by a few of the Marines in Charlie One hollering, "Get some!" and other invectives.

By that evening the feelings of victory had passed and had become just another taste in my mouth, a memory filed away in my mind. Events in the Vietnam War had a bad habit of repeating themselves. The same bad things happened over and over, redundant in their surprise and shock. But in the absence of the phantom mortar crew, the slow-paced life at Lang Co Bridge overtook Charlie 1/5 again—the warnings from the village chief, the uneventful night ambushes, the daytime boredom. Time, again, crept by interminably. The phantom mortar crew never returned.

With the bothersome exception of our contest of will and wits with the phantom mortar crew, our only real problem for the next few days was the fact that we were no longer able to get resupplies. Highway 1 was shut down, so there would be no convoys to bring us the beans, Band-Aids and bullets we needed to survive and fight, and all of the helicopters stayed busy with medevac missions and resupply missions for units engaged with the enemy. We ran out of C-rations within a couple of days and had to scrounge to avoid starvation; we ate the village out of rice in a couple more days, and then we just went hungry, until finally a resupply chopper brought us a pallet of C-rations a couple of days before we left Lang Co village for good.

While the Marines of Charlie Company struggled to deal with our isolation at Lang Co, the Marines of Delta Company fought for their lives at their firebase, and the remainder of the battalion struggled valiantly to defend Phu Loc 6 Combat Base. During the month of January 1968, a total of 17 Marines serving with 1/5 lost their lives, and nearly 150 suffered wounds, most of them seriously enough to require medical evacuation. After the major battles that resulted in the loss of two battalion commanders, Lieutenant Colonel Van Den Berg and Lieutenant Colonel Whalen, the fighting at Phu Loc 6 Combat Base continued unabated. Then, late on the afternoon of 2 February 1968, Maj. R. H. Thompson, USMC, arrived at the 1/5 combat base, assuming command of 1st Battalion, 5th Marines while under enemy fire. The first two weeks of February proved costly for the Marines of 1/5. Starting with the major battle on 1 February through the 9th, a total of 20 Marines of 1/5 lost their lives. The situation seemed to get worse on a daily basis; what we didn't know was that the worst was yet to come.

The platoon of Marines called Charlie One was fifty-one men strong when we survived our time at Phu Loc 6 Combat Base and the phantom mortar crew's attacks. Not one of us was scratched during those long and hazardous days. But by the end of that month, February 1968, only thirteen Marines from 1st Platoon, Charlie Company, including myself and my two navy corpsmen, were still in action. All the rest were either dead or severely wounded and medevaced. On 13 February 1968, the Marines of 1/5, with my Marines of Charlie One on point, walked into the edge of a deadly steel hurricane of hot shrapnel and small-arms fire in the ancient citadel fortress in a city called Hue. We did not survive it intact.

Afterword

According to research data, approximately 8.7 million Americans served in the military on active duty during the war years (August 5, 1964–March 28, 1973). Of those, approximately 2.7 million trudged daily across the soggy rice paddies and struggled through the mountainous jungles of the Republic of South Vietnam or provided direct support in the skies over North and South Vietnam or offshore in the South China Sea.

Strangely, according to census figures reported in August 1995, the number of Americans claiming to have served in-country during the Vietnam War was nearly ten million. This is a somewhat surreal statistic and is very confusing to most of us Vietnam veterans because of the very cold reception we received upon our return to the United States after serving there. At that time, *no one* wanted to be a Vietnam veteran. Even those of us who did not get directly spit on or otherwise disrespected felt a pervading contempt from many of our fellow Americans that stuck with us for decades. Most of us managed to move on with our lives; like others, I simply tucked my memories, good and bad, down as deep as possible and seldom if ever brought the subject up.

As you will recognize from my acknowledgments, death has struck the combat veterans of the 1st Battalion, 5th Marines many times since the war. Of the two dozen or so contributors to this book, five have passed away in the few short years since I recorded their stories or wrote about them. David Babb, Joe Cody, Buck Darling, Pat Polk, and Dale Hatten—all great Marines—are gone. I am grateful that I got to know them and call them my friends while they lived, and most important, I am grateful that I was able to capture their stories for posterity before they departed this earth. I honor their service to our Corps and country and acknowledge that their involvement in this book project has made this a better history. I mourn their loss; to me, they were all heroes.

The writing and publication of this book could not have been possible without the creation of a new veterans' organization, the 1/5 Vietnam Veterans, which was created by many of those US Marines and US Navy corpsmen whose stories are told in *Charlie One Five*. I am honored to be a part of that organization. We started organizing annual reunions in 1997, after the publication of my first book, *Phase Line Green; The Battle for Hue, 1968*. Although I had not contacted any of my fellow Marines who served in the 1st Battalion, 5th Marines, when the book was published, word started getting around and the phone started ringing. Within a year, our loose-knit group had found the 1st Marine Division Association, a grand old veterans' organization created by Guadalcanal veterans in 1947, and we had found a home. We have conducted a reunion every year since 1998 in conjunction with the Old Breed, a name given to the veterans of the 1st Marine Division by a Marine Corps legend, Lt. Gen. Lewis B. "Chesty" Puller. A regular attendee at these reunions, I began to meet Marines, US Navy corpsmen, surgeons, and chaplains who served before me and after me in the 1st Battalion, 5th Marines during the Vietnam War.

Marines, especially combat veterans, love to tell stories. Listening, I quickly became fascinated with stories of places and events such as Hill 51, Hill 110, the Que Son Valley, the rescue of Staff Sgt. Jimmie Howard's recon team, Operations Union I and Union II, and, the deadliest action of all, Operation Swift. My fascination with these stories led to the writing of this book. To all the members of the 1/5 Vietnam Veterans, especially those who remembered and told those stories, I owe you a huge debt of gratitude.

The multifaceted mission of the 1/5 Vietnam Veterans, chartered in 2003, is to support the 1st Marine Division Association and its scholarship program; preserve incidents and memories of the Marines and sailors who served with 1/5 during the Vietnam War; foster, encourage, and perpetuate the memory and the spirit and comradeship in arms of the 1/5 Vietnam Veterans; perpetuate the spirit and traditions of the United States Marine Corps; and support the Marines and sailors who are currently serving in the 1st Battalion, 5th Marines and the Fighting Fifth Marine Regiment.

Since the beginning of the War on Terrorism, the 1st Battalion, 5th Marines has deployed seven times to combat zones, and the Marines and sailors serving in my battalion have been in the thick of the fighting in both Operation Iraqi Freedom and Operation Enduring Freedom in Afghanistan. As has always been the case in all wars we have fought in, 1/5 has been assigned many difficult and challenging combat missions over the past decade, and in every instance the Marines and sailors have served honorably, professionally, and with great distinction, despite the politicization of those wars and in many cases despite extremely restrictive rules of engagement. The 1/5 Vietnam Veterans are committed to a Care Package Program for the young Marines serving in the 1st Battalion, 5th Marines whenever and wherever they are deployed overseas. It is the very least we can do to support these magnificent young Americans who are giving their all and risking everything to serve their country.

One project worthy of note is the Sgt. Rodney M. Davis, USMC (Medal of Honor) Memorial Monument and Scholarship Program, in Macon, Georgia. Arriving in South Vietnam just before Operation Swift, Sergeant Davis had to get up to speed quickly with his duties as a platoon right guide in Bravo Company. He barely knew the four or five Marines he shared a muddy trench with, but when that enemy grenade plopped into the midst of those Marines, he did not hesitate even for an instant. He threw himself on top of the grenade, covered it with his body, and absorbed the terrible force, saving all the others. Rodney willingly gave his life for his fellow Bravo Company Marines.

Rodney's shattered body was delivered in a closed casket to his broken-hearted parents, siblings, wife, and daughters in Macon, Georgia. He was posthumously awarded the Medal of Honor for his incredible act of courage. His family was informed that the US Marine Corps would see to it that Sergeant Davis could be buried, with full military honors, in our National Cemetery in Arlington, Virginia. However, the Davis family wanted Rodney to lie at rest with them in their community, so he was buried in the Davis family plot in a historic African American cemetery called Linwood Cemetery. Unfortunately, over the ensuing years Linwood Cemetery became overgrown and fell into disrepair.

The 1/5 Vietnam Veterans led an effort to erect a permanent granite memorial monument commemorating Sergeant Davis's heroism and to revitalize Linwood Cemetery. The monument itself, which was fittingly dedicated on the 237th birthday of our Corps, 10 November 2012, provides a memorial worthy of the Marine whose memory we honor. In conjunction with erecting the memorial monument, the 1/5 Vietnam Veterans initiated and funded the Sgt. Rodney M. Davis, USMC (MOH) Memorial Scholarship Program, which will benefit graduating high school students in Macon.

Vietnam veterans' thoughts also often turn to the people and country of Vietnam. It was truly an incredibly scenic place, and the people we met during our combat tours, both friendly and enemy, were in many ways unforgettable. Some of us, especially those of us who enjoy travel adventures, have returned for brief visits, drawn by our memories of an incredibly beautiful if somewhat unfortunate land.

In February 1998 my wife, Pamela, and son, Brenton, traveled with me to Vietnam, and together we followed my footsteps from my first visit. We spent time in Hoi An, Phu Bai, Hue, An Hoa, and other locations, and many of the wounds caused by the war to my heart and soul were healed. I found no resentment from those whose lives we disrupted; I found very little physical evidence of warfare. Most Vietnamese we met were happy to meet Americans, as they are naturally a gregarious, warm, and friendly people. We visited eleven different families, in their homes, in eleven different cities and villages. On 13 February 1998 we enjoyed tea with the family now living at 72 My Thuc Loan Street, inside the citadel fortress of Hue, the scene of so much death and destruction three decades before.

Much has changed in Vietnam, most for the good. The people there have somehow managed to create a hybrid form of life; they are ruled by the communists from the north, but the black market of capitalism that cropped up after the war is apparently there to stay, and today it is pretty much above ground and thriving. The average Vietnamese person doesn't have much in the way of possessions, at least in comparison with the average American, but they all seem very happy with their lot in life.

Nowhere in our travels did the healing of this beautiful country appear more profound than at the site of Phu Loc 6 Combat Base. As we traveled north up Highway 1, over the Hai Van Pass and through the thriving village of Lang Co, I was determined to find, visit, and remember that lump of dirt our battalion called home for nearly two terrible months. In truth, it was difficult to find, despite the fact that it is only about two kilometers off Highway 1 and was situated right on a secondary road, Route 591, atop a slight rise just before the road goes steeply up the side of mountainous Bach Ma. It was difficult to find because it was nearly unrecognizable.

Today, the green vegetation on that low hill is profuse, there are many shade trees there, and they all provide a beautiful landscape of flowers and greenery that would be suitable for the headquarters of one of our national parks. In fact, the site of Phu Loc 6 Combat Base now shelters the headquarters compound for the Bach Ma National Park.

Semper Fidelis!

Appendix A. Navy Cross Citation

Corporal John E. Rusth
United States Marine Corps

For service as set forth in the following CITATION:

The President of the United States of America takes pleasure in presenting the Navy Cross to John E. Rusth, Corporal [then Lance Corporal], United States Marine Corps, for extraordinary heroism while serving as a Fire Team Leader with Company C, First Battalion, Fifth Marines, First Marine Division (Reinforced), Fleet Marine Force, in the Republic of Vietnam on 10 May 1967. During Operation UNION, Corporal Rusth was moving with the lead elements of his company, as they secured the crest of Hill 110 in Suoi Cho Valley, advancing against an estimated battalion of North Vietnamese Army regulars. Accompanied by other elements of his company, he was leading his fire team to secure the military crest on the northeastern slope, when they came under intense enemy fire from positions concealed in hedgerows, tree lines and cane fields at the base of the hill, sustaining numerous casualties. Immediately assessing the situation, Corporal Rusth moved among the wounded to ensure that all had received proper care, while he steadfastly remained exposed to hostile fire on the bare hillside. He displayed outstanding leadership, courage, and tactical skill, as he aggressively led his men in the grenade and bayonet assault down the hill against the North Vietnamese positions, routing the enemy and forcing it to flee to alternate ground. Corporal Rusth, completely disregarding his own safety, fearlessly moved down the hillside on nine occasions to assist casualties up the slope to safety. Although painfully wounded in his thigh from an enemy round when he began his tenth trip to rescue a wounded Marine, he quickly bound his injury and, displaying exceptional physical stamina and courage, assisted the stricken man to safety before collapsing from the effects of his painful wound and heat exhaustion. By his prompt and courageous action, he was instrumental in saving several Marines from further injury or possible death and contributed significantly to the successful accomplishment of his unit's mission. By his bold initiative and unswerving dedication to duty at great personal risk, Corporal Rusth inspired all who observed him and upheld the highest traditions of the Marine Corps and the United States Naval Service.

Appendix B. Medal of Honor Citation

Captain James A. Graham
United States Marine Corps

Citation: For conspicuous gallantry and intrepidity at the risk of his life above and beyond the call of duty as Commanding Officer, Company F, Second Battalion, Fifth Marines, First Marine Division, in the Republic of Vietnam on 2 June 1967. During Operation UNION II, the First Battalion, Fifth Marines, consisting of Companies A and D, with Captain Graham's company attached, launched an attack against an enemy occupied position, with two companies assaulting and one in reserve. Company F, a leading company, was proceeding across a clear paddy area, one thousand meters wide, attacking toward the assigned objective, when it came under heavy fire from mortars and small arms which immediately inflicted a large number of casualties. Hardest hit by the enemy fire was the second platoon of Company F, which was pinned down in the open paddy area by intense fire from two concealed machine guns. Forming an assault unit from members of his small company headquarters, Captain Graham boldly led a fierce assault through the second platoon's position, forcing the enemy to abandon the first machine-gun position, thereby relieving some of the pressure on his second platoon and enabling evacuation of the wounded to a more secure area. Resolute to silence the second machine-gun, which continued its devastating fire, Captain Graham's small force stood steadfast in its hard won enclave. Subsequently, during the afternoon's fierce fighting, he suffered two minor wounds while personally accounting for an estimated fifteen enemy killed. With the enemy position remaining invincible upon each attempt to silence it and with their supply of ammunition exhausted, Captain Graham ordered those remaining in the small force to withdraw to friendly lines, and although knowing that he had no chance of survival, he chose to remain with one man who could not be moved due to the seriousness of his wounds. The last radio transmission from Captain Graham reported that he was being assaulted by a force of twenty-five enemy; he died while protecting himself and the wounded man he chose not to abandon. Captain Graham's actions throughout the day were a series of heroic achievements. His outstanding courage, superb leadership and indomitable fighting spirit undoubtedly saved the second platoon from annihilation and reflected great credit upon himself, the Marine Corps, and the United States Naval Service. He gallantly gave his life for his country.

Appendix C. Medal of Honor Citation

Lieutenant Vincent R. Capodanno
United States Navy Chaplain

Citation: For conspicuous gallantry and intrepidity at the risk of his life above and beyond the call of duty as Chaplain of the 3d Battalion, in connection with operations against enemy forces. In response to reports that the 2d Platoon of M Company was in danger of being overrun by a massed enemy assaulting force, Lt. Capodanno left the relative safety of the company command post and ran through an open area raked with fire, directly to the beleaguered platoon. Disregarding the intense enemy small-arms, automatic-weapons, and mortar fire, he moved about the battlefield administering last rites to the dying and giving medical aid to the wounded. When an exploding mortar round inflicted painful multiple wounds to his arms and legs, and severed a portion of his right hand, he steadfastly refused all medical aid. Instead, he directed the corpsmen to help their wounded comrades and, with calm vigor, continued to move about the battlefield as he provided encouragement by voice and example to the valiant Marines. Upon encountering a wounded corpsman in the direct line of fire of an enemy machine gunner positioned approximately 15 yards away, Lt. Capodanno rushed a daring attempt to aid and assist the mortally wounded corpsman. At that instant, only inches from his goal, he was struck down by a burst of machine gun fire. By his heroic conduct on the battlefield, and his inspiring example, Lt. Capodanno upheld the finest traditions of the U.S. Naval Service. He gallantly gave his life in the cause of freedom.

Appendix D. Medal of Honor Citation

Sergeant Rodney Maxwell Davis
United States Marine Corps

Citation: For conspicuous gallantry and intrepidity at the risk of his life above and beyond the call of duty while serving as the right guide of the 2d Platoon, Company B, in action against enemy forces. Elements of the 2d Platoon were pinned down by a numerically superior force of attacking North Vietnamese Army Regulars. Remnants of the platoon were located in a trench line where Sgt. Davis was directing the fire of his men in an attempt to repel the enemy attack. Disregarding the enemy hand grenades and high volume of small arms and mortar fire, Sgt. Davis moved from man to man shouting words of encouragement to each of them while firing and throwing grenades at the onrushing enemy. When an enemy grenade landed in the trench in the midst of his men, Sgt. Davis, realizing the gravity of the situation, and in a final valiant act of complete self-sacrifice, instantly threw himself upon the grenade, absorbing with his body the full and terrific force of the explosion. Through his extraordinary initiative and inspiring valor in the face of almost certain death, Sgt. Davis saved his comrades from injury and possible loss of life, enabled his platoon to hold its vital position, and upheld the highest traditions of the Marine Corps and the U.S. Naval Service. He gallantly gave his life for his country.

Notes

About the Maps

1. Active-duty Marine infantry regiments during the Vietnam War were the 1st through 9th and the 26th through 28th; the artillery regiments were the 10th through 13th. Units from all of them except the 2d, 6th, 8th, 10th, and 28th Marines saw combat service in Vietnam.

Foreword

1. The abbreviation NVA is for North Vietnamese Army, the name the United States used at the time. The actual name of this force was People's Army of Vietnam (PAVN), but the Marines always referred to them as NVA.

Chapter 2

1. A save-a-plane area was a designated no-fly zone where mortars, artillery, and naval gunfire dominated the battlefield.

Chapter 3

1. Gerald Turley later served with distinction as an advisor to the ARVN in the spring of 1972 and wrote a fine book about his experiences during the NVA's notorious Easter Offensive late in the war.

Chapter 6

1. Rural settlements in Vietnam are organized in districts, which contain villages comprised of hamlets. Districts and villages are named, but hamlets use the name of the village followed by a number. Thus, Nghi Thuong (4) is the fourth hamlet in the village of Nghi Thuong.

2. The Snake Eye is a 250-pound high-explosive fragmentation bomb, equipped with pop-out fins that slow the bomb's rate of descent, allowing the delivering aircraft to avoid self-inflicted damage.

3. The military crest is an area on the forward or reverse slope of a hill or ridge just below the topographical crest. From the military crest maximum observation and direct fire covering the slope down to the base of the hill or ridge can be obtained.

4. Air panels are colorful cloths that ground troops lay out to signal aerial observers and attack aircraft, indicating the troops' location and proximity to the enemy forces the aircraft are about to attack.

Chapter 8

1. A punji pit is a pit dug with sharpened sticks in the sides pointing *downward* at an angle. A Marine stepping into the pit would find it impossible to remove his leg without doing severe damage, and injuries might be incurred by the simple fact of his falling forward while his leg is in a narrow, vertical, stake-lined pit. Such pits would require time and care to dig the soldier's leg out, immobilizing the unit longer than if the foot were simply pierced.

Chapter 9

1. A short round is an artillery or mortar round that falls short of its target.

2. A frag order is an abbreviated form of an operation order (verbal or written), usually issued on a day-to-day basis, that eliminates the need for restating information contained in a basic operation order.

3. Maj. C. H. Black, USMC, the 1/5 operations officer, received the Silver Star for his acts of courage during Operation Swift.

Chapter 11

1. On 11 March 1965 the US Navy created a combined force, the Coastal Patrol Force, later designated as Task Force 115, and launched Operation Market Time with the objective of interdicting enemy efforts to move supplies to South Vietnam by sea. The Junk Force was the South Vietnamese Navy's component in the US Navy's Coastal Patrol Force; they were considered to be one of the most effective counterinsurgency units in South Vietnam's armed forces.

Index

1st Anti-tank Battalion, 195
1st Battalion, 3rd Marines (1/3), 90, 94, 106, 123, 125
1st Engineer Battalion, 195, 247, 251
1st Marine Air Wing (1st MAW), 69, 124, 195
1st Marine Division, xvii, 7, 33, 36, 38–39, 80, 87, 113, 225–26, 249, 278, 293
1st Marine Division Association, 293
1st Medical Battalion, 91, 131, 218, 236
1st NVA Regiment, 190, 198, 216
1st Reconnaissance Battalion, xiv, 80
1st Support Battalion, 195
1st Tank Battalion, 195
2nd Battalion, 11th Marines, 69, 118, 195, 253
3.5 inch rocket, 48, 140
3rd Battalion, 5th Marines (3/5), 65–68, 88–89, 147–50, 191–92, 195, 198, 200, 214
5th Marine Regiment (5th Marines), xii, xvii-xviii, xxi, 20, 28, 64, 69, 122, 150, 154, 164–65, 187, 190, 198, 214, 225–26, 257
60 mm mortar, 44, 48, 92, 94–95, 128, 140, 170–71, 200, 263, 265, 285–87, 289.
81 mm mortar, 35, 112, 116–18, 125, 145, 151–52, 180, 183, 190, 193–95, 199, 216, 221, 226, 228, 242, 257, 265–66, 269, 271
82 mm mortar, 100, 110, 212, 258–59, 261, 263, 266–67

A-1H Skyraider, 38
A-4 Skyhawk, 41, 136
air panels, 129
AK-47, 22, 29, 47, 71, 107, 110, 135, 193–94, 200, 280
Alger, Maj. Dick, 33–35, 39, 165
Alpha Company, 1st Battalion, 5th Marines (A/1/5), 8–9, 30, 65, 67, 81, 84, 87–89, 107, 116–17, 119–24, 126–28, 138–40, 143, 150, 165, 171–73, 179, 182, 192, 210, 264, 268–71
Amphibious Warfare School, 38–39, 42, 128
amtrac (amphibious tractor), 53, 56, 59, 218
Arc Light mission, 86
Army Intelligence School, Fort Haliburton, Maryland, 214
ARVN (Army of the Republic of Vietnam), xiv-xv, 44, 69, 96, 138, 165, 199, 226, 242, 275, 278, 280, 283–85, 303
Attack Carrier Wing 2, 38

B-40 rocket launcher, 110, 200, 267
B-52 bomber, 13, 86,
Babb, David, 91–93, 292
Babich, Capt. R. G., 150, 171–72, 179, 183

Bach Ma, 15, 148–49, 249–50, 255, 295
Bach Ma National Park, 295
Benware, Lance Cpl. Benny, 233–35, 237, 239, 243, 280, 288
Best, Sgt. Delbert L., xxvii, 54, 73–74, 99, 109, 129, 138
Bianchino, Lt. Col. Richard, USMC (Ret), xxviii
Black, Maj. C. H., S-3 Officer, 202, 215, 220, 304
Blades, Lt. Gen. Arthur C., USMC (Ret), xxvii, 26–30, 35
Bohn, Col. Robert D., xviii
Boice, Cpl. Larry L., 229–32, 234, 236, 240
Bouncing Betty (anti-personnel mine), 68, 237
Brackeen, 2nd Lt. John, 209
Bradley, Pfc. Loren E., 18
Bravo Company, 1st Battalion, 5th Marines (B/1/5), 10, 49, 107, 171, 186, 188–92, 195, 200–202, 204–5, 264, 294
British Royal Marines, 39
Brodie, Capt. B. K., 183, 186
Browning automatic rifle (BAR), 47
Burke, Capt. E. M., 195
Burrow, Capt. Edward B., 226, 229, 232, 276, 280–81, 283–84

C-4 plastic explosive, 17, 48, 86, 237
Cam Ranh Bay, 135, 214
Camp Lejeune, North Carolina, xvii, 91, 158, 220
Camp Pendleton, California, 7, 36, 38, 53–54, 79, 92, 113, 161, 172
Cap Ferrer, 8
Cap Saint Jacques, 8, 193
Capodanno, Lt. Vincent R. (MOH), 191, 214, 301
Carty, Col. J. J., USMC (Ret), 35, 42, 44, 70, 113
Caswell, Maj. Russell J. "Jim," USMC (Ret), xxvii, xxviii, 35, 37–49, 55, 62–63, 66–68, 72, 89–94, 98–100, 105, 107, 110–12, 117–19, 127–29, 132, 137–42, 144–46, 151–52
CH-34 helicopter, 8, 20–21, 84, 114, 166, 196, 203, 234–35
CH-46 Helicopters, 8, 40–41, 66, 74, 84, 134, 234
CH-47 Helicopter, 194
CH-53 Helicopter, 234, 246, 253, 262
CH-54 "Sky Hook" helicopter, 87
Chau Lam (3), 200–201, 210, 212
Chau Lam (4), 188, 197–98
Chau Lam (5), 170, 212
Chu Lai, x, xxi, 11, 16, 19–20, 24–25, 31, 37, 39–40, 53, 55–56, 59–60, 63, 65, 69, 81–83, 88–89, 92, 113, 163–65, 223, 242
Cigar Island, 55–58
Coastal Patrol Force, 304
Cody, Lt. Col. Richard L. "Bill," USMC (Ret), iv, vii, xv, xxviii
Cody, Lt. Col. Joe, USMC (Ret), 292
Coffman, Lt. Col. H. L. "Al," USMC, 8, 14–15, 19, 27–28, 30–32, 34
Colvin, Lance Cpl. David, 12
Combined Action Platoon (CAP), 24, 238, 242, 257
Connors, Lance Cpl. Don, 209
Cooper, Lt. General Matthew T., USMC (Ret), 35, 37
Coxen, Cpl. James K., xxvii, 30–31, 75, 89, 95, 99, 108–9, 137, 143

Da Nang, x, xiii, xviii, 7–8, 19–20, 54, 60, 69, 80, 89, 91, 131, 134, 163, 187, 217–18, 225, 235–36, 246, 252, 254, 264, 273, 284
Dam Cau Hai (bay), 15, 264
Darling, Col. Marshall Buckinghgam "Buck," III, USMC (Ret), xxvii, 7–9, 14–17, 19–21, 27–28, 30–32, 35–36, 39, 41, 49–50, 59–63, 67, 137, 292

Davis, Sgt. Rodney M., USMC (MOH), ix, xxviii, 204, 209–13, 294, 302
Delta Battery, 2nd Battalion, 11th Marines (D/2/11), 118, 139
Delta Company, 1st Battalion, 5th Marines (D/1/5), ix, 44, 106–7, 112–15, 121, 140, 147–50, 166–67, 170, 173–76, 178–81, 184, 186, 188–92, 194–95, 197, 201, 203–6, 215, 218, 248, 254, 256, 263, 274–75, 279, 283–84, 286–90
Demory, Staff Sgt., 192, 196, 203
Dong Son (1), 188–90, 197–98

Enaiko, 2nd Lt. Rob, 20

F-4 Phantom jet, 98, 122–24, 136
Faught, Pfc. David. L., 30
Fleet Landing Support Group B, 51
Fowler, HN William R. "Doc", 130
frag order, 125, 200, 304
Fulford, General Carl, USMC (Ret), 188

Gall, SSgt. John, 20
Giordani, Capt. Floyd S., 183, 186
Gummere, Sgt. David D., 18
Gustafson, Cpl. "Gus", 206–7

Haddix, Cpl. Douglas B., 30
Hai Van Pass, ix, 15, 246, 249–52, 254, 256, 263, 276–77, 279–81, 283–84, 295
Hall, Cpl. Worley Wayne, 59
Haskins, Pfc. Harry D., 18
Hatten, Sgt. Maj. Dale, USMC (Ret), xxviii, 192–93, 195, 199, 264, 269, 271, 292
Hawk (antiaircraft missile) battery, 24
Heinz, Lt. Bruce, 216
Hiep Duc, 68–69, 89–90, 114–15, 154
Higbee, Cpl. Robert D., 30
Highway 1, ix, xviii, 69, 95, 113, 154, 164, 187, 222, 225–26, 248–50, 252, 254, 263–64, 268–69, 274–76, 280, 283–84, 290, 295
Hilgartner, Col. Peter, USMC (Ret), xxvii, xxviii, 32–35, 39, 42, 44, 52, 60–65, 68, 70, 72, 93, 106, 112–15, 117–23, 126, 140–41, 145, 147, 154–55, 170, 173, 179–80, 182–83, 187–88, 191, 194–95, 198–99, 201, 215–16, 220
Hill 110 (see Nghi Ha Sa), vii, x, xx, 66, 71–72, 75, 89–91, 93–101, 103–7, 109–12, 115–16, 122–23, 125–27, 129–41, 143–47, 152, 157, 165, 220, 251, 293, 297
Hill 185, 66, 143
Hill 488, x, 24
Hill 51 Combat Base, 115, 149–52, 154, 156–57, 169–70, 181, 185, 188, 192, 200, 210, 217
Hill 54 Combat Base, ix, 19, 34, 56–57, 69, 83, 88, 95, 113
Hill, Pfc. Richard K., 11
Hinz, Capt. D. W., 190
Ho Chi Minh Trail, 29, 249
Hoi An Combat Base, ix, 218, 221, 223, 265
Hoi An TAOR, x, 217, 220, 222, 227–28, 242, 246
Houghton, Col. Kenneth J., 64, 106–7, 114, 141, 165, 173, 183
Houser, Pfc. Dorian, 99, 137
Howard, Staff Sgt. Jimmie E., (MOH), x, 20, 20–23, 29–30, 293
Hue, xxi, 54–55, 205, 218, 234, 273, 283, 291, 294–95

Jackson, Sgt. Craig, xxvii, xxviii, 157–158, 162, 165, 169, 175, 183, 186–188, 192, 195, 201–2, 215, 218–19
Jackson, Pfc. Eddie L., 240–42
Jennings, Capt. Ferdinand, 186
Jewell, 1st Lt. Jack, 57–58, 72–73, 220
Johnson, 2nd Lt. Richard, 80–81
Johnson, President Lyndon, 49, 159
Johnston, Capt. H. C., 186
Junk Force, 264, 304

KA-BAR knife, 22, 102
Kelly, Col. Jack, USMC (Ret), 224–25
Kennedy, Lance Cpl. Jack, 85
Kit Carson Scouts, 96, 195
Knuth, 1st Lt. Lawence D., 5, 16–18
Krulak, Lt. Gen. Victor H., USMC (Ret) - CG, III MAF, 42

Lang Co Village, viii, xix, xx, 252, 263, 274–75, 283, 290
Lauff, Pfc, 127, 129–30
Leedom, Randy, xxviii, 209
Long Thanh Peninsula, 8
Lopez, Pfc. Richard, 187
Loudermilk, "Doc" John, 233–34, 239–42
Lyles, Capt. H. Gaylen, 60
Lynch, Sgt. John, 53–54, 75, 99, 108
LZ Condor, 66, 68, 90, 156, 170
LZ Crow, 15
LZ Robin (Operation Jackstay), 8–9
LZ Robin (Operation Union II), 156, 170
LZ Sparrow, 8

M1 carbine, 47
M1 Garand rifle, 47
M14 rifle, 41, 50–51
M16 rifle, 50–52, 66, 80, 82, 84, 111, 128, 241
M60 machine gun, 45, 85, 110–111, 113, 177, 232, 235, 266, 282, 288–89
M79 grenade launcher, 45, 177, 228, 241
Manion, Cpl. Tom, 85, 87
McCamble, Cpl. Robert L., 78
McInturff, Lt. Col. Dave, USMC (Ret), xxvii, xxviii, 112, 147, 149–50, 169–71, 173–75, 179, 186, 190–91, 216
McKay, Brig. Gen. Jerry, USMC (Ret), xxvii, 117, 119–20, 122–23, 125–27, 150
McNamara, Secretary of Defense Robert Strange, 49, 185
Med Cap program, 44, 221
Meyer, 2nd Lt. Ronald W. "Stumpy," 20, 22–23
MiG-17, 38
Morgan, Capt. Ronald F., 186, 188, 192
Morris, Rich, 203
Morton, 1st Lt. Bruce C. "Cole," xxviii, 252, 258, 270–71
Mullan, Staff Sgt. John "Mother," USMC (Ret), x, xxviii, 226–27, 229, 232–33, 235, 237–39, 241, 243–47, 251–52, 260, 278, 280, 282, 287
Munns, Cpl. Walter, 58–59
Murray, 1st Lt. D., 195

Nelson, Scott A., iii, vii, x, xviii, xxi, xxviii, 277, 283–84, 286, 288
Nghi Ha Sa (see Hill 110), 66
Nickerson, Maj. Gen. Herman, 60, 80–81
NVA (see PAVN), xix-xxi, xxiv-xxv, 20, 22–23, 28–29, 62, 69, 71, 74, 76, 88, 90, 94, 96, 98, 102, 104–9, 111, 114–18, 122–24, 126–30, 134–36, 138–43, 148, 153, 156–57, 165–67, 170, 172–75, 178–79, 181–86, 188–91, 193–94, 196–99, 201, 203, 205, 208–10, 215–16, 221, 227, 234, 247, 250–51, 253, 266–69, 273, 283–84, 303

Operation Adair, 186–87
Operation Cochise, 186–87
Operation Colorado, vii, 19, 27–28, 30, 32, 37
Operation Desoto/Deckhouse V, 19
Operation Desoto/Deckhouse VI, 63, 113
Operation Jackstay, vii, 7–8, 10–11, 14
Operation Market Time, 304
Operation Onslow, 220
Operation Osage, 15, 18
Operation Starlite, 7
Operation Swift, viii, x, 185–86, 188, 190, 192, 195, 197–98, 200–201, 205, 210–12, 214–16, 220, 266, 293–94, 304

Operation Union I, vii-viii, x, 52, 63–71, 74–77, 82, 87–88, 93, 109, 113–14, 120–21, 123, 140, 143, 145, 149, 152–54, 157, 165, 176
Operation Union II, 156–57, 171–72, 175, 178–79, 183, 185, 187, 299

Parks, Sgt. Frank, 67
PAVN (see NVA), 303
Pellizzari, 1st Sgt. Louis U., 4, 17–18
Petrous, Lance Cpl. Gary "Pete," xxviii, 204–5
phantom mortar crew, viii, 274, 287–91
Phu Bai, x, 15, 254, 273, 284, 294
Phu Loc 6 Combat Base, viii, x, xviii-xix, 149, 247–52, 254, 256–59, 261–63, 265–67, 270, 272–74, 276, 291, 295
Phu Loc district, 15, 248
Pierson, Lance Cpl. William E., 240–42
Pogre, HM2 Bob E. "Doc," 18
Polk, 2nd Lt. Pat, 228–32, 239–41, 292
Posey, Staff Sgt. Ron, USMC (Ret), 209
PRC-25 radio, 16, 272
Puff the Magic Dragon (C-47 gunship), 86, 200
Puller, Lt. General Lewis B. "Chesty," 293
punji pit, 169, 302

Quang Nam province, 221
Quang Ngai province, 19–20, 63
Que Son Valley, ix-x, xx, 65–66, 69–71, 73–76, 84, 88, 96, 109, 115, 143, 154, 156–57, 170, 172–74, 181, 185–86, 188, 214, 217, 222, 246, 293

Redic, Terry, 19, 22
Reese, Capt. T. D., 186, 188–89
Republic of Korea Marines (ROKs), 44–45
Rivera-Cruz, Gunnery Sgt. Marcelino, ix, 40, 67, 97–98, 100–102, 105, 111, 146
Rogers, Roy, 33
Rohring, Pvt. Kevin, ix, 56, 58–59
Rolle, Pfc. Melvin, 30
Route 538, 222, 225, 243
rules of engagement (ROE), 49, 293
Rung Sat Special Zone, ix, 8–9, 14
Rusth, Lance Cpl. John "Rusty," ix, xxvii, 36, 54–59, 71, 75, 95–96, 98, 102–3, 133, 140, 220, 250, 297–98

Salinas, Pfc. Antonio, 187
Sanchez, Sgt. Juan, 45–46, 94, 139, 144
save-a-plane, 19, 21, 303
Sawaya, Cpl. John, 233, 235, 237, 240–42, 288
Schlagel, Pfc. Richard L., xxvii, 54–55, 76, 96, 131
Scott, Fred, 176, 178, 196, 202
SKS .30-caliber rifle, 89, 110
Snaggletooth Island, 24, 53, 55–59, 113
Snowden, Col. Larry, 33–34
Song Ly Ly (Ly Ly River), xiii, 89, 167, 188, 196
Song Thu Bon (Thu Bon River), xii, 217, 225, 237
South China Sea, xxiv, 38, 53–54, 118, 222, 237, 262, 264, 274–75, 292
South Vietnamese Regional Forces (RF), 19
Sparrow Hawk, vii, 19–21, 24, 32, 66
Spawn, SSgt. Warren, 30
Special Landing Force (SLF), 7, 90, 123
Steiner, HN Lawrence T. "Doc," 30
Strickland, 2nd Lt., 192, 218
Suapaia, Lance Cpl. David, 134
Subic Bay, Phillipines, 8, 11
Sudsbury, Pfc. Paul E., 30
Sulick, Carl, 87

Tam Ky, x, 21, 28, 49, 51–52, 59, 65, 69, 74–75, 114, 135, 156, 165–66, 170, 187, 193
Task Force 115, 304
Tate, HM3 John C. "Doc," 130

Tate, Lance Cpl. Fred, 100–102, 104–5, 132
Tenny, Capt. W. R., 195
Thang Binh Valley, 69
The Basic School (TBS), xvii, 7, 45, 79, 80, 91, 113, 253, 258
Thrasher, Sgt. Harold L., xxvii, 52–53, 76–77, 99, 103, 130–31
Troui River bridge, 184
Trung Tin (village), 39, 41
Turley, Maj. Gerald, 33–34, 303

UH-1E (Huey) helicopter, 189
US Army Air Cav, 215
US Naval Academy, 33, 37, 42
USS Gaffney, 36
USS Midway (CV-41), 38
USS Princeton, 8, 13–15
USS Repose, 103, 131
USS Upshur, 54

Vacca, 2nd Lt. Bill, 81–82, 84, 88, 117, 121, 171
Van Den Berg, Lt. Col. Olver W. Jr., 216, 220, 226, 257, 268, 291
VC Valley (see Que Son Valley), 16, 65, 73, 76–77
Velardo, LCpl. Anthony G., 12
Viet Cong (VC), ix, xxiv, xxv, 5, 8, 10, 14, 19–20, 22, 24, 28–30, 42, 45–47, 62–63, 65, 69–70, 72, 89–90, 96, 154, 156, 169, 217, 221–22, 226–28, 230, 235, 239–40, 243, 246, 249–50, 254, 256, 275, 283–84, 290
Viet Minh, 39, 47, 253–54
Vinh Huy (2), 157, 174, 180, 183
Vollendorf, Keith, xxvii, 9, 15–18, 23–25, 27–28

Walt, Gen. Lewis. W., CG, III MAF, 138, 140–42, 221
Warr, 2nd Lt. R. Nicholas, x, xx, 224, 225, 232, 245, 277–78
Washington, Pfc. Clarence, 72, 131–32
water buffalo (waterboo), 45, 62, 71, 74–75, 202, 225, 279
Westmoreland, Sgt., 18
Widdecke, Col. Charles F., 28–29, 60
Willy Pete (white phosphorous), 21
Wiskur, Pfc. James C., 18
Wunderlich, Col. Len, USMC (Ret), xix, 272

Yankee Station, 38
York, Sgt. Alvin, 25
York, Sgt. Hillous, xxvii, 25–26, 28, 52, 54, 59, 66–67, 70, 72–73, 78, 98, 100, 105, 107, 133, 135, 140, 145

Zell, Capt. Rick, xxvii-xxviii, 78–80, 84, 87–88, 116, 150, 171–72, 174, 191, 214–15

About the Author

Nicholas Warr, formerly an account executive and marketing manager in the high technology industry, lives in Hendersonville, North Carolina. His first book, *Phase Line Green: The Battle for Hue, 1968*, was on the Marine Reading List for over a decade and was a Featured Selection of the Military Book Club. He was a 2nd Lieutenant in Charlie One Five.